RICK PERRY

CLIFTON AND SHIRLEY CALDWELL TEXAS HERITAGE SERIES

RICK PERRY

A POLITICAL LIFE

BRANDON ROTTINGHAUS

University of Texas Press

Austin

Publication of this work was made possible in part by support from Clifton and Shirley Caldwell and a challenge grant from the National Endowment for the Humanities.

Requests for permission to reproduce material from this work should be sent to:
  Permissions
  University of Texas Press
  P.O. Box 7819
  Austin, TX 78713-7819
  utpress.utexas.edu

♾ The paper used in this book meets the minimum requirements of
ANSI/NISO Z39.48-1992 (R1997) (Permanence of Paper).

Library of Congress Cataloging-in-Publication Data

Names: Rottinghaus, Brandon, 1977– author.
Title: Rick Perry : a political life / Brandon Rottinghaus.
Other titles: Clifton and Shirley Caldwell Texas heritage series.
Description: First edition. | Austin : University of Texas Press, 2024. | Series: Clifton and Shirley Caldwell Texas heritage series | Includes bibliographical references and index.
Identifiers: LCCN 2023029347 (print) | LCCN 2023029348 (ebook)
    ISBN 978-1-4773-2889-7 (hardcover)
    ISBN 978-1-4773-2890-3 (pdf)
    ISBN 978-1-4773-2891-0 (epub)
Subjects: LCSH: Perry, Rick, 1950– | Perry, Rick, 1950—Influence. | Governors—Texas—Biography. | Texas—Politics and government—21st century. | Texas—Politics and government—1951–
Classification: LCC F391.4.P47 R68 2024 (print) | LCC F391.4.P47 (ebook) | DDC 352.23/213097640092 [B]—dc23/eng/20231106
LC record available at https://lccn.loc.gov/2023029347
LC ebook record available at https://lccn.loc.gov/2023029348

doi:10.7560/328897

To my students. Texas is in your hands.

CONTENTS

Photographs follow page 126.

RICK PERRY

—1—

A POLITICAL REBIRTH AT THE DAWN OF THE MODERN TEXAS REPUBLICAN PARTY

As he neared the end of his final term as governor of Texas in 2014, Rick Perry stood with a small circle of family and friends at the edge of Little Rocky Creek near Independence, Texas, to be baptized in a private outdoor ceremony at the historic spot where Sam Houston had been baptized 160 years earlier. His spiritual rebirth at that boggy creek was a nod to both his past and his future—political rebirth across moving waters would be a frequent occurrence in his life.

James Richard "Rick" Perry is the Zelig of Texas politics, his career a reflection of the ways in which politics evolved in Texas and nationally over the nearly forty years he spent in the political arena. Over the decades his political instincts served as a radar primed to identify future political opportunities, and in doing so plotted the arc of Texas political change: from a rural, conservative "Blue Dog" Democrat, a species as numerous as fleas on a farm dog in Texas between the 1950s and the 1980s, to one of the most conservative politicians the state had ever elected, overseeing the enactment of controversial congressional redistricting, voting, and abortion measures. Yet his evolution was complicated and incomplete, as his stands on such topics as immigration, vaccine requirements, and the use of state funds to attract business ran into opposition from a growing and evermore conservative wing of the Republican Party in Texas—and the nation.

The charming rancher, pilot, and politician from West Texas is one of the most important but polarizing figures in Texas history. "What I've found is people either really love Rick Perry or they just have no use for him at all," a friend and former state senator said. Her view is that those who don't like Perry don't understand him, and in many ways that suggests a greater blind spot: "They may not understand Texas totally."[1]

Rick Perry profoundly shaped the powers wielded by the modern Texas governor, and along the way he oversaw the rebuilding of the Texas Republican Party, changed the face of state politics, and invigorated the role of Texas politics on the national stage.

Often derided as "Governor Good Hair," just a good-looking good ol' boy—a charge that was hard to disagree with as he hee-hawed across the stage on *Dancing with the Stars* following a short-lived second presidential campaign in 2016—his impact on state policy, politics, and the Republican Party ranks among the most consequential in Texas history, on par with influential leaders like Sam Houston, Jim Hogg, and Allan Shivers, who ushered the state and their parties through tumultuous times. Dismissed as the "accidental governor" when he rose from lieutenant governor to the governor's office in 2000 after serving governor George W. Bush left for the White House, Perry was a master of the bold move, a trait that transformed a little-known former Democratic lawmaker from tiny Paint Creek into a political powerhouse.[2] His longevity in the governor's office (fourteen years—as of this writing the longest tenure of any governor in Texas history) provided him with unprecedented accumulated political power to sway Texas government in an ideologically conservative direction, tracking the bend of political changes in the state.

Yet Perry's political career is more than the story of one man: it both rode and led the social and political transformations of Texas over three decades, some of the most eventful in the state's history. Its shift to a red state, concurrent with the slow withering of the Democratic Party statewide, was a function of economic gains produced through a growing service sector, the emergence of the state as a global energy hub, and the rapid suburbanization of its major cities. This book describes a state in transition through a critical period and charts the political changes that accompanied it.

"You heard his accent," said Justin Egner, a twenty-five-year-old Amarillo voter and Army National Guard specialist who came out to see Perry during the third of his four successful gubernatorial campaigns. "It doesn't get any more local than that. He's a man of the state."[3]

Voters, journalists, analysts, and other politicians all have tried to explain Perry's persona and political allure—the "all-American boy," as Joe Holley, a journalist and former staffer for Jim Hightower and speechwriter for Ann Richards, described him.[4]

He was charming, but not everyone considered him a serious student of government. "Serving in government was like a different form of being Most Handsome Man or Most Popular Boy," said veteran journalist Dave McNeely. "He was more interested in the glitter of it than the substance."[5] Perry later called politics a "form of show business" and said that he wasn't really interested in governing until he was in his midtwenties.[6]

Perry's image was Texas-town-square solid—a political life built on pastoral Texas and its tenets: faith, military service, farming. Patricia Kilday Hart described him as he nominated George W. Bush as the Republican presidential candidate in 2000: "He was tall and lanky, with dark, wavy hair, and lively eyes framed by crinkly lines that testified to long days spent under the West Texas sun. A rakish smile crept across his face to balance the hard set of his jaw."[7]

Despite the attention given his looks, few dispute one of Perry's most formidable political skills: no matter whom he met along the way—elderly grandmother, high school student, or sophisticated businessman—he was comfortable with them all.[8] Like his looks, that West Texas twang and easygoing persona obscured something tougher.

Perry brought a steely resolve to both politics and life that impressed those around him. "He never backed down from a fight," said Ron Lewis, a former member of the Texas House and a longtime Perry friend. "[I was] amazed how he took things on." Perry relished these fights, Lewis added, and has "a strong side of him that isn't afraid."[9]

Journalist Jay Root got a personal view of Perry's take-charge approach during the 2010 gubernatorial campaign, as the campaign plane flew into Orange, Texas, amid an East Texas storm that left most of the passengers white-knuckled and tense. Perry (sitting with Root and press secretary Ray Sullivan) was unflappable and "talk[ed] the whole time" while the others were "as white as sheets." The storm knocked out the lights at the small airport and left water standing on the runway, but Perry was determined to carry on, calling on the Texas Department of Public Safety to light up the runaway so they could head back to Austin. "Root, I'm going to get you home tonight," the governor boasted.[10]

It was an acerbic journalist, the late Molly Ivins, who bestowed the nicknames that stuck: "The Coiffure" and "Governor Goodhair." This "affectionate abuse," as one former journalist put it, dramatically undercut Perry's political cunning.[11] Throughout his career, Perry played the country politician, generating low expectations that he always exceeded. Recalling a speech Perry gave to a conference of the Texas Federation of Women when he served as the state's agriculture commissioner, journalist R. G. Ratcliffe reflected on this popular perception of Perry. As he stepped away after the speech, a woman in the crowd gave voice to that perception: "Damn that Rick Perry's good looking, but he's dumber than a post."[12] The nicknames and good-looking good ol' boy image tempered the hard edges of his political gamesmanship.

Perry leaned into it, at least a little, and continued his steady rise in Texas politics. The truth was he did have a bit of the country hick about him—no one was going to mistake him for a brain surgeon or a rocket scientist, and he didn't come anywhere near a Phi Beta Kappa roster. But he had shrewd political instincts and a reputation for not playing games.[13]

Compared to his predecessor in the governor's mansion, Texas transplant George W. Bush, Root recalled Perry as "so different, so Texan, so *authentically* Texan. There was so much Bush could rightly claim about being Texan, but there was so much about him that wasn't Texan. The difference between being *from* Texas and *of* Texas.

"Perry was the real-deal Texan."[14]

The real deal, a people- and dog-loving Texan who didn't hesitate to jump into the fray. From leading parades through his West Austin neighborhood to whistle-stop campaigning in Abilene to sharing vodka shots at the traditional sine die party marking the end of each legislative session, Perry's skills as a politician were among the best the state has seen.

Laura Tolley, then capitol bureau chief of the *San Antonio Express-News*, was with her pug, Dash, on the Austin Hike and Bike Trail when she ran into Perry during his campaign for lieutenant governor. As a huge, unleashed dog came bounding towards them, Perry, in running shorts and a T-shirt, jumped to scoop up the diminutive pug, raising it above his head as the massive interloper's muddy paws climbed Perry's chest. Gifted politician that he was, Perry never forgot the moment. "How's that pug?" he would ask for years to come.

He was the genuine article to most people who met him. It wasn't a show or a facade. "Who doesn't like Rick Perry?" exclaimed Debra Medina, an opponent in the 2010 gubernatorial primary, decades later. Perry just engages people in conversation, in typical politician fashion: "He loves the interaction, that's what makes him a good politician."[15] While Perry's shoot-from-the-hip style resulted in plenty of misfires—he once leaned in to assure capitol journalist Jonathan Tilove at a governor's mansion Christmas party that "Jesus has a plan for you," apparently not realizing that Tilove, whom he had just met, was Jewish—the net effect of his irrepressible personality was not lost on the state's voters.[16]

Neighbors recall the "ol' Aggie," while governor, leading Fourth of July parades in a West Austin neighborhood in his "tight jeans and Aggie boots."[17] When he'd go out and speak to people in Abilene, he was clearly "one of them." Former staff fondly recall Perry talking about making a coffee-table book of all the marriages he helped facilitate among staff. "You can't teach that. It's instinctive," according to a former consultant.[18]

His skills as a retail politician are on par with the state's best, according to observers. After forty years in politics, Democrat-turned-Republican consultant David Weeks deemed Perry "still the best retail political person I've seen."[19] Perry liked the "people part of politics."[20]

In every interaction, Perry sought a personal connection. His longtime political consultant Dave Carney said Perry has the ability to remember every person he meets, finding something in common—the military, sports, schools—to form a connection. "I've never known him to meet a person a second time and not remember details about that person." He added, "When you meet him again, it's like you're old friends."[21]

Perry was at his best in this performative role, an action hero for the voting public, inadvertently fueling a mistaken belief on the part of detractors and even some supporters that he was just, in his own words, "a great head of hair."

He had a welcome sense of humor, both giving and taking barbs at a 2011 roast of longtime friend State Representative Senfronia Thompson. Senator Rodney Ellis joked that "Rick Perry was the only governor in Texas history who spent more money on hair products than Ann Richards."[22]

He infused the traditional rope line with small, intimate moments, ensuring his continued popularity with many Texans. At fundraisers he seldom sat to eat, instead shaking hands and working the room.

A big part of the job in a politically diverse Texas is to navigate competing interests and big egos. According to one journalist, "I've seen him wear some expensive cowboy boots. He waded through a lot of BS but didn't get any on him."[23] He wears his heart on his sleeve and comes from a part of the world where people can see through your lies. "You know when he's lying. You know when he's trying to fib. He doesn't have it in him. That's a West Texan. It isn't in his DNA."[24]

Which isn't to say Perry never made people angry. His fellow conservative Democrats may have understood his switch to the Republican Party in 1989, but his decision to campaign against House members with whom he had spent time in the trenches still smarted.

Mark Stiles and Alan Hightower, both conservative Democrats, pushed back when Perry campaigned for their Republican opponents in 1992. The men had been in a dozen legislative battles together, and they had hunted and camped around the state.

Perry's response: I have to prove myself to the Republicans.[25]

That stung, but the effect was fleeting. According to a former Democratic state senator, "You can't stay mad for very long at Rick Perry."[26]

It is, however, possible to doubt the depth of Perry's convictions, and many did, pegging Perry, in the words of legendary journalist Paul Burka, as "more about politics and ideology than governing."[27] And as the state GOP grew increasingly conservative, members of his own adopted party began to doubt Perry's "ideological compass," contending that many of his positions were more a matter of expedience than fealty.[28] "He wasn't that interested in governing, as such," recalled former state Republican Party chair Tom Pauken. "It was more 'let things run as they're running' and if there's a jam or a problem, send your expert aides over to try to fix it."[29]

Contrasting Perry to previous governors, the late political writer (and coauthor of *Bush's Brain*) Wayne Slater said Perry never gave the impression of deeply caring about specific issues. He supported and opposed specific issues, but they weren't "deeply in him."[30]

"I don't know what Rick Perry really believes. He came here as a conservative Democrat. He then becomes, without changing his politics much, a mainstream Republican, sort of in the Bush line, but that's only through happenstance and the coincidence of them running together," said Ken Herman, a former *Austin American-Statesman* columnist. "Then he sees the world change and he goes with it. Is he following a trend or is he helping create that trend? It's certainly a little of each."

"When you're governor, you have a pretty good pulpit, and he became increasingly aggressive about things."[31] To some degree, Texas politics caught up to his personal beliefs, and he could be more expressive in leading the party.

Perry also had something else going for him: luck.

Longtime friend Ric Williamson once called Perry the "luckiest politician" he'd ever seen.[32] And his timing was legendary.

"Perry has been a risk taker," said Kent Hance, a former US congressman from West Texas and another Democrat-turned-Republican who later became chancellor of the Texas Tech University system. "And if you look at Perry's timing in every race, he's been the golden guy."[33]

Rick Perry's tenure in office coalesced three primary themes: firsts and lasts, harnessing the institutional powers of the governor's office, and navigating Texas's ever-changing political landscapes.

Perry became the first Republican lieutenant governor since Reconstruction, at a time when the Republican Party was hungry for strong leadership. Before Perry, the joke around the Capitol went, Republicans could hold caucus meetings in a phone booth.[34] He was the first Aggie

(Texas A&M class of 1972) to become governor, although not all of his many friends from those days went on to become political supporters. He may well be the state's last rural governor, a reflection of the growing concentration of both population and political power in Texas's urban and suburban areas.

Perry's career symbolizes the sea change in Texas politics charted between 1990 and 2016. He became a statewide official just as the Texas Democratic Party's power was crumbling and the party's bench was emptying. In 1990 he defeated liberal stalwart Jim Hightower in the race for agriculture commissioner. He was elected lieutenant governor in 1998, just as the Democrats relinquished their last hold on statewide office after Attorney General Dan Morales announced he would not run for reelection. His tenure as governor coincided with the symbolic death of the Democratic Party in Texas: party stalwarts Bob Bullock, Ann Richards, Lloyd Bentsen, Preston Smith, John Hill, and Billy Clayton all passed away while Perry was governor.

In his seminal book on Texas gubernatorial leadership, *The Chief Executive in Texas* (1964), Fred Gantt Jr. wrote that key characteristics are shared by most strong governors: "Good luck; great energy and drive; above-average intelligence; likeable personality; vanity; love of the limelight; a sense of knowing what the public wants, fears, or approves of, and a willingness to identify with felt needs; and a talent for collecting more credit than is their due."[35] This description of an archetypal Texas governor, written five decades before Perry moved into the governor's mansion, fits Perry to a T.

The formal powers of the Texas governor are weak, at least on paper. Governors have the veto, the line-item veto, the power to issue executive orders (rules to government agencies), and the ability to appoint members to dozens of state boards and commissions. They lack the power to appoint other executive officials or to submit their own budget plans, tools that governors in other states have used to amass power. Appointed officials can't be fired by the governor and, once appointed, might be pesky independents in office. Limited by a Texas constitution that doesn't trust executive power (it was ratified following a bitter arrangement with Reconstruction-era governors), modern governors have struggled to metaphorically toss their weight around. But a new breed of Texas governors emerged as the twentieth century summoned the governor to fill a new role.[36] The public now looks to governors for leadership. Crises mandate quick gubernatorial action. Governors' agendas are only won with an active hand in legislative affairs.

Still, no special session can be called, no convict pardoned, no appointment to state boards or other offices made, no special elections called, and no militia mobilized without the Texas governor's say-so.[37] Longevity also aids Texas governors—after the state moved to unlimited four-year terms, governors began serving longer. From 1845 to 2000, the average tenure of a governor was three years and nine months—Perry shattered this record. "Most didn't have time to get their suitcase unpacked real good," Perry joked.[38] Perry, who had served longer than any governor in Texas history at the time he left office, appointed nearly every official in state government, the judiciary included.

Perry's later authoritative use of power got off to an inauspicious start. Elected lieutenant governor in 1998, he led with a steady but light hand, emphasizing bipartisanship and a "let the Senate work its will" model, while playing second fiddle to Gov. George W. Bush. He had "played the good scout," in his words, while running as a ticket with Bush in 1998. (The ticket approach fell out of favor in later years as statewide executives focused on their own ambitions.) Perry was comfortable in the role, gaining leverage he wouldn't otherwise have from these political alliances—until he could amass power on his own. Not everyone was a fan of the go-along approach: when US House majority leader Tom DeLay got Texas legislators to agree to a rare redrawing of congressional district lines between censuses, the actor Alec Baldwin suggested delivering dog biscuits to Perry for "acting like DeLay's lapdog."[39]

Perry's conciliatory approach shifted as he moved into the governor's office following George W. Bush's election as president in 2000. He transitioned into the muscular, aggressive governor he would become by spending state funds to lure business to Texas, driving hard bargains with the legislature (especially Democrats), frequently calling special sessions, accelerating appointments to executive and judicial offices, and enacting an aggressive and historic use of the veto power. This approach would make him the state's most powerful governor ever, helped in part by the Republican-controlled legislature, which gave him the power to act in many cases. There, as in so many other instances, Perry's personality made a difference.

"The comfort level with Perry because of his personality" let him get away with expanding these powers.[40] So too did the rapid expansion of his (new) party's political power.

Texas had been solidly, almost solely, Democratic from the 1930s to the 1980s. "We have only two or three laws, such as against murdering witnesses and being caught stealing horses, and voting the Republican ticket," iconic writer O. Henry once said of Texas.[41]

But by the 1960s the Republican Party was trying to break the Democratic Party's stranglehold on the South, Texas included. George H. W. Bush served as chairman of the Harris County Republican Party in 1964, and two decades later, the resurgence took root for good, with a new generation of Republicans embracing the modern party ideals of supply-side economics and tax cuts and deregulation, bolstered by an alliance with Christian conservatives who made up one-fifth of the expanding Texas electorate.

Rural Texas Democrats, after the party realignment in the 1960s, were attracted to the new Republican message as delivered by Ronald Reagan, and they began shifting their votes. And they weren't alone. Other Texas Democrats—either temporarily, as with the "Boll Weevils," who supported Reagan's economic policies, or permanently, as they switched parties completely—also backed the new brand of conservative fiscal Republican orthodoxy with small government and big tax cuts, leaving a dwindling number of Democrats to demand a return to a broader social safety net promised by the New Deal but never fully delivered. Reagan's barnstorm through Texas in the 1976 Republican primary encouraged Republicans and "indicated a conservative direction for the party in the state," according to former party chair Tom Pauken. In the 1980 presidential election, Reagan nabbed 55 percent of the Texas vote, besting moderate Democrat Jimmy Carter, who had won the Lone Star State by 3 percent just four years earlier. "Reagan was the key to the philosophical change."[42]

When Reagan ran up the score against Walter Mondale in 1984, winning Texas by 28 percent (the second highest lead among the old Confederate states), it was clear that Texas was in transition. Perry remembers that Reagan finally made it safe to be a Republican in Texas.[43] Voters felt out of sync with the national Democratic Party, and Texas Democrats were unable to separate themselves from their national party.

Even so, Perry's move from three-term Democratic member of the House to standard-bearer of the Republican Party was, to say the least, "a bold move," as Mike Toomey, one of the few Republicans in the House in the late 1980s and a future Perry chief of staff, put it.[44] Soon, however, Perry was riding the wave he had helped create, as Texas voters remained conservative and the Democratic Party and its candidates drifted to the left.[45] Suddenly, candidates for school board, city council, and other local and state offices were running as Republicans in the 1990s.

"It's not that the state has changed, it's that the label has changed," Ken Herman said. Voting Republican gradually became an option, and Perry helped make that happen.[46]

Rebirth, it turns out, wasn't just about the religious grounding symbolized by that baptism on the banks of Little Rocky Creek. For Perry, rebirth was about politics, too. He began his career as a conservative Reagan Democrat and ended as a conservative Republican.

"He wasn't a die-hard conservative, cultural conservative," consultant Matthew Dowd said. "He became more of that over time as it was politically expedient."[47]

He was part of a group of fiscal "pit bulls" in the Texas House, members of the House Appropriations Committee who pushed for more austere budgets in an early foreshadowing of the Tea Party. Yet he also voted for the $5.7 billion tax increase pushed by Republican Gov. Bill Clements and liberally used state funds as governor—some argued they were "slush funds" designed to pick winners and losers—to lure business to Texas. He supported federal healthcare reform in 1993 but then spent much of his time as governor railing against federal intrusion into Texas's healthcare system through the Affordable Care Act signed into law in 2010. He argued for repeal of the Seventeenth Amendment to the US Constitution, allowing the direct election of US senators, and teased about Texas seceding from the United States.

Political operative Jon McClellan watched Perry play a central role in changing the Republican Party: "He pushed it to the right, more conservative, but he also had a little maverick in him where on certain issues now people look negatively at, he would not toe the party line."[48]

The decade of the 1990s presented its own dichotomy. The stock market exploded with a tech boom, crime rates plummeted, and much of America benefitted from the years of peace and prosperity, while the decade also gave birth to a tribalism and a "partisan fervor and level of sordidness previously unseen in modern politics," according to Steve Kornacki, author of *The Red and the Blue: The 1990s and the Birth of Political Tribalism* (2018).[49] Politicians like Newt Gingrich and Pat Buchanan ushered in new cultural politics and established a market for an edgy brand of nationalist politics. In Washington, DC, George H. W. Bush's broken promise to not raise taxes drew the ire of conservatives. Some on the far right echoed Buchanan's call to end all immigration.

All of that was felt in Texas; by 1996, Republican primary voters outnumbered Democratic primary voters. Rural Texans saw the changing landscape as a threat not just to their political power but to their very way of life.[50] As Democrats fought among themselves, a new breed of Republican saw an opportunity, Perry first among them.

In his 1990 race for the obscure office of agriculture commissioner, his first race as a Republican, Perry ran to the right—and ran negative. Perry called it the most pivotal election in Texas history.[51] Painting Democratic incumbent Jim Hightower as a "whole hog" liberal and as corrupt, following the conviction of three Hightower aides on bribery charges, Perry's first statewide campaign would mirror future campaigns for governor: conservative and nasty. The position of agriculture commissioner is not political in any way, but under Perry a new foe emerged: the federal government. These themes continued over Perry's entire political career.

The Texas Republican Party didn't have many stars in its political galaxy in the early 1990s, but a more conservative electorate and the emergence of George W. Bush, son of a famous political dynasty whose father was president from 1988 to 1992, gave Republicans the push they needed. Rick Perry was again along for the ride: at the right place at the right time but with the political instincts to strap in and reap the benefits. While his tenure as the state's lieutenant governor did little to distinguish him from the rest of the Republican pack, his charm, coupled with a hard-hitting campaign style, made him seem destined for a key role in the state's strengthening Republican Party. As lieutenant governor, as during his time as agriculture commissioner, he generally governed in a bipartisan, consensus-building way, highlighting the differences between his bare-knuckled campaigns and his style in governing. At that point he had to—Democrats still held power (if dwindling) in many corners of state government. But by 1998, all the statewide elected Democrats were gone.

When Perry became governor three years later, he veered towards a more conservative line, overseeing the enactment of controversial voting and abortion measures, a reflection of the same instincts that led to his switching parties, a recognition of where the crowd was headed. "I think we all in politics had to adjust to where the (Democratic) Party was going and where the state was going," said a conservative Democrat who served in the state House with Perry. "I think Perry made those adjustments, reading where the state was moving and the public perception was moving."[52]

Although early political putty, Perry later hardened into a partisan rock. He morphed into a divisive figure within his own party, drawing primary challengers in his 2006 and 2010 races for governor and accusations of bringing "Washington-style politics" to Texas. Yet he was also the last governor powerful enough to hold the diverse factions of the Republican Party together. He campaigned hard, pushing conservative and polarizing issues in campaigns, but he managed to govern in a way that kept his friendships intact.

The election of a Democrat as president—Barack Obama in 2008—ironically helped his cause, uniting the Republican base and lessening the focus on contentious issues pushed by Perry, including the Trans-Texas Corridor and a vaccine mandate for HPV.[53] Perry pushed back on expanding Medicaid through Obamacare (a nickname for the Affordable Care Act of 2010) and challenged federal government's policies on, well, everything from gun control to environmental regulations. Rural Democrats, meanwhile, lost in big numbers in this era, even seats the party had held for decades. Tapping all that pent-up anger in the Republican electorate, Perry casually floated the idea that Texas might secede from the Union, a patently illegal notion but one that resonated with a small but vocal segment of the Republican electorate that was increasingly dictating who ran and what issues they ran on.

There was a flip side, too: his stands on immigration and vaccines ran into opposition from an ever-growing conservative wing of the Republican Party when he ran for the Republican presidential nomination in 2012 and 2016, even as he faced pressure at home from Republicans on issues like a "fetal pain" bill that banned abortions after twenty weeks, drug tests for people applying for unemployment benefits, and concealed handguns in classrooms. The dominant Republican Party Perry had helped engineer was now wracked with infighting. Perry's stillborn 2016 presidential campaign met a similar fate; a civil war led to the emergence of more radical, grievance-filled politics in the party—and President Donald Trump.

Perry was underestimated his entire political career—all "hawk and no spit," as famous Texas journalist Molly Ivins used to say. The perception was that Perry was a lightweight, but opponents consistently underestimated him and the appeal of his brand of politics. "Rick has always been under-credited for his accomplishments," Republican political consultant Bill Miller said. "People have written him off because he's a good-looking guy who can meet and greet well. Where's the meat? But the truth is he has a super work ethic, and he is smart enough to not diffuse things. He focuses on things, and he sees them through. He doesn't get credit for that because he's too good-looking."[54] This was the undoing of many political opponents, emphasizes former chief of staff Ray Sullivan.

Ken Luce, who managed Perry's 1990 campaign for agriculture commissioner, said, "When Rick's been the best, it's when there is no expectation of Rick Perry."[55] People underestimated him, but when they looked closely they came away with a sense that he was "really good at what he does."[56] It was a knack to be underestimated, observed former roommate and legislative deskmate Cliff Johnson. He was good at getting people to "the place where they wanted to help him. That is the key to relationships, and it's everything in government. You've got to have your pals."[57]

But Perry set his hook in deeper water and became a prize angler, among the most effective the state has ever seen. For all those political elites who thought he was a country bumpkin and "rough around the edges" and couldn't win, by the end he had proved the naysayers wrong.[58] According to one journalist, "His political opponents typically make the fatal mistake of underestimating him."[59] Said one House member who has known Perry since his early political days: "Don't let that country-boy look fool you."[60]

—2—

THE HOUSE YEARS, 1984–1990

Democrat from "The Big Empty"

Perry's childhood in an isolated pocket of West Texas offered a firm grounding in the state's agrarian history. Paint Creek—"Pint" Creek to the locals—was a small, unincorporated farming and ranching community in Haskell County, about fifty miles north of Abilene, the nearest large city.

"Halfway between Abilene and the end of the earth," as Anita Perry later put it, or simply "the Big Empty," in the words of Perry's father, Ray Perry.

That meant hardscrabble conditions almost unimaginable in modern Texas. The Perry house had no indoor plumbing until the future governor was six; he left for Texas A&M University in College Station a dozen years later with his bag packed with underwear his mother had sewn by hand.

"He had a horse, a dog, and a full belly," Amelia Perry, his mother and a bookkeeper by trade, once said. "He didn't know there was anything else you could want." "Paradise," he later said in describing growing up on the High Plains.[1] They weren't poor, but being dryland cotton farmers, they were certainly frugal. He also took with him his mother's admonition to make a friend everywhere you go—be nice, be respectful, be friendly. "That paid great dividends for me over my thirty years of elected office."[2]

The university, the Air Force, and politics broadened his horizons substantially, but at his core, Rick Perry remained a product of Paint Creek, its name arising from the reddish clay on the creek's banks used by Native American inhabitants for adornment. Ricky, as he was known growing up, was an Eagle Scout who attended both the Baptist and Methodist churches in town, the beginnings of his religious beliefs guided by several factors, including his understanding of scripture and conversations with faith leaders. "His walk of faith is a lifelong journey of a sinner who has accepted the grace of God," said one supporter.[3]

At the Paint Creek school Perry graduated at the top of his class—thirteen students total—and, in his first election, was chosen Most Popular and Beau of the Future Homemakers of America. "Beau" or not, high school romance in Paint Creek was almost painfully wholesome. Perry's first date with classmate Anita Thigpen was fittingly to a six-man football game—he was on the team, but a horse-trampling accident left him unable to play. When a hard-nosed coach insisted he ride the team bus to the game in Moran, forty-five miles away, Anita traveled to the game with his parents and sister. "I figure that's about what every girl dreams about for her first date," she later joked.

Sixteen years later—separated while they attended different colleges (she went to Texas Tech University in Lubbock) and by his stint in the Air Force—with the blessing of her father, she agreed to marry him. They wed in 1982, as Perry juggled trying to farm, fix airplanes, and fly.

There wasn't much else to do. Reb Wayne, a Republican consultant for four decades, recalls driving through the area in the mid-1980s and seeing state representative-elect Perry playing *Pac-Man* at a Town & Country gas station in Stamford.

Paint Creek may indeed have seemed like paradise to young Ricky Perry, a bucolic underpinning to a values-based childhood grounded in scouting, church, and family. But that Spartan rural upbringing also shaped his future mindset about following the money, an outlook that informed both his political path and the policies he undertook while in office.

"For Perry, it's always about the money," said journalist Gary Scharrer.[4]

The meager salary of a state legislator and lean times at the farm almost pushed him out of politics and into a more lucrative lobbying job until friends talked him into running for statewide office.[5] Perry was "loyal to his country, and he's a patriot and the rest of it, but he's also an enterprising, on-the-make kind of guy," remembered Harvey Kronberg, who from the beginning followed Perry's career from his perch at the *Quorum Report*, an insider's source for news on Texas politics.[6] Case in point: Perry would later come under scrutiny for drawing his state pension while still in office. While legal, it certainly raised eyebrows.[7] This "double dipping" (taking a state salary and a pension at the same time) was outlawed by the legislature after Perry left office.

Perry's political career mirrored—and sometimes led—Texas's transformation from a rural Democratic stronghold to an urban state of increasing Republican strength and national relevance, but in some ways the former governor never left that rural patch of West Texas.

"Perry likes a good fight. Perry still shows signs of coming out of Paint Creek," said Democrat John Whitmire, dean of the Texas Senate. "I doubt if [current governor Greg] Abbott knows where Paint Creek is. Abbott is very urban."[8] So is the rest of the state, which boomed as a result of post–World War II prosperity. In 1950 Texas had 7.7 million residents. By 1960, that number would reach almost 10 million. Houston had half a million people in 1950 and double that by 1960. Texas was already very urban by 1950 (62 percent of the population lived in urban areas), but that number would grow to 75 percent just ten years later.[9]

Perry dreamed of being a veterinarian, but his college grades steered him in other directions. "Organic chemistry changed my life," he recalled years later. "Me and organic chemistry didn't jehaw very well."[10]

His charm and leadership ability suggested another calling.

He was elected yell leader by the A&M student body in his junior and senior years (1971–1972), a position held in high esteem in a university culture steeped in tradition, faith, and sports. And at A&M nothing personified tradition more than membership in the Corps of Cadets, a military-style organization that was established in 1876. Membership in the Corps had been compulsory until shortly before Perry's arrival, and he ultimately was elected social secretary of the group, gaining the Corps' influential backing when he ran for yell leader. Perry was in his milieu. Hector Gutierrez, commander of the Corps of Cadets when

Perry was a freshman, recalled Perry as "charismatic and energetic" and "smarter than people think he is." And he was loyal to his friends. "If I need[ed] him right now, he would find a way to do that."[11]

By Perry's own admission, the structure at A&M, and in the Corps, saved him. "I was probably a bit of a free spirit, not particularly structured real well for life outside of a military regime," he said in a 1989 interview. "I would have not lasted at Texas Tech or the University of Texas. I would have hit the fraternity scene and lasted about one semester."[12] But his time in College Station was formative in other ways, too: Perry said later that he hadn't met any Black or Jewish people until he went to A&M, an experience that broadened the narrow beliefs that were common in Paint Creek. And even aside from organic chemistry, grades weren't the primary concern for Perry and his friends. Why make straight As when the prospects of Vietnam might cut life short, classmate and future Marine Corps general Joe Weber recalled.

Perry learned other lessons during a summer job in 1969 as a Bible book salesman in Festus, Missouri, population about 7,000. The product was a set of four books of Bible history, stories, and an encyclopedia—a combination they called "a superset." He, along with classmate and future Washington County Judge John Breeden, got a crash course in sales from the company, basically a pyramid model where more sales benefited each person up higher on the ladder. Going house to house, repeating the same canned speech again and again, was a crash course in handling rejection, he said, but he also realized he didn't want to fail. "That's where I really learned about cold selling," Perry said. Working all day, he could keep up with the daily soap operas by listening at each door, Perry recalled. "It was a really hard but interesting summer."[13] Perry, strapped with his dad's military B4 garment bag and living in a rented room with no air conditioning, got firm life lessons in rejection and tenacity ("stick-to-itiveness" he called it). A very effective salesman, he saved enough to buy a new car, a 1967 Catalina.[14]

Experience by experience, Perry was learning to use his winning personality as an asset. "The same kind of personality that draws you to cheerleading is the same that draws you to the human side of politics," suggested a future Texas House classmate.[15]

Politics, however, wasn't first on his mind after graduating from A&M; instead, he joined the Air Force. He trained as a tactical airlifter, flying transport planes in faraway places like Germany and Saudi Arabia. It was perhaps a disorienting experience, moving from the insular worlds of Paint Creek and College Station to the beaches of Rio de Janeiro, the Arabian Peninsula, and the old cities of Europe.[16]

Once his tour in the Air Force ended in 1977, he headed home to Paint Creek, where Ray Perry made him an equal partner in the family business. Rick ran the ranching operation, about 6,000 acres, and Ray ran the farm, which was about 2,500 acres. "We had a few rocky months there as I was transitioning from being a captain in the Air Force and he thought I was still the dummy that had left ten years before," Perry joked years later. "Over about a year's period of time, in his eyes I matured, and he got a bunch smarter from me."[17]

Still, Perry was clearly restless and considered interviewing as a commercial pilot with Southwest Airlines. He was bored, he admitted.[18] Then another calling emerged: politics. Years later, Kronberg, who publishes *Texas Energy Report* along with the influential *Quorum Report*, recalled talking to Perry at a Texas Medical Association event about the decision to enter public service. "Well," Perry intoned, "all I can tell you is that I spent most of my youth sitting on a tractor, and I'm not doing that again."[19]

Politics, like farming and military service, ran in his blood. His great-great-grandfather, D. H. Hamilton, was a Confederate veteran who served in the state legislature. His great-grandfather was a Haskell County commissioner. His grandfather Hoyt Perry ran unsuccessfully for county commissioner in the 1940s. And his father, Ray Perry, served as Haskell County commissioner for twenty-eight years. All were southern Democrats: comfortable with government up to a point, socially conservative, and tight with money except when it came to aiding a cause.

Texas was chock-full of these conservative Democrats from the 1930s to the 1970s, and they ruled the roost. "I never met a Republican, or anyone who admitted to being one, in Haskell County. There were a few people you kinda looked at," Perry remembers.[20] Wallar Overton, Perry's former scoutmaster, told a journalist it didn't matter what people in Haskell believed 364 days a year. "But on Election Day, you better be a Democrat. That describes Ray Perry pretty well—I don't know that he would have been a Democrat in another county."[21]

Indeed, Haskell County politics could be rough-and-tumble, and a grand jury investigating Ray Perry for misappropriation of county funds described the elder Perry's political style as "aggressive, unyielding, occasionally vengeful." He later worked to abolish the county auditor's office after the auditor refused to reimburse Amelia Perry for a business trip to Amarillo.[22]

Family history and his experiences in the late 1970s lobbying with fellow Haskell farmers over commodities prices had given the younger Perry a formal taste of politics. It didn't hurt that he was easy on the eyes. Perry was "this good-looking young thing," Reb Wayne recalled.[23]

But between the ranch and daily life, Perry wasn't tracking local politics closely. A massive ice storm in March 1983 had kept him inside for days before he arrived in Stamford to hear Democratic US Senate candidate Kent Hance speak. "I had kind of lost touch with what was going on," he said. At that event he was approached by "Big" Bill Lonley, who worked for US representative Charlie Stenholm and who asked if he'd run for State House District 64.

"Gosh, no," Perry told him. "I'd never run against Joe Hanna."

Lonley informed him that Hanna, who had held the seat for fifteen years, had announced a month earlier he wouldn't run for reelection.

That afternoon Perry told Anita he was thinking about running. What did she think?

"You're going to do what you want to do anyway," she told him. "I'm going to be for you."[24]

On January 12, 1984—a day before the filing deadline—he made it official in the community building of the Haskell National Bank. Identified as a "Haskell County farmer and rancher," a "Texas A&M graduate with Air Force service," and "from an old Haskell County family," favorable reports enthused that he had "the dress and demeanor of the classic young man running for office."[25] The 64th district was large, even by rural district standards. Indeed, it held more land than people: the "Big Country" of Callahan, Haskell, Hood, Palo Pinto, Shackelford, Stephens, Throckmorton, and Young Counties.

Stenholm, like Perry a conservative Democrat and a family friend and neighbor, talked with Perry for hours outside the area cotton gin in his pickup truck as Perry asked about campaigning in a rural district. Stenholm, whose congressional district included the 64th, offered his contacts, his mailing lists, and his endorsement. Perry was a good fit for the district, he reasoned, and had "all the character, all the ambition, all of the enthusiasm" he needed.[26]

But as their politics changed, so did the relationship between them.

By the early 1980s, there were functionally three parties in Texas: liberal Democrats, conservative Democrats, and Republicans. Conservative Democrats were called the "Texas Regulars" (sometimes called "Shivercrats" for their loyalty to conservative Democratic governor Allen Shivers), and from the 1940s to the 1980s these Democrats fractured the Democratic Party over the New Deal programs and later over advancing civil rights.

By the 1980s Ronald Reagan was making inroads in earnest. Reagan, a conservative governor of California, Barry Goldwater acolyte, and B-movie actor, used his rising profile to challenge Gerald Ford for the Republican presidential nomination in 1976. Texas was a primary battleground, and Reagan was successful in activating the Democratic Party's conservative wing, generating enthusiasm among newer suburban Texans, and converting rural Texans from the Democratic Party to the Republican. Ford lost the Texas primary with a surge in support for Reagan, including among conservative Democrats hoping Republicans would continue to be favorable to business interests. Ford eventually won the nomination but lost Texas to Democrat Jimmy Carter by 7,232 votes in the general election.

Ford lost, but "two-party Texas" won—the state was developing more fixed ideologies that meant voters now would have clearer ideological choices. Increasingly, Republicans benefitted from that choice. A book by Nixon aide Kevin Phillips, *The Emerging Republican Majority* (1969), called on Republicans to exploit conservative sentiment in the South and Southwest. Demographic change, a favorable business climate (low wages, weak unions), and an erosion of Democratic support in Sunbelt states like Texas netted a growing GOP advantage.[27]

A similar internal Democratic split helped elect Republican Bill Clements as governor in 1978. Progressive attorney general John Hill had ousted conservative incumbent Dolph Briscoe in the Democratic primary—Briscoe had backed George Wallace for the Democratic presidential nomination in 1968—and Clements beat Hill by twenty thousand votes to become the first Republican governor of Texas since Reconstruction.

The 1971 Sharpstown scandal—in which businessman Frank Sharp bribed members of the legislature, including House Speaker Gus Mutscher Jr., into supporting favorable banking legislation—had already crippled the Democratic Party brand. Gross inflation and economic stagnation, an unholy combination that had created "stagflation" across Texas and the nation, killed it. Anger over rising crime rates and cultural changes, such as efforts to pass the Equal Rights Amendment and expand abortion rights, drove wedges between people. Blue-collar workers long loyal to the Democratic Party because of economic concerns feared losing their place in society.[28]

When Perry first ran for the legislature in 1984, however, most of the competition was still inside the party primaries. The issues didn't matter much in the end—the local Democratic establishment backed Perry over his two primary opponents, and he won the nomination almost unanimously and later easily topped Republican oilman Sam Newcomb of Breckenridge, a twenty-year Army veteran whose stances differed little from Perry's.

The frugal rancher from Paint Creek spent $13,000 on that race, which he called "cheap" compared to others at the capital who racked up more than $100,000 in campaign debt.

But Perry also brought a bit of panache to the campaign trail, using the flying skills learned in the Air Force to campaign across the sprawling 64th district in his 1952 Piper Super Cub. Friends respected Perry's skill at the controls and would often join him in the years to come. That plane, on the other hand, was a subject of both jokes and trepidation, its mismatched green paneling leading friend and deskmate, House member Cliff Johnson, to suspect the plane was a mash-up of Super Cub and John Deere tractor.[29]

"Is Rick flying his plane?" future state senator Ken Armbrister asked upon hearing plans for Perry to fly a group to Austin. "Break out the bailing wire." The doors would barely shut.[30]

The two-party system still hadn't fully matured when Perry entered the House, even though redistricting in the 1981 session had crafted districts that were more or less winnable by one party or the other.

In fact, a slight edge went to Republicans as districts reflected significant growth in Republican-leaning areas.[31] Republicans hoped to pick up nineteen House seats in 1984 as demographic changes favored the party and the Republican brand became more distinct from that of conservative Democrats. For open seats like the 64th, lines drawn to protect Democratic incumbents made that a challenge. But times were changing; the 64th was one of about thirty seats where the Democratic primary suggested a party struggling with its identity.[32] Moderates and liberal Democrats typically voted together, bound by a fraying party. But moderates increasingly voted with Republicans, even on redistricting matters. That trend would reverse a decade later as Republicans began to dominate statewide elections.

"If the Republicans are going to help build a two-party system (which all but the most partisan of us would like to see), I believe the Elephants are going to have to put up more candidates," wrote a local paper.[33]

Changes were coming. Sixteen members of the legislature called it quits in 1983 and 1984, which led to a large freshman class in 1985, thirty-four-year-old Rick Perry included. "We were young, and we didn't know what to expect, but we were full of piss and vinegar," said former House member Ron Lewis.[34]

The class of 1985 was unique—thirty-three new members, among them future leaders including Dan Morales, Gene Green, Sam Johnson, Dr. Mike McKinney, Ric Williamson, and Lena Guerrero. "New type of legislators. Hard working, smart legislators," Perry recalled. The group bonded as members ate, drank, and went hunting together.[35]

The chamber was also more conservative than it had been in recent sessions. Democrats controlled 98 of the 150 House seats, but Republicans had gained 18 new seats, many of them flipping districts from conservative Democrats and all riding on Reagan's long coattails. Even so, people got along both politically and personally: "It wasn't just bipartisan, it was nonpartisan," recalls one member who served with Perry.[36] Your partisan label wasn't as important as where you were from, Perry reflected on this era.[37] As a new member, Perry "wasn't particularly partisan at all," recalled Harold Cook, who worked for the most liberal member at the time. And although Perry's critics over the coming decades would consistently downplay his intellect, Cook saw it differently. "He was a perfectly delightful guy, real smart."[38]

Newlywed Perry showed up for that first session with braces on his teeth, and he roomed with fellow freshmen and conservative rural Democrats Cliff Johnson of Palestine and Ric Williamson of Weatherford. After Perry won the office of agriculture commissioner in 1991, Johnson and Williamson kept the same apartment for twenty years. Johnson recalls the group was so broke back then "they couldn't pay attention," leading them to sleep two to a room.[39]

What kind of roommate was Perry? Beyond the usual roommate foibles, he was a good companion, tidy (usually) and chummy with fellow lawmakers. Cliff Johnson laughed remembering that Perry wouldn't "flush the commode," and when confronted, the future governor said that growing up on a dryland cotton farm encouraged saving water, including flushing toilets. "Still a problem," Perry joked years later.[40] The group was tight. Williamson was the "$E = MC^2$" guy; Mike McKinney was a medical doctor who kept the group balanced; Mike Toomey was the straight shooter, no-nonsense.[41]

Friend Ron Lewis first met Perry at legislative training. He recalled that Perry was "suave" and a "good-looking guy" and added that "he'd probably kill me for saying this," but he also "wore outfits that dictated where he was from"—sleeveless sweaters with his jackets and cowboy boots.[42] He was as "common as dirt," a compliment from roommate Cliff Johnson relayed years later. "He could walk into any honky-tonk or hunting camp or anything else and fit right in."[43] Perry got a jumpstart on the session because, after he won the primary, outgoing representative Hanna invited him to Austin to observe the special session that had just been called on education reform, including "don't pass, don't play" and teacher testing. There he saw "dealmaking at its finest": teachers' groups and legislators engaged in ample arm-twisting to pass these reforms.[44]

Perry was immediately a player in the process. "As solid as a freshman can be," remembered Ed Emmett, a Republican member from Houston who was chairman of the energy committee, of which Perry was a member. His personality and ability to read the room made this work. Unlike many members who arrived thinking they were smarter than everyone, "he quickly figured out 'these are the people I needed to help and get along with.'"[45]

And when it came time to pick a seat in the chamber, he asked for and got one closest to the media section, allowing him to chat up the assembled press corps who watched the floor action. At first the journalists viewed him as "ambitious but quiet."[46] It didn't take long, however, for the gregarious former Aggie yell leader to hit his stride, instantly recognizable for his tight jeans, movie-star looks, and quick smile.

More than that, "He was the guy you wanted to sit next to at a baseball game. Friendly and engaging and fun," recalled Leticia Van de Putte, a pharmacist and longtime Democratic legislator from San Antonio who was close to one of Perry's childhood friends. "He's devastating one-on-one."[47] And he wasn't shy about using those one-on-one skills on anyone he happened to meet. Exiting the House chamber one day in 1985, Perry ran into two women with name tags reading "Older Women's League," there to lobby for a bill allowing divorced and widowed women to remain insured for a year under their former husbands' group policies. "Oh, you're not an older woman," Perry assured one of them, taking a fact sheet and smiling broadly.[48]

Perry decided early on that he would prefer to block bad legislation rather than carrying his own bills, although he did work on one issue important to his district—a bill to protect commodity-buying businesses such as grain elevators and auctions.[49]

He was appointed to the House agriculture and livestock and energy committees—important committees for the 64th district—and wanted to "be part of the system, not just punch a button and go to committee meetings. He wanted to be in the mix," remembered a House colleague.[50]

Former House Speaker Gibson "Gib" Lewis (1983–1992), then in his second session with the big gavel, rated Perry a good member who brought more than charm and a farming background to the chamber. "He learned leadership in the military, and I might have been partial to him because of it. He was solid as a rock."[51]

But while you could take the boy out of Paint Creek, you couldn't take Paint Creek out of the boy—his habit of wearing (and frequently adjusting) tight pants earned him the unfortunate nickname "Crotch."[52]

Perry called his first session "stimulating" and "overwhelming." He learned that quiet committee negotiating was better than being heard on the floor: "The House floor is not where law is made," he told reporters after.[53] He learned from leadership, especially Jim Rudd, a longtime legislator from Brownfield.

"He got a taste of power. He was beginning to learn the exercise of power very early on," said a future Perry chief of staff. "He treated people with respect, and respected their opinion, not necessarily always agreed with them, and I think that's one of the traits that he had that made him so special—that he didn't dog people for their opinion or anything. Now he would argue with you, but he wouldn't dog you for your opinion. He never would make you out to be somebody evil."[54]

Fellow freshman legislator and roommate Cliff Johnson at the time ranked Perry among the top two or three of the freshman class. "I think the sky is the limit."[55]

For his part, Perry kept his ambitions modest—possibly becoming the executive assistant to Lewis, becoming chair of the House Energy Committee, maybe running for state senate.

The class of 1985 was unique in another sense, too—the political careers and fortunes of the budding Texas politicians who entered office that year would be forged in the fire of a relentless budget crisis driven by a massive oil bust and puckering droughts that damaged the state's revenue. Banks failed and real estate values plummeted. As Texas celebrated its sesquicentennial in 1986, oil prices dropped to ten dollars a barrel, dramatically reducing the revenue collected by the state and pushing the unemployment rate to almost 10 percent, 3 percent higher than the national average. At the time, the state's finances were so strongly tied to oil prices, one member recalled, that a dollar drop in the price of a barrel cost the state $100 million in revenue. Comptroller Bob Bullock, the wizened, hardnosed keeper of the state's checkbook, dubbed it a "crisis by anybody's definition." Texas was "on its back," Perry remembered. "You literally could stand on the third floor of the Capitol looking south and see through a lot of buildings."[56]

Desperate times meant possibly higher taxes.[57] "The question is not if there will be a tax bill," one observer told reporters at the time. "The question is how big it will be."[58] Predictions from economic forecasters, including Bullock, were that Texas would need a state income tax by 1995. Most politicians were against an income tax, including Mark White, the well-dressed and camera-friendly Democratic governor, who promised to veto any bill instituting an income tax. (Bullock later repented, saying the state would sooner see a Russian submarine in the Houston Ship Channel than a state income tax.)

Russians or no, the state needed money. Finding it would not be pretty, but the ongoing crisis, including months of special sessions and deal making, helped sharpen Perry's views, offering the first hints of his future fiscal conservatism.

Conservative House members objected to increasing taxes to make up a $2.3 billion budget shortfall. Groups like the Texas Association of Taxpayers stressed "fiscal responsibility" and favored spending reductions.

White and other Democrats were still smarting from a $4.6 billion tax increase passed in 1984 for public education and highway improvements, and the governor turned to the Bible and a passage from the book of Mark to insist that, even in a dire budget environment, that money would be protected. "Train up a child in the way he should go; and when he is old, he will not depart from it." But White quickly joined the call to cut spending before considering raising taxes.[59]

Perry agreed. "If we come as a group and cut state spending to a point we can live with, it will get us to the point where we're not going to be floating little heaters (hot checks) in November," he reasoned.[60] His conservative views were reinforced by those of other members of his legislative class, including Williamson and Toomey. These conservative Democrats "were Republicans without having 'Republican' by their names," Toomey recalled. "They believed what Republicans did back then with limited government. Make government run efficiently. Things needed to be appropriated but no more than that, no gains."[61]

Perry certainly had a conservative stripe, but few people watching at the time would have predicted his coming change of philosophy. "If you told me then that he would take a hard right turn, along with the rest of his party, and become hyper-partisan and become far right, I would not believe you," according to Harold Cook.[62]

Democrats still ran the House in 1986, but Republicans were making steady electoral gains—taking fifty-five seats and requiring Speaker

Lewis to dole out a few key committee positions to Republicans—and winning six seats in the thirty-one-member Senate.[63] A second sales tax increase in two years gave Republicans leverage, and while White and other Democrats got credit for their courage in facing an impossible financial crisis, the political fallout would cost them. Republican political consultant Karl Rove said White "expects to be crowned with a garland and given a reward. His actions are an indictment of his lack of leadership, not a symbol of leadership. I think he is (politically) dead."[64] Republicans took to calling him the "Governor of *Taxes.*" Bill Clements, a blunt and often cranky Republican who in 1979 had become the state's first GOP governor since Reconstruction before losing to White four years later, beat White by six points in their November 1986 rematch.[65]

Perry's voting record continued to be conservative with a nod towards protecting his district and those like it—for example, voting against a 1985 repeal of the state's Blue Laws (which had been in effect since 1863 and prohibited the sale of dozens of items on Sunday in the name of protecting family values) and pushing an amendment to exempt passengers in larger pickup trucks from a mandatory seat belt law that instituted $50 penalties for noncompliance.[66] "These are work pick-ups. They're used out in the country. You're in and out of them a lot." Representative Mark Stiles (D-Beaumont), who was called by his mostly good ol' boy colleagues "the Bubba of Bubbas," reportedly flashed "Bubba likes this" on lawmakers' desk video screens to show support of bills he favored.[67] Senate Democratic colleague Bill Messer was not impressed: "Bubba has written me" and thinks "he has got a right to ride out there on the roads any way he wants to." Republicans agreed. Perry's "Bubba amendment" failed, even as the seatbelt law passed.

This isn't the stuff of a political firebreather. Perry was rare creature in Texas in the late 1980s. His approach reflected the tempered political times of the era.

Meanwhile, Perry had become comfortable with the perks of serving in the legislature, even as questions began to be raised about legislators' close financial ties to businesses. A private plane, a ranching operation, oil holdings, and serving as a bank director in Haskell gave the appearance of financial success. Other legislators from West Texas had similar ties: Rep. Charles Finnell of Holliday had oil holdings, more than thirty pieces of property in Archer County, and homes and several cars in Austin. Rep. Steve Carriker owned Galaxy Farms, a consulting business with his wife, and shares in farming and co-ops.[68]

Perry loved to travel on state business in his single-engine airplane. When the legislature was not in session in 1987, he reported spending $8,719 on travel, hotels, and meals, according to House vouchers. He also traveled more miles in 1987 than any other lawmaker—15,062 by plane and just 66 by car.[69] It wasn't graft, Perry insisted, it was a time-saver. "I don't make any apologies because of where I live," he said, explaining that the one-hour drive from his home to the airport in Abilene, coupled with a layover in Dallas before a second flight to Austin, cost more and took as long as flying his own plane to Austin. Besides, he argued, that allowed him to spend more time with the "folks back home" and his family, which at that time included a four-year-old and a one-year-old. That, he said, was "more important to me than the Legislature."[70]

Given the part-time nature of the Texas legislature, members had long mingled public and private funds for political and personal purposes—it has been one of the longest-standing traditions under the Capitol's pink limestone dome. Getting caught was the second longest-standing tradition.

Most members didn't think twice about mixing these funds. Clements was nabbed for charging taxpayers $20,000 for round-trip weekend flights aboard his private plane to Dallas. Even so, more than a few eyebrows were raised when Speaker Lewis named Perry co-chair of the State Air Transport System, an interim committee charged with examining the cost difference between the use of private planes versus commercial air transportation by state officials. "It doesn't look good to appoint the people who are billing the big bills," Carriker noted at the time. But he, too, rationalized the practice, suggesting that Perry's use of his private plane made it possible for him to serve in the legislature, since his family remained back on the ranch.[71]

The episode, frankly, had little effect on Perry's standing back home.

The 70th legislature, which convened in January 1987, had even bigger problems than the prior session—a continuing budget crisis from cratering oil prices, a record-setting 9.5 percent unemployment (meaning eight hundred thousand Texans were out of work), and brinksmanship politics among the "Big 3" (the governor, lieutenant governor, and Texas House Speaker). Clements, the newly elected Republican governor, tried to convince the legislature to expand overcrowded Texas prisons without raising taxes in the face of a huge budget deficit. Half of the state's spending was in the executive agencies, and Clements wanted deep cuts.[72]

Those who wanted to spend more were "prairie chickens . . . just doing their little dance," the governor argued. The prairie chickens viewed him as an ostrich, sticking his head in the sand and ignoring the needs of a modern Texas.[73] Lawmakers printed shirts reading "Proud to be a Prairie Chicken" and passed a Senate resolution expressing "heartfelt and sincere gratitude for the contributions of the prairie chickens of Texas." Democratic lieutenant governor Bill Hobby called for a voice vote on the resolution: "All in favor, signify by thumping."[74]

The new-again governor also wanted education improvements and more prison funds but "didn't want to pay for it," said grim-faced Bill Hobby.[75] Everybody knew tax increases were on the horizon, and Clements, who claimed that only a businessman could fix Texas, was going to have to draw a shaky line in the sand. House member and close Perry friend Cliff Johnson, who then served as legislative liaison for the governor, stopped wearing blue shirts because telling the governor bad news would cause the staff to sweat when the governor chewed them out.[76]

The rural-urban divide shaped legislative battles throughout the 1980s, especially when the state had to balance a fiscal shortfall of almost $6 billion in 1989. "There is definitely a discrimination against rural Texas," said Perry. More than $135 million in cuts were made to county extension offices, 4-H programs, and farm-to-market programs, and "on the backs of rural Texas."[77]

Perry voted his district. A former member remembers taking a picture with Perry and other members—each person wrote a message. Perry wrote on Ron Lewis's picture, "Remember me when you're speaker and I'm in the lobby."[78] The members knew Perry would "strive to do something else" after his time in the House. The financial picture would run him out of the chamber—similar to many members who served in the part-time legislature.

In a sign of the chamber growing more conservative, the House voted in 1987 to require majority approval from both chambers and from voters in a statewide referendum in order to adopt a state income tax. Republicans made up one-third of the House, and tax increases were an easy target. "A litmus test between Republicans and Democrats would be to vote for tax bills—Republicans should never vote for a tax bill," recalled a prominent Republican member.[79] It was also a way to force a conservative governor to keep his promises on not raising taxes.

This was grim news for a state facing a $1 billion revenue shortfall for the prior two-year budget (even after the budget was cut to the bone in the special session in October 1986) and a whopping $4.6 billion shortfall for the next budget. Clements applauded the action. Perry and many other rural Democrats voted in favor, but most everyone realized some taxes would have to be raised to meet the impending deficit.[80] Clements called in fixer H. Ross Perot, who had helped navigate education reform in 1983, to help broker agreement: "I'm in my classic role, a grain of sand. I'm down here irritating the oysters a little bit. They'll make the pearl," Perot said.[81]

These intense budget battles shaped the ideological divide within the Democratic Party, pitting conservative members against more liberal ones. After the House approved a $40 billion budget in 1987 built on higher taxes than Clements had agreed to accept, Perry was one of only a few Democrats to vote against it and one of two West Texas Democrats to vote against (three voted in favor). Toomey, a Republican state representative from Houston who was later to serve as chief of staff to both Clements and Perry, urged the House to send the bill back to the appropriations committee for substantial cuts. Toomey—called "Mike the Knife" for his budget-cutting zeal—was a serious, intense, and private figure, the intellectual leader of the conservative group, the "shock collar," recalled journalist Dave McNeely.[82] Perry softened this, calling Toomey a mentor to the group of young legislators.[83] "Partisanship just wasn't as big an issue then," Toomey said of his alliance with Perry and other conservative Democrats.[84] His approach—no new taxes—became a Republican battle cry: "That good old Toomey line/That good old Toomey line/We'll never spend a penny more/'Til Toomey says it's fine."[85]

Perry's evolution as a politician was under way, influenced in no small part by Toomey. His reputation as a fiscal conservative had earned him a spot on the powerful appropriations committee in 1987, along with a group of other conservative Democrats, a move Toomey recalled as reflecting the speaker's acceptance that the budget would have to be cut.[86] Observers remembered that Perry "ha[d] natural conservative instincts on a lot of fronts." He had "that West Texas skin flint in him." He wasn't "afraid to spend money, but he [was] politically cautious in that regard."[87] "All of them were very conservative guys and had a good head on their shoulders, and that's how I picked 'em," the Speaker recalled. "When he first came to the legislature it was predominately white, Democratic, conservative. He was one of them, and I was, too."[88]

These budget hawks—a core group of nine legislators led by Williamson, a Democrat from Weatherford who would switch to the Republican Party several years after Perry—were collectively known as the "Pit Bulls," who would sit in the lower dais of the committee room and snarl at large budgets.[89] Their charge from the speaker: "Quiz the agency heads and make sure that whatever they wanted to spend was going to benefit the people of Texas."[90] "We were just a bunch of thirty-year-olds," reflected an astonished Cliff Johnson years later. They asked, "Is this a people thing or a money thing?" The group resisted cutting useful parts of the budget that benefitted people, but they were willing to trim financial excess.[91]

The questioning was vigorous, even "downright rude."[92] Perry, however, tended to spare agency heads who were, like him, graduates of Texas A&M, appointing himself the defender of his alma mater on appropriations, looking after their budgets and gently asking questions to spur more funds for their agencies. At one point seatmate Debra Danburg, a Democrat from Houston, unaware her microphone was on, covered her mouth, leaned over, and joked, "You're such a fucking suckass." Perry laughed so hard he nearly fell out of his chair.[93]

"We felt we were really something else, but we got our britches cut a few times, thinking we were bigger than we were. We were educated real quick," recalled Ron Lewis, a fellow Pit Bull. In one episode the Pit Bulls tried to reject an amendment by the appropriations chairman Jim Rudd that would have funneled money to Rudd's district. "We just showed the chair of appropriations," Lewis remembered bragging. Several members of the group, including Perry, were soon summoned to

Speaker Lewis's office. In the wood-paneled office sat the Speaker and Rudd. "So we were very well educated. That afternoon, we went back to appropriations, and we all voted for the amendment," Ron Lewis chuckled.[94]

But the Speaker also saw young, hard-working, smart members who cared about spending and the budget and how government ran—the same things he believed in. Like Gib Lewis, many of the Pit Bulls were conservative Democrats from rural areas. Perry was among the most conservative of the group.

The group was serious about the fiscal problems facing the state, but its members didn't panic. Debra Danburg, a liberal Democrat from Houston's Montrose neighborhood, was the only female (and liberal) in the group—the "pit bitch," she laughed. The group "was classically conservative" in that they didn't want to stick future legislatures with a big bill.[95] The group would meet in Williamson's office—he had his own computer, better than the state-issued equipment—until two or three in the morning to plan the state's fiscal future.

This was a big moment for members of the group, who were still relatively new to the legislature and were expected to be "seen and not heard," according to a former representative.[96] To his credit, and to Perry's political education, he gave the group plum assignments on Appropriations and Calendars.[97] The group was close, bound in part by the knowledge they could make a difference. "You had to deal with them. They couldn't be ignored," remembered longtime political consultant Bill Miller of the Pit Bulls.[98] The group was starting to have a significant effect on state policies, even as the Senate "went about their knitting," comfortable in its Democratic majority, according to Bill Ratliff, one of the few Republicans in the upper chamber.[99]

For Perry—known for his enthusiasm for the task if not as a "worker bee," the role was a nod that he was an up-and-comer.[100]

The group wore mobile pagers, cutting-edge technology at the time, so they wouldn't miss a vote. One member would stay to monitor committee hearings and contact the others if they were needed. Hearing the beepers go off in other committee hearings, one committee chair remarked, "Well I guess the Pit Bulls have a vote." The *Dallas Morning News*'s Sam Attlesey called them the "beeper bunch." "We know what's important is the votes [on the individual agencies]. We know if we can outlast them [liberals] physically or technologically, then we win. That is where the idea for the beepers grew out of," one West Texas lawmaker said.[101]

The group would "fight like hell" with other members (even those of their own party) on the House floor but get beers together after at the Cloak Room, the Austin Club, the Quorum Club, or the Cidadel at the Driskell Hotel (a members-only club where LBJ used to hold court). "There was nothing personal about it, it was business," remembered a former member.[102] Confronting a bill brought by colleague and friend Rep. Colonel James Adams, Cliff Johnson admitted they'd "rip the fur out of each other" behind closed doors, but in the end they needed each other's votes so the group would find a way to work out differences.[103]

Hard thinking about the state's fiscal health came just in time—by 1987 the state was immersed in an oil bust and money was tight. "We were broke. We had to cut the budget something fierce," Perry lamented years later.[104] The Pit Bulls cast an estimated four hundred votes as a block against higher state spending, often siding with Republicans and antagonizing committee veterans—Democrats—with their questions.[105] Many of the votes were for naught since the Senate shot down many of these cuts. Privately, many members with more seniority referred to the Pit Bulls as the "Pit Puppies."[106] Regardless, the relationships Perry forged in that lower tier of the hearing room would shape Texas politics for decades.

Clements had campaigned on not raising taxes. Once in office and faced with a steadily worsening budget picture, he first called for $2.9 billion in new taxes and then suggested he would support a higher number, prompting angry House Republicans and the media to call him out for hypocrisy. Eventually, he was forced by the state's miserable finances to relent. The budget bill narrowly passed, 78–70, with the $5.7 billion tax increase the largest in modern Texas history, worth some $11 billion today.[107] Faced with little choice, Perry voted in favor of the hard-to-swallow tax increase. Republicans turned on Clements, claiming they didn't see any difference between him and Mark White. Clements assumed Republicans would lockstep vote for the bill, but they did not, even with a Republican-stacked Ways and Means Committee. One Republican legislator said that the tax reversal would define Clements as "one of the worst governors this state has ever had," a comment that marked the beginning of hard-line Republican opposition to tax increases.[108]

During Perry's first term, after another emergency special session in September 1987, lawmakers had slashed $582 million in spending, about 1.5 percent, along with increasing sales and gasoline taxes. The cuts to transportation, social services, and higher education meant smaller paychecks for 4,500 state workers. Perry sided with Democrats supporting a revamped tax plan that raised the sales tax from 5.25 cents on the dollar to 6 cents and increased taxes on selected items and some businesses, along with a 15-cent increase for the gasoline tax. Without the needed one hundred votes, the tax increase would not take effect until November 1, 1987, and would have left the budget about $313 million short. Legislative bargaining was at play—a controversial "doomsday" provision reduced state revenue by $90 million, primarily targeting districts with conservatives who opposed the tax bill. In the name of expediency over politics, Perry voted to support the tax bill and its fast-tracked application.[109] He was the only member of the local delegation to switch his vote from opposition to support. (Fellow Democrat Foster Whaley from nearby Pampa held firm voting against.) The bill passed, and Texans immediately awoke to higher sales and gasoline taxes. This was supposed to be a short-term legislative fix but was extended indefinitely in the next session.[110]

This, too, hurt fragile relations between the parties, although to make it politically palatable, Lewis removed the doomsday language and let Republicans vote against the tax bill but for a separate measure to put the legislation into immediate effect. But the tinder box was lit—primarily from the respective party chairs—and the resulting explosion "cast a pall over the statehouse for years to come."[111]

The boot was on the other foot now. Republicans—fifty-six in total in the House, many of whom had campaigned on promises to nix any tax increases—now had to defend against record-setting tax bills, even if most of them had voted against the increases. Seven Republicans voted for the bill.[112] The chair of the state Republican Party, George Strake, said the party would use votes for higher taxes as a campaign issue.[113] Perry was one of those targets. The growing Republican base was becoming agitated—members of an "Ad-Hoc Citizens Committee for Fair Property Taxes" rallied on the steps of the Capitol in May 1987 decrying higher taxes.

Republicans were gaining ground in elections in the late 1980s, running against members forced to take the hard votes on budget issues. Future Republican activists and candidates saw this as a perfect political opportunity to purify the party.[114] Partisanship began to set in. Some conservative Republican legislators who sat near the "back mic" would jump up and raise points of order on Democratic bills.[115]

But it wasn't just Republicans versus Democrats. The Democratic Party in Texas had a split personality heading into the 1990s. It was tied—too tied, according to some more conservative party members— to labor and trial lawyers. A delegation of these new-generation Democrats met at a hotel breakfast in Dallas in late 1989 to urge the party to focus on the "forgotten American" to win back middle-class voters from Republicans. One local Democratic precinct chair carried a small American flag in his coat pocket, tired of seeing the party pummeled on the flag issue. "It's just to show that Democrats are patriotic, too," he said.[116] On election night in 1988 at Lloyd Bentsen's watch party, Democratic-turned-Republican strategist Matthew Dowd looked at the data and informed people that the senator—who was running for reelection at the same time as he was on the ballot as the Democratic vice presidential nominee (on a ticket with Walter Mondale)—"just lost the white vote" to his opponent, an obscure congressman from Amarillo. "So get ready, this state is gonna move." The rural and suburban demographic change was unavoidable. "It went really fast. I mean '90 was a good year, but that was the last really good year [for Democrats]" recalled Dowd.[117]

Perry wasn't always on the winning side, but his hard work paid off. He received the highest marks from the Young Conservatives of Texas, who ranked members on issues such as supporting private prisons, stopping a personal income tax, and chemical castration of those convicted of sex crimes.[118] He sided with Democrats backing efforts to move the 1988 Texas primary to March from May in order to join the Super Tuesday states, a moved opposed by all Texas House Republicans. He also backed Democratic efforts to propose a constitutional amendment to funnel more than $1 billion in state bonds and revenue to water projects across the state.

The 1989 legislature, Perry's third and final, didn't have the drama of past sessions. A welcome respite from economic bust years, the 71st regular meeting of the legislature was significantly less divisive. But the 1990 election was on the horizon (both Clements and Lieutenant Governor Hobby had announced they would not seek reelection) amid increasing party competition and redistricting battles to come. "It's going to be a routine session, I hope," said the typically understated Hobby. A normally crabby Clements reflected on the previous session, perhaps the most acrimonious in Texas history, saying that "maybe a good lesson was learned by all."[119]

Even so, early in the session Comptroller Bob Bullock estimated lawmakers would need an additional $1 billion to balance the budget, even while the "costs of educating young Texans, caring for the handicapped, housing prisoners and providing other state services also have risen in the meantime."[120] House member and Perry roommate Cliff Johnson called the score: the legislature was an independent body with significant power, but the comptroller held the money so they were "constantly sending flowers" to keep the comptroller happy.[121] The flowers might have worked. The modest resurrection of the Texas economy later cut the estimated budget shortfall to less than $600 million. Clements doubled down on his "no new taxes" pledge, snuffing out a proposed cigarette tax; he later signed a $289 million corporate franchise tax bill that he insisted wasn't a tax but rather a "redefinition" that closed loopholes. Perry, along with Ric Williamson, was among the leading voices on state budgetary issues. Perry had an unusual assortment of allies, having a personality that helped him forge friendships and long-term alliances in the House. "The Pit Bull sessions were tough and grueling," Danburg recalled of the work that paired a liberal Democrat from Houston with a conservative rancher from West Texas. "It could have been a horrible time. We told stories, so at least it was bearable."[122]

Democrats were consumed by infighting, while Republicans quietly built reserves led by Ronald Reagan's popularity, another Republican (Texan George H. W. Bush) in the White House, an influx of new state residents in the late 1970s and early 1980s, and millions in campaign spending. By 1989 Republicans held eight of the thirty-one Senate seats and fifty-seven of the 150 House seats. Republicans finally formed their own party caucus to organize members.

Perry ended his six-year run in the House with his charm and relationships intact and his political character seemingly moving to the right. Perry authored the first tax break for the oil and gas industry passed in the history of the Texas legislature, providing severance tax exemptions on new wells that used enhanced recovery techniques. Perry carried the bill in the House for Democratic railroad commissioner John Sharp, an old friend of Perry's from their days at Texas A&M.

Perry also flashed his tough-on-crime credentials, previewing a harder conservative stance on criminal justice issues as he wrote a constitutional amendment to deny bail to parolees accused of committing new crimes, reacting to a dramatic murder in the state. Kenneth Reed Smith was out on bail when he was charged with abducting and killing fourteen-year-old Amy Lynn Thatcher on her way home from school. Based on a New Mexico law, the amendment would have given judges the option to deny bail to those accused of committing a violent crime while still on parole. "This is not just an emotional, knee-jerk reaction. This is a very sensible approach," Perry said, claiming Amy would have been alive still if this no-bail amendment had been in place.[123] The amendment failed, but a broader tough-on-crime agenda, pressed by Governor Clements, was born.

In a rare tone-deaf maneuver, in the same 1989 session with a looming financial disaster, Perry coauthored legislation to triple legislators' salaries, citing financial hardships and the difficulty of recruiting new members who could afford to serve. Legislators hadn't had a raise since 1975, and, frankly, Perry needed the money for his growing family; Anita Perry worked as a registered nurse, earning too little to support them. "He was about starving to death," said one old friend.[124] Voters rejected the proposal in a statewide referendum, and Texas legislators would continue to be among the lowest paid in the nation.

Foreshadowing what was to become a key plank in the GOP platform, Clements also hinted at a special session on abortion after the US Supreme Court ruled that states could ban the use of public funds and facilities to provide abortions. Lieutenant Governor Hobby opposed the session, saying, "The fact is, most Texans believe the Legislature should mind its own business."[125]

Some Republicans agreed—the 1990 state Republican convention included a debate questioning government intrusion into private decisions versus those who preferred a "tough-as-nails" antiabortion platform.[126] "Putting a record vote on the table right before the election will scare the hell out of every legislator from Liberty to El Paso," said Phyllis Dunham, director of the prochoice Texas Abortion Rights Action League. "The Supreme Court gave that fence that some legislators and some candidates have been sitting on a good shaking."[127] In November 1990 twenty thousand people—including State Treasurer Ann Richards and actresses Cybill Shepherd and Morgan Fairchild—rallied at the Texas Capitol to keep abortion rights intact, chanting "Take our rights, lose your jobs" at legislators.[128] Clements ultimately chose not to call a special session on the politically charged topic before his term ended in 1991.

Other complex issues couldn't be ignored. In *Edgewood ISD v. Kirby*, the Texas Supreme Court found that the state's school finance system was unconstitutional, favoring students in property-rich districts. The court gave legislators until May 1, 1990, to fix it.

Three consecutive special sessions later, the legislature had taken a step towards equity in public school finance. The problem, as it had been for most of the previous decade, was money—how much to spend and where it would come from. Clements pledged to veto any bill that increased taxes or spent more than $300 million. Republicans had the numbers to slow any veto override should the governor break out his stamp. But in the House, Speaker Lewis had an increasingly difficult time keeping conservatives in his party in line. Bucking his party, Perry was the sole member of his west central Texas delegation to vote against a $553 million school finance bill that redistributed state money to Texas's more than one thousand school districts, partially funded by a quarter-cent sales tax and a ten-cent increase on a pack of cigarettes, along with increasing a number of state fees.[129] The governor vetoed the bill, and the House was eight votes shy of overriding the veto. Perry voted against the override.[130]

Ultimately, a final funding plan that took four months and four special sessions in June 1990 to produce and upped Texan's sales and cigarette taxes to among the highest in the nation was ruled unconstitutional. A new governor and a new legislature would have to sort that out in January 1991.

The legislature—which was in session longer than the US Congress that year—weighed on Perry; his daughter Sidney was born during one of the earlier special sessions. He was home for her birth, but he stated, "I started seeing some real clear evidence that I needed to go do something else. For the bottom line, for my family, it was not in their best interests."[131]

Reports were mixed but generally favorable about his time in the House. "He was like your friendly fraternity brother," recalled Wayne Slater, then a reporter at the *Dallas Morning News*. As his fellow Pit Bull member Danburg dryly put it, "Some of the people in the group were not known for their seriousness."[132]

She oversaw the group's voting when others were off hunting or playing golf. "All the guys in the group were conservative," so for votes on women's rights or racial issues, she'd clear it with them before voting. "Vote me like a Democrat," Perry would say. Except on abortion issues—they would vote against expansion of choice measures or find a way to avoid voting.

But Perry had his strengths, and Danburg singled out his work on the appropriations committee as an example. He had a knack for the politics of the hearings, understanding the backstories of witnesses who came before the committee. "He knew who slept with who to get to be the head of this agency, and whose daughter was so-and-so, and that's the reason they are the head of this agency," Danburg said.[133] The details were more than idle chatter. "Gossip is too light a word. He wanted to know what was happening with people both personally and professionally. He stored that information. He knew who he needed to help, he knew who was in trouble, and he knew what was coming around the corner a lot of the time. It made him better as a politician," one insider said.[134]

There was, however, the occasional flash of arrogance that threatened his reputation. As a sophomore legislator on appropriations, he was tasked with reading a section of the budget from the front mic. "Thinking it would be cool to just go up there and mumble," he caught the ire of "Mrs. T" (Senfronia Thompson, D-Houston), who was a Democratic stalwart and knew the legislative process better than most. She sat dead center in front of the podium. "She knew what I was doing," Perry recalled. She asked him to repeat something. "Why don't you listen better," was the smart-aleck response. Sensing danger, Cliff Johnson saved the day by literally stepping between the podium and Mrs. T, telling Perry to "go apologize to her right now," with a gaze at Perry that strongly implied she could make his legislative life miserable. On bended knee, Perry apologized. Mrs. T and the future governor became (and remain) dear friends.[135]

Even after three terms, Perry didn't take on big issues, sticking to issues important to his district and making sure to take care of the folks at home, according to fellow Pit Bull Ron Lewis. But he did his homework. He wasn't always the "guy whose name was on the bill, but if he had an interest in it, he was always involved in the negotiations," often serving on conference committees on bigger issues, said Lewis. Younger members deferred to older members, especially on important issues. Perry never "tried to be something that he knew he wasn't." Said Lewis, "There were people in the legislature doing everything they could do be recognized by *Texas Monthly* as one of the best" legislators, and others who felt "if we're not on any list, we're doing a good job."[136]

Nonetheless, Perry could tout significant accomplishments, many of them behind the scenes. He served on important House committees, including on the 1989 budget conference committee and the agenda-setting calendars committee. He was appointed by the Speaker to the Southern States Energy Board, a regional group focused on energy-related environmental concerns. He spearheaded a move to make state agencies more efficient using technology. Gone would be the days of the "green eyeshade," where state checks were processed by hand—Perry worked with Ann Richards, then state treasurer, to streamline government payroll.[137] The *Dallas Morning News* put him on the honor roll of members after what would be his final legislative session, calling him "a bright new star" for his role on appropriations and in crafting a compromise on the agriculture department's sunset bill.[138]

He was also on the House conference committee team for critical legislation during the infamous 1989 special session to reform workers' compensation insurance, when East Texas poultry king Lonnie "Bo"

Pilgrim brazenly handed out $10,000 checks on the floor of the Texas Senate to sway senators to make the rules more employer friendly. Democrats charged that Republicans were more concerned with helping Pilgrim cut costs than protecting workers from grave injury. House members charged that the Senate was too beholden to trial lawyers, and the Senate claimed the House was too probusiness. Amidst the political turmoil, a *Houston Chronicle* investigation found that lobbyists, including the Texas Association of Business, had given money to all five House conferees, including Perry. During the tense negotiations, he tried to lighten the mood by donning a bicycle helmet as the conference committee convened. Another member walked by Perry, saw the helmet, and asked, "Where's your tricycle?"[139] He was just having fun, trying to lighten the mood, but the committee couldn't resolve the differences and the bill died.[140] Later reforms establishing the Texas Ethics Commission and banning political contributions while the legislature was in session were forged from this work.

His tenure prompted high praise from some news outlets and recognition by the Texas Farm Bureau, Texas Southwestern Cattle Raisers Association, and Texas Association of Wheat Growers. He also got high praise from the Texas State and National Rifle Associations.[141]

"Let's face it, if you represented a rural district in Texas in the late 80s, the needs his district had were NOT . . . the sort of needs that garnered a bunch of big headlines," a Democratic consultant and former House staff member said. "You don't get famous taking care of that business."[142]

The Democratic Party in Texas was used to a wide ideological spread, so Perry's conservative record wasn't particularly alarming to Democratic leaders. Working closely—and, yes, compromising—with the opposition party was a hallmark of politics in this era, especially after rough-and-tumble sessions like Perry survived. But a coming move to the Republican Party would fully liberate him from concerns about backing party leaders' efforts to fix the state's budget problems by raising taxes.

Perry truly excelled back in his district. That meant showing up at an endless string of community events: the Young County 4-H Achievement Banquet, a branding board ice cream social ceremony in Graham in conjunction with the fiftieth anniversary of the placement of a centennial marker commemorating the formation of the Southwestern Cattle Raisers Association at the American Legion. He handed out awards to top 4-H'ers. When a tanker exploded into a huge fireball in Eastland, prompting the evacuation of more than a thousand residents, Perry traveled to the area to report back to the state.

Even his gaffes seem almost quaint in retrospect. A taped presentation on the dangers of drug abuse—sent by Perry's office to the twenty-six schools in his district—contained an awkwardly spliced thirty-second scene of a nude couple, taken from the film version of George Orwell's *1984*. The tape was a reused personal copy of the movie from the director of House Technical Services. The tapes were immediately recalled by Perry's office.[143] "I hope everyone will overlook this mistake. It happened. I'm sorry," Perry said. A staff member ultimately took the blame.

Perry forged cozy relationships with lobbyists in Austin during his time in the House, as well. In the years before tighter ethics regulations, members frequently dined with lobbyists or traveled at the expense of lobbying organizations. Some called them "sponsorships." Others called them "freebies." Whatever your term of choice, almost every night when the legislature was in session, there were five or more receptions at which members were expected to make an appearance at the Austin Club, the Stephen F. Austin, or the Van Grundy Hall. It was free food and drink for legislators who were paid $600 a month by the state, and members routinely made the rounds, Perry included.

He took constituents for meals at the swank members-only Austin Club on lobbyists' tabs. "I don't see this as an influence-peddling problem," Perry said. "I see it as a problem of perception, that people may think there's something wrong down here even though there isn't." He added, "If there are actually members going up and saying, 'Hey, Mr. Lobbyist, will you take me to dinner tonight?' then that may be stepping over the line."[144] Appropriations committee chair Jim Rudd easily won approval to spend state money to study a bullet train and promptly took a ski trip to Utah with lobbyists promoting the project and embarked on a fact-finding trip to West Germany (paid for by the German High-Speed Consortium). Perry went on the latter trip but reported that it failed to convince him the state should fund a full study.

"But it's a good example of where members went on a junket, a freebie, and it didn't influence opinions to benefit those who paid for the trip," he said.[145]

This was the world of members in the late 1980s—close associations with lobbyists and little oversight on the money spent to woo them.

By September 1989 Perry saw a brighter political future with the Republican Party. He wasn't alone. The number of white Democrats over forty—WD40s, as they were called—bolting out of the Texas Democratic Party for the blossoming Republican Party increased threefold during the 1990s. Between 2008 and 2013 alone, more than two hundred Texas Democrats at all levels of elected government switched to the Republican Party as the Democratic Party swung to the left.[146]

Few were surprised by Perry's switch, although opinions differed on the cause. "He was always politically ambitious. He saw what everybody was watching, which was that Texas was becoming more of a Republican state," recalled Dowd, the one-time Texas Democratic strategist who later worked for Republican George W. Bush.[147] Local Democrats in Haskell, Perry's home county, were also unsurprised, even if many people thought the county remained solidly Democratic. Perry thought differently—"[President] George [H. W.] Bush carried this district by 62 percent," he said. "I would suggest to you that I am as popular as George Bush in my district."[148] Upon reaching Speaker Gib Lewis and roommate Cliff Johnson vacationing in New Mexico with other members, Lewis said, "Hey, guy, it's your district, just do what you think is best for your district."[149]

Perhaps more to the point, he felt the only realistic path to winning *statewide* was to switch. When Danburg asked why he switched, Perry told her bluntly: "I can never go anywhere unless I switch parties, and they [Republicans] have made it clear to me that if I did I would have all the money I'd need to run for whatever office I want."[150] Toomey recalled of Perry and other conservative Democrats: "They were like Republicans, but they couldn't run as Republicans in their areas, it was still pretty rural."[151] Leaving the House made financial sense too—farming was lean back then, and the Perrys were not wealthy.

Democrats pushed back, with the executive director of the state Democratic Party predicting, "Republican honchos will use Perry as a boasting point and then discard him when his usefulness is finished."[152] The liberal *Texas Observer* called Perry the "Benedict Arnold of the Democratic Party" for siding too often with Clements, the Republican governor, and too seldom with his Democratic colleagues.[153] But of course it was more complicated than that. Gib Lewis was in the middle of a five-term run as House Speaker, and Perry had been passed over for a leadership role in 1989. The "ledger above him was crowded with good members," said Cliff Johnson, who worked for Governor Clements at the time. "But he was not going to be a chairman anytime soon."[154] Perry wanted the coveted chair of House Calendars Committee, which went to Hugo Berlanga from Corpus Christi.

Perry had backed Jim Rudd, the chair of appropriations, for House Speaker in a challenge to Lewis. "Team Rudd" fizzled, the kind of political bargaining that can put members on the outs with leadership if they back the wrong horse. Most of the Pit Bulls, who, like Perry, backed Rudd, had moved on within a session or two.

Perry always claimed he didn't leave the Democratic Party; instead, the party left him. At the time there wasn't much difference between Republicans and conservative Democrats. But from a strategic future position, he read the tea leaves well. The national Democratic Party was seen to be out of step with Texas Democrats, especially in rural areas, which held outsized influence in elections. "He timed it just perfect. The Republican Party was looking for young, conservative people."[155] Everyone else is taking the stairs, but Perry took the elevator, observed Bill Miller. Craven? "Malleability in the service of power" is how one observer characterized the change.[156]

There was some bitterness: notably, his friend and political mentor US Representative Charlie Stenholm was angered by the switch. US Representative Mickey Leland from Houston, one of a vanguard of liberals in the party in the late 1960s and early 1970s, called the Boll Weevils (conservative southern Democrats) a "tumor in the Texas Democratic Party." Other Democrats claimed to be happy to see him go.

He "never supported the trial lawyers' agenda, he never supported labor's agenda, so they were happy to see him go," said one former Democratic member.[157] He wasn't a big star and was not well known outside the capital or his district. "It was not an earthquake. But it turned out to portend one," said one journalist covering the events.[158]

Republicans, meanwhile, were happy to have him. The party was "lusting for people with talent and attractiveness," remembered a Republican consultant. "I don't know that they were all that crazy about Rick himself, but for what he represented I think they were delighted."[159] The Republicans wanted to win. In a transition period, anyone willing to join was welcome.

Welcoming him on the Capitol steps in Austin for the announcement was US Senator Phil Gramm, himself a former Democrat turned Republican. The two-term senator crowed about the party's newest convert, making it "clear today that we are not welcoming a private into the army. We are welcoming a person who is an instant new leader in the Republican Party." Others were nonplussed. "If Rick feels like it's time to come out of the closet, I don't have any criticism of that. It takes a lot of courage to declare you are a Republican when the vast majority of your friends and neighbors in Haskell County overwhelmingly vote Democratic," Carriker deadpanned.[160] Within a decade, Haskell County would be as red as a stop sign.

Nevertheless, Perry's switch moved the GOP to sixty Republicans in the 150-member Texas House, stinging Democrats who were losing electoral steam across the state—especially in rural areas. The timing of his announcement was important, too. Perry's announcement took place after the 180-day legislative session was over and just as he was planning his next political step.

—3—

REPUBLICAN AGRICULTURAL COMMISSIONER, 1991–1998

"Jane Fonda—That Was Stretching It"

Perry was the new fair-haired boy for the Republican Party, but he didn't completely self-select into the role.[1] Wayne Slater, the late coauthor of *Bush's Brain: How Karl Rove Made George W. Bush Presidential*, reported years later that Rove picked candidates for the Republican Party back then. "He picked Perry. He picked Kay Bailey Hutchison." He controlled the money, siphoning money for Republicans away from conservative Democrats, so he could shape the field. Rove wanted an ideological party and people tied to the business community, and "Perry was that candidate."[2] But it was clear that Perry couldn't beat Jim Hightower, the liberal incumbent, in a Democratic primary, necessitating his party switch.

Perry officially announced his run for agriculture commissioner on December 6, 1989, striking out at Hightower, a populist with a biting sense of humor, as "a political animal of the extreme left with bizarre ideas." He promised that "this race will be a black and white contrast. It will be a socialist versus a capitalist. It will be a man who believes in family values versus a man who believes in who knows what?"[3] Perry painted himself as a farmer and rancher who would represent the conservative mainstream of Texas and would not use the office to further his political career.

"My heart has always been close to agriculture and the people who farm and ranch," he said, capitalizing on a qualification the populist Hightower didn't possess. "That's where [Perry] came from. He could talk their lingo," said one friend.[4]

Even some conservative Democrats were skeptical of Hightower: "The only thing 'ag' about Hightower was his cowboy hat," said one former conservative representative.[5] When Hightower cut his finger on a lawnmower blade, Perry disparaged his background: "It's probably a good thing Hightower is not a farmer, because there are machines much more dangerous than lawnmowers on the farm, like shredders and bush hogs and balers."[6]

But Hightower wasn't a hayseed from the back forty. "Rick Perry? Oh, I thought you were talking about Gaylord Perry [the former baseball player]. Oh well, I'll wait to see who finally comes crawling out" of the Republican primary, Hightower scoffed in response. Instead of offering his own program, Hightower's spokesman wrote, Perry felt pressured to make up for lost time by attacking the jocular incumbent and was at best "the third dog in the hunt."[7] Seeking his third term, Hightower may have underestimated Perry.

Posters of Perry dressed in chaps and a Stetson, looking like a *Gunsmoke* character standing next to a horse may have given people the wrong message, but the cowboy swagger mattered. "Rick is just an exceptional retail politician," said Bill Miller, a longtime Republican consultant. The campaign projected a "charismatic sexiness that wasn't captured in any of the other races. None of the other candidates of any stripe had that *oomph*. It's an authentic Texan swagger. It's not this big-belt-buckle bullshit. He felt, looked, and sounded authentic."[8]

These campaign posters of Perry wearing tight blue jeans, his foot strategically poised on bail of hay, sprouted up in offices around Austin. Miller remembered *Texas Observer* editor Kay Northcott asking him if Perry "wore a sock" in his pants. "What that told me was he was inside her head. He had already gotten in the heads of people on the other side just by being who he was."[9]

"I'd be a rich man right now if I had a bunch of those," Toomey joked years later. "I could sell them to women who still want them."[10]

Only a few television ads aired, but Perry appeared to have been custom-made for the role as the only farmer-rancher on the ballot, throwing rope, fixing a saddle, riding a horse, and sipping from a steaming cup of coffee on the wild West Texas plains. He could have easily been the Marlboro Man, straight out of Hollywood.[11]

The brand mattered. He presented himself as a consummate Texan, and that was ultimately enduring—and endearing.[12] The campaign was shot on film, so it was warm and rich and "better than any Marlboro ad from Madison Avenue," Perry remembers of that shoot. "I looked like a cowboy, which [I] was at that point in my life."[13] Perry would get away with things other politicians couldn't: "Nobody could have pulled it off like he pulled it off." He was the first candidate in Texas to be pictured on a horse, consultants remembered. "Everybody wanted to be on a horse after that," recalled David Weeks.[14]

Or *was* it the right message? While certainly attention-getting, Perry also benefitted from a host of missteps by Hightower, from pursuing unpopular farm policies to a political scandal that engulfed his office.

Opponents painted Hightower as out of touch, an advocate of impractical and ideological experimental policies, such as stricter regulation of pesticides and an aggressive promotion of beef raised without hormones, which angered many of the state's farmers and ranchers.[15] Hightower's attacks on corporate agriculture alienated the office's core constituencies. "The entrenched powers feel alienated," Joe Rankin (then president of the Texas Farm Bureau) said at the time. "Jim won't get into bed with the good ole boys."[16] Hightower's push to reduce pesticide use angered farmers who believed they couldn't grow crops without them.

Central to the Perry strategy were accusations that the Department of Agriculture was racked by scandal and abuse of the public trust. Perry raised questions about Hightower's use of cars and credit cards from the department's Crop Inspection Program, racking up more than $7,000 in expenses from restaurants in San Francisco and New York, as well as at the Democratic National Convention in Atlanta in 1988.[17] Undercutting Hightower's populist message, his aides were also involved in a plot to pressure seed dealers subject to the agency's oversight to contribute to Hightower's reelection campaign. After the election, a federal grand jury indicted Hightower aides Mike Moeller and Pete McRae, among others, charging that they had used USDA funds for political work.[18] Three aides were convicted and served time.

In fact, the Republicans began sharpening their blades to go after Hightower even before the 1990 election. In a show of Republican strength during the 1989 session, the legislature passed (and the governor signed) a bill to force Hightower to share rule-making authority over pesticides with a panel of scientists and physicians. Clements, who pushed for the change, said it would give experts a voice in pesticide regulation, "as opposed to some ex–magazine publisher." (Hightower was the former editor of the left-leaning *Texas Observer*.) Hightower argued that the decision would prolong decision-making times, making it a bad deal for Texas farmers: "If a horde of locusts descends on your fields, you have to have a response in a matter of hours," he said.[19] Perry, then still a Democrat, cosponsored the legislation in the House. Republicans also briefly pushed to turn the elected position into one *appointed* by the governor. Hightower retaliated by bringing in country music legend Willie Nelson to argue against it at a legislative hearing. The matter was dropped, but Perry was impressed by the maneuver from his future adversary.

"People like celebrities," he said. "I don't think it will have a lot of effect on the membership of this body [the Texas House]. It will have a positive effect on the electorate as a whole. It's very much in Hightower's favor to keep the spotlight on himself. That's name identification he doesn't have to buy at a later date. He's making lots of hay while the sun is up."[20]

Competition in the 1990 race was unusually heated for a usually quiet office, with six Republican candidates, including Perry. On the Democratic side, the Farm Bureau political action committee paid the $3,000 filing fee for several farmers to challenge Hightower, although it failed to persuade Texas Rangers star pitcher Nolan Ryan or former Dallas Cowboys player Walt Garrison to jump into the race. ("They couldn't get a major leaguer, so I guess they'll settle for six bush leaguers," said Andy Welch, Hightower's spokesman.) Each of them said they were so upset with Hightower that if he won the nomination, they would vote for a Republican in November.[21]

In fact, in the fall of 1989, Perry talked to Nolan Ryan in Houston, who was sill pitching for the Texas Rangers, about the politics of a run (the nicest person "unless you piss him off"). Perry told the intimidating fast-baller, "I'm not fool enough to run against you"—and remembers telling him that "he's an icon" but once he picked a team, half the state would say "screw you. And you're not wired for that."[22]

Perry eventually won the primary in a runoff with help from Rove, who was setting up the chessboard for Republican wins across the state. Rove saw the future, and it was Republican. "The state was in the midst of a pretty phenomenal partisan shift. . . . This change was also mirrored in a shift in most rural counties from Democratic to Republican, or at least competitive for Republicans," he said at the time.[23] (Perry once explained the difference between himself and the GOP guru by describing his brain as chicken pot pie, whereas Rove's was a well-organized refrigerator.)

But building out the Republican Party infrastructure would take time. Back home in Haskell, Perry had to establish a Republican primary since the county hadn't previously run one; his grandfather boasted about being the first person to vote for a Republican—his grandson—in Haskell in decades.[24]

Few thought it would be a tough sell to convince members of the party that a Democrat-turned-Republican like Perry was truly conservative. "Hell, everybody that was a Republican that was on the scene had recently shifted from the Democrat Party," campaign consultant Jim Arnold said.[25]

That didn't mean people believed Perry was likely to win. Hightower campaign staff met every morning at Katz's Deli on West 6th Street in Austin, plotting strategy against an opponent they considered a lightweight. But the Hightower campaign underestimated the resentment many rural Texans felt towards their candidate. Hightower saw himself as a champion of the little man, "keeping the jam on the lower shelf so everybody could reach it," recalls Hightower's speechwriter Joe Holley. Rural Texans, however, saw him as a hippie liberal, out of touch with their conservative values and way of life.[26] They saw a writer for the progressive *Texas Observer* who couldn't connect with many conservative Democrats. "The agriculture community considered him a liberal intellectual, a socialist, if not a downright Communist," said Kronberg.[27]

By the time Hightower's campaign realized they were behind, with little money in the kitty, it was too late for a statewide television advertising push, about the only thing that could have saved him.

Perry, meanwhile, campaigned hard. He was disciplined. He was on message. He was better than most candidates at raising money.[28] He could work a crowd, singling out people he knew to make a point. All candidates get tired of campaigning, a former campaign consultant said, but Perry never did. "He thrived on it."[29] If Perry found out there was a Boy Scout troop meeting in Muleshoe, he would be there. "All he needed was money for gas." To save money, he would fly to different airports to price-shop cheaper gas, pushing the lever to empty too close for comfort more than once. He would land on a postage stamp, joked roommate Cliff Johnson, who recalled Perry's plane leaking oil all over the state.[30] His campaign focused on targeted television advertising in larger cities to blunt Hightower's high name identification, coupled with old-fashioned retail politics, including phone banks and yard signs, in the vast reaches between the cities. Perry ran ads highlighting Hightower's appearance with Jesse Jackson, whom Hightower had endorsed for president in the 1988 Democratic primary. "It was a taboo at the time" to back Jackson, and Perry exploited it, recalled House legend Senfronia Thompson.[31] (Hightower brought down the house at the convention with his comment that George H. W. Bush "was born on third base and decided that he'd hit a triple.")[32]

Larry Evans, a Houston Democrat and leader of the Texas Legislative Black Caucus, warned Perry the ads veered dangerously close to race-baiting and asked the campaign to stop running them. "Given the foregoing, and in the spirit of genuine racial harmony and cooperation, please refrain from campaign tactics which appeal to the worst in us all," Evans wrote. "My request is based upon my knowledge of you as an honorable and racially sensitive man."[33] Another ad targeted the Hightower scandals, and the campaign also sought to link, without any supporting evidence, Hightower to anti–Vietnam War activist and actress Jane Fonda. Perry later acknowledged that may have crossed some ethical lines: "Jane Fonda: That was stretching it a little bit. That was trying to show that he was a liberal, and I was a conservative. There were some times that, quite frankly, we stretched it."[34]

But it all worked. In a down-ballot race, "if you can get voters to remember one thing about a race, it's mission accomplished."[35] Voters had several juicy items to snack on: Perry as poster boy, Hightower scandals, and the incumbent's liberal, pesticide-hating ways.

The powerful Farm Bureau—kingmaker for candidates running in rural areas—was also ready for a change at the Texas Department of Agriculture, citing battles with Hightower over pesticide regulation and hormone-free beef. "He's gone off on tangents. He wants to produce antelope meat and Christmas trees," said the organization's spokesperson. New Republican Perry nabbed formal backing from the Farm Bureau, although not from the Texas Farmers Union, which backed Hightower.[36] The Farm Bureau support was critical. Hightower and the Farm Bureau were like oil and water, and the bureau was used to getting its way with agriculture commissioners.[37]

Hightower viewed the campaign as a referendum on the future of Texas agriculture, as he promoted not just the Christmas trees and antelope farms the Farm Bureau complained about, but also pushed vineyards and fish farms, promoted the direct sales of commodities, and worked to reduce chemicals in crop production. Although farfetched for Texas in the 1990s, the agency would wade into these waters in later years.

But Hightower didn't take the race seriously enough. A reluctant fundraiser, he expected to raise a million dollars. In his previous race for agriculture commissioner, he presented the State Democratic Party Executive Committee the three-thousand-dollar filing fee in a bushel basket filled with $1 bills, collected by a supporter from Happy, Texas, from two hundred working farmers and ranchers throughout the state.[38] Hightower sought tougher measures to combat pollution from hazardous waste;[39] he received an A from the Texas Environmental Voters Watch Group, a coalition of environmental leaders. Perry scored an F.[40]

Polls reported a sizeable gap for Perry in May 1990, as he trailed Hightower by 35 percent, with 21 percent undecided. Republican support was the problem: among Republicans, 41 percent planned to vote for Perry but nearly as many, 38 percent, supported Hightower. The Republican Party, for all the gains, still wasn't seen as a viable political choice, even in a down-ballot election. Independent voters favored Hightower almost two to one, and Hightower was popular with both blue-collar workers and professionals. Polling showed that 67 percent of Texans were comfortable with split-ticket voting, and it was hurting Republicans in 1990. This was especially true in the lieutenant governor's race, where conservative Democrat Bob Bullock held a twenty-point lead over Republican Rob Mosbacher—a quarter of Republicans said they would vote for Bullock.[41] Perry didn't ultimately win the rural vote, but he cut the margins enough to win his race.

Painting Hightower as a corrupt liberal worked to bring Republican voters to Perry's side. It was a national strategy—corruption or salacious sexual allegations crippled Colorado senator Gary Hart's 1988 presidential campaign; brought down US House Speaker Jim Wright of Fort Worth; and hit Arkansas governor Bill Clinton in the 1992 presidential election, although it did not derail his victory. Hightower recalls the impact of these hits: "They ran ads of me endorsing Jesse Jackson—ran that in East Texas. One ad showed a hippie setting a flag on fire and throwing it on the ground, and my picture came up out of the flames. So I had supporters in Dallas and Houston and East Texas who said, 'Well, I liked ol' Hightower but I didn't know he burned flags.'"[42] If it hadn't been before, politics was now blood sport. The Perry campaign clawed steadily to dead even with Hightower in surveys in early November 1990. He picked up the endorsements of six famers who had run against Hightower in the Democratic primary in the spring: "Jim Hightower and the seven Republican dwarfs," as Democratic Party officials called them, embracing the liberal Hightower.

Republicans hoped to ride national sentiment (Reagan had won the state with 64 percent of the vote in 1984) and Sen. Phil Gramm's popularity (he won 60 percent of the vote in 1984). The money was rolling in, too—a Gramm fundraiser at the Astrodome in 1989 pulled in $2.4 million (worth about $5.5 million in 2022 dollars). Republicans held a record number of county primaries—247 in the state's 254 counties, besting the previous high of 235 in 1988.[43] The Republican Party emphasized unity with a series of campaign visits across West Texas towns, including Amarillo, Lubbock, Midland, and Abilene. Gramm, gubernatorial nominee Clayton Williams, lieutenant governor nominee Rob Mosbacher, attorney general nominee J. E. "Buster" Brown, and the rest of the GOP ticket reminded voters of their conservative values and drew a contrast to the disarray the Democrats currently found themselves in. They called it the "Footprints of Texas" tour.

Rick Perry did his part by shooting clays with Clayton Williams and his wife, Modesta, as Williams picked up the Texas State Rifle Association endorsement in the fall. Williams tried to boost the rest of the ticket in remarks to a crowded ballroom on the Texas Tech campus in Lubbock. "You've all seen that television series *Lonesome Dove*? It sure would be bad if I got elected and the rest of the ticket didn't. You'd be calling me lonesome guv." Williams couldn't resist taking a shot at his Democratic opponent, Ann Richards, accusing her of wanting to raise taxes, flip-flopping on flag burning, and being indecisive about death penalty for child murderers. In short, he painted her as a gay-loving, Jane Fonda liberal. "She is a Hollywood liberal running in our conservative Texas. There is no room for that."[44]

Richards, a two-term state treasurer, wouldn't be outdone. She went dove hunting in Kaufman County on opening day, emphasizing she wouldn't take anyone's sporting guns away.[45] She questioned Williams's business ethics—succeeding in getting under his normally thick skin. Clements, the outgoing Republican governor, was also a bit of a drag on the ticket, with a low 34 percent approval rating—attributed to his tax increase and his role in the Southern Methodist University football payoff "Pony-Gate" scandal. (Clements had been a member of the private university's board of governors.) This was despite near record-high approval for President George H. W. Bush in Washington.[46]

Perry flew himself around the state to small farming communities, visiting rural newspapers and taping radio spots at a time when radio was both local and influential. He walked into Rotary Club meetings and came out having made a roomful of friends. "He was one of the first to understand the strength of rural voters who tended to be conservative," said one journalist.[47] Many didn't like Hightower's liberal bent, and "Hightower didn't do Rotary clubs," Kronberg said.[48] But the largest newspaper closest to Perry's hometown paper didn't endorse him, instead favoring Hightower. "Hightower's ultra-liberal politics is troublesome" the *Abilene Reporter News* wrote, but he has "demonstrated freedom of thought that has made the office effective for promoting markets for Texas agricultural products," the newspaper wrote.[49] Hightower didn't think these were *his* voters.

Hightower leaned on his celebrity friends, with actor and environmentalist Robert Redford headlining the post–Labor Day "Jim-Bob's

Kick-Ass Populist Back-to-the-Ranch Political Extravaganza," featuring Texas music and barbecue. Bob Bullock, Dan Morales, and John Sharp attended. House Majority Leader Jim Wright and Ann Richards spoke. Gary P. Nunn and Ruben Ramos and the Texas Revolution provided the soundtrack. Later in the campaign, Hightower called for reforms to the nation's "critically ill" healthcare system, which had significantly impacted rural Texas.[50]

Despite his easygoing demeanor, Perry was feeling the stress. He even said his hair had started to fall out as it appeared until the last few days before the election that he was unlikely to win.[51] Ray Sullivan recalled Perry would be so tired he had forgotten how he got from stop to stop.[52] He ran a lean campaign—Rick Perry the prodigious fundraiser didn't yet exist, so the budget was modest. The campaign kept track of every penny. Then came the "Claytie collapse" in October, threatening to sink every Republican statewide candidate. Williams bragged that he hadn't paid taxes, setting off alarms about what else he might be hiding. "Boot-in-mouth disease," some Republicans called it after a string of awkward statements from the irascible Williams. Perry's friends in the House didn't think he would win, and at least one planned to attend the election night party to support his friend in his loss: "I thought he was going to lose." At the party Rove took in the trappings—country music, barbecue, and a cake with Hightower's face on it—and, convinced Perry was going to come up short, slapped a grim-faced Perry on the back. "You fought a good fight."[53]

But Perry pulled it out. Hightower was dumfounded by the loss, taken by surprise and with a quarter million dollars in unspent campaign cash. "He didn't know he was going to lose until two or three days before the election," remembers Perry's campaign consultant.[54] There were a lot of angry farmers out there, ready to oust Hightower. After the dust settled, Perry had won a tight victory, with 49 percent to Hightower's 47 percent.[55] Hightower was "small in stature" but was loved by the progressive wing of the Democratic Party—a Goliath of the party—so the win gave Perry instant credibility in Republican circles.[56] At the same time, Hightower was so disliked by conservative Texans that Democrat Niki Van Hightower (no relation to Jim but running for state treasurer against Kay Bailey Hutchison) lost, possibly because of her last name.[57] Even Yellow Dog Democratic areas like

Perry's hometown crossed over to side with Perry, where he won 1,536 of the 2,395 votes.

Perry credits Rove but also Republican women and the Farm Bureau for the win. One rural group pulled their cotton trailer onto the shoulder of the interstate and displayed a handmade sign: RICK PERRY FOR AG COMMISSIONER. But even Republicans—including GOP state party chair Tom Pauken—still chalked up his win to more of an anti-Hightower vote than a pro-Perry vote, downsizing Perry's role in the party's growth.[58]

But those two statewide wins—agriculture commissioner and state treasurer—marked 1990 as a seminal moment in Texas politics. The campaign was the first consequential fight of Perry's political career, and he came out on top, if a little bloodied by a bruising campaign that set a new tone for rugged two-party politics in Texas. Three Hightower aides went to prison. Perry instantly became seen as an instrument of party change, even before George W. Bush played savior.[59]

"Rove only knows one style of campaigning," a longtime Democratic operative said. "That's just insult the other guy to death. By election day hopefully (voters) will believe you."[60]

The job of agriculture commissioner was a lot tamer than the campaign to get there. Most agriculture commissioners rarely make headlines. "Most people in the state of Texas probably didn't even know we had an agriculture commissioner, let alone who it was," Perry recalled.[61] That gave him time to breathe and focus on business, not politics, dealing with everything from wildflowers to fire ants in a state where agriculture remained an important economic driver. Still, he did what he could to raise his statewide profile. He penned letters to the editor of local papers supporting 4-H Clubs, citing his personal experiences and extolling the program's virtues in teaching commitment and providing experience, even as the state was becoming more urban, with youngsters in Dallas as likely to be tending rooftop gardens as they were to attending livestock shows.[62] Agriculture was an $11 billion industry, accounting for one in five jobs statewide and pumping more than $32 billion a year into the state's economy—a substantial revenue stream. Perry vowed to bring agriculture processing back to Texas, creating thirty thousand new jobs.[63] He did draw a ripple of attention when he appointed a vegetarian to head the agency's beef promotion projects. "It was a little gutsy," an observer recalled.[64] Executives at the Texas and Southwest Cattle Raisers Association had no objection.

A big part of the agency's responsibility was overseeing grants and protecting Texas crops. Under its aegis, Perry funded a project to determine if Big Bend bluebonnets could be commercially sold to further boost the multimillion-dollar business in Texas.[65] Fire ants—the scourge of Texas picnics everywhere—also threatened crop production and ranching, and Perry's Texas Department of Agriculture went to war against the red menace. "Some of the most brilliant minds in the country assure me we will be able to eradicate fire ants—right after we teach pigs to fly and coyotes to tend sheep," Perry noted, tongue firmly in cheek, in one summer press release. The department also developed a program to control an outbreak of armyworms, a hard-to-spot pest that threatened the state's beet and cotton crops.[66]

Ants weren't the only pest. One TDA backfire involved a plan to mate "unladylike" (according to a press release) Africanized bees with the mellow European honeybees to more vigorously pollinate crops. Unlike Hightower's push for pesticide-free agriculture, Perry supported proper management of pesticides, along with pheromone research to eliminate queen bees, and TDA was there to help.[67] These new bad-attitude bees channeled their excess energy into reproducing more bees with delinquent demeanors. Because of the importance of bee pollination to Texas crops and the production of hive products including honey, the legislature appropriated more money for TDA to hire inspectors to monitor the buzzing problem.[68]

Perry's early efforts to transform the agency included a reorganization that cut jobs, consolidated offices, and saved $3 million over two years—all within his first six months in office. Critics complained it was a smoke screen to purge employees left over from the Hightower administration, "absolutely" political, according to the fired director of the Food Assistance Program.[69]

And in a suggestion notable for its unpopularity across a number of constituencies—though not, perhaps, with rural Texans—Perry suggested in 1993 that the agency be moved from Austin, "away from the Capitol and the ivory towers disguised as pink buildings," an allusion to the pink granite used to construct the state capitol building.

One plus, he said, would be to send jobs to the state's heartland. Employees were not enthused, with one, Jeanne Carter, calling it "absolutely the most ridiculous idea Rick Perry has ever had since he's been in office." "A true nightmare," another employee said, citing the implications to related agencies.[70]

Such a move would have been unprecedented, requiring a constitutional amendment. The suggestion prompted state senator Gonzalo Barrientos (D-Austin) to suggest Perry quit Austin and leave the agency and staff in the city.[71] The idea went nowhere. Twelve senators signed a letter to block the proposed constitutional amendment, but Perry was undeterred, saying he was "proud to hold the mirror" to how state government does business.

In other legislative fights, Perry mostly stayed in his lane. He bragged about the 1991 budget, which gave his department $2 million less than the previous budget, emphasizing doing more with less. He lauded Richards, the Democratic governor, for using the line-item veto for a budget rider that would have eliminated inspections of vegetable and citrus commodities. He worked with the legislature to oppose transferring regulation of pesticides to another agency but applauded them for lowering workers' compensation insurance rates to put more funds back into the hands of working farmers and ranchers.

Perry wasn't only about cutting, however. He also drove efforts to modernize through investing in new technology: the Internet. The agency joined the digital revolution in mid-1995, establishing a political website with photos, a biography, and information about Texas agriculture. The website was paid for with political funds, but Perry embraced the idea of using technology to communicate with farmers. "We're seeing a lot of agricultural applications for home computers," he said.[72] He later embraced privatization, turning over the inspection of gas pumps to the private sector to "save taxpayers' money and enhance efficiency."[73] Like the Pit Bulls' embrace of beepers for connectivity and computers to accurately assess budget woes, technology drove progress in TDA.

For Perry, the issue of jobs in Texas hit on two important themes: bipartisanship in legislative negotiations and job creation as a major goal. "We brag that we produce more cotton, cattle, goats, wool, and mohair than any other state," he said. "But that bragging stops when it comes to processing those products—and reaping the resulting profits."[74] He also worked with Democratic senators to allow food stamp recipients to use their benefits at farmers' markets. He was "welcoming" and easy to work with.[75]

Other goals may have been less tangible but still often yielded measurable results. Perry justified an ag literacy campaign because modern Texas kids were more likely to visit grandma at her condo at the beach than on the farm, but the campaigns also made it easier to promote Texas products and expand avenues for international trade.[76] Part of the campaign involved encouraging local Texas school districts to review bid specifications for food purchases and remove barriers to buying Texas produce. Only a fraction of the six hundred thousand school lunches served in 1992 featured Texas produce, something TDA wanted to change.[77] Several schools followed Perry's lead, including the Houston Independent School District, which switched to buying orange juice grown and produced in Mission, Texas.

Much of the unglamorous work of state agencies is enforcing rules. In 1997 spot checks found that many milk cartons contained sips and swallows short of the advertised amount. The state's sample was tiny, but Perry, standing beside a test beaker of milk, cracked down on measurement compliance.[78]

Serving as agriculture commissioner gave Perry a taste of what would come to play a growing role in governing Texas—navigating relationships with the federal government. "Politically, it's never a bad move to be against the federal government," he later recalled. "They're a useful foil," but they earn it because of a lack of response to the average citizen.[79] Perry gave speeches around the state in 1993 and 1994 with the same theme: bad government policies resulted in overregulation and infringed on private property rights. Both came from a lack of understanding of farmers' lifestyles and created confusion, frustration, and added compliance costs.[80] Agriculture had fallen for that old "just trust government" line for too long.[81]

Perry fought back against regulations he felt were too expansive, especially from the US Environmental Protection Agency. Among the regulations receiving pushback was one that limited the time of day certain chemicals could be sprayed and required special protective gear to be worn by those doing the spraying. He acknowledged that protecting farm workers was a legitimate goal but argued that the policy was overly broad and was not backed by funding to enforce it.[82] These fights drew high praise for Perry from producers, with one saying, "We're not very political, but Rick Perry and his group are probably the best thing going for Texas agriculture." These fights drew high praise for Perry from producers, and the accolades weren't limited to those in Texas. "After seeing and comparing the secretary of agriculture for California and the commissioner of agriculture for Texas, Rick Perry just outshines what we've got in California."[83]

Perry also pushed back against 1993 Clinton administration rules to reduce pesticide use, favoring the inclusion of economic impacts, and not just public health, to determine standards for allowing certain pesticides to be used.[84] He also rejected federal efforts to regulate the use of water from the Edwards Aquifer, the underground water source for much of Central Texas that provides critical habitat for several endangered and threatened species. Litigation initiated by the Sierra Club alleged the US Department of the Interior and US Fish and Wildlife Service failed to enforce the Endangered Species Act as it related to water from the aquifer. Perry said he supported environmental protection but endorsed what he called a "balanced" solution, negotiated locally by water districts, as the best course.[85]

He argued that bureaucrats shouldn't be in charge of protecting natural resources, going so far as to compare regulations to collectivism in the former Soviet Union. Private citizens, he said, were more likely to care for those resources than government agencies. "It's a question of stewardship versus bureaucracy."[86] The federal judge ruled against Texas.

As the 1994 election approached, the federal-government-as-whipping-post became a frequent Perry theme. In remarks to the Nacogdoches County Extension Program Council, he spoke out against the Endangered Species Act and the overregulation he saw as threatening private property rights, contending that burdensome overregulation left producers unsure how to comply with the law. Addressing the Texas Agricultural Aviation Association at the Adam's Mark Hotel in Dallas in early 1993, he accused the EPA of "regulation by the government, for the government." And he argued at the Dumas/Moore County Chamber of Commerce Industrial Banquet in 1994 that "excessively broad regulatory definitions make landowners adversaries by their mere presence on the land."[87]

The way to help Texas agriculture, he argued, in what was becoming a Republican talking point, was to "put common sense back into government."[88]

Washington faced a serious budget deficit and economic crash as Bill Clinton took office in 1993, and Perry quickly went on the offensive against some of the proposed solutions. One proposal called for increasing an energy tax on British Thermal Units, or BTUs, of natural gas. Higher BTU taxes would have meant higher heating bills for agricultural greenhouses, as well as higher costs for fertilizer and other chemicals, which are made using components of natural gas. Texas, as the nation's leading producer of natural gas even back then, arguably would have been hit disproportionately. Perry put the price tag at up to $2 an acre. "Somebody must have told the President farmers work for free," he said in a crowd-pleasing sound bite. "Somebody must have convinced him that agricultural producers don't send their kids to college. They don't have mortgages to pay. They don't have the right to a fair and reasonable profit." Bureaucrats, he suggested, collect taxes, while agriculture pays the price.[89]

Perry's solution echoed his arguments regarding regulating the Edwards Aquifer: landowners, not government bureaucrats or lobbyists, should determine how to use the land.

But back in Texas, not even politics could control the boll weevil. The pest threatened cotton farmers in the warm winter of 1991 and spring of 1992, and Perry wanted increased funding to fight the scourge. The bill, however, ran afoul of revenge politics. Rumors held that state senator Steve Carriker, a Perry foe, buried the bill in the 1993 regular session in order to punish Perry for switching parties and beating Hightower two years earlier, even though Carriker's own cotton crop had been devastated by the pest. Perry noted that the fear of pushing the issue to a special session was that other issues (like school consolidation) would get in the way, but he still planned to ask Governor Richards to put the item on the call: "The governor got some bad advice from staff, from Carriker, but that's behind us. It's spilled milk," he said.[90] Letters to the editor complained about the "bad blood and bad politics" on the Rolling Plains, with farmers in the middle of the skirmish. Perry and

Carriker crossed swords again in the final days of the prior legislative session in 1991, when Carriker added an amendment on the final day for changes to the TDA budget that moved $1.5 million collected by the agency to the state's general fund. Perry accused Carriker of lying about Perry's backing of the move: "State law doesn't say the crop inspection fund should be raided to pay for welfare, legislative salaries, or anything else."[91] Perry subsequently backed Carriker's Republican challenger, Tom Haywood, in the 1994 election, which Haywood won.

While Ann Richards and New York governor Mario Cuomo watched the 1994 Super Bowl rematch between the Dallas Cowboys and Buffalo Bills at the White House with President Clinton, Perry took advantage of the publicity to grab a bit of the spotlight himself, betting New York's agriculture commissioner over the outcome, with the loser sending the winner a cheesecake. Victory for the Cowboys the prior year had netted Perry a case of wine produced in New York—and the opportunity for some grandstanding. "We really enjoyed winning the mediocre New York wine last year," he crowed. "It cleaned those saddles up real nicely."[92]

Thanks to the Cowboys' repeat victory in 1994, that cheesecake gave Perry another chance to gloat. It was a fun moment for a politician who enjoyed the camaraderie of politics but also an indication of the low-hanging fruit Perry could grab.

The agriculture commissioner's job wasn't particularly ideological, but, as Hightower had before him, Perry periodically threw a little red meat to his base. Decades before most people had even heard about vegan diets, animal rights activists launched the Great American Meat Out, celebrated every March to promote the benefits of a meat-free diet. Perry launched his own counterprogramming in 1992, calling it the Great American Misjustice and contending that quality of beef protein and the potential for beef to reduce iron deficiency in young women globally, along with the industry's billion-dollar impact, deserved greater respect and appreciation.[93]

Long before the Trans-Texas Corridor (a proposed network of all-in-one supercorridors made up of toll roads, railways, and utility easements that would have connected most major Texas cities by rail) became a political thorn in Perry's side, he opposed efforts to build a bullet train and supported efforts opposed to the Texas High Speed Rail. "I'm not opposed to progress" he stated, but he argued that the proposal put Texas agriculture—fourteen thousand acres of it—at risk by taking the land out of production. A rail line bisecting agricultural lands would be "just money out of your pockets" for farmers. The noise would disrupt livestock and pastoral settings. "Folks, that's more than a 600-mile runway cutting through the Texas countryside," Perry said at a press conference.[94] He shifted positions on this issue later as governor when he embraced a similar network linking the state's major cities.

The next political step was never too far away. Perry announced in late 1993 that he would run for a second term, saying he had fulfilled his 1990 campaign promises to trim agency staff and increase efficiency. The next four years, he said, would focus on processing more Texas commodities within the state and helping farmers and ranchers cash in on the pending North American Free Trade Agreement, which took effect in early 1994 and which Perry hailed as the beginning of a new era in freer trade with Mexico. Sales of pork across the border would soar.[95]

But even then Perry was thinking ahead. Campaign manager Jim Arnold and longtime Perry friend and ad maker David Weeks signed on in anticipation of Perry making a run at a different statewide office, although what office that would be remained unclear. The one thing they knew was that they didn't want to mess with Bob Bullock, the irascible and powerful Democratic lieutenant governor. Perry "damn sure didn't want to say, hey I'm coming after you."[96]

The 1994 election looked to be a good year for incumbents—that fall, the Texas Poll had challengers winning support from only between a fourth and a third of those polled in the five statewide races. Bullock pulled 54 percent of the vote to 23 percent for Republican H. J. "Tex" Lezar. Dan Morales, the incumbent attorney general, had a twelve-point lead over Republican Don Wittig. Perry had the support of 42 percent of Texans, over a relatively unknown Democratic challenger, Marvin Gregory, an East Texas dairy farmer. Perry remarked he knew what it was like to be lonely: "Try being an Aggie and a Republican in Austin, Texas, today."[97]

But Republicans wouldn't be lonely in Austin for long. Already,

Perry was in high demand. When he was first elected agriculture commissioner—becoming with state treasurer Kay Bailey Hutchison one of just two Republicans to hold statewide office—Perry suddenly was headlining all the Republican events, just a few years after switching parties. "All of a sudden, he was the guy," Weeks said, "a hero" for beating Hightower.[98]

Perry flew himself, other Republicans, and members of the media around the state in small planes.[99] Agriculture commissioner might not have been a natural attention-getting post, but Perry continued to build his political network, holding fundraisers and doing "all the mechanical stuff you needed to do to reach for higher office." Kronberg recalls Perry stopping into the Texas Chili Parlor, which is close to the Capitol and popular with lawmakers, journalists, and lobbyists. "This is my pathway to the governorship," stated a blunt Perry. He sat sipping iced tea and carefully mapping out his course. George W. Bush would be elected governor in 1994, with Perry ascending to the lieutenant governor' office in January 1999 after a second term at agriculture and then moving up to governor when Bush left Texas for the White House.[100]

As the Republican incumbent in a state that was growing more conservative, Perry had little to worry about. Between 1984 and 1994, fewer liberals identified with the Republican Party and fewer conservatives identified with the Democratic Party.[101] Polls revealed that 78 percent of Texans called themselves conservatives or moderate rather than liberal. Of the moderates, 10 percent leaned liberal and 22 percent tended conservative. "There is no question that conservative these days in Texas and most places is a better thing to be," pollster and Republican consultant Bill Miller noted at the time.[102] Both Texas parties began running candidates with clearer ideological differences and who fell more in line with the goals of their respective national parties.

Having George W. Bush at the top of the ticket for Texas Republicans in 1994 certainly helped. First-time Republican candidates drafted off Bush's conservative positions, such as expanding prisons, overhauling the juvenile justice system, cutting the state budget, and privatizing some state services. A longtime friend, Perry was happy to be on the ticket with the surging Bush. "The kind of person he is, and the kind of candidate he'll make, are basically the same," Perry said. "He's got a great sense of humor, and he's not hung up on who he is, who his father is, what he's done." Bush's political inexperience and reform agenda were seen as positives by Republicans.[103]

Efforts to attract Latino support for the Republican Party commenced in earnest. Tony Garza, a Republican running for judge in Hidalgo County, had introduced Perry to the heavily Democratic Rio Grande Valley in 1990. When Garza ran for attorney general in 1994, Perry returned the favor by campaigning with Garza in a crowded Republican primary field. "Hispanics are bright and moving up fast in the world," he said. "They will be the leaders of the state of Texas. Tony is the vision of Texas' future."[104]

The push for Latino support didn't always go smoothly on the campaign trail, however. Perry, lamenting the growing number of lawsuits filed in the state, remarked at one campaign stop that "every José in town wants to come along and sue you for something," prompting the Wichita County chapter of Mexican American Democrats to call for his resignation. Perry apologized the next day, addressing it to the intentionally vague "to anyone that is offended."[105] The battle for Texas's Latino vote continued unabated, but the moment also marked the beginning of another noteworthy step in Perry's political evolution: a career-long crusade in favor of tort reform and against large legal judgements. He viewed tort reform as a critical issue: "The trial lawyers are trying to use this for their own political gain, and that should be offensive to all of us."[106] *Houston Post* columnist Lynn Ashby joked that Perry plea-bargained and should be sentenced to "two months in Wichita Falls."[107]

Perry had previously weathered a minor scandal involving one of his top lieutenants, Deputy Commissioner Dick Waterfield, who established the Texas Agriculture Finance Authority and was accused of using a racial slur while meeting with two Abilene businessmen seeking a loan. The remarks reportedly involved whether it would make a difference in receiving the loan if the company's board of directors included a minority member. Waterfield denied the charge but resigned anyway, "for the good of the agency." Perry accepted the resignation but called the allegation "vile and offensive."[108]

Despite a solid record as agriculture commissioner and such attention-getting antics as Super Bowl bets and attacks on federal regulations,

Perry remained relatively unknown to most Texans. By 1996, well into his second term, only 6 percent of Texans could name him as agriculture commissioner.

That was a problem for someone with higher political aspirations, but Perry's primary constituents—farmers and others in the state's agricultural community—knew him well, and that's what counted on Election Day. His informal 1994 reelection bid started just six months after he was elected, spearheaded by Karl Rove. Strengthening the Republican brand was high on the list of Rove's actions, including raising money and broadening the base of support. Tickling the ideological effect raging across the state, a mass-mail piece from the Perry campaign dismissed liberal Democrats and their "ilk" and expected nothing but trouble from them. Hightower responded that there was little truth to these letters and added that "it's a typical Karl Rove scare type of letter."[109]

Perry's first campaign had focused heavy criticism on Hightower's personal use of government money, but that didn't affect his own spending while in the office. He was consistently the top-spending officeholder in Texas during his tenure, racking up more than $80,000 in state-reimbursed travel. The trips included a 1994 borer trade alliance meeting in Mexico; a 1995 agriculture trade mission to France and Germany; a 1995 trip to West Palm Beach for the Southern Association of State Departments of Agriculture; and dozens of smaller trips to rural parts of the state. His spokesman at the time, Ray Sullivan, defended the travel, noting Perry's visits to areas affected by drought and his efforts to find new export markets for Texas products. Governor Bush came under similar criticism from Garry Mauro, his Democratic opponent in the 1998 gubernatorial election.[110]

Perry's time as agriculture commissioner was solid but unremarkable. Modest accolades accrued, such as being named to "Who's Who in Food and Wine in Texas" in 1992 by the *Dallas Morning News* for his efforts to promote those industries. But there wasn't much trouble to get into, and the state—politically purple at the time—didn't have the same friction that would come to dominate politics in the next few years.

The office of agriculture commissioner was seen as a political parking space, often an early stop for the more politically ambitious, but it came with a built-in consistency that could be counted on for support and political money, should one choose to move up.[111] Perry's ambition was no secret, and as early as 1993—still in his first term as commissioner—rumors were swirling that he would run for higher office. He turned down the chance to throw his hat into the arena to replace Senator Lloyd Benson, who was slated to become the US secretary of the treasury. He also sidestepped an opportunity to run for governor after his first term as ag commissioner. "I'm sure some day in my life I will be interested in running for governor, but it will not be in 1994."[112]

—4—

LIEUTENANT GOVERNOR, 1998–2001

"Together We Can—Juntos Podemos"

He was willing to wait until the timing was right to run for governor, but Perry had no plans to end his political career as agriculture commissioner. After eight years in the low-profile spot—years he spent making contacts and learning how Texas fit into national issues, such as trade and globalization—he needed to take the next steps to keep his political career in motion and harness the fast-moving changes in Texas politics. He wasn't a lawyer, so attorney general was out. Republican superstar George W. Bush had a lock on the Republican nomination for governor, and the comptroller and land commissioner positions were as obscure as the one he already had. That meant his best option was lieutenant governor. Team Perry had really been thinking about this moment for years. Perhaps it was inevitable.

But from a wider view, this moment in Texas politics was striking: here was Rick Perry, eight years out from being a Democrat, running for the second-most important position in Texas government as a *Republican*. Luck would again bless Perry—Democratic Party stalwart and political powerhouse Bob Bullock (who served as lieutenant governor 1991–1999) was stepping aside, leaving the position open. Most around the Capitol couldn't imagine the office without Bullock, but times were changing.

The trouble was that the Democrats, while wounded, were not yet dead, and Perry's old running buddy John Sharp, then the state comptroller, was standing in his way. Sharp and Perry went back decades to their years at Texas A&M and Squadron 6 of the Corps of Cadets—thrown together "by the grace of God," a wistful Perry later recalled. "He and I have been married and divorced more times than Bob Bullock."[1]

The political clash between Perry and Sharp was unavoidable as their ambitions led each up the political food chain and as Texas was jolted into a two-party state. At Texas A&M, Sharp was elected student body president and Perry had been elected yell leader. "John took the governance route, and I took the showbusiness side," Perry acknowledged.[2] Sharp sat in the state Senate when Perry served across the rotunda in the House. Sharp was elected comptroller in 1990, the year Perry was first elected agriculture commissioner. Now both were thinking about running for lieutenant governor. The big difference? Perry had switched parties. Former Democratic strategist Matthew Dowd, who later worked for Bush and as a national political commentator for several networks, recalled Sharp's decision not to switch parties, to "stay in, an independent Democrat, more of a moderate-to-conservative Democrat."[3] That choice defined the "hand-to-hand combat" of the 1998 race.[4]

The political establishment, still leaning Democratic in that era, wasn't sure it was Perry's time. Sharp was able to raise significant amounts of campaign cash and had collected favors from people around the state. Bill Miller, the Republican consultant, remembers calls from the Texas Retailers Association, the Texas Association of Automotive Dealers, and the Texas Restaurant Association all urging Perry to run for comptroller instead, offering to help him win the lower office and essentially telling him to wait his turn.

"Fuck that, I'm running for lieutenant governor," a shocked Perry reacted.[5] The Perry camp also had to talk fellow Republican David Dewhurst, a wealthy candidate from Houston, out of running for lieutenant governor. Dewhurst ran for land commissioner instead. (He later held the office of lieutenant governor from 2003 to 2015.)

The race for lieutenant governor—by most accounts a position more powerful than the governor's office—drew attention, but most eyes were on the top of the ticket in 1998, as Bush campaigned for a second term as governor amid rumors that he would run for president. Bush had cemented Republican popularity in Texas with his 1994 trouncing of Ann Richards—the last of the state's Democratic stars—by 37 points, the biggest win for Texas Republicans ever. Across the country Republican gubernatorial candidates were poised to be the major Republican victors following the bitter Clinton impeachment fight that alienated many from the Republican Party. The GOP had its own ethical issues, as Newt Gingrich and Bob Livingston—the key architect and manager of the impeachment, respectively—were felled by scandals of their own. Bush's family name gave him instant credibility and a large network of donors. His engaging if sometimes goofy personality let him sell himself as a "uniter not a divider," and his theme that government could be the solution to some problems, just not every problem, was pitch-perfect for the emerging Texas GOP. Bush represented another milestone in the state's partisan shift—the last politician whom Texans of all political stripes wanted to succeed, Harvey Kronberg reflected.[6]

Like Perry, Bush was outstanding at retail politics. His popularity translated into down-ballot support for other Republicans, a needed boost for candidates like Perry, who either had switched parties, hadn't run before, or were running against Democrats with piles of money and strong track records. Republicans were happy to hitch their wagon to Bush, the popular former managing general partner for the Texas Rangers, all the way down the ballot to local positions. (Bush sold his ownership stake in the baseball team in 1998.) Just one example: Nancy Rister, running for Williamson County Clerk against write-in candidate Joan Green, used telephone banks to remind voters: "Nancy Rister is a George Bush conservative. . . . When you vote to re-elect Gov. Bush, vote to keep hard-working Nancy Rister as our county clerk."[7]

Bush's conservative shift in the governor's mansion changed the tenor of Texas politics and gave Republicans, long in the wilderness with few statewide wins, something to cheer about. The reshaped Republican Party of the 1990s made significant inroads into a booming Texas population, especially in rural areas that had long favored Democrats and in shiny new suburban areas around the state's major cities.

Republicans rallied around a well-funded Leadership Texas '96 coordinated campaign to handle communicating with the growing spread of conservative suburban voters.[8]

Conservative Republicans, and especially the religious right, had organized successfully beginning in the early 1990s to win local party leadership positions, including at the precinct and county levels. Their reach extended to membership on the state executive committee and, ultimately, to state and national conventions. They directed the focus of the party towards abortion issues, harnessing the influence of the religious right and taking an increasingly hard line against abortion. The Magic Circle Republican Women's Club, which counted Barbara Bush as a member, had worked to remove any mention of abortion from the Republican state platform. Dolly Madison McKenna, running for party chair and facing a slightly hostile crowd at the 1994 Texas Republican Party Convention, practically shouted, "There are those people in this audience that want the Republican Party to be a church," eliciting boos and catcalls. "You are very welcome in the Republican Party. But the Republican Party is not a church."[9]

"Boy, was she ever wrong," journalist R. G. Ratcliffe said decades later.[10] Tom Pauken, a Dallas lawyer endorsed by the Texas Christian Coalition, was elected over McKenna, in part by emphasizing his strict antiabortion views. "This election is about setting the future course in the long term for the Republican Party," he told conventiongoers. "This is the time for choosing sides between those who believe in the conservative values that make America great versus a leftist agenda which is leading our country down the road to socialism."[11] Pauken recalls that abortion was the "turning point" in the Republican Party in that period. The coalition of Goldwater and Reagan acolytes and Evangelical Christians brought Pauken to victory, and he worked to bring them into the party—to the temporary alienation of some big donors and outgoing chair Fred Meyer, who would have taken a more moderate course. But the pro-life position took hold, making it the position of the party, and "it's been that way ever since."[12]

The "righteous right," as some (self-identified) mainstream Republican delegates called those focused on social issues, was slowly taking over the party—a process that began as a grassroots effort from married conservative women in Dallas and Houston.[13] Before the 1990s, a veteran of '90s Republican campaigns said, abortion had drawn little attention: the candidate was against it except in cases of rape, incest, or a threat to the life of the mother. "That's it."[14] Two of the seven 1990 Republican gubernatorial candidates were pro-choice. One, former secretary of state Jack Rains, said in ads that he wouldn't impose his personal views on his wife or daughters or the other women of Texas: "It's a very private issue. I don't believe in government intervention."[15] By the 2000s, opposing abortion was a cornerstone of the Texas Republican social agenda, driven by activists but also by the emergence of single-issue organizations like Texas Right to Life.

Perry and Bush were never close. While friendly, they were not intimates, according to Ray Sullivan, who worked for both.[16] But Perry knew the smart political move—he stuck tighter than bark on a tree to Bush during the campaign. He hit the airwaves with television commercials featuring Bush and his parents, former president George H. W. Bush and First Lady Barbara Bush, both of whom were wildly popular in Texas. The campaign was largely a sidecar to Bush's high-profile race, but Perry could campaign on his eight years at the Department of Agriculture, touting his judicious staff and budget cuts, his elimination of hundreds of regulations, and a 24 percent increase in agricultural exports.[17] The themes were catnip for Republican voters, but overall, the office of agriculture commissioner didn't have much resonance with the general public. As a measure of the political times, Perry even sold himself to some audiences as a former Democrat who could work with both parties, a nod to bipartisanship that had the virtue of being true, at least for a while. Still, the Bush campaign was where the real action was, and Bush was the best chance for down-ballot Republicans, including Perry, to win. Bush also helped behind the scenes, reportedly asking Bullock refrain from endorsing Sharp, paving the way for a Republican lieutenant governor to take Bush's place if he was elected president.[18]

Democrats weren't sold. "They have nothing else to say except, 'I'm a Bush groupie and vote for me.' The voters aren't going to fall for it," quipped Harold Cook, then the political director of the Texas Democratic Party. Voters "are interested in issues like education, not who hugs George Bush the tightest." Sharp tried to have it both ways, promising in television ads to be more independent than Perry—"I won't be anybody's man but yours"—while showing video of Sharp and Bush sharing a handshake, a subtle promise that he would have the governor's ear.[19] In reality, the two Aggies had more in common than not. "There wasn't two dime's worth of difference" between Sharp and Perry, according to one campaign operative.[20]

Early polls showed a close race, with Perry leading Sharp 45 percent to 36 percent in September 1998, while Bush led Democratic land commissioner Gary Mauro by a commanding 70 percent to 21 percent.[21] Despite a lead in the polls, insiders saw the Perry campaign struggling, recalled Ray Sullivan, who had crossover voters ("Bush and Sharp yard signs popped up all over the state") and the endorsement of the Texas Farm Bureau.[22] Bush told Sullivan, who was working for the governor, he needed Perry to win since he was planning on running for president and needed a Republican lieutenant governor to hold down the fort once he was gone.

Bush was certainly doing his part. By October, Bush still held a 45-point lead over Mauro, but the lieutenant governor's race had closed. Partisan activity late in the race narrowed the distance between the candidates, despite their similarities. Other statewide offices were close, too, reflecting a state in political transition—Democrat Paul Hobby led Republican Carole Keeton Rylander (later Carole Keeton Strayhorn) 36 percent to 33 percent in the race for comptroller, and Democrat L. P. "Pete" Patterson had a 35 percent to 33 percent lead over Republican Susan Combs in the race to succeed Perry as agriculture commissioner.[23] A surge of support for Bush at the ballot box sealed the deal for many Republican candidates, Perry included.

Despite the candidates' similarities, the race for lieutenant governor turned heated over several issues, prominently among them criminal justice and punishment. Sharp released ads late in the campaign claiming Perry had voted in the House in 1987 for legislation allowing prisoners to collect extra credits for good behavior, a legislative change that led to an early prison release for Gary Wayne Etheridge, who was released from prison in 1990 and later convicted and executed for the 1990 murder of a fifteen-year-old girl in Brazoria County. The law Perry supported, according to the ad, "freed Etheridge and thousands of others to strike again."

An angry Perry shot back: "This weekend I discovered that John

Sharp will indeed say or do anything to get elected." Perry accused Sharp of a shameless attempt to exploit the death of a child for his political ambitions. The Perry team also did their homework. While still a state senator, in 1983 Sharp had voted for a similar law that allowed early release for prisoners.[24] Perry hit Sharp hard on this, running ads in Wichita Falls that attacked Sharp for senate votes that had led to the early release of more than fifteen hundred criminals, had paid prisoners minimum wage, and had provided telephone services for prison inmates. Which law was to blame? Sharp claimed not one prisoner was released as a result of the 1983 law (although it was in effect when Etheridge was released). Perry got cover, too, from local Republican sheriffs who slammed Sharp.

Criminal justice had become a big issue nationally in the 1990s as Republicans and Democrats both positioned themselves as the toughest on crime. The issue rose to prominence with good reason. Crime rates had spiked in the 1980s, especially rates of violent crime. Surging populations in Sun Belt cities such as Houston saw crime rates double from 1970 to 1980—one out of every thirty-two Houston residences was burglarized in 1980.[25] Murders in El Paso jumped from the teens to more than fifty per year by the mid-1980s. Officials in Odessa blamed the jump in homicides on an influx of people during the oil boom, as homicides per capita in the dusty West Texas town surpassed those in Miami.[26]

Subsequent state and national policies would drive these rates down. Putting more police on the streets helped, as did ramping up incarceration rates. Finally, economic improvements in previously crime-ridden neighborhoods made crime less attractive. But in the elections of 1998, crime was the number one issue for Texas voters, and politicians in both parties followed along.

Tough-on-crime talk wasn't new for either party by the time Perry and Sharp faced off in 1998. In his unsuccessful 1990 primary race to regain the governor's seat, former governor Mark White ran ads of himself strolling past larger-than-life photos of prisoners executed while he was governor.[27] Sharp relied on the same dog-eared playbook eight years later, running ads featuring retired members of law enforcement's storied Texas Rangers, who accused Perry of distorting Sharp's record on criminal justice. "It was Perry, not John Sharp, who voted for the law that opened the floodgates and let thousands of criminals go free before their time," one retired Ranger intoned in the ad.[28] Perry countered with a plan to toughen penalties for drug traffickers who used children to sell drugs, increasing the punishment to twenty-five years in prison, with a mandatory minimum of eleven years. Sharp, endorsed by police associations in Houston, Dallas, and Austin, earlier in the year had released an anticrime plan calling for the death penalty for major drug dealers and those convicted of repeat aggravated child sexual assault.[29]

It got personal, too. Sharp took to calling Perry "pretty" during the campaign, a not-so-subtle swipe meant to raise in voters "the subconscious stereotype that no serious thought could come from a noggin sporting so lovely a face."[30]

The two also tussled over public education—or more accurately, how *private* to make *public* education. Perry proposed allowing parents to take the share of public funding allotted to public school districts for each enrolled student and use the money for private school tuition. "The issue of parental choice is very simple," said Perry. "I want to give them every tool that we have. . . . And if a pilot program voucher is going to work, I'm going to stand up and say let's try it."

Sharp responded during a debate in El Paso that there were not sufficient funds for families to take money out of public schools to create a multimillion-dollar private school program.[31] "What's really happening is a bunch of people that I think want to destroy the public school system, want to do away with it and want to make money off of tax dollars. And that I think is very dangerous in the state of Texas," he said, claiming that Perry—whose campaign raised $8 million from voucher supporters, two-thirds of his total $12 million war chest—was beholden to his benefactors. Records released following the election revealed that ten days before the election, Perry's campaign got a $1.1 million loan backed by three voucher advocates.[32]

Sharp didn't entirely rule out a voucher program, although he said it should be the last option, prompting Perry's campaign to point out the fence-straddling. "If Mr. Sharp is so opposed to parental choice in education, he should just say so instead of trying to have it both ways."[33]

The two had been close during their College Station days, drawn together by the Corps of Cadets and sharing in such classic dorm hijinks as flushing fireworks down toilets. Even back then—more than twenty years before they faced off for the state's second-highest office—the two were intensely competitive. "They either love each other or hate each other," their former corps commander recalled. "It's always been a marathon race about who is going to be the best."[34]

As pals at A&M, "as close to roommates as you can get without being roommates," Perry recalled, the two hatched a get-rich-quick scheme to raise frogs they would sell to restaurants.[35] "We had thousands of frogs," Sharp said. "I was going to be a millionaire frog farmer" with the intention of selling these to fancy eateries in Houston and Austin. Just one problem: "All of the frogs died," apparently because they overstocked the pond, which couldn't support so many frogs. Sharp jokingly blamed Perry, who was in charge of the frog selection and breeding.

The childish barbs continued over the decades, with the two men acting more like bickering brothers. "When I first saw him, I thought he looked stupid," Sharp said, and he didn't hesitate to tell Perry that. "No more stupid than you're going to [look]," Perry responded.[36] Sharp had to protect a wild Perry from himself on occasion. At an away football game in Waco, Perry mouthed off to some rough-looking bikers in the parking lot (Banditos, as Sharp told it). A worried but quick-thinking Sharp scooped up a handful of crickets hopping around on the ground and ate them, causing the bikers to back off.

Any Aggie bond between the two was severed by partisan politics after each won his respective primary. "On any given day, we could ruin each other's political future," Perry said in a 1988 interview.[37] This was both a measure of their political competitiveness and evidence that the men had enough dirt on each other to sink both. Both men were talented retail politicians, although Perry in particular earned high marks. "Hands down the best retail politician I've seen in Texas or nationally," one Republican operative said. "He gets it. It just comes naturally to him."[38] Still, Sharp was no slouch. He was a strong campaigner and better with a shotgun than Perry, remembered journalist Dave Mc-Neely, who had covered, and hunted with, both men since the 1980s.

Sharp went negative first, and Perry took it personally. "The contrast between Rick Perry's positive campaign and Mr. Sharp's mudslinging has never been sharper," said Perry campaign spokesman Ray Sullivan in slamming the new ad. Years later, Sullivan remembered that the ad was brutal and stung the Perry campaign.[39] Sharp's camp defended the ad—in which he claimed Perry would be "in lockstep" with Bush, to the detriment of the state—as factual.[40] They maintained Sharp was a true independent candidate who would break with the Democratic Party when necessary. "The next lieutenant governor better put Texas first. He better put Texas before party, before other elected officials, before friends," Sharp said. Looking into the camera, he declared, "I'll work with any governor for the good of Texas, but as your lieutenant governor I won't be anybody's man but yours."[41]

Other Sharp ads hit Perry for accepting a state pay raise and traveling extravagantly on the state's dime as agriculture commissioner, although the reality was more a matter of degree: Perry had billed the state for $84,355 in travel expenses since 1991, compared to Sharp's $61,194 during the same period. Another Sharp ad accused Perry of spending time in "pricey hotels in Europe (and) four-star resorts back East" (to the soundtrack of Willie Nelson's "On the Road Again")—more than any other state official. As the shadow of a jet moved over the pink-domed Capitol, the narrator delivered the punch line: "So when Perry says he'll go far in politics, he's not kidding."[42] Perry noted that the comptroller's office—that is to say, Sharp's office—approved the travel (or at least signed the checks) and claimed that the Perry family had donated the pay raise to charity.

Sharp's campaign spokesperson didn't buy it: "We're simply showing voters what the record is. . . . Rick thinks any discussion of his record is negative. Frankly, if I had his record, I would, too."[43]

Perry's campaign dismissed the barbs as "Washington-style, attack-style politics"[44] but held off on its own negative ads for strategic reasons not entirely of their choosing. Ads run without authorization from the Perry campaign accused Sharp of being "a Dukakis-Clinton, tax-and-spend Democrat" who backed a $4 billion income tax on business and who "coddl[ed] criminals." Sharp's campaign responded that the ad was wrong and misleading—that it aired in only smaller media markets like Waco—and claimed that the comptroller had prevented a state income tax with money-saving proposals and had been endorsed by several law enforcement groups.[45]

Internally, the Republican Party, still relatively new to competitive statewide elections, was trying to see how all the pieces fit together. More specifically, Karl Rove was trying to see how the pieces fit together. Rove was the key—he handpicked the candidates, set them up with consultants, controlled the flow of money. But Perry, who had been comfortable with Rove's role in his 1990 and 1994 campaigns for ag commissioner, was suspicious about what Rove's work for Bush might mean for the down-ballot races.

Perry campaign manager Jim Arnold said the Perry campaign almost got "sacrificed to the aspirations of Bush" and nearly became "collateral" damage as Bush—and Rove—pushed for a big turnout and an overwhelming victory, with a goal of receiving 70 percent of the popular vote in anticipation of a run for the White House in 2000. More than a big turnout, the Bush camp wanted bipartisan support and a rainbow coalition of racial support.[46] Rove made the Perry campaign tap the brakes on negative ads it had planned to run against Sharp, including one on personal tax issues, which polling had suggested would be effective. Rove said no: the Bush camp wanted a positive campaign filled with "flowers and light."[47] And Rove's "no" came with a not-so-veiled threat: unless the Perry campaign cooperated, a planned ad with former president George H. W. Bush endorsing Perry would not air. Frustrations boiled over, and a Perry campaign official punched a hole in the wall during the meeting.[48]

Bush's goal of a big turnout had another potential drawback for Perry—more Democratic voters meant more Sharp voters, and polling showed a very close race in October 1998, just a month before the election: the candidates were tied at 37 percent. The Bush campaign considered its ability to play rainmaker for other Republican candidates to be a test of its strength and poured resources into shifting Bush voters and undecided voters to Perry.[49] Perry also got a $1 million boost from a major backer—Jim Leininger, a San Antonio physician and businessman and an ardent backer of vouchers for private schools. Insiders say Perry has been repaying the loan ever since—in the 1999 legislative session, his first as lieutenant governor, he pushed hard for vouchers, only to have the bill die after an ailing state senator hospitalized in San Antonio asked that the bill not be passed in his absence. Perry agreed.[50]

The fight over vouchers, however, continued during and after Perry's terms as governor.

Both Bush and Perry won on Election Day, although the margins of victory differed. Bush won by more than one million votes, getting the blowout he wanted; Perry won by just 69,000 votes. Ultimately, Perry's secret weapon over Sharp turned out to be a comfortable spot on the ballot, just below the popular George W. Bush. "Basically, Rick Perry is on top of George Bush's shoulders," said Miller, the Republican consultant.[51] The sweep was complete, as Republicans painted the state red from top to bottom, winning every statewide race for the first time in modern history. More than five hundred mayors backed Bush's bipartisan approach to government, an indication that the Republican Party's ground game was growing and early efforts to win local elections had paid off.[52] Former GOP state chair Wayne Thorburn called the 1998 election "a turning point in the emergence of a Republican majority in Texas."[53]

What happened? Sharp had pulled his negative ads with only days to go, hoping to end the campaign on a positive note. Cook considered that to have been a big mistake, and Miller agreed, saying winning the lieutenant governor's race required staying "bitter to the end. It was just enough time to let Perry off the mat, but it was enough."[54] You don't take your boot off their neck when you have them pinned, Chad Wilbanks, a Republican Party operative, said. "You don't stop until election day."[55] But Sharp may have had no choice. Perry campaign aide Ray Sullivan tracked down a family member featured in Sharp's brutal tough-on-crime ad and persuaded her that the content was wrong. The Sharp campaign may have been worried about the veracity of the ad, since the Perry campaign was furiously sending out press releases about the recanting participants. The campaign stopped running it.[56]

For its part, the Perry campaign maximized its available funds, crafted a good message, and stayed focused on old-fashioned campaigning. Jim Arnold, the campaign manager, believed doing less could have cost Perry the race, although he acknowledged that Perry might have won regardless, considering Bush's popularity and state trends that favored Republicans.[57]

Demographic change in the form of shifting party loyalties and major Republican inroads into rural Texas were simply too much for Sharp to overcome. "Texas was changing too fast for him," said Dowd, who had run Bullock's 1990 campaign and later worked for the lieutenant governor's office under Bullock.[58]

The Democratic Party stumbled. Bush dominated, and his fellow Republicans and conservatives racked up margins of nine to one in exit polling, winning moderates, older voters, and women and nearly carrying the Hispanic vote. Bush's 37 percent margin of victory was the largest by a Republican candidate in Texas; remarkably, he also carried almost one-third of the Democratic vote, up from 10 percent in 1994,[59] along with 27 percent of the African American vote and 70 percent of independents.[60]

Republicans also made gains in traditionally Democratic medium-sized counties, including Jefferson (Beaumont), Nueces (Corpus Christi), and McLennan (Waco).[61] This robust coalition further fueled speculation about a White House run for Bush, just as Rove planned.

Perry and the rest of the ticket did not do as well among Hispanic voters; Perry drew 31 percent, still respectable for a Republican not named Bush, while Cornyn received 29 percent of the Hispanic vote. Both won by narrower margins than Bush had,[62] fanning the argument that the Sharp campaign, believing he was going to win, had taken South Texas for granted when an extra $50,000 spent in the region might have made the difference.[63]

The Democrats were also hampered by the absence of a unity ticket, with each candidate riding the campaign trail alone. A politically changing Texas had warped the political alliances that once held the Democratic Party together, at least tenuously, as being a Democrat now meant playing defense against an increasingly conservative electorate. Conservative Democrats who had dominated state politics since the 1940s were spooked as voters turned to the Republican Party for policies that conservative Democrats had pushed for decades—low taxes, minimal regulations, favoring state power over empowering the federal government. Republican branding was simply better.

Sharp even distanced himself from President Clinton, who came to Texas to stump for his old friend Garry Mauro in Mauro's bid against

Bush. While about a third of Bush voters also voted for Sharp, Perry's strong support in East and West Texas carried the day. Mauro ran strongest in Houston and South Texas, but Bush carried both regions by more than three to two. Democrats still held a significant edge among elected officials overall (more than three to one in local offices), but the political tide was turning.[64]

It was the toughest campaign of Perry's political career, and he learned several lessons. Flying around the state solo in a "cowboy-built" airplane, as he had in the early days, was no longer practical. Ready money was necessary.[65] So was a good campaign staff, especially in a big state like Texas and as Republicans were beginning to see the pay-off from local organizing efforts. "People can call it George W. Bush's coattails, and some of it probably was," said Ron Lewis. "But [Perry] worked hard. Nobody gave him a chance to beat John Sharp. He was totally underestimated."[66] As had happened so many times before—and would again and again in the coming years—those who underestimated Rick Perry did so at their peril.

Despite his victory, Perry took the bruising campaign personally; he didn't talk to Sharp, his former college pal, for more than ten years.[67] The backslapping, easygoing Perry didn't take the friction with his old friend well. The race did, however, give him a thicker skin in future campaigns.

The campaign cemented Rove's vision of Texas as a Republican powerhouse, with Perry's rise to the dais of the Texas Senate cementing the concentration of Republican power that began when the party took a majority of Senate seats in 1996. Two questions remained: What kind of leader would Perry be in the Senate? Would Bush's presidential ambitions leave Perry an accidental governor?

The nasty campaign behind them, Bush and Perry headed back to Austin for inaugural ceremonies and the start of the 76th legislative session in January 1999. Bush's brief speech was big on aspirations but light on policy. "The 21st century will be one of great opportunity," he told the crowd bundled up for the chilly day. "Our economy will be strong, so long as we pursue free markets, free trade, low taxes, and limited government." Bush emphasized compassion for young criminals, the need for a more literate Texas, ending the social promotion of students, and embracing Texans' diverse heritage. He opposed "promiscuity and having babies out of wedlock."[68]

Perry largely parroted and praised Bush in a burst of optimism and conservative values on the front steps of the Capitol. "Gov. George W. Bush—he's done in office what he said he'd do. He's brought respect, civility, and unity to state government. He's cut taxes. He's restrained government growth. And he's improved the health, education, and welfare of the state of Texas." Once basic education, criminal justice, infrastructure, and human service needs had been met, Perry said, tax cuts should come next.[69] He had his own agenda—it just happened to dovetail with Bush's, including his proposed master reading program to reward expert teachers, echoing Bush's emphasis on improving reading skills and ending social promotion of students who weren't academically ready for the next grade level.

Perry's predecessors as lieutenant governor, including Bill Hobby and Bob Bullock, were tough acts to follow. As the first Republican lieutenant governor since Reconstruction, he stressed inclusive decision making and an optimistic attitude in tackling issues of importance to all Texans—investing in public schools through increased academic standards and local control and improvements in the criminal justice system through crime-prevention efforts. He was a backslapping presence in the chamber, and members reported easier access to the lieutenant governor than in previous sessions.[70] He stressed bipartisanship, but he didn't shy away from the occasional partisan jab.

"There are a lot of senators and a lot of egos, and he didn't want to necessarily upstage them. He wanted to get things done. He realized he was not the heavyweight in the job," said Christy Hoppe, then a reporter for the *Dallas Morning News*.[71] Indeed, recognizing this was a talent in itself. Bullock, the grizzled incumbent and longtime capitol insider, had high hopes: "He's going to make a fine lieutenant governor. You watch him."[72]

Still, the contrast with Bullock was inevitable and occasionally unfavorable. He didn't always live up to expectations in administrative routines, such as keeping members informed about the flow of bills through the process. But "in all the ways that counted, Perry did pretty well," said Harold Cook, the former Democratic operative. Certainly, he tried to master the job; embarrassing reports at the time said Perry practiced wielding the oversized gavel in the empty Senate chamber.[73]

Despite Perry's efforts, longtime senators were hard to impress. Affectionately nicknamed Obi-Wan Kenobi by his peers for his zen attitude and adroit legislative skills (and selected by his fellow senators as interim lieutenant governor when Perry moved to the governor's office after Bush was elected president), Sen. Bill Ratliff (R-Mount Pleasant) assessed Perry as a laissez-faire leader in contrast to his Democratic predecessors: he was "much more interested in his future" than the day-to-day workings of the Senate. Bill Hobby, son of former Texas governor William P. Hobby, had also been something of a hands-off leader, Ratliff said, "maneuvering the Senate in a quiet, behind-the-scenes way." He would pick three or four issues he cared about; otherwise, his attitude was "Y'all work it out." Bullock, on the other hand, had been a "micromanager, who wanted to know exactly what was going on and when and why, who was dating who, and who was having an affair with whom. He was the ultimate hands-on guy," Ratliff said.[74]

With a nearly evenly divided Senate—sixteen Republicans and fifteen Democrats—senators of both parties tended to ignore Perry, and Ratliff said that didn't seem to matter to the new lieutenant governor, who was obsessed with the political fallout of any potential legislation. "We hardly ever talked about what was good for the state."[75]

Republicans did have a modest advantage, but Senate rules required a two-thirds majority, or twenty-one votes, to bring up a bill for consideration, meaning the new lieutenant governor would have to hustle for votes on most issues, and many of the senators weren't inclined to let an upstart they considered little better than a rube from West Texas run the Senate. "Don't make them mad," Hoppe admonished the new lieutenant governor. "They can jerk the rug out from under you at any time. They write the rules."[76]

The tight partisan balance required careful diplomacy. Democrat Hector Gutierrez, whose relationship with Perry stretched back to their days at Texas A&M, was brought on as policy director for the lieutenant governor's office. "The only way you could pass any legislation was to have twenty-one [members]. You had to schmooze the Ds [Democrats] to pass legislation," Gutierrez said. "He would be a total failure if he didn't get D backing for legislation we hoped to pass. Sometimes we had to pass D bills to get D votes on our key issues."[77] This included issues on which the parties agreed: higher education (expanding university systems to other parts of the state), economic development, and transportation.

Perry's interim charges, the framework for an agenda during the session, included studying education issues, especially addressing college preparation and the teacher shortage; a NAFTA-related trade corridor and its impact on urban and rural areas; a water plan for the border; and economic development. They were modest goals, reflecting acquiescence to a popular governor with political ambitions and a divided Senate where few large, controversial policies could get enacted. "I think until one party reaches twenty-one (members), we will continue to have a very good, bipartisan Legislature," Sen. Florence Shapiro (R-Plano) said.[78]

Flexing their modest political leverage is a privilege for lieutenant governors, Perry included, and he appointed Republicans to head nine of the fifteen committees, with Democrats heading six. He stripped two Democrats of their chairs, including from the powerful finance committee, thus opening vacancies for friends and allies. Republicans held majorities on ten of the fifteen committees. Similar to Bullock and other lieutenant governors before him, Perry emphasized bipartisanship with a side of sharp partisan elbows. He was, after all, the first Republican in modern times to hold the office, which has considerable power to shape legislation.

In reality, Perry both hewed to the bipartisan traditions of the Senate and kept his eyes keenly focused on his political future, being willing to "carry whatever water Bush needed carrying because Bush was his pathway to the governorship," Kronberg said. Bush made it easy: he was "the kind of guy who would drop into a senator's office or a House member's office, put his boots up on the receptionist's table."[79] But Bush and Perry were also wary of one another's ambitions, and hard feelings from the campaign—Perry felt the Bush campaign had run roughshod over his own plans—had not entirely dissipated. Another point of contention was Bush's rejection of Perry's suggestion to name Joseph E. Thigpen, Anita Perry's brother, to an opening on the state appellate court. Thigpen was a former district attorney in Haskell and had been fired in 1993 for not showing up to work.[80]

A divided Senate limited Republican policy ambitions, forcing bipartisan solutions, and the session ended with substantive policy wins, from cutting taxes (including creating a three-day sales tax holiday on clothing and other back-to-school items), to increasing spending on public schools and expanding health insurance options for low-income children. Across the aisle, the House was also closely divided, with seventy-eight Democrats and seventy-two Republicans. In theory that meant House and Senate should work well together. Veteran Speaker of the House Pete Laney (D-Hale Center) stressed the practical adage that members should "vote their district," a philosophy he expected would inform cooperation with Perry. "Most members of the Legislature want to represent their district and do what's best for their district and work to solve the problems of the state of Texas," said Laney at the time. "I think there's more of those than there are of the people that would like to divide the aisles."[81]

Perry seemed to agree. "We grew up in West Texas on cotton farms and with a belief that you should do your best for Texas," he said. "I expect to have a very good working relationship."[82]

But working together proved difficult. Laney was a Bush backer, so his relationship with Perry was professionally workable, focused around a common agenda, but their personal relationship never warmed up. Understanding West Texas, Laney was immune to Perry's charms. Laney felt that Perry came off as arrogant and that he feigned a closer partnership with Bush than the Speaker. Perry thought that Laney believed him to be an "accidental governor" ("How'd he beat Sharp? was a headscratcher for some") and the mentality was that some legitimate candidate would come along to beat him. Perry's party switch aggravated Laney more than most Democrats.[83] Despite the seismic partisan power shift in the early 2000s, Laney wanted rural Democrats to hold on to power—an impossible goal in a rapidly changing Texas. Laney later said he wasn't invited to Perry's office during the two years after Perry became governor, while Laney was still speaker.

The friction grew more heated after Perry became governor, when Laney and Ratliff, now the interim lieutenant governor, met with Perry for the long-standing Wednesday morning breakfast meetings (started in 2003) of the "Big 3"—the governor, lieutenant governor, and speaker—to preview the week's issues and generally "smooth the process." The breakfasts grew "pretty heated" between Perry and Laney, Ratliff recalled. What started as a political issue steadily turned personal. The only "thing we ever talked about was whether a John Deere tractor was better than a Farmall tractor," Ratliff said. "They never could be civil to each other.[84] The joke around Austin, Kronberg said, was that because of his close relationship with Bush, Laney had been to the White House more often than to Perry's governor's mansion.[85] Despite this, "There's supposed to be a natural tension. That's healthy. What is unhealthy is when it is so divisive, when it becomes a personal battle instead of the system battle."[86]

But certainly Perry and Laney found ways to work together during Perry's first and only session as lieutenant governor, when bridging the divide, or at least ignoring it, was made easier by a multibillion-dollar stimulus from a bustling economy and a $17.3 billion settlement with Big Tobacco.

Perry's new role brought new scrutiny. Reports swirled after the election that lobbyists were expected to either contribute $50,000 to the new lieutenant governor's campaign fund or raise that amount from clients. Perry's spokesman denied it. "It sounds like a bunch of disappointed lobbyists whose guy didn't win," spokesman Ray Sullivan said. "There are no fixed limits and certainly no assessments or quotas in our fund-raising."[87]

Whether the pressure was explicit or implicit, Perry's fundraising prowess became even more lucrative as he more frequently served as acting governor while Bush campaigned out of state for the White House. He raised $4 million in the second half of 1999, after a state ban on raising money during the legislative session was lifted. Stepped-up fundraising efforts were just one hallmark of Perry's ambition—he also began aggressively courting the capital press corps. Jay Root, bureau chief for the *Fort Worth Star-Telegram* at the time, recalled seeing Perry at a downtown Austin BBQ spot as part of his efforts to reach out to journalists: "They were trying to let all of us know 'I'm here, and I'm not going anywhere, and I'm ambitious.'"[88]

Despite the occasional skirmishes, Perry was typically bullish about the Senate's successes as the 76th legislative session neared sine die.

"When it comes to hard work and dedication and, I might add, bipartisan cooperation, this Senate has excelled. I would say that it has been the most successful legislative body and session to date in the world," he said after the Senate adjourned for a long Easter break after passing a record high 241 bills.[89] "I've always found that if you bring people together and try to find some common ground, that it generally makes you sleep better at night and your stomach hurt less," he said.[90]

Perry's governing style had meshed easily with the reality of the Senate, which is that the members run the chamber because they control the rules. Thirty-one members is really like "thirty-one independent contractors," said Ken Armbrister, who was in the Senate during Perry's time as lieutenant governor and later served as legislative director in the Perry gubernatorial administration. Perry gave input but allowed senators to negotiate. He also held weekly meetings with committee chairs to discuss the legislative calendar, all of which helped to keep things running on time and with less friction.[91] Also, staying out of the way let Perry look bipartisan.

In fact, he earned high marks as a consensus builder from veteran senators in both parties, John Whitmire among them. "The state's diverse. The Senate's diverse," said Whitmire, longtime chair of the Senate's criminal justice committee. "I think he's kept a lid on the partisan competitiveness about as well as anyone could have."[92]

Perry also retained his ability to get in on the joke. When Whitmire wisecracked that he was a victim of legislative "chunking"—prison slang referring to prisoners hurling excrement—during one debate, Perry responded by asking Whitmire to approach the dais from his back-row desk. Whitmire declined, chortling, "I don't know if I can chunk quite that far."[93] Perry also played favorites, cultivating his inner circle, including appointing childhood friend Troy Fraser to plum committees to engage in "bill rustling," which meant taking over bills (and often the spotlight) from fellow senators who'd sponsored them.[94]

The rookie lieutenant governor got points on style but sometimes missed on substance. Several top priorities failed to pass. Senate Bill 1, which set a higher standard for passing grades on standardized tests and had been designated the top Senate priority, flew through the Senate but failed in the House. The Senate did not vote on a proposed voucher pilot program, something both Perry and Bush favored. Vouchers were dead on arrival in the legislature, even a pilot program proposed by Senate education committee chair Teel Bivins (R-Amarillo) that would have allowed limited vouchers for students in the state's largest counties. Opponents were concerned that the plan would funnel taxpayer funds to private schools and convinced eleven of the thirty-one senators to object, enough to block the bill.

Perry had similarly mixed luck on other issues. He spent hours conducting shuttle diplomacy between Sen. Rodney Ellis (D-Houston) and key Republican senators over the James Byrd Jr. Hate Crimes Act, named for a Black man who had been dragged to death by White supremacists in Jasper, Texas, in 1998. The bill would have strengthened criminal penalties for crimes motivated by a victim's race, religion, sex, disability, or sexual preference. Perry was caught between support for the bill—or at least shepherding a bill he knew had support—and bottling up a bill Bush didn't want passed before he ran for president.[95] It passed the House but, despite Perry's efforts, died in the Senate, in part because it didn't have support from Bush, whose team worried it would hurt his chances in a Republican presidential primary. The bill was passed the following session and signed into law by Governor Perry.[96]

Not everything he supported passed, but Perry developed a deft touch that did not go unnoticed. He was even willing to sacrifice a political issue backed by Bush when a bill requiring background checks for guns purchased at flea markets ran into opposition, choosing the Senate's bipartisan tradition. Ratliff, the Senate's resident Jedi master, was impressed: "The first criteria [sic] for a lieutenant governor is you don't have the wheels come off. I don't think he's had any such disasters," Ratliff said. "The second one is, I believe he's widely perceived as having overseen a bipartisan Senate."[97]

Bullock had exercised more control over the process and the members, but Perry allowed for more breathing room, essential in a politically divided Senate. Neither side had the ground forces to win an all-out war. With two-thirds of the chamber needed to bring a bill to the floor for debate, it was risky to anger colleagues if you wanted your own bills to get a hearing. Perhaps an even bigger factor was the looming question of whether Perry would be a short-term lieutenant governor who would move across the street to the governor's mansion if Bush was elected president. Conservative Democrat Eddie Lucio, introducing Perry at an event in Corpus Christi following the session, praised Perry's management style. "Never before have we had such dynamic leadership take place in the Texas Senate." Perry was coy. "We're going to be back, Lord willing," he said. "Senator Lucio's going to be in the Senate, and I'm going to be somewhere."[98]

Two of the session's biggest bills—tailor-made for the Republican primary electorate Bush needed for his budding presidential run—highlighted the GOP's new approach to policy and politics in Texas. The legislature passed and Bush signed into law a bill to require a doctor to notify a minor's parents before performing an abortion.[99] A compromise allowed abortion providers to skip notification if a judge decided the girl was mature enough to make the decision on her own. The second involved deregulating the state's electric utility market, thus introducing retail competition and giving consumers the ability to shop for their power provider. Unlike most states, Texas would have separate electricity generators, transmission companies, and retail firms to provide power to consumers. Deregulation was intended to keep energy prices low, but in 2021 a deep freeze crippled the grid and created havoc for consumers who had variable rate plans. The grid failure led to massive increases in their energy bills as wholesale prices soared.

Despite the friction between the Bush and Perry camps,[100] it was a good session for Perry, who used it to raise his profile and establish his own political identity. The chamber's one-vote margin meant he had to be diplomatic and finesse tough votes. Reading the temperature of the chamber, a skill learned during his days in the House, let him understand where to push and where to retreat. Pushing the Bush agenda, which was becoming more polarizing, also required keen legislative skills. Unlike Bullock, Perry sought the spotlight. "Bullock would tell senators, leave partisanship at the door when you come see me. Perry was the opposite of that," said Dowd, who had worked for Bullock. "Bullock had no other ambitions, and Perry did. The lieutenant governor's office was always temporary for Perry."[101]

On June 14, 1999, Bush made it official. He was running for president. Perry indicated that if Bush won, he would run for governor in 2002. Taking a page from Bush, Perry carefully honed his message, noting he would continue to focus on the core issues of education and transportation. "I know what I'm going to be doing," he said. "I just don't know where I'm going to be doing it from."[102]

Texas ultimately sealed the Republican presidential nomination for Bush—as the primary polls closed on March 14, 2000, the Lone Star State allotted 124 delegates to its governor. Referring to his father's loss to Bill Clinton in the 1992 presidential election, the younger Bush remarked he was "halfway to ending the Clinton-Gore era in Washington, DC. To get there we must face one more Clinton-Gore campaign," a reference to his Democratic opponent, Al Gore, who had been Bill Clinton's vice president.[103]

Perry, head of the state party's nominating committee as it met in humid Houston that June, showed no signs of the testy relationship he and the governor shared. "All I want to do is to help George any way that I can," he said.[104] The convention itself illustrated a changing Texas Republican Party. There was a prayer room, something absent from the Democratic state convention, prompting state representative Rick Green (R-Dripping Springs) to declare that GOP stood for "God's Own Party." The Log Cabin Republicans, a group of gay Republicans who had been excluded from the convention, set up a mobile information booth outside the convention center. Still, choosing delegates was less contentious than it had been in 1996, when convention-goers tried to block Sen. Kay Bailey Hutchison from a place in the delegation because she didn't oppose abortion in all instances.[105]

Perry did put his boot in his mouth at least once. "Wherever your political philosophy might be, if you're not for George Bush being the next president of the United States, I consider that to be almost treasonous if you're a Texan." Just a joke, his staff clarified, after some of Perry's own donors, who had supported Bush opponent US Sen. John McCain, objected.[106]

Bush prevailed in the 2000 presidential election. Eventually. A tight election nationwide and voting irregularities in Florida followed by an extended court battle delayed the final victory for several weeks. Bush wasn't the only one waiting. Perry wasn't sure what job he'd have come January 2001. "The governor's direction to me was to . . . 'Be a good

Boy Scout. Be prepared.' I said, 'Yes sir,'" Perry said. Time was tight—
the legislative session was set to start a short nine weeks after the November election, and hundreds of bills had already been filed.[107]

The bipartisan spirit of the prior session was now a distant memory. Grievances with other Texas state leaders swelled. The usually
mild-mannered Speaker of the Texas House, Pete Laney, blasted Perry
for campaigning against House Democrats in 2000, a violation of the
gentlemen's agreement between legislative leaders, which held that they
would not get involved in races involving incumbents. "This campaign
by Perry and others in his party fails to measure up to the kind of leadership Gov. Bush and former Lt. Gov. Bob Bullock gave our state, the kind
of leadership that Texans respected and admired," Laney said.[108] Perry's
spokesperson noted that Laney campaigned for several incumbents.

Supporters saw the flap as simply another reminder that Perry viewed
politics like football. "He roots for his team, but after the game is over,
he makes a strong, bipartisan effort to build consensus and to accomplish the objectives that Texans elect members of both parties to
accomplish."[109]

In the end, the fuss didn't amount to much at the ballot box. Republicans still held a sixteen-to-fifteen majority in the Senate, and the
Democrats held seventy-eight of the 150 seats in the House. Both parties claimed victory, with Democrats holding on to majorities in the
state House and in the US congressional delegation. Both promised to
reload for 2002.

The cooperative spirit was bound to end. It was an election year, after all. Partisanship was on the rise in Texas and across the nation.
The coming legislative session would largely dictate how future political districts were drawn. Texas Republicans had a taste of winning
and committed to gaining a majority in the House to choose the first
Republican Speaker to complement Perry as the first Republican lieutenant governor.

"When President Bush got to Washington," Perry changed, according to one-time political mentor Charlie Stenholm. And the hardening
partisan lines weren't limited to Texas. Before 2001, Republicans and
Democrats in Texas could work together on most issues, and Stenholm
optimistically told his fellow Blue Dog Democrats in Congress that
Bush was "a president like Ronald Reagan (that) we can work with."[110]

That middle ground disappeared. When the Bush White House un-veiled its first tax plan, Vice President Dick Cheney told the Democrats he was "with them or against them" on the tax policy and everything else. There would be no negotiating or working together.

Perry changed, too, in both his political philosophy and his persona after Bush moved to Washington, according to Stenholm, who had known Perry since before his first run for office in the 1980s. Perry went for the political money, which was all on the right. (Stenholm said he had declined the opportunity.) "Rick drank the Kool-Aid on what has now become the current Republican Party," Stenholm said.[111]

The new governor would chart his own course with a legislature that knew and generally liked him. But questions remained: How would an unelected, first-term governor deal with contentious issues like growth, redistricting, and, although no one yet knew it, a budget crisis brought on by terrorism from the sky?

—5—

GOVERNOR, 2001–2002

*Into the Governor's Mansion
and the First Gubernatorial Campaign*

A mid the traditional "Whoop!" yelled by the Aggies assembled at Reed Arena in College Station, Perry—the first graduate of Texas A&M University to reach the governor's chair—took the stage. "It's good to be home," he said. "There's always been one constant in my life, and it's this place."[1]

It was Perry's first return to Aggieland as the state's chief executive, and he played on the storied loyalty that students and alumni hold for the place. He shared stories of serving in Saudi Arabia during his time in the US Air Force and of watching people on their journey to Mecca, the holy Muslim shrine. "I told them I know a place like that, where pilgrims come back year after year."[2]

Famously, Perry was not a stellar student. As an animal science major and member of the Corps of Cadets, he earned passing grades, but sometimes just barely. His D in a class named "Meats" would seal his place in Texas lore as an intellectual lightweight, reliably drawing laughs from his former professor when he teased, "I know you never thought you were educating a governor."[3] His devotion to the maroon and white, however, was unwavering. Later, when asked to name his favorite book, Perry picked *The Standard*, which spelled out the rules and regulations of conduct at the university.[4]

One indication that Perry was in politics for the long haul—and was serious about building on Bush's support with Hispanic voters—came when he was set to study Spanish in Mexico. He used the language briefly during his swearing-in ceremony in December 2000, after Bush left for Washington, DC, but he was far from fluent and opened himself up to ridicule from opponents. The left-leaning *Texas Observer* suggested he learn key phrases like "'El año pasado' (last year) mandé ejecutar (I ordered the execution of) muchos presos (many prisoners)."[5]

In most other ways, Perry was eager to declare his independence from Bush, an effort complicated by the new president's enduring popularity in Texas. "Rick Perry walks in after John Wayne. That's a hard task," said former senator Leticia Van De Putte.[6] The 77th session of the legislature, which convened just one month after Perry's inauguration with a renewed focus on economic development, provided ample opportunities.

After thirteen years of positive growth, by the early 2000s the Texas economy was "softening" (to use a term from the Dallas Federal Reserve): employment numbers were lower, interest rates were higher, and sales were slumping.[7] Perry was on the case. Among his first actions was to establish a Boeing Company task force to try to lure the aerospace company to North Texas from its longtime headquarters in Seattle.

Although Boeing ultimately chose Chicago as its new home, the efforts were the start of Perry's aggressive use of state funds to promote the "Texas Miracle," a phrase denoting the rapid growth of the Texas economy. Fresh off two legislative sessions that had responded to the state's budget surplus with tax cuts, lawmakers became more adamant that extra money should be invested in other priorities as the Legislative Budget Board projected a $1.5 billion surplus and projected economic growth of 14 percent for the 2002–2003 budget cycle.[8]

Becoming the yell leader for Texas—promoting the state's economy, job growth, and education system—would be central to Perry's political life over his three terms as governor. "I want Texas to be the engine of innovation, of job creation for decades to come," he said at an event in Houston. "Today Texas is looked at as the model of how you can make it work better."[9]

Building alliances in the private sector proved considerably messier, as stories emerged about an email from Dallas insurance executive Robert Reinarz claiming a lobbyist persuaded Perry not to appoint a Senate committee to study insurance industry deregulation in exchange for a $25,000 campaign contribution from the industry. Insurance deregulation was not on the list of interim charges, and Perry did receive about that amount from insurance interests at a fundraiser shortly after the email was sent. Perry insisted that there was no evidence, and the lobbyist denied speaking to Perry about the issue. Perry aide Eric Bearse stated: "What is alleged in the memo is total fiction." More instances followed. In September, Perry's campaign sent invitations to the Austin lobbying crowd for a fundraising reception and suggested donations of up to $25,000. The invitation was read as a warning: We're tracking who your clients are, and you are responsible for ponying up. "I learned that appearance is awfully important," Perry says of his experience with the fundraising letter.[10]

Such practices have many names, depending on your perspective. Corruption. Crony capitalism. Honest graft. Corporate welfare. In each case, the effect is the same: The Texas Miracle had a price. It had been around for a long time, but "with Perry, pay to play became a cottage industry" in Texas, according to one longtime journalist.[11] Businesses and politicians didn't see it as corruption, just business as usual.

The ghosts of George W. Bush's legacy as governor remained, even as lawmakers attempted to "de-Bush" Texas: they shored up areas of the budget that had been neglected in the rush to cut taxes, banned new charter schools, and overhauled the criminal justice system (especially the death penalty) to make it more equitable. Partisanship had come to Texas. Anything that smacked of Bush was rejected by an emerging polarized Democratic Party.

Republicans generally supported Bush's efforts to cut taxes on the federal level, but many worried more about the $3 billion hole left in the prior biennial budget inherited from the governor-turned-president. Democrats complained about paying a price for the tax cuts amid a fever of electing a Texan to the White House. "I think his sole purpose was to show people across the country that he could do a tax cut, and he did it at our expense," said Sen. Mario Gallegos (D-Houston). Democrats, who had a majority in the House, also passed legislation delaying the ban on social promotion—a major Bush initiative—saying it was unfair to students, especially when combined with the tougher TAAS tests set to be instituted that year and a ban on new charter schools.[12]

This friction was partly why Perry vetoed a record number of bills at the session's end. One journalist referred to Perry's time in office as "George W. Bush on steroids."[13] But Perry was only partially to blame for the transition from the "uniter-not-divider" tactics of the state GOP—the Republican Party was changing, too.

Perry set out a commonsense agenda in his first State of the State address on January 24, 2001, while also laying the groundwork for the battles that would consume the coming months. He even suggested an interest in putting an old rivalry behind him, thanking not just his wife— standard political fare—but also "a man . . . who has guided this House with an even hand and a calming temperament, who shares my farming roots and that optimistic West Texas outlook."[14] He would need both that optimism and an assist from House Speaker Pete Laney if the legislature was to continue in the relatively bipartisan spirit of the prior session, especially considering upcoming decisions about redistricting.

He noted that worsening traffic posed a risk to economic growth: "Even out in Haskell County these days, Dad has to actually look before he pulls onto Farm Road 618." He called for a conservative budget and robust Rainy Day Fund (then projected to top $1 billion), giving consideration to what looked to be a slowing economy.

Overall, Perry set out a purposely modest agenda: improving access to higher education; raising teacher pay and improving reading and math skills for students; expanding enrollment in the Children's Health Insurance Program; and increasing funding for transportation, nursing homes, and Child Protective Services, priorities that could have been proposed by a Republican or a Democrat.

"Lighter than helium," *Texas Monthly* later proclaimed of the new governor's legislative program.[15] Light, perhaps, but also a nod to how much of the emerging conservative philosophy could be accomplished in a divided legislature with an unelected governor.

Pushing harder would risk revolt from moderate Republicans in the Senate or from the Democrats who ran the House, especially in a year that would require all available goodwill to draw new political lines after the 2000 census without ending up in court. Pushing less would signal the new governor was too timid, and it also risked squandering the emerging political strength of the Republican Party. Laney claimed the concern about redistricting was "hype," but he was being disingenuous. "Everyone is kind of hypersensitive to the redistricting issue," acknowledged Max Sherman, longtime dean of the Lyndon B. Johnson School of Public Affairs at the University of Texas at Austin and a former Democratic state senator from Amarillo.[16] Perry tried to lower the temperature after the contentious 2000 election, but nothing could stop the political assault that was to come.

Light agenda or looming political assault aside, Perry spent much of the session's first few months building his name ID, visiting with the editorial boards of small-town newspapers, and doing talk-radio interviews. By the time he returned to the Capitol, he'd missed much of the narrative of the session.[17]

That's not to say that Perry—and especially his staff—wasn't paying attention. Governors, after all, are chief executives, and like other governors before him, Perry surrounded himself with trusted staff who could be relied on to oversee both the politics and the policies of key issues.

Governors pick the policies they want to pursue, aware that they will be judged by the results. "If you highlight six policies in the State of the State, that's what reporters are going to judge you on. Did you get them done?" said Mike Toomey, who served with Perry in the House and went on to serve as his chief of staff from 2002 to 2004. "You're not going to pick something you're going to lose on."[18]

Toomey, described as "part adviser and part enforcer," had known Perry for decades, stretching back to their service in the House together. The two worshiped at the same megachurch, and when Perry bought a chunk of land but was unavailable to sign, Toomey signed in his stead.[19]

While cynics viewed Perry's travels across the state as an effort to build name recognition for the next campaign, Toomey took a different view, suggesting that Perry was selling his policy goals. "Perry gets a bit of a knock because he wasn't attuned to the details, but he didn't need to be," Toomey said. "Staff is in charge of the details."[20]

Perry's strength lay in picking effective people and bringing them together. "He's not a policy wonk. He's not the smartest guy in the room. But he always managed to get the smartest subject matter experts and get their advice, and he would pay attention to them," said Leticia Van de Putte, a San Antonio Democrat who spent almost a decade in the House before moving up to the state Senate in 1999. "That's a really great leader."[21] Perry had enough friends in the House and Senate to get things done. Cliff Johnson, then senior adviser to Perry, would tell the governor, "'We need to go see somebody,' and [it] didn't take two seconds until he was ready to go."[22]

Journalist R. G. Ratcliffe likened Perry's leadership style to that used by Captain Jean-Luc Picard aboard *Star Trek*'s USS Enterprise. The governor's staff assembled to discuss some policy issue, Perry heard everybody out, and then he made a decision based on those recommendations. After the decision had been made, "there was no question that was what they were going to do."[23]

Staffers analyzed and tracked every bill filed, and Perry didn't need to wallow in minutiae. He had "nerds working for him who were very detail-oriented [and] he knew who to pick to surround himself with," said Perry's former policy director Hector Gutierrez.[24] He had a short attention span sometimes, sure, but he could focus on the agenda items he cared about.[25]

The contours of Perry's style as governor quickly snapped into place. The day after the inauguration, he invited the Legislative Black Caucus to the governor's mansion for breakfast. The next day he invited the Mexican American Legislative Caucus. "These brand-new legislators, second day in office, 'I'm going to the governor's mansion,' telling their spouses, 'Rick Perry invited me to the governor's mansion,'" Van de Putte said. "Everybody's a hug. Everybody's *un abrazo*."[26]

Perry earned a reputation for trolling the halls at all hours when a major state bill was up for consideration, walking into committee hearings, inviting members over for meetings. "The legislature is all about relationships," Toomey said. "A lot of votes happen on the House floor based on the reputation and relationships with the members right there."[27] Perry himself pointed to building relationships, understanding the system, and spending his early political life as a Democrat as keys to his longevity.[28]

Senfronia Thompson, an experienced legislative knife-fighter after decades in the House, knew Perry would negotiate based on trust. Thompson wanted to raise nursing home funding for people with special needs, about $39 billion worth. The Perry administration was pushing through a Section 1115 Medicaid waiver to fund the state's federal Medicaid needs on which Thompson had raised points of order to kill the bills.

"Senfronia, I *need* your help."

"Governor, I *need* your help."

The two old legislative hands went back and forth, making their case over a day. At the end of the last conversation, Perry bluntly asked, "So are you gonna kills those two bills?" "As sure as God sends the sun to warm us during the day and the moon to give us light at night," punched back Representative Thompson. "Well, I talked to my people, and I think we can help you. We'll put the money in the budget." "Well, ok then, if you can help me, I can help you." All of the bills passed and were signed by the governor. When Perry's approval began to slip weeks later, he bragged in a press release about the budget increasing nursing home funds.[29]

State Republican Party chair Tina Benkiser recalls an invitation to an impromptu dinner at the governor's mansion with Carly Fiorina, CEO of Hewlett-Packard, whom the governor was trying to convince to move to Texas, Republican state senator Jon Lindsay, and famed economist Arthur Laffer, along with Rick and Anita Perry. The talk was about policy, not politics, and the impact of economics on people's lives—and a little football talk, too.

"I recall thinking how easily the conversation flowed at a higher intellectual level than most political conversations," Benkiser said. "Most political conversations these days take place at the sound bite level, but that night I was really impressed, and I don't impress easily."[30]

On some issues, however, Perry would "draw a line in the sand." On issues of statewide importance, "he wanted to be nuts and bolts, on the ground, in the meeting or running the meeting." He wanted to set up budgets for success, especially oversight over departments, such as knowing in advance what each agency's legislative appropriation requests (LARs) would be before they submitted them to the legislature. "Who knows that minutia? Somebody who's been in the Lege. He didn't demand it. The way he did it was his staff said they wanted to be helpful" to agencies that needed specific program funding. "He didn't write the budget, but he got to see and influence" the process. Those small things mattered. Ann Richards had tried the same approach but wasn't as successful—the chairs of the finance and appropriations committees politely sent the same letter back to the governor. "Rick Perry said it in a different way that [was] meant to be helpful"—the process worked because "he knew how to do it."[31]

More than a decade in Austin paid off, as Perry knew most of the players and tended to those relationships, allowing him to guide competing interests on both sides of the aisle to common ground.

His early experiences in the military and in the House helped prepare him for this next step. "I always loved the fact that he was open to suggestions, but he would let you know 'not going there, can't go there, nope.' That way you don't waste your time." "If he didn't feel like he had all the information he needed, he would ask for it." Military training prepared him for this, insiders said. "You just don't go and fly into a combat situation not knowing what you're flying into. Until he was satisfied with those questions' answers, we would take the time it took to get the job done." "We had many, many meetings just for the purpose of vetting whatever the issue *du jour* was. 'I heard such and such was happening in Beaumont. Get us some information.' So he knew if he was asked to do something on that he had all the facts."[32]

His time in the House trained him, as one capital insider recalled, as a "student of the process."[33] Governors who were "House trained," they said, consistently made good governors, or least governors who knew the process. "He sure knew how things worked, he knew the basis, which is saying something. Bill Clements didn't understand how things worked when he was governor until after a little while. Governor Bush probably understood the basics just from paying attention in government class, but he never got inside the system quite the way you have to be as governor. So Perry was versed in that way."[34] Having been in the legislature and run an agency, he worked on "building consensus. It wasn't 'my way or the highway.' Let's try to get it home."[35]

Former chief of staff Mike Toomey summed up Perry's approach in one word: relationships. "The legislature is all about relationships. He handled that expertly." "A lot of votes happen on the House floor based on the reputation and relationships with the members right there."[36] They would dispatch Perry to the legislature to work the floor, aided by staff work that hashed out the details. As one former legislator put it, Perry "put his agenda out on the line and he fought for it," he said. "And he worked with legislators. His executive team would work with legislators on key pieces of legislation and he'd talk you through if you had some concerns about it, to keep the office from vetoing a bill. He would just come into your office and say, 'Hey, if you could change this for us, that would help us.' It gave more direction."[37]

He primarily engaged in issues that mattered to him and didn't try to "micromanage" the members or the legislative agenda. "He would come to the floor. He had a personal relationship with everybody."[38] He wasn't strictly a transactional politician, but knowing the players helped. "It's all about cultivating relationships—you don't know when you are going to need them or how." In legislative negotiations, finding common ground and issues of interest can get the job done, even across the aisle, a skill that Perry handled well: "If you can find some issue with someone who opposes you that you [both] agree on or at least come together on, you'll always find common ground. I think he realizes that," recalled a former legislative staffer. "Many times he'd say, 'Hey you know I haven't talked to so-and-so [member] in a while. Think they can come by and just visit?'" recalled a former legislative director. "Perry was in politics to make things better," not throw bombs.[39]

These personal relationships were genuine. "He had a big heart. He's not mean enough to be a national politician," said Van de Putte.

The two seldom agreed on policy, but she came to respect his "West Texas, no bullshit" style. "He's very affable, but if he's not with you, he's going to tell you. We disagreed with great respect and never lost the friendship," she said.[40]

By observing and working with Perry, Van de Putte learned an enduring lesson. "It's about how people feel first. Not about how great the numbers, the data, are. It's about how you feel. Rick Perry could make you feel shitty. He could make you feel wonderful. And he could make you get on his side very quickly." He understood that sometimes, the personal trumped policy differences. In 2012 Democratic senator Mario Gallegos was dying of liver failure in a Houston hospital when Harold Cook, who had been asked to manage media calls during Gallegos's final days, received a call from the governor. Perry offered to help in any way he could, but one family member wasn't impressed. "Rick Perry is so chickenshit I bet he won't even lower the flag to half-staff when Mario dies."

Cook conveyed the message, albeit more diplomatically: "There's already been a discussion that they would consider it a really a nice act of respect if you made a big honking deal of lowering the flags to half-staff whenever Mario does pass."

Gallegos died a few days later, and within an hour, the governor's office put out an effusive statement and ordered the state's flags lowered. "It's just those little things. And that adds up over time," said Cook. "I think it made up for a lot of these really sharp, hard campaign messages."[41]

Perry's formidable personal skills might have seemed more remarkable had he not followed George W. Bush in office. "In contrast to Bush, who made a show of running down hallways and stopping into offices to say hello, Perry didn't do that all that often," said Gardner Selby, a longtime capitol reporter.[42] He wasn't "as active as Bush [with the legislature] or as standoffish as [Gov. Greg] Abbott. He just let the process go."[43]

The media noticed another shift, as the rising political star who'd been eager to court reporters on the House floor and at Austin watering holes became more distant. His office stopped releasing his schedule, as previous governors had done. He used his private email account and not his official state account in an effort to sidestep public records disclosures.

"He very much had the notion that the press was not his friend. The more of the ball you can hide, the better," said Christy Hoppe.[44]

Harvey Kronberg headed into a Perry fundraiser at the Four Seasons in Austin, where he'd sat in on previous fundraisers for other politicians, only this time he was told that no press were allowed. "There's a new sheriff in town," Perry's communications director, Ray Sullivan, told him.[45]

Times were changing, and candidates didn't spend as much time courting the mainstream media. Social media allowed Perry to communicate directly to his preferred voters, making an end run around traditional news sources.

Perry didn't make the same mistake other governors made. Campaigning and governing were two different things. "How you run a state is not by campaigning. Rick knew that, he understood that." The politics were kept at the door when negotiating. "We kinda prided ourselves that we weren't Washington," remembered Perry's legislative director, former senator Ken Armbrister. "We didn't care who had a solution. You got a solution, and we were willing to work with anybody on it. Let's do something for the state. As opposed to if the Ds had a solution the Rs won't vote for it, or if the Rs have a solution the Ds won't vote for it. We can still all go to Friday night football. If you have a solution, we don't care" what party you belong to."[46]

That first, partial term was a balancing act, requiring Perry to carefully weigh his own agenda against that of the popular former governor who was now president. He was cautious but remained committed to his pet programs.[47] "He probably agonized over more things in the two years he filled George W.'s terms than all the other years. Any decision he made was going to be scrutinized by his enemies."[48]

The bipartisanship of the previous session carried over, and Perry helped push through a key bill that had failed in 1999, the James Byrd Jr. Hate Crimes Act, which strengthened penalties for crimes motivated by race, religion, color, disability, sexual preference, national original, or ancestry.[49] Extending the hate-crime designation to crimes committed against LGBTQ Texans was politically charged, a sticking point for many Republicans.

Perry stepped up and "forged that deal," according to insiders, offering political cover for members willing to make a vote that might be unpopular with their core voters back home.[50] "That was one thing he was very good at," recalled Van de Putte. "He said, 'I'll have your back.' It meant, if you get challenged, I'll come to your district and help you campaign."[51] Republican senator Tom Haywood bucked his party and voted for the bill, and as promised, Perry campaigned for him to take some of the heat.

But legislative pressure helped too. "Perry knows me. He knows that if I get behind something, I'm going to keep on it," according to the bill's author, Rep. Senfronia Thompson. The bill's biggest opposition was another Democrat turned Republican, Warren Chisum. Thompson approached Chisum one Friday during session: "Are you going home this weekend?" The two members and their staff worked over the weekend to find a compromise to nail down the language and hammer out a policy to include LGBTQ protections. The two pulled a fast one on a shocked House, pretending arch conservative Chisum was against the language but in fact was in favor of a "friendly" amendment to add the protections to the bill.

After the bill passed both Houses, Perry had to either veto, sign, or let the bill become law without his signature. "I'm sure he's making this evaluation," Thompson remembered. "He looked down the road politically and the impacts. What are you trying to accomplish with this bill, and . . . [do] you think it would alienate people if I don't do it?" It became a message bill: hate has no place in Texas.[52]

Support for the bill was also a way to show some independence from Bush, who had not supported the bill. Perry "put some energy into showing some independence from 'Bush world'" once he was governor, and he wanted to "show he was not 'Bush's guy,' he was going to be his own person."[53] Republican senator Haywood bucked his party and voted for the bill, and as promised, Perry campaigned for him to take some of the heat.

"In the end, we're all Texans," Perry said at the bill signing, joined by James Byrd's teary-eyed family.[54] Extension of hate crimes to LGBTQ Texans was politically charged and was the sticking point for many Republicans. Was the signing politically motivated? Opponents claimed it was, but Perry said it was "the right thing to do." "He knew he was going to get hammered by a certain element of the Party," so he agonized over the decision. Ultimately, he "stuck to his principles."[55]

His priorities, as detailed in his first State of the State address, got attention, including expanding access to higher education and the first moves towards a state transportation plan, which would become one of Perry's signature issues.[56] But criminal justice reform consumed much of the session.

Perry signed legislation to overhaul the state's indigent defense system, to ban racial profiling, and to give inmates easier access to post-conviction, state-funded DNA testing that could exonerate them. Calls for expanded use of DNA testing had grown louder after flaws of the application of the death penalty in Texas were highlighted by Democrats during Bush's presidential campaign. Joined at the signing by members of both parties, including bill architects Robert Duncan (R-Lubbock) and Juan "Chuy" Hinojosa (D-McAllen), Perry called DNA technology "an important tool. It must be utilized to shed light on cases where there is cause for doubt."[57]

But like Bush before him, Perry maintained a breezy confidence that no innocent person had been executed in Texas. "I think we have an appropriate process in place from the standpoint of the appeals process to make sure that due process is addressed," Perry said.[58]

The legislature wasn't so sure, and it passed a bill to ban the execution of inmates with mental disabilities. The US Supreme Court was similarly unconvinced, voiding the sentence of Johnny Paul Penry, who had been convicted of a 1979 murder but had the intellectual capacity of a seven-year-old, according to testimony. Perry, pressured on all sides to sign, vetoed the bill on the last day before it would otherwise have become law without his signature. He argued that the state already had numerous safeguards in place and that he trusted the state's jurors to get punishment right. Seven inmates with cognitive disabilities were on Death Row that year, and Rodney Ellis, the Houston Democrat who had sponsored the bill in the Senate, decried the veto as giving Texas "the appearance of being barbaric."[59]

The House also forwarded a resolution to ask voters if the nation's most active death penalty state should halt executions for two years. "We need to ensure that we execute the guilty and let the innocent go," said Rep. Juan Hinojosa (D-McAllen), chair of the Criminal Jurisprudence Committee. "For me, it's just a disservice to victims and their families to place a blanket moratorium on the death penalty," said Rep. Terry Keel (R-Austin).[60] Ultimately, despite legislative support and polling that revealed Texans were concerned that innocent defendants might be executed even as they supported the use of the punishment, the resolution was met with a lightly attended funeral in the House Calendars Committee.[61]

Some of the efforts, including allowing wider use of DNA in appeals, positioned Texas—and Perry, to a degree—as a leader on criminal justice reform. But the state had a mixed record on executions, an issue that dogged Perry's time as governor. He didn't fully embrace reform but nibbled at the edges. He refused to stay the 2004 execution of Cameron Todd Willingham, who had been convicted of the arson deaths of his three daughters in 1991; when evidence emerged after the execution raising doubts about Willingham's guilt, the governor's office replaced three members of the independent state forensics panel investigating the case. (A spokesperson said the decision was motivated solely by the fact that the members' terms had expired.)[62]

When Perry did commute a death sentence, it was often because the US Supreme Court had ordered him to do so.[63] In another case, an inmate named Anthony Graves served eighteen years for murdering a family in the Central Texas town of Somerville, despite limited evidence to suggest his guilt. Convicted in 1992, a federal appeals court overturned the conviction in 2006 after an investigation revealed prosecutorial misconduct, and he was released in 2010. These high-profile mistakes added up and, combined with the cost of executions—running into the hundreds of millions of dollars—motivated reform efforts.

The politics of capital punishment required a firm public posture. Privately, though, these executions were not easy for Perry. Van de Putte was Senate president pro tempore in 2001, serving as acting governor while Perry was out campaigning and the lieutenant governor was traveling abroad, when one controversial execution was scheduled. Real concerns had been raised about the defendant's mental capacity, but there was no question about his guilt in a brutal slaying.

Van de Putte called Perry and asked, "How do you handle this, knowing that when you say, 'You may proceed,' you are ending a person's life?"

His answer stayed with her. "Even if I know and am certain this person is guilty, I fall on my knees and beg for forgiveness."

"And that's what I did."[64]

The first in his family to go to college, Perry pushed to expand access to higher education through grants for first-generation college students and to reorganize the state-funded Hinson-Hazlewood loan programs. He signed bills that tripled the Toward Excellence Access and Success (TEXAS) grant, from $100 million biannually to $300 million.[65] He signed bills to simplify access to Medicaid and increase funding for education, infrastructure, and healthcare in border communities, along with legislation giving the state education commissioner more power to shut down or oversee failing schools and allowing state universities and colleges to set up an unlimited number of charter schools, even as it capped the total number and increased regulations on other charter schools.[66] Members who carried those bills recall meeting with a disinterested Perry in the governor's office. Fixing a Bush problem wasn't high on his to-do list, but the legislature had to do it, and he recognized that the unchecked explosion of charter schools was a problem.[67]

He also made suggestions that would have gotten him drummed out of the GOP in future years. Ratliff, elected by his fellow senators to replace Perry as lieutenant governor until the next election, drafted a school funding formula that included a statewide property tax, an idea Perry agreed to consider. "We'll put all options on the table and take a look at them and have a good and open debate" about the potential for a more equitable tax system, he said, noting the change would require voter approval. A reasonable suggestion for any governor, perhaps, but a death wish for Republicans in the coming years. Even the 2002 Democratic nominee for governor, Tony Sanchez, rejected the idea. "Taxes are off the table," he said at a fundraiser.[68] The Senate did reduce franchise taxes, the state's de facto business tax.

A number of major issues emerged during the 2001 legislative session, but none would come to define Perry's terms as governor so much as transportation.[69] While he was still lieutenant governor, Dell Computers approached Perry with a problem: they needed an off-ramp for their facility north of Austin. The bureaucratic challenges of working through the Texas Department of Transportation (TXDoT) to get that built, however, were myriad. The issue stuck with a development-minded Perry, recalls Ray Sullivan a future chief of staff.[70] When he was elected governor, he appointed Ric Williamson, a friend since their years together in the House, to the Texas Transportation Commission in 2001, and threw his support behind Williamson's vision of a massive transportation network connecting the major Texas regions.

Nicknamed "Nitro" for his effusive personality and grand ideas, "Ric was very, very smart but often very, very wrong," Harold Cook said, and the Trans-Texas Corridor—a system of supercorridors comprising toll roads, highways, railways, and utility lines linking the state's major population centers—was proposed with much fanfare but little vetting.[71] Republican consultant Reb Wayne summed up the reality, which would require navigating funding from federal and state sources, the complicated bureaucracy at TXDoT, and the challenging politics around toll roads ("people hate them").[72]

Nevertheless, Perry was all in. "We're way behind," he said, raising the alarm at an October 2001 event in Houston. "After a heavy downpour, the roads wash out so fast an emergency vehicle can't get in or a school bus can't get out," he said. "How can a child in this state reach for the stars if he can't even reach the classroom?"[73] A business-friendly, transportation-accessible Texas was necessary for economic growth in the state, aides believed.[74]

A few months later he unveiled a sweeping new proposal for an invigorated road and rail plan, including high-speed trains and thousands of miles of new highways, funded with both public and private money and projected to cost $175 billion over the next fifty years.

Transportation was a priority for Perry, and for he and Williamson to achieve his vision, they needed consensus in the legislature. Under his watch came the first major expansion of toll roads in Texas. Ken Armbrister recalled, "People for better or for worse complain about it, but the last time we had a gas tax increase was under Clements [in 1991]. We raised it a nickel, and nobody even said a thing because they could see we needed transportation. With the makeup of the legislature they'd say, 'Oh, I can't vote for taxes.' Well, B.S."[75] They created these "little animals" that ceded some local control over transportation funding.

"[Williamson] is a bright, shining kind of guy. He likes ideas, and he'll grab onto ideas and run with [them]," Miller said.[76] But "Williamson was contagious," and his ideas often "sounded great because he was a great salesman."[77] Rick and Ric were very different people—Perry the implementer and Williamson the intellectual force—but they shared an interest in mobility and an ownership stake in Williamson's MKS natural gas company (run by Mary Ann, Williamson's widow, whom Perry later appointed to the Texas Lottery Commission).[78] The bugaboo ended up costing Perry some of his conservative credentials as opponents railed against the aggressive development of new toll roads and the land-gobbling, property-rights-stomping Trans-Texas Corridor, which would have expanded existing highway and railway capacity between large cities across the Texas prairies and through forests and arid deserts.[79] The plan had a massive footprint that would have removed millions of acres from private hands and off county tax rolls. "You don't understand, they don't want the money; they don't want you on their place," Armbrister said, encapsulating the opposition from landowners.[80]

The idea was good, but the execution was not, and the project was shelved by the end of the decade. "The Trans-Texas Corridor, had they played the politics right, could have been enormously consequential in economic development," Kronberg said.[81] Perry sought consensus, as was his style.[82] The governor reached out to his former House committee chair Ed Emmett, who was at the National Industrial Transportation League in Washington, DC. "Mr. Chairman!" Perry exclaimed on the phone, before explaining the idea. After reviewing it, Emmett thought it a bad idea—not the politics, necessarily, but the logistics of route selection and railroad easements. Perry and Williamson, whom Emmett had stayed with while campaigning for the Railroad Commission, put out too many possible options, angering everyone who might have been in the path. "They didn't talk to me for over a year," Emmett said.[83] Without rural buy-in and a larger campaign to attract interest, the Trans-Texas Corridor became a dead end.

That first term also marked the start of another of Perry's most enduring legacies, with more than three thousand appointments to the state's courts, boards, and commissions. The Senate unanimously confirmed San Antonio appellate attorney Wallace Jefferson as the first Black justice to the Texas Supreme Court, filling the seat vacated by Alberto Gonzales, who left to serve as White House counsel.

Controlling who served on state boards and commissions would, at least in theory, allow the governor more say over state agencies and allow more coordination among agencies that might otherwise work in different—or even opposing—directions. Staffers said Perry spent more time on appointments than any other single topic besides natural disasters.[84] Staff used these appointments to protect the governor by deploying political surrogates to run political defense.

Appointments were important because "the bureaucracy runs that place. And they know it," Perry reflected. Agencies could hold their breath for as long as a governor might serve (since most governors didn't get more than one term). "I changed that trajectory."[85] The first priority was to replace Ann Richards's appointees on boards and commissions as soon as their periods of appointment ended. After that, the Perry camp had a simple rule—Bush appointees could serve two terms if they wished. Finding the right people was key, since by statute some roles were specifically defined.

For new appointments, Perry gave each appointee a card listing seven principles that he or she needed to "keep in mind." Prospective appointees were vetted, and Perry looked to his friends, to Aggies, and to those who had "shown something in life," according to senior adviser Cliff Johnson. "That's a governor's legacy, and governors are always fearful of making mistakes."[86] Perry later admitted he would have been firmer with university regents, asking them to presign a letter of resignation that the governor could execute if they didn't follow his directives.[87]

Perry followed an informal chain of command in making appointments, choosing people who were loyal to him, even over loyalty to the Republican Party.[88] In that, he was following a time-honored practice. "Who are they supposed to appoint?" a longtime journalist asked. "People who didn't support them or vote for them?"[89]

Perry trumpeted his legislative successes, but they took a backseat to the new governor's heavy-handed use of the veto pen.

Legislators awoke on June 17, 2001, the Sunday after the session ended, to news of the "Father's Day Massacre," as Perry vetoed an unprecedented seventy-nine bills in a single day. In all, he vetoed eighty-two bills, another record.

The fallen bills spanned a gamut of issues, from requiring racial and ethnic awareness training for state judges to equal access to public places for protected classes and the expansion of legal charitable bingo games. One bill would have allowed undocumented immigrants to obtain driver's licenses, and another created low-interest loans for building energy-efficient housing. Perry's reasoning ranged widely. He claimed some bills were duplicative, such as a bill banning establishments from denying admission to people wearing "motorcycle clothing," a protection already covered by federal law. He said other laws overstepped the proper scope of government, intervening in areas where local authorities should have greater say, such as a bill limiting the amount of paperwork required of public school teachers. Many, he argued, were simply bad for Texas.[90]

Why did Perry do it? The state legislature had spent time and taxpayer money crafting the legislation, some of which passed with overwhelming support. Most of the vetoed bills had been sponsored by Democrats (fifty-six out of the eighty-two), but not all. And many legislators had not received a courtesy call warning of the governor's plans, a longstanding tradition.[91] Charges of a power grab and political payback echoed throughout the Capitol. Members had grown complacent with Bush at the helm, and this was a new approach—or at the least a show of force.[92] Perry blamed Speaker Laney. The House sent a bunch of "bad bills," not caring whether the governor was for or against. "Laney was just being Laney," sending signals that Laney, not Perry, ran the show.[93]

In any case, the message was clear: Rick Perry would be a strong and active governor. Lieutenant governors succeed by letting the senators run the show and giving them credit. Being governor is different. "It wasn't spiteful," Perry said. He knew the process and needed to express to the legislature he was willing to work with them, but if they tried to "cram this down my throat," he would act, Perry remembers.[94]

Bill Miller, the Republican consultant, saw it as Perry demanding respect from the legislature. "'You guys better start respecting me, and you better start doing what I want.' It was a pure, clear, unmistakable signal." And with the vetoes, "he got their respect."[95]

"When he became governor, he began to express that anxiousness and impulsiveness—it was a mark of who he was. It was at rest when he was in the Senate." The legislature did not think he had the "political guts" to pull the trigger, recalled press secretary Ray Sullivan. Members ignored him, underestimating the new governor.[96]

He also intended to invigorate the Republican Party at a time when Democrats and Republicans were vying for control of the legislature. But the vetoes were more than ideological. As Miller suggests, they were a warning that he was in charge, would settle scores after the players left the field to keep order in the legislative process. Perry was determined to cement the concept of a strong Texas governor, even though historically the Texas executive branch has been weak. Perry could play hardball in a way that Bush could not. "Bush needed Pete Laney, he needed the Democrats," said Wayne Slater, while growing Republican power in the legislature meant Perry didn't have to negotiate in the same way that his Republican predecessors did.[97]

Without a heads-up from the governor's office, the vetoes caught many legislators by surprise, leading some to argue that Perry was too focused on politics. Successful governors, they sniffed, didn't have to veto—they instead let legislators know they wouldn't approve a bill and worked with them to change it. Perry's methods, they said, were "a case of macho."[98]

"That is not policy-making. It's the Father's Day Massacre, with blood running in the streets," Rep. Garnet Coleman (D-Houston) lamented.[99] Sullivan agreed, in part. "Some of those bills didn't *need* to be vetoed," but Perry and the staff wanted to send a clear signal to the legislature that they were coequal branches. Inside the governor's office, some staff members were angry with the legislature for not heeding warnings and wanted to punish them. But Perry, a former legislator, was "eyes wide open" about what the vetoes would mean to the legislature. Yet he also realized how it would strengthen his hand in future legislative sessions.[100]

Rep. Senfronia Thompson of Houston, "Mrs. T" to multiple generations of legislature watchers, remembers Perry calling her about a bill he was going to veto. They were mad at each other about something that session—"I was on him like white on rice." Perry said, "I'm letting you know you've got four bills here I'm going to veto." "'Well, Governor, I don't give a fats rat.' What could I do? There is nothing I would be able to say to him to make him change his position." The whole episode was about respect for the executive, she believed. "I am the governor," was his mindset.[101]

Perry dismissed criticisms from some members about the lack of communication: "I think I've been very open with members of the Legislature about issues that we have had."[102] His staff was more blunt: "That's bullshit." The members, they said, ignored what the governor wanted and ignored the advice of the governor's staff.[103] But the episode changed how Perry was seen in the legislative process. From then on, members earnestly checked in with the governor's office before filing bills.

The outrage wasn't confined to legislators. Interest groups that pressed for passage of the vetoed bills protested, too. "*Veto Perry!*" chanted dozens of people gathered outside a meeting of the Southwest Voter Registration Education Project, where Perry was the first Republican to give a keynote address. This particular group was upset at Perry's veto of a bill that would have boosted staffing at correctional facilities. "Honk if you are with the Hispanic community." (Well aware that Hispanics were an important demographic group for Republicans, Perry touted his approval of a bill that would add 150,000 low-income families to Medicaid.)[104]

Physicians were angry about his veto of a measure intended to speed payment of physician claims by insurance companies. One lobbyist said they got "sandbagged, sucker-punched."[105] Perry attempted damage control days later at an industry workshop at the Texas Department of Insurance, fussing that insurance companies needed to do better to pay claims promptly, but supporters of the bill were not pleased. Advocates for border residents were angered by the veto of a living-wage bill at a time when most migrants lived on far less than the $5.15 per hour set as the state's minimum wage. They also decried the veto of the bill to make it easier for Mexican immigrants to obtain Texas driver's licenses. "We don't know who the governor is listening to if he's not listening to the people of Texas," said a spokesperson for the Texas Immigrant and Refugee Coalition.[106]

The Father's Day Massacre certainly expanded gubernatorial power, the veto being one of the few powers on paper that governors have. And it changed his governorship: it was "the singularly most effective thing I did. 'What's the governor think about this?'" members would ask of the governor's chief of staff or legislative director.[107]

Despite the bloodbath, most people rated the session as more fruitful than expected. There was no stalling over controversial abortion regulations or school voucher issues. The shift in legislative power to suburban areas rankled rural members, including House Speaker Pete Laney, who feared losing influence to fast-growing metropolitan areas. Yet even Laney called the session "very positive for Texas," including the establishment of programs to enhance access to high-speed Internet healthcare.[108]

The positivity was perhaps enhanced by the lack of any huge battles over redistricting, largely because the session adjourned without adopting new political lines. The last three decennial redistricting plans had ended up in court, and this round would be no different, as massive demographic and regional changes continued to reshape the Lone Star State. Rapid suburban growth in counties like Williamson (north of Austin), Collin (north of Dallas), and Montgomery (north of Houston) would mean those areas would gain representation, but inner cities and rural West Texas stood to lose up to a dozen seats in the state House of Representatives.

With no plan passed during the regular session and Perry hearing mixed reports on the likely success of a special session, he was content to leave the line-drawing to the Legislative Redistricting Board, which drew the new state House and Senate districts, and to the federal courts, which produced a congressional redistricting plan. "It turned into a huge, bloody battle," Lt. Gov. Bill Ratliff recalled years later.[109] Redistricting would be a messy affair in the years to come, but for now, Perry was happy to fight that battle another day.

The relative harmony shifted to political jockeying as soon as the session ended. Laney had been held up as a model of bipartisanship by Bush, even introducing the new president when Bush spoke from the House floor to accept the presidency after Al Gore conceded in December 2000. But now, less than six months later, Laney faced revolt from House Republicans, who figured they could sink the Democrats, who held a tenuous six-seat majority.

"My concern is that we'll be more like DC, in that we'll divide the aisle," said Tommy Merritt, an ally of Laney. "And I think that is a very significant change in Texas."[110]

It was the last session in which conservative social issues were "background noise" and economic and fiscal matters were central, where the business of legislating was "more than just abortion and voting rights."[111]

Previously, campaign messages were based on the challenges facing the state—gang violence, child support, welfare reform, tort reform for medical malpractice. But by the early 2000s, that had reversed. Political messaging led the agenda.[112]

Perry launched his 2002 gubernatorial campaign back home in Paint Creek, in front of three hundred supporters, twelve of whom graduated with him from the Paint Creek rural school. "As I look out across this room today, I am mindful of a common bond we share: the privilege of being Texans."[113] His hometown was important to Perry. He used the family ranch brand as his campaign symbol. He vowed to improve public education, make advances in transportation, promote Texas business, and innovate in healthcare.

"I've been tested, and I have experience," he said. "I am the strong leader who can lead Texas forward for the next four years."[114]

According to polling, Perry was riding high in the saddle. Fifty percent of registered voters approved of his handling of the job as governor, compared to 24 percent who disapproved and 26 percent who were unsure. He started with a ten-point lead over his Democratic challenger, but with 23 percent responding "not sure," it would be a race to define himself before the deep-pocketed Democrat did so for him. Mixed economic success was part of the issue—45 percent of Texans said the state was in "good" economic times, compared to 43 percent who rated the economy bad."[115]

Democrats, meanwhile, saw 2002 as their best chance to stop Perry before he could stake a stronger claim to the governor's mansion. But Tony Sanchez was an unlikely Democratic candidate, a Laredo banker who had made millions in the oil and gas industry, a major donor to Bush's gubernatorial campaigns, and a Bush appointee to the University of Texas System Board of Regents. He was a seventh-generation Texan, but political veterans saw some immediate downsides. "He doesn't have a willingness to engage. He doesn't have a passion for the issues, and he is not working very hard."[116]

Sanchez calculated his political positions carefully. Donations to Bush? Those symbolized his "middle of the road" personality. The death penalty? He supported it but objected to Perry's veto of the ban on executing mentally incapacitated inmates. Abortion? As a Catholic, he objected, but he backed a woman's right to choose.

But in other ways, he was a perfect Democratic candidate. He grew up picking pineapples and melons in fields along the border and later became the first in his family to graduate from college and earn a law degree. The growing Latino vote was emerging as a political force, and Sanchez's efforts to court that vote would set the stage for future Democratic success.

Education was his top issue, especially fixing the state's underfunded and inequitable educational system. "Texas is a 'can-do' state that will no longer tolerate a 'do-nothing' governor."[117]

Just as Perry had, Sanchez kicked off the general election in his hometown (Laredo), followed by a trip across the state. "We can have better schools. We can have better health care. We can have a better environment. We can have more jobs at better pay so that every Texan can live a life with dignity," he announced.[118]

Standing in his way was one of the few remaining Democrats still capable of credibly running a statewide race: former Texas attorney general Dan Morales. Morales was the last Democratic official to hold statewide office, choosing not to run for reelection in 1998 and ending the Democratic Party's reign not with a bang but with a whimper.[119] Morales had flirted with a bid for US Senate and jumped into the governor's race literally minutes before the filing deadline. One of the two would become the first Latino Democratic nominee for Texas governor. Neither man, nor the Democratic Party, would come out unscathed.

In an historic, televised Spanish-language debate, Sanchez accused Morales of being "embarrassed" to be Hispanic because he opposed affirmative action and favored English as the state's "principal language."[120] Morales bragged about his role in the state's historic $17.6 billion settlement with the tobacco industry.[121] Later, questions were raised about his contracts with private attorneys on that case, who investigators claimed did little or no work. Morales was charged in 2003 with twelve counts of conspiracy and of using political money for private purposes; he pled guilty to a reduced charge and served time at a federal prison in Texarkana a year later.[122]

Boosted by his saturation of the airwaves and backed by $20 million in campaign dollars, Sanchez won the nomination with 61 percent of the primary vote, including 70 percent of the Latino vote, which accounted for more than one-third of total Democratic turnout. The Democratic "Dream Team"—Sanchez; US Senate nominee Ron Kirk, the mayor of Dallas; and John Sharp, running for lieutenant governor just four years after he had been beaten by Perry—headed an all-star ticket featuring money, influence, experience, and diversity.

The slate tried to have it both ways, boasting that the Democratic ticket "looks like the face of Texas" while simultaneously urging voters to judge them on their records, not their skin color. But the group walked a fine line on race, with Kirk backtracking on claims that ethnic and racial minorities did most of the fighting in the Iraq conflict after Republican opponent John Cornyn called the comments "unnecessarily divisive." Sharp proclaimed the ticket the most "centrist, pro-business" ticket in twenty years. "The middle of the political spectrum? I can tell you who will be there—the next senator and next governor of the state of Texas," said Kirk.[123]

Not all Democrats were impressed. "I continue to think if they take a don't-rock-the-boat, middle-of-the-road, try-not-to-offend-anybody-and-sneak-in strategy, that they're doomed," said Hightower, the liberal stalwart who unsuccessfully faced off against Perry in his 1990 race for agriculture commissioner.[124] But the mainstream party persisted, contending that a fiscally conservative ticket with progressive values on social issues would appeal to Texans.

Perry, who had been unopposed in the Republican primary, appeared unconcerned. "You've heard the other side brag about a certain so-called 'Dream Team'? Well, on November 5th, when the dream is over, they will be in for a rude awakening," he prophesied of Election Day 2002.[125] He was by now a seasoned campaigner and had risen through the ranks of Texas state politics without ever losing an election.

"I'm going to try to be as open and as positive and as visionary as I can be," he said. "I've got a track record."[126] He also had $13 million on hand when the primaries were over, and that increased to $20 million before the general election rolled around. This was as much as Sanchez spent in the primary, making raising money important for Perry against a self-funding millionaire. Morales eventually endorsed Perry, in part because he said he disagreed with efforts by Sanchez and the Democratic Party to court the Latino vote over white voters.

Sanchez struggled in the general election. He'd never held elected office, and campaigning—the handshaking, chitchat, and constant media questions—were often "trying" for him. "I like to call myself a raving moderate," he said, bragging about working for another moderate who occasionally ruffled feathers, then lieutenant governor Ben Barnes. "Extremisms don't work in business, and they don't work in government." His personal wealth of around $600 million allowed him to spend "whatever it takes" to beat Perry.[127]

Sanchez planned to focus on the issues and hoped that Republicans would, too. His hopes were quickly dashed. The Republican Party of Texas said Sanchez was "short on talking about the issues and long on negative campaigning." "I think the Republican Party has got a well-deserved reputation of being very, very partisan and that can get out of hand sometimes and I hope it doesn't," a Sanchez spokeswoman later said.[128] Banking on the hope that that the public was frustrated by leadership and wary of war with Iraq, he played up claim that he was an "entrepreneur, an innovator, a salesman" and Perry was "a professional politician."[129]

This was a transition moment for the Republican Party in Texas. Bush had moved on to the White House. Republicans hoped to consolidate their wins and push Democrats out for good. Many seasoned Democratic officeholders, seeing troubled times ahead, chose to move into the private sector, but the party wasn't quite ready to give up. Still, Republicans smelled blood.

The chair of the state GOP at the time likened the previous years' efforts to building a farm team of Republican leaders. Now, she said, they were "well prepared to step forward and grasp the reigns of leadership."[130] Four years earlier, led by the popular George W. Bush, Republicans had swept every statewide office. Two years earlier, Democrats didn't field a credible candidate for the US Senate race against Kay Bailey Hutchison, offered only a handful of candidates for the state's two high courts, and ran no candidates for Texas Railroad Commissioner, the only other statewide offices that were up for election.

By summer 2002 polling showed Perry with a 20 percent lead, and he wasn't the only Republican ahead in the polls: John Cornyn, the incumbent attorney general, led Democrat Ron Kirk in the US Senate race by 5 percent; Land Commissioner David Dewhurst led John Sharp in the race for lieutenant governor by 7 percent; and the Republican former state supreme court justice Greg Abbott led Democrat Kirk Watson, the former mayor of Austin, by 6 percent. But with as much as one-third of the electorate undecided, no one was taking anything for granted.[131]

Ethnic breakdowns told the story about Republican success in crafting a statewide advantage. Perry got 63 percent of the white vote and

27 percent of the Latino vote in early polling, compared to 60 percent Latino support and 25 percent of the white vote for Sanchez.[132] Republicans had successfully courted Latinos in past campaigns—Bush was particularly popular with Texas Latinos—and Perry, working on his Spanish, attempted to continue the trend. His campaign targeted the Latino vote with a Spanish-language ad called "El Gov," set in a classroom as a teacher promised that Perry cared about Texas schoolchildren and their education. Sanchez appeared in his own Spanish-language ads, proposing raising teacher salaries and scrubbing the budget for savings that could be spent on education.[133]

Statewide polling suggested that a durable Republican coalition was beginning to come together: older male college graduates who appealed to middle- to upper-income voters. Republicans strongly backed Republican candidates, and Democrats were likewise loyal, hinting at rising polarization that had largely eluded Texas politics to that point. But not always—Republican support for Sharp, running for lieutenant governor against Dewhurst, was higher than for other Democrats, at 20 percent.[134] Republicans expected to win between eighty and ninety seats in the legislature, with a record 185 candidates running. Democrats, who held no statewide seats but led most of the major cities and the Texas US congressional delegation, conceded nothing.[135] But math and geography were becoming a challenge. As the "Tony Express" tour bus—a forty-five-foot luxury bus adorned with Sanchez campaign logos—rolled into rural East Texas, Yellow Dog Democrats lamented the loss of ground they once dominated.

East Texas was not the only trouble spot for Democrats. Sanchez worried publicly that his last name would be a drawback in parts of North Texas and West Texas. "I don't think I'm accepted there," he said. He had reason to worry—his campaign was greeted by protesters on a stop in Canyon, home of West Texas A&M University, including a student waving a sign reading, "SANCHEZ IS PRO-AFFIRMATIVE ACTION!! (ANTI-WHITE!)." Ethnicity played an ambiguous role in the campaign, as Sanchez's business record would later be connected to violence south of the border.[136]

The election marked a turning point for Perry, who previously had been able to win in a Republican primary ignoring controversial red-meat issues.

The coming interparty rift was starkly illustrated by the rise in 2002 of a far-right political action committee, the Free Enterprise PAC, or FreePAC, which targeted moderate Republicans and accused them of promoting "radical liberal and homosexual agendas."

Perry, Cornyn, and a handful of other Republican leaders, including Comptroller Carole Keeton Rylander (later Strayhorn), Agriculture Commissioner Susan Combs, and Railroad Commissioner Michael Williams denounced the group, as did the state party. Bill Ratliff, one of the targeted legislators, said statements by Perry and others were "less than satisfactory."[137]

"It slowly became clear that as Republicans started taking power, there were going to start to be tests," Matthew Dowd said. "Perry was never a culture candidate; Perry became one. That's when he started really going after the cultural issues."[138]

Even in a state with a history of muddy, brutal gubernatorial campaigns, 2002 was one for the record books. It was also pricey: both sides collectively spent a record-setting $72 million, mostly on television advertising, including $60 million of Sanchez's own money, smashing the previous record of $53.4 million, set in 1990 as Ann Richards faced off against Clayton Williams. Politics-weary Texans saw more than seventy thousand ads during the 2002 campaign season.

All the mud that could be flung was flung. Sanchez called Perry both a "do-nothing governor" and an "accidental governor" who inherited the job after Bush became president.[139] Sanchez ads showed people unable to respond when asked about Perry's record as governor. "Nothing," was the usual response, or nothing good, at any rate.[140]

The basic Sanchez message: "Rick Perry. We didn't elect him. We don't have to keep him." Perry fired back: "No vision. No leadership. No clue. Shame on you, Mr. Sanchez."[141]

Sanchez also blasted Perry's transportation platform, accusing him of supporting the Trans-Texas Corridor at a cost of $24,000 for every Texas household. Perry responded that the plan would be funded by bonds and tolls, with existing roadways exempt from new tolls. And Sanchez blamed Perry for a whisper campaign that Sanchez had been a draft dodger during the Vietnam War. (Sanchez received a deferment in 1968 while in law school.)

Perry, in turn, unleashed a volley of attacks stemming from San-chez's business dealings, including serving as a director for eleven busi-nesses in poor standing with the state for tax delinquencies or failure to file proper tax information (Sanchez called that a paperwork prob-lem), and of hiding his stake in Conoco, the state's second-largest pro-ducer of natural gas, when Sanchez-owned stock didn't appear on his personal financial statements.

Perry surrogates criticized Sanchez for using his post as a regent for the University of Texas system to promote a contract between the sys-tem and Enron, a high-flying Houston-based energy company that filed for bankruptcy in December 2001 amidst a major accounting scandal. Sanchez ridiculed Perry for accepting campaign contributions from the Enron officials. (Perry eventually donated a $25,000 contribution from Kenneth Lay, then-chair of Enron, to a scholarship fund for families of laid-off Enron employees.) Sanchez also needled Perry for appoint-ing former Enron executive Max Yzaguirre to chair the Public Utility Commission of Texas the day before the Lay donation.[142] Yzaguirre re-signed seven months after the appointment.

Much as it had during Sanchez's primary race with Morales, Te-soro Savings and Loan, the failed thrift he had once owned, served as a flashpoint. Perry harped on an apparent violation of government su-pervisory rules and the $161 million federal bailout; Sanchez blamed the institution's failure on the economy and government regulation.[143] Reports that the IRS, in a crackdown on aggressive tax shelters, de-manded $4 million from the International Bank of Commerce in La-redo, which was controlled by Sanchez, didn't help. The bank paid but disputed the IRS's claims.[144]

In the campaign's final days, Perry ran television ads linking San-chez to the Mexican drug dealers accused of murdering an agent for the US Drug Enforcement Administration working in Mexico. The ads accused Sanchez's bank of laundering $25 million for the drug cartel involved in the torture and death of Enrique "Kiki" Camarena in 1985. Sanchez was livid. "Never in the history of Texas politics has an office-holder, politician, or candidate ever stooped so low and into the gut-ter as Rick Perry has this time," he said at a San Antonio press confer-ence, accusing the governor of using Camarena's murder for political gain.[145] In a borderline racist tactic, the Texas Republican Party had a staffer dress up as a "Mexican drug lord," and follow Sanchez to campaign events sporting a briefcase.[146] Issues of national security in the post-9/11 world were a potent political weapon.

Not that Sanchez was above negative ads. The same week the Camarena ad began airing, Sanchez launched an ad featuring raw video from the patrol car of a female state trooper who'd stopped Perry's vehicle when his driver was clocked going twenty miles per hour above the speed limit. Perry was captured on video getting out of the car and urging her to "let us go down the road." She wrote a ticket anyway. Perry objected to the characterization that he was disrespectful of law enforcement but admitted, "I could have been better served had I sat in the vehicle."[147]

Sanchez's "both sides" strategy was a tougher sell on abortion. He described himself as a Catholic who personally opposed abortion but who would veto any bill that interfered with a woman's right to choose. "He can't be pro-abortion and be Catholic," said the head of the Amarillo Right to Life organization. By the 2002 election the Republican Party had sorted into a distinctly antiabortion party, and Perry's personal philosophy easily squared with the required political position. He opposed abortion except in cases of rape or incest, or when the life of the mother was at stake.[148]

The candidates even sparred about whether to sit or stand at the two debates agreed to by the campaigns—Sanchez, the shorter by about six inches—wanted to sit, obscuring Perry's height advantage. In the end, they compromised, sitting for one debate and standing for the other.[149]

The *New Braunfels Herald-Zeitung*, in endorsing Perry for governor after the bloodletting campaign, wrote: "If both candidates had spent more time on the issues rather than attacking each other's character, Texans would have been much better served."[150] Postelection polls showed 63 percent of Texans found the ads to be very negative, hurting both men. Seventy-three percent said the ads caused them to like both candidate less, but Sanchez was more damaged.[151]

One thing they agreed on? The other candidate lacked vision.[152] Both promised to tackle looming budget problems without new taxes, and both favored a fairly implemented business tax.

Sanchez favored relieving teachers of administrative responsibility, lowering class sizes, cutting the budget to pay for higher teacher pay, and providing a computer for every public school student.[153] He demanded accountability from charter schools and a reinvestment of money spent on charter schools back into public schools.[154]

Perry stuck to a familiar line of improving education, infrastructure, and the state's bottom line. He objected to the state's Robin Hood school finance system, which redistributed property tax funds from wealthier districts to poorer districts, and argued for a $200 million school reform plan that included a prekindergarten program, measures to reduce dropout rates, and higher salary for teachers. Hinting at an agenda to come, he lashed out at lawyers: "You shouldn't have to operate your schools with a personal injury trial lawyer standing over your shoulder," he said, implying that frivolous lawsuits had hurt public education.[155] But Perry also strayed into the culture wars, praying with students at an East Texas high school and defending the act by saying he disagreed with a US Supreme Court ruling banning organized prayer at public school events.

Sanchez hoped to use his ambiguous partisanship to his advantage, with ads suggesting support from President George W. Bush. The Republican National Committee issued a cease-and-desist letter, but the campaign declined to pull the ads, which featured images of the two men and mentioned their ties. Another mentioned the bipartisan working relation between Bush and his lieutenant governor Bob Bullock. "That's my model," Sanchez said.[156] He backed Bush's plans to invade Iraq and pledged to protect hunters' rights, saying Texas didn't need more gun laws.

A group called Republicans and Independents for Sanchez formed but gained little political traction in a rapidly polarizing Texas.

The race was never close. Only one public poll showed Sanchez within ten points of Perry at any point in the campaign, and the final numbers had Perry trouncing Sanchez by 18 percent (58 percent to 40 percent). Sanchez and the rest of the Democratic Dream Team won in South Texas (two to one in the Lower Rio Grande Valley's Hidalgo County, and nine to one in Sanchez's home of Webb County.) Exit polls showed 87 percent of Hispanics backed Sanchez, but just 11 percent of Hispanics turned out to vote, lower than expected in an already low-turnout election. About 35 percent of registered voters showed up at the polls. And Sanchez lost white Democrats. Democrats were wiped out in heavily populated North Texas, where Perry grabbed 60 percent of the vote, and in the Panhandle he won by more than two to one.[157]

The Perry campaign also got lucky—again. *Dallas Morning News* reporter Wayne Slater asked the campaign in September if he could review a particular campaign ad—communications director Ray Sullivan sent an intern to drop the videos off without looking at the tape. Upon reflection, Sullivan worried, "I wonder if I should have watched that tape before I sent it." Sullivan, normally calm and sophisticated, yelled "Fuck!" from his office down the hall. He realized the media firm had put *all* the campaign's ads on the tape—including yet-to-be-run attack ads. "I think I may have just killed the campaign," a guilty Sullivan assumed. Spinning the situation, the campaign worked a deal to give the paper an exclusive to the story. The paper ran the story in condensed form, summarizing the ads, and ended up getting massive coverage using the backing materials.[158] Ken Herman wasn't so sure it was an accident since it happened to him, too. Their protestations didn't stick. "To this day, I think they knew what they were doing. They went through all the right motions." The campaign got what it wanted out of the negative ads without having to buy any airtime.[159]

That new pugnacious style was a significant legacy of the 2002 election, as was the move into more polarizing social issues. Perry wasn't milquetoast. He wanted to win but was unconcerned about winning big. He was engaged in campaign planning, asking questions, and caring about every dollar being spent, to the exasperation of campaign staff. "He was a cheap motherfucker," longtime campaign adviser Carney joked years later.[160]

From 2002 on, rough campaigns would be the norm. Perry had his own ideas but was "willing to put himself in the hands of professional campaign people and do what they told him to do and be who he needed to be to win."[161] "We'd rather be the ones throwing the punches than taking them," Carney said.[162]

His former allies took note. "It's one of the biggest disappointments that I had in Rick, when he listened to them," said Charlie Stenholm.[163]

Texas A&M was eye-opening for young Rick "Ricky" Perry; there he met people who were different from his friends and family in Paint Creek. Being in the Corps led to a military career and broader horizons, too. (Cushing Memorial Library and Archives, Texas A&M University)

Perry's House career (1985–1989) was short but impactful. As a "Pit Bull," he was an effective budget cutter, exposed to the workings of Texas government and to friends who would help shape and fulfill his political ambitions. (Courtesy Texas House of Representatives)

**TO GET INVOLVED IN THE
RICK PERRY CAMPAIGN
Call 512-478-FARM**

Perry's swagger and farming and ranching background persuaded voters in
Democratic-leaning Texas that he was right for the part. This set the new
Republican on a path to elevate the GOP in Texas but came with a cost—brutal
campaigns. (Courtesy Ron Johnson)

Governor Bush and then–Lieutenant Governor Perry had a solid but not close working relationship. The two had different goals and constituencies, making joint campaigning a challenge. (Agence France-Presse)

On the fringes of politics at first, the Tea Party became a monumental force in Texas politics, with Perry both leading and following the grassroots effort. (M. Cotera/Bob Daemmrich Photography, Inc. [BDP, Inc.])

Perry received high marks for his disaster-recovery efforts as Texas faced floods, droughts, wildfires, and hurricanes during his years in office. (Courtesy Texas State Library and Archives Commission)

Governor Perry's exit from the political stage took him to the small screen as a contestant on ABC's *Dancing with the Stars*. Perry admittedly had two left feet but learned to dance for his daughter Sidney's wedding. (ABC/Eric McCandless)

–6–

FIRST FULL TERM, 2003–2006

The 2003 Session and the Democratic Walkout

For the first time in state history, Republicans ruled Texas largely unimpeded. Following the 2002 state elections, the GOP held nineteen of thirty-one seats in the Senate and eighty-eight of 150 in the House. The lieutenant governor, David Dewhurst, was a Republican, as was House Speaker Tom Craddick, elected almost unanimously by the Republican majority. Some of the leadership stability eroded when Perry nemesis Pete Laney lost his House seat. The process would spin nearly out of control, leading to Democrats—out of power in the House for the first time since after the Civil War—literally fleeing the Capitol.

Reflecting these changes and his role in them, Perry's tone at his inauguration on January 21, 2003, was almost giddy. He thanked the elementary school teacher who'd traveled from Paint Creek rural school for teaching him life's greatest lessons. He referred to ceremonies that make US citizens of immigrants from dozens of nations who come to Texas for a better future. "Today we remain a people living under the light of that 'one star,' venturing down a single path toward one future, one Texas."

But he was also pointed in his criticism of big government, indicating a new, harder line defining Republican priorities and positioning Texas as a leader in national Republican thought. "The larger government grows, the smaller the circle of our freedoms," he said. "We limit government so that opportunity is unlimited." He spoke out against new taxes. He admonished those worried about the revenue shortfall and counseled fiscal discipline, saying even a $100 billion budget was big enough (the 2002–2003 budget was $111 billion). How to get there? Jobs, low taxes, a twenty-first-century transportation system, reforming insurance laws, and tort reform—a succinct summation of the defining issues that Perry would pursue over the next four years.

Before Larry Gatlin sang "Texas, Our Texas" to end the ceremony, the governor quoted the Biblical prophet Isaiah—urging Texans to stand resolute, as so many veterans, clergy, and peace officers had before them: "Here am I, send me."[1]

A confident Perry ascended the House speaker's rostrum a month later for the State of the State address, standing before more Republicans than the chamber had seen in its history. An old hand by now at the lever of state government, Perry referenced the civility and friendship he had learned in both wings of the Capitol. And he had jokes: "Even when we disagreed, we did so with civility. If a colleague refused to vote our way, we would shake their hand, give them a pat on the back—and then quietly switch the lights on their voting machine. It's no wonder they vote by voice in the Senate."[2]

The state was spending more on transportation, more children had health insurance, student test scores were improving, the state was better prepared for emergencies, and Toyota was coming to Texas, expanding the job base. Citing a December 2002 article in the *Economist*, he crowed: "The future is Texas." Perry rode that horse for a decade, using his pet project, the Texas Enterprise Fund, to recruit companies and emerging industry to the state.

The future also included a $1.8 billion hole in the prior budget and an $8 billion crater in the upcoming budget, caused by the ongoing national recession that followed the 9/11 attacks and ensuing drop in sales-tax receipts. Perry leaned on his extensive "middle school, high school, college, and graduate" education platform from years of time in office during the roller-coaster Texas economy.[3] Carol Keeton Strayhorn, the comptroller, noted that the state had boasted billion-dollar surpluses for the past six years. "The last several revenue estimates have begun to look a lot like Christmas," she reported. "This year, the stockings are empty."[4] Filling those stockings without raising taxes was simple, according to the Republican line—low taxes, small government, and fiscal responsibility, following the example set by millions of Texas families: cover the basics, even if it means no cable TV and taking your lunch to work. Agencies reduced spending by 13 percent, and more cuts were coming. Through closing loopholes, scrutinizing spending, restricting agencies, and upgrading technology, the state could save its budget from disaster.

Critics asserted Perry was overly focused on balancing the budget, enacting tort reform, and reforming homeowner insurance, paying back conservative business leaders who'd backed Republicans up and down the ballot. "My greatest fear is that we will balance the budget on the backs of the poor," said Sen. Judith Zaffirini (D-Laredo).[5]

Those fiscal decisions drew a line on state spending, the loudest signal yet on the coming Republican orthodoxy about limited public spending. But what Perry *didn't* emphasize—school finance and tax reform—would also shape the state's future.[6] With so many new members, those problems promised to take longer to solve, and Perry didn't seem to devote much effort to addressing them beyond proposing reducing state mandates and paperwork, thus allowing money spent on compliance to be returned to the classroom in an homage to an idea still professed by many Republicans—local control.

One emergency item Perry designated was insurance reform, especially automobile and medical malpractice insurance. Members were concerned about rising homeowner insurance premiums, but most policies are written by subsidiaries of national companies and are exempt from state regulation. Texans paid the highest homeowner premiums in the country, even more than other large, weather-battered states, such as California and Florida. The governor called for giving the state insurance commissioner more regulatory power over homeowner and auto insurance rates and capping noneconomic damages in medical malpractice lawsuits at $250,000. The Texas Trial Lawyers Association vowed to fight the bill, saying it was unfair to people with legitimate claims.[7]

Texas was at the center of this new legal maelstrom—litigants called the state a "judicial hellhole," where enforcement of personal property rights was applied arbitrarily, depending on the court and which attorney was at the bench. The problem reached back to the 1970s, when elected leaders and reformers created the Keeton Commission to propose a cap on damages for medical malpractice. The Texas Supreme Court struck down the cap in 1988, arguing it violated the state constitution's open courts provision, spiking the number of lawsuits and, according to opponents, forcing medical providers out of the state because of rising malpractice claims.

Passing tort reform would be a massive political effort. Laney and other key Democrats had blocked it for several sessions, but that obstruction drove money from the business community into the campaign chests of Republican candidates.[8] Organizing for a fight was critical, especially for a policy that affected the whole state. "The hardest bill to pass is one that has statewide impact. What works in El Paso may not work in Texarkana. What works in Amarillo may not work in Brownsville," said a former Perry legislative director.[9]

Was Perry up to the task? Said one former senator, "What I find is the governors who don't succeed, it's a combination of their personality and noncommunication."[10]

The Texas Trial Lawyers Association girded for a fight.

Roiling beneath these once-in-a-generation issues was a concern that was familiar to anyone who had been in office as long as Perry: the projected revenue shortfall. Due to a slowly rebounding economy and higher-than-expected enrollment in Medicaid and other health and human services, the state's two-year budget was in rough shape. Perry tried to deflect, suggesting it could be worse. "I get up every day and thank God I don't live in California," he joked. Hilary McLean, chief deputy press secretary to California governor Gray Davis, shot back, "I'm sure there are millions of Californians who wake up every day and are glad of that too."[11]

The comptroller's revenue projection was off by several billion dollars, alarming Republicans who promised not to raise taxes in their 2002 campaigns. Perry called for reduced spending, and Talmadge Heflin, the fiscally fastidious chair of the budget-writing House Appropriations Committee, offered an analogy: "If I run out of money at home in the middle of the month, I'm not going out and hiring some-body to cut the grass," he said.[12]

Even some Republicans appeared open to new taxes, but only as the last option. Perry recognized the potential for political disaster if taxes were raised after Republicans finally gained control of state govern-ment, and he was reminded daily about the obligation he had as gov-ernor to hold the Republican Party line. Perry recalled the beating Bill Clements took as governor in the late 1980s. But this was a newly con-stituted and larger party with more hardened priories than the one Perry joined just a decade before.

The proposed budget cuts ran deep: programs for at-risk students, funding for public school districts to pay off debt, and layoffs at the Texas Education Agency and at the signature math and reading pro-grams championed by Bush and Perry. Democrats, now in the mi-nority, had little recourse but to play for a better deal. Sylvester Turner, a Houston Democrat on the appropriations committee, criticized the proposed cuts but played ball, gamely smiling as Craddick projected bi-partisan cooperation. "I think everyone understands where we are in a budget crisis and that everyone's going to have to take cuts, whether it's my district or Sylvester's district," said Craddick. "I'm with you, Mr. Speaker," Turner responded.[13]

Other Democrats were less sanguine. "This is hardball," said Rep. Garnet Coleman, Turner's fellow Houston Democrat.[14]

Complicating matters was the fact that the Big 3 didn't necessarily agree on a solution, despite their shared party identities. Perry offered to pro-pose a joint budget with Lt. Gov. Dewhurst and Speaker Craddick after the governor's office drew chuckles for proposing an initial draft budget with all zeros, illustrating his belief that the state budget should be re-built from scratch. Zero-based budgeting was something the state had never done. The effort was met with lukewarm praise. When Dewhurst announced bipartisan support to tap the Rainy Day Fund, the state Re-publican Party Executive Committee urged members to call their sen-ators and object. Perry compared the one-time accounting measure to the character Wimpy from the old Popeye cartoons, who promised, "I will gladly pay you Tuesday for a hamburger today."[15]

Perry and Craddick were close, while the governor and his lieutenant governor, Dewhurst, had what was better described as a cordial working relationship. While Perry and Craddick both hailed from
West Texas and had taken part in hundreds of battles in the House,
Dewhurst was a wealthy urbanite from Houston who had no significant legislative experience prior to being elected lieutenant governor in
2002. Perry was prompt, a throwback to military discipline. Dewhurst
was frequently late to meetings. Perry was outgoing; Dewhurst was
stiff. They had different legislative priorities, too, with Perry focused
on economic development and Dewhurst on higher education scholarships. A tight budget meant that many things were on the chopping
block, Perry's signature Texas Enterprise Fund included. He asked for
$139 million for the fund; the House and Senate budgets offered no
new funding, although they allowed it to retain carryover funds. Dewhurst, siding with Democrats, pointed to a lack of transparency over
how the fund was used and proposed letting the fund dry out.[16] Tensions boiled over when Dewhurst skipped a leadership breakfast with
Perry, Comptroller Strayhorn, and Craddick the next week after making the proposal, leaving his warm cheese omelet and home fries un-
touched.[17] Eventually Perry cut a deal with Craddick for the Enterprise
Fund money. "It's a story about how committed he was to those funds,"
recalls Mike Toomey, Perry's chief of staff. "Craddick and Perry get
along famously, and two out of three rules over there."[18]

Craddick's commanding, win-at-all-costs style was new to a party
accustomed to being an underdog. He dug in over cuts to the Children's
Health Insurance Fund (CHIP) and Medicaid, calling some Democrats "obstructionists" for holding up the process as deadlines loomed.
"It's the Democrats, not the Republicans," Craddick said. "They're the
ones, in my opinion, who have made the House partisan."

"Debate," Coleman responded, "is the reason why we're here."

But Craddick wasn't so sure, contending that victory at the ballot
box meant the GOP deserved the final word. "The people of Texas have
made a change in the leadership and their philosophy," he said.[19]

Craddick understood how dissent worked—he was one of a few reb-
els in the 1970s who spoke out against corrupt leadership as part of the
"Dirty Thirty," a bipartisan group of House members who forced out
then speaker Gus Mutscher shortly before Mutscher became embroiled

in the Sharpstown stock scandal. In 2003, however, some Democrats followed the leader; leadership-loyal Democrats, known as "Speaker Ds," who sided with Craddick were rewarded with high-ranking committee assignments.[20] On the other side of the Capitol, brokering deals came easy for Dewhurst, who was naturally less combative than Craddick and found security in rules requiring bipartisan support before contentious issues could be brought to the floor for debate.[21] Interchamber differences made for rough skiing, especially on school finance. "I learned a lot of things this session. One of the things is to make sure you're coordinated with the House on school finance," said Dewhurst at the end of the session, drawing laughs. "I'm not commenting," Craddick grinned.[22]

Perry stayed close to the legislative process during the complicated session, and his close relationship with Craddick earned him the facetious nickname "Speaker Perry." Others called them "The Towers," since virtually no daylight was found between them politically. The "aloof" Perry of the prior session—emotions still raw from the Father's Day Massacre and the bruising 2002 election—was replaced with a hand-shaking, backslapping, engaged Perry in the 78th session. He met privately with legislators, his staff were often on the House and Senate floors, and he offered (or threatened) to use executive power to call a special session or veto a bill.[23]

Perry was growing into his own as governor.

The final version of the state's $118 billion budget for the 2004–2005 biennium, about $6 billion more than the 2002–2003 budget, passed just hours before the deadline as exhausted legislators sighed in relief through gritted teeth.[24]

Neither party got everything they wanted. "With this budget we mark the passage in Texas from compassionate conservatism to just plain old mean spiritedness," said Sen. Eliot Shapleigh (D-El Paso).[25]

Democrats, who in late March had walked out of a budget committee hearing, complained the budget would reduce rural healthcare and mental health services. Republicans worried about cuts to prisons and provisions allowing colleges and universities to set their own tuition rates, taking it out of the hands of the legislature. Some conservatives groused about $14 billion allocated for business and economic development, including $200 million for the governor's Enterprise Fund to lure businesses to Texas.

Then Strayhorn rejected the budget in June 2003. She acted between the end of the regular session and the start of the called special session June 30, sending the two-year spending plan back to the House for revisions and claiming the budget wasn't balanced, as is required by the state constitution. "I cannot certify this budget because it is $185,900,000 short."[26]

That shortfall, as it turned out, was related directly to funding for one of Perry's pet projects: the budget moved $236 million out of the general fund and into the Trans-Texas Corridor, a spending choice that shortchanged the budget by $185.9 million.

Strayhorn's decision surprised legislators and dealt a serious blow to members who'd spent most of the 140-day session on the grueling work of setting a two-year budget while facing a $10 billion revenue shortfall that gave them 10 percent less money to work with than the prior budget. Strayhorn said she was troubled by technical issues, such as the transfer of funds from one source to another, and provisions to automatically balance the budget by empowering the Legislative Budget Board to make additional cuts. She was concerned about more than the bottom line—she objected to using the Rainy Day Fund to fill budget gaps and questioned cuts to public safety, prisons, and higher education. Strayhorn also favored a larger cigarette tax, even considering Perry's pledge to veto one. The comptroller claimed such an increase would not violate her no-tax pledge because "it's also an additional revenue stream that does good. As a mama and a grandmama I want to deter young people from smoking."[27]

Inside the governor's mansion, Perry fumed. "This is crazy."[28] He and his staff were already privately preparing for what was likely to be a contentious special session on redistricting. Publicly, he needed to fix the problem. "While the announcement is disappointing, I believe legislators can quickly address her concerns," he responded. "I will continue working with the leadership of both chambers and with Comptroller Strayhorn, and I am confident we can address this issue quickly."[29]

It was "minute-by-minute warfare," and Perry had multiple conversations with Strayhorn about the budget.[30] Rodney Ellis and some other Democrats saw an opportunity to undo some of the cuts and suggested starting from scratch. The suggestion was rejected. Both sides lawyered up, and Strayhorn hired a constitutional scholar to assist her staff. Greg Abbott, as attorney general, threatened a lawsuit to force Strayhorn to certify the budget.

Strayhorn backed down. The Perry team had to wake the chief clerk up in the middle of the night to certify that a bill "she was complaining about" did in fact pass on a certain day. She accepted that and certified the bill. What fueled the ruckus? Strayhorn's ambition, at least in part. Toomey, Perry's chief of staff, believed she received bad advice from her political consultant. "Clearly it was just political," he concluded.[31]

This intraparty strife was not what Republicans, in charge of state government for the first time in 130 years, wanted. It made the party look uncoordinated in its first show at running the state, and the immediate fallout was nasty. Republican lawmakers attempted to strip Strayhorn's office of control of the e-Texas performance review (the one Perry bragged would save the state money) and school district audit programs. Estimating the state's revenue, one of the "fundamental duties" of the office, was being neglected: "Revenue estimating in your office needs improvements," said Sen. Steve Ogden (R-Bryan), who sponsored the legislation. Strayhorn claimed she was being unfairly targeted for saying the budget was not balanced and argued that the state should have designated $700 million that was available to lawmakers to restore funding for healthcare for the elderly and needy children. "And I was telling the truth when I said new fees, charges, and out-of-pocket expenses were going to cost Texans $2.7 billion over the next two years. You can take away every desk and every chair and every program in the Texas comptroller's office, and I will still tell the people of Texas the truth," said Strayhorn.[32]

Perry denied that the move was personal. "Carole is my friend, and I hope that she will focus on her duties," he said. But the effect was clearly personal—and political. Strayhorn did not rule out running against Perry in 2006, and she sure sounded like she was running, criticizing him for leaving more kids without health insurance, spiking transportation woes, and imposing hidden fees all around.[33]

The final budget (again) squeaked through the chambers and made its way to Perry's desk across the street by the end of August.

The rest of the session focused on decidedly conservative matters, even as what would become the defining issue of the session loomed ominously in the background. "We kept the trust by keeping our promises," said Perry, joined by Dewhurst and Craddick at the Capitol.[34] Every conservative group—paralyzed and pushed away for so long— now had a seat at the table under the pink dome. Legislation allowing parents to opt out of vaccine requirements for "reasons of conscience" passed, as Texans for Vaccine Choice became a more prominent player in conservative politics.[35] The recognition of same-sex unions performed in other states was banned under the so-called Defense of Marriage Act, making Texas the thirty-seventh state to pass such a law. Jeff Wentworth, a Republican senator from San Antonio, sponsored the bill, saying he considered it "more of a legal matter, where Texas claims its right to set its own policy in that important area of family law. It defends and protects the institution of marriage that, candidly, has been under attack the last 25 years." "It's about politics," said Ellis, executive director of the Lesbian/Gay Rights Lobby of Texas. "It's about scapegoating gays and lesbians."[36]

Perry, led in part by the legislature, was beginning to make good on delivering conservative outcomes. About 40 percent of Republican primary voters were religious conservatives, meaning a candidate would need only one out of five other Republican votes to win his or her primary.[37] Perry's shift to the right captured that dynamic—he claimed the shift was sincere, but others saw it as pandering.[38] Regardless, many voters were more than willing to be pandered to, making the overtures successful.

Marriage wasn't the only conservative issue addressed. Fetuses were given legal standing in a new bill defining an embryo as an "individual" and allowing criminal prosecution or civil court action in case of injury or death to the embryo. A twenty-four-hour waiting period for abortions was passed. A minute of silence (not necessarily prayer) was required for students in public schools, along with a pledge to the US and Texas flags. The old joke about the legislature raising fees as the first order of business every session held, too; in this case lawmakers increased fines for first and second offenses of driving while intoxicated. Government *was* shrinking under the Perry governorship. He got the budget austerity he wanted, and the legislature reorganized or downsized several agencies.

Perry also scored on a second signature agenda item—tort reform. An opinion piece in the *Wall Street Journal* heralded the change as "Ten-Gallon Tort Reform." The *Dallas Morning News* called it "Open Season on Plaintiffs." Jury awards against physicians, hospitals, and other institutions were capped at $250,000, and there was a maximum overall cap of $750,000 per claim. Perry framed it as maintaining access to healthcare. If doctors left the state, hospitals and nursing homes would suffer, as would patients. Advocates complained it was a serious setback to legitimate claims in civil courts, disrupting the balance of power in Texas courtrooms in favor of insurance and corporate defendants.[39]

Texans for Lawsuit Reform—the premier group founded by Houston real-estate developer Dick Weekley to stem runaway litigation costs—had friends in high places, from the governor's office on down. But advocates for tort reform still needed support from Democrats in both chambers, especially to get the hundred votes needed in the House and twenty-one votes in the Senate. It was a grassroots battle, a minicampaign outside the legislative process to influence members.

It was futile to fight a resurgent Republican Party in a climate in which trial lawyers had few friends. "We've lost a lot of battles," said one member of the Texas Trial Lawyer Association team. "Now we're just trying to keep them from coming back and bayoneting the dead."[40]

Perry appeared to be ending the session on top: his signature legislation passed, and good defense blocked undesirable bills. The Texas Enterprise Fund was richly funded and moved under direct control of the governor's office. While Perry focused on successes, including Toyota's decision to locate a plant in Texas, Democrats focused on failures like the millions spent to woo Boeing (which ultimately moved to Chicago) and claimed the Texas Enterprise Fund was little more than a slush fund for a spend-happy governor, money that would be better spent on public schools or programs for the needy.[41]

Reorganization of state government, especially the newly consolidated mega-agency Department of Health and Human Services, would allow the governor to appoint more people to state boards and commissions. The legislature trusted Perry, and Perry in turn used this to expand the role of the governor. "Obviously we did change the structure, we changed some laws, we changed some mindsets. Even if you have a lot of laws, regulations, and what have you, unless you have the personality to get the legislature and others to work with you, you're not going to be as successful as you could be."[42]

But despite the accomplishments of the session, the biggest story was what legislators didn't get done.

Redrawing the state's congressional districts was the most notable item on the Republicans' legislative to-do list. After the legislature had failed to agree on redistricting during the 2001 session, new state Senate districts were drawn by the Legislative Redistricting Board, and a federal court produced a plan for the state's congressional districts.

That wasn't good enough for US Rep. Tom DeLay, nicknamed "Hot Tub Tom" for his partying ways during his years representing Sugar Land in the legislature. By 2003 DeLay was majority leader in the US House. The court plan left Democrats in control of seventeen of the Texas delegation's thirty-two seats. Republicans were the majority party at every level, DeLay argued, so why should Democrats control the delegation?[43]

His plan, not coincidentally, was drafted to result in the defeat of as many as five Democratic incumbents. In his view, the fact that Democrats retained control of the delegation was proof that the lines were unfairly drawn, more art than geography.[44] *Texas Monthly* described his plan thus:

> A Jackson Pollock masterpiece? Or a Picasso in Silly Putty? De-Lay totally disregarded Texas' interests; he put Fort Hood [based in Killeen] into a district anchored in San Antonio, forcing the world's largest military installation to compete with San Antonio bases for funding, and carved Austin, a major research center, into four districts, two of which ran to the perimeter of the state.[45]

Fireworks boomed as Joe Crabb (R-Humble), chair of the House redistricting committee, asked Attorney General Abbott if the legislature was even allowed to revisit redistricting in the middle of a census decennial cycle. Short answer: Yes. Perry concurred, saying Texans would prefer that the elected legislature make those decisions rather than a federal court.[46]

Democrats cried foul. Caught off guard by a midsession bomb, they argued that the current plan was already court-approved and should stay in place. The process was being managed by Republicans in Washington, DC, the Democrats argued, an attack on the bipartisanship that had governed Texas for more than a decade. One insider said, "All of the Republicans—Dewhurst, Perry, Craddick—got rolled by DeLay." Despite protestations early in the session that they wouldn't do it, "DeLay came and broke some arms. If it would have been left to them, they wouldn't have done it."[47] DeLay had the power and the money, so Texas leaders went along. The 2001 redistricting didn't lead to significant gains, so DeLay wanted a redo. Rising polarization and party ties were among the reasons Perry went along. "Perry stood with his party," reflected one longtime House Democrat.[48]

Redistricting ate away at that bipartisan spirit, and Perry joined DeLay at the helm of this turning tide. Emboldened by his resounding victory over Sanchez and his successes during the session, Perry had come to see himself as a master political strategist. Was the goal to elect more conservative lawmakers? "No question about it," recalled former lieutenant governor Bill Ratliff.[49]

So the Democrats bailed. On May 12, 2003, fifty-one House Democrats fled the state, leaving the House without a quorum and killing the Republican-backed redistricting bill set for a hearing that week, along with hundreds of other bills.[50] The House parliamentarian locked the voting machines of the absent Democrats—who became known as the "Killer Ds"—and Craddick alerted the Texas Department of Public Safety (responsible for statewide law enforcement) and then locked down the chamber so no other legislators could leave. The remaining House members lobbed toy balls, whistled, or gossiped while waiting. Republicans accused Democrats of fleeing the Battle of the Alamo and spent legislative days throwing wads of paper at one another and distributing playing cards sporting likenesses of the absent Democrats in an echo of the most-wanted terrorist cards then being circulated among US troops in Iraq. DPS troopers first checked the Cloak Room, a dimly lit basement bar at the heel of the Capitol frequented by members, lobbyists, and staffers. Perry personally instructed troopers to search for Rep. Craig Eiland at the hospital neonatal intensive care unit in Galveston, where his premature twins were receiving medical care.[51]

Democrats had gathered at an Austin hotel in the preceding days, planning a four-day trip that would span the deadline for preliminary passage of House bills. Jim Dunnam (D-Waco) was leader of the House Democratic Caucus and engineered the walkout; he didn't initially think there were fifty representatives who would leave, but after a few discussions many Democrats agreed to walk. Texas Democrats publicly hailed the move as a courageous stand against a partisan power grab. Perry declined to tip his hand about whether he would call a special session to consider redistricting, but he was quick to issue a statement disparaging the action. "These legislators . . . are asked to work for 140 days every two years—not to hide out because they don't like the way the debate is going." Other Republicans also rushed to condemn the missing Democrats. "I have never turned tail and run," DeLay said. "Even when I'm losing, I stand and fight for what I believe."[52]

Even former state senator Carlos Truan, one of the original "Killer Bees" (a dozen liberal senators who broke quorum in 1979 to stop legislation they opposed), was cautious. "They better be prepared to pay the political consequences for their actions, because there will be a hell of a price to pay," he said.[53]

Craddick called the group "Chicken Ds." But he had his own loyal Craddick Ds who stayed behind, including Sylvester Turner—"crossdressers," they were called by some fellow Democrats.[54]

Leader Jim Dunnam recalled years later that it was about fairness— you can keep drawing the lines until you win. It wasn't about saving the seats of some Democrats who weren't well liked. "Nobody was going to go to Ardmore [Oklahoma] to protect Lloyd Doggett. But they saw it more as a fundamental attack. At some point it ceases to be a democracy."[55]

Other Democrats stood in solidarity with more than a hundred people who gathered in the rain on the front steps of the Capitol holding signs that read "TOM DELAY, GO AWAY," and "SIEG HEIL, TOM DELAY." "I wish I was out there with them, wherever they are," Sen. Rodney Ellis announced at the gathering.[56] Willie Nelson sent the Oklahoma Democrats red bandannas, whiskey, and a note saying, "Way to go. Stand your ground."[57]

Democrats spent their days in Oklahoma working in cramped conference rooms, at tables stacked with papers, notebooks, and laptop computers, eating at the Denny's next door. "We have a message for Tom DeLay: Don't mess with Texas," said Dunnam. "We did not choose the path that led us to Ardmore, Oklahoma. Tom DeLay chose that path."[58]

They were discovered just a few days after they fled the state, but Texas troopers had no jurisdiction in Oklahoma, meaning the Killer Ds were safe for the moment. The US Department of Homeland Security was even briefly invoked after reports that a plane believed to be carrying the Texas lawmakers had crashed.[59] The tactic drew attention both inside Texas and beyond. "I have been with the force for 25 years, and I can honestly say that this is about the strangest thing I've seen," said DPS captain Mike Caley.[60]

Some newspaper editorials praised the move, calling it a "strategic retreat" that built support for outnumbered Democratic legislators, although the hometown publications of some absent lawmakers were less charitable. An editorial in the *Lufkin Daily News* reflected, "The 'Filthy 50' will win acclaim from the media and the history books, but in gambling their dwindling reserve of clout, they probably doomed the chances for any remaining items on their legislative agendas."[61] (Lufkin was represented by Jim McReynolds, one of the walkouts.) Democrats offered to return if Craddick promised not to bring up redistricting. A response from the speaker, happy to let the Democrats dangle as negative publicity mounted, was not immediately forthcoming. "He's taking his wife out for a night of dinner, dancing and frivolity," said Craddick spokesman Bob Richter.[62] In any case, he wasn't inclined to negotiate, and the stalemate continued. Republicans asked the Oklahoma attorney general to have Texas Rangers arrest the lawmakers there without a warrant. The AG declined. They asked the Bush DOJ to intervene. Officials there declined, as well.

The Democrats' plan eventually worked, at least temporarily. The House redistricting plan died, along with hundreds of other bills. "Now that we have been able to kill redistricting, we are able to go back and finish the business of this state," Eiland said, still furious over DPS troopers being sent to the hospital where his newborn twin daughters were in the NICU. With eighteen days left in the session, the Democrats returned to an acidic political climate in Austin—they took two charter buses, one for smokers and one for nonsmokers.[63] Crossing the Red River, the group stopped at the Texas Welcome Center, greeted by a dozen Denton County Democratic Party supporters. Back at the Capitol, some were greeted with open arms by their Republican friends, but others reported a chilly reception, perhaps among those members who wore bright red suits or ties (matching onlookers in red T-shirts) to show party unity. Outside, those demonstrators who were angry with Democrats for leaving wore chicken suits and held signs proclaiming, "CHICKEN DS." "We've weathered a few things. We've weathered some troopers; we've weathered a tornado, and we weathered Denny's," said Dunnam, who emerged as the group's ringleader. "No matter what happens, democracy won."[64]

Dunnam got word DeLay was encouraging Republicans in other states to engage in redistricting in the same way. "We figured if we could muck it up enough and make it have a PR price on it, it would back down these other states."[65]

Perry announced he would call a special session on school finance at some point during the interim but had remained mum about a second round for redistricting when the session reached sine die on June 2. It was his call alone whether to add the contentious redistricting fight to the call.

But Dunnam didn't believe their hearts were in it; they were just running the political playbook. No lasting harm was done in his relationship with Perry. He liked him, even when they didn't agree. Years later Perry gave Dunnam's daughter monogrammed champagne glasses for her wedding.[66]

Two weeks later, Perry made the call, and legislators returned to Austin on June 30, four weeks after the regular session had adjourned, for the first special session since 1991. Perry's call also included administrative housekeeping matters, such as streamlining the process for state permitting and legislative action to settle civil claims about asbestos, as well as several items meant to increase the governor's power.[67]

The real action, however, was on redistricting. "The recently completed regular session clearly demonstrates that legislators—regardless of political party affiliation and philosophy—can work together to address issues important to Texans," Perry wrote. "I am confident that Democrats and Republicans can likewise work together to develop a map that is fair, compact and protects communities of interest."[68]

Democrats were dubious of his motives, referring to the attempt as "Perrymandering." Martin Frost, an endangered Democratic congressman from Arlington, labeled Perry "the most overtly partisan governor in Texas history."[69]

Support for redrawing congressional lines didn't fall entirely along partisan lines, even as the legislature's historic collegiality was dimming. Bill Ratliff, the Republican senator from Mount Pleasant, joined Democrats in opposing a motion to bring redistricting up for debate, citing little concern in the proposed plan for communities of interest in East Texas and claiming to speak for other Republicans who opposed the legislation but felt compelled politically to back it. Dewhurst worried about upsetting the equilibrium in the Senate: "[Redistricting] is not the most pressing issue," he said. "Lots of good will is threatened by redistricting."[70]

He demanded the Senate use a long-standing procedure requiring two-thirds of the chamber to agree to move forward in order to ensure bipartisan support. In practical terms, this meant eleven of the twelve Senate Democrats could kill GOP efforts to redraw political lines mid-decade.[71] The two-thirds rule saved bipartisanship—and the Democrats—once again.

That's exactly what happened—eleven Democrats and one Republican blocked the redistricting bill following approval by the Republican-led Senate Jurisprudence Committee. "The likelihood of passage this session is very, very slim and grows more dim as the days and hours go by," reported committee chair Todd Staples, admitting the proposed lines would give Texas Republicans as many as twenty-two seats, compared to ten for Democrats.[72]

But the battle wasn't over. Democrats began to openly mull breaking quorum again if another special session was called.

Perry called a second special session to begin July 28, taking a more aggressive tone and perhaps bowing to pressure from national Republicans, who saw a red Texas as key to moving the South completely to Republican control and cementing the national conservative trend. "This is an important issue to the leadership and, I think, to the people of the state," he said, even as he tried to balance the competing tensions.[73] "My recommendation to folks in Washington, who have an interest in this, I'm sure, is to stay up there and take care of your business, and we'll take care of these congressional lines."[74]

Could a reasonable bill pass? Ratliff, under pressure from the White House—including Karl Rove, a key architect of the Republican takeover of Texas—demurred. "Reasonable is in the eye of the beholder," he said.[75]

Dewhurst, too, signaled a change of heart, agreeing to alter the process so a simple majority, not two-thirds, of the Senate could approve a vote in favor of debate. Bob Bullock had done the same in a 1992 special session on redistricting, so why not? Dewhurst also pointed to George W. Bush's ongoing popularity as justification: if most Texas voters support the Bush agenda, why shouldn't Republicans make up a majority of the congressional delegation? To do otherwise was "not fair," he said.[76]

Outnumbered twelve to nineteen, Senate Democrats couldn't stop the legislation from moving forward.

Without a clear legislative path to stopping the redistricting process, Democrats again abandoned Austin, flying in private planes to Albuquerque, New Mexico, acting on a tip that Perry was about to call a third special session early to surprise them and lock down the Senate to force them to stay.

This time the quorum-busters were eleven Senate Democrats. "It's not about Democrats, it's about democracy," Sen. Gonzalo Barrientos said from an Albuquerque hotel.[77]

"It really is sad to see the Texas Legislature so divided, and at the same time we felt validated because we accomplished what we set out to do," Judith Zaffirini said as Democrats watched the session adjourn online.[78] She even threatened to stay until Christmas if needed: "Some of us are learning to ski."[79] The move ended Zaffirini's record-setting 834 consecutive legislative session days and 29,577 consecutive votes.

Ken Armbrister, the lone Senate Democrat who didn't leave, sat on the floor of the stately chamber as his fellow Democratic senators approached.

"Hey, we're walking out," they told him.

"Welp," Armbrister responded. "Good luck to you."

"You've got to come with us."

"No, I don't."

"We're all in agreement."

"Obviously," Armbrister said dryly, "we are not all in agreement. What is your exit plan? If y'all think the governor is not going to keep calling special sessions, what is your exit plan?"[80]

Without a quorum, legislative business halted, and the legislature adjourned a day early.

It was a radicalizing moment for Dewhurst, who had been criticized by Republicans for being too accommodating to Democrats: "We cannot in good conscience stand here when there is work to be done and not be able to do the job we were elected to do when our eleven colleagues are effectively thumbing their nose at the process." It would pass sooner or later, he reasoned. "I've said this before, that Lieutenant Governor Dewhurst is abusing his power. Now he's abusing the truth," said Sen. Juan Hinojosa (D-McAllen).[81] The second called session had to adjourn a day early with an insufficient number of lawmakers present. "It's kind of like baseball. You play by the rules. The rules say you have to have a quorum, you can't blame them for using the rules to their advantage."[82]

Democrats pledged to take the first flight home if legislative leaders agreed to pull debate or reinstate the two-thirds rule. Two Republican senators flew to New Mexico to meet with Democrats, but nothing came of it. Lawsuits were filed to force lawmakers home. Perry was initially quiet, hoping the chamber would work it out, but he grew increasingly unhappy with what he saw as a constitutional crisis: "You leave on redistricting, then there's something else they don't like and they leave on that. That's like negotiating . . . for hostages," he said.[83]

Ensconced in New Mexico, Van de Putte, in turn, called the Texas Republican Party a puppet for the national GOP—not a big leap with a Texan in the White House surrounded by a Texas-based political team.

"Is there anything, Senator, that you can say positive about Rick Perry?" one reporter asked.

Van de Putte, who had always maintained a strong personal relationship with Perry, despite their policy differences, responded tartly. Perry was "not the brightest porch light on the block, [but] he really looks good in jeans."[84]

Years later, she lamented the comments made in the heat of the moment. But when Perry called the next morning, he offered a reminder of their friendship. "So, you still think I look pretty good in jeans, huh?" he asked after her sheepish "Good morning."

"Yes," she joked, "but you wear those damn suits that are too long, so no one can see that cute butt of yours."[85]

Their relationship was intact, but the issue was far from resolved. Democrats spent their time at an Albuquerque Marriott plotting strategy. Partisanship that normally was left inside the dusty Capitol spilled out. They posted a "Come and Take It" flag to provide a warlike vibe and worked among balloon bouquets sent by supportive constituents, along with a banner sent by Barrientos's constituents: "EAST AUSTIN SUPPORTS GONZALO Y LOS TEJAS 11."

Willie Nelson repeated the support he had offered the Killer Ds in Ardmore, inviting the senators to a sold-out concert at the Isleta Resort and Casino in Albuquerque. "I think they're great. I think they're heroes, and we're all very proud of them," said the Texas icon.[86] Family members sent fresh clothing, and some of their Republican colleagues clandestinely fed them information, including tips about potential traps to forcibly end their boycott. Valley senator Eddie Lucio ironed for his fellow senators, having picked up the skill in the military, charging his former bunkmates for the job.

Sen. Bob Deuell (R-Greenville) sent each Democrat a book by the late columnist Lewis Grizzard called *Last Bus to Albuquerque*.[87]

Without a quorum, the second called special session ended. Perry indicated he would call a third. "If there is work to be done, I expect the Legislature to be here," he said.[88]

Trying to tempt the Democrats to return, Republicans offered a vote on increasing Medicaid spending, needed to tap hundreds of millions of dollars in federal funds. It didn't work. Fearing arrest in Laredo, where a federal court was hearing arguments about the case, the

Democrats hunkered down in Albuquerque. "Surely, he wouldn't be that stupid," Van de Putte said. "That would exactly prove our point, [which] is they will trap us, they will do anything whether it's unethical or immoral to try and please partisan Republicans."[89]

The Democrats signaled they would stay away from Austin for another thirty days if needed.

The Democrats' monthlong boycott was broken when one of their own—Sen. John Whitmire of Houston, the "dean" of the Senate as the member with the longest tenure—returned to Austin on September 2, a week after the adjournment, and agreed to appear for a third special session. Celebrating his fifty-fourth birthday in New Mexico with a candlelit chocolate cake, Whitmire was feeling philosophical about the whole affair. "After being in my district for five days, I have concluded my constituents are opposed to redistricting, but they also believe the fight should be on the Senate floor," Whitmire said. He was quickly given the nickname "Quitmire."

Perry called a third special session for September 15, two weeks after Whitmire returned to Texas, as Democrats scoured the playbook to stop redistricting. Court appeals didn't work; a three-judge federal court panel dismissed the lawsuit Democrats had filed challenging the abandonment of the two-thirds rule a few days before the third session began; and it was all over except the crying. Spectators in the Senate gallery wore T-shirts with individual letters spelling out "QUITMIRE." Fourteen senators voted against the redistricting—all twelve Democrats and two Republicans, including Ratliff. In a forgiving mood, the Senate voted to lift the thousand-dollar-per-day fines assessed against the Democrats and restore the office privileges (like staff cell phones and parking spaces) that had been revoked during the quorum break.

Perry signed the new plan into law. The GOP hoped to topple the slight advantage Democrats held and pick up seven additional Congressional seats. Two months later, the Department of Justice precleared the plan, casting aside concerns that it illegally diluted minority and rural voting power and, according to Perry, "validating our efforts to draw fairer districts that reflect the voting patterns of Texas."[90]

As the fight shifted from the Capitol to the courthouse, the final lawsuit (*Session v. Perry*, 298 F.Supp.2d 451, 478 [E.D. Tex. 2004], which sought to have the mid-decade redistricting ruled illegal) resulted in a favorable ruling for Republicans in early 2004, affirmed months later by the US Supreme Court.

President George W. Bush lauded the plans. Perry took a victory lap as well, despite having less to do with the final outcome—DeLay was flying the plane on this one. Actor Alec Baldwin, in Austin for a fundraiser for House Democrats, brought a box of dog biscuits for Perry, whom he dubbed "Tom DeLay's lapdog." But Perry spokesman Gene Acuna got the last word: "I have no doubt that Texans will give the comments made by the star of *Beetlejuice* all of the attention they are due."[91]

Three times was the charm for Republicans—after three attempts, the Texas legislature redrew the state's congressional lines in the middle of the decade. The results paid political dividends as the state moved full circle, from domination by one party to domination by the other. Republicans would go on to win seventy-six seats in the Texas House in 2008 and ninety-nine seats in 2010. (Another three members switched to the Republican Party that year, giving Republicans an all-time high of 102 members, the largest margin for any party in the Texas House since 1984, the year Perry was first elected to office. At that point, of course, Democrats held the massive numbers advantage.) The Senate was more balanced, with Republicans hovering around 19 seats through most of this time, but incumbent Republican senators drew fewer Democratic opponents since the lines were drawn to predominantly favor Republicans.[92]

Yet the party was changing. Some long-serving members of the old guard grew weary of the hand-to-hand partisan combat that had overtaken political issues in the legislature. Ratliff openly contemplated resignation. "It's a day-to-day or month-to-month decision," he said. "I'm getting to the point that I'd rather be playing golf." The political hostilities had escalated, he lamented, and it was all predictable and avoidable. "I don't think it's going to blow over. I think it may be a generation before the scars from this are healed."[93]

Inside the GOP, the divide between moderate and more conservative members was widening, a precursor of the schisms that continue to dog the party in the 2020s.

Lessons learned? DeLay had his win, with a handful more congressional seats to bolster Republican margins. Texas Republicans had shown they wouldn't back down. Democrats had ramped up the stakes and shown some backbone, but their actions helped set the stage for partisan battles to come. And no matter how hard they fought, nothing could stop the Republicans' legislative blitzkrieg.

The mid-decade redistricting marked an inflection point in Texas politics. With the 2003 redistricting, and DeLay's heavy hand in the proceedings, the nationalization of Texas politics had begun in earnest.

"We thought ourselves so special," Van de Putte says of those pre-2003 days. "We didn't succumb to the political paranoia of DC. We could work together, and we were Texans above Republicans or Democrats. I don't know that I can say that right now." DeLay's constant presence in Austin during the 2003 legislative battles convinced her things were changing. "Washington called the shots."[94]

The holidays brought a much-needed pause and a little rock and roll. Just before Thanksgiving 2003, the rock group ZZ Top took the stage at the Compaq Center in Houston, closing out the facility's days as a concert and events venue just as the band had opened it more than twenty-five years earlier, with one notable addition.

Rick Perry sat in on drums, his long-sleeved black shirt and sweatpants looking a bit out of place compared to the ornate matching hats, jackets, and boots worn by lead singer Billy Gibbons and bass player Dusty Hill. Years later, asked if he played drums, he grinned. "Well, I did that night."[95]

But it would take more than a rock concert to repair the hit his foray into so many hot-button issues had dealt to Perry's public image. Two-thirds of Texans had approved of Perry when he moved up to the governor's mansion; that dropped to 40 percent after the marathon sessions of 2003.[96] He blamed "uncorroborated filth" spread by long-swirling rumors about his personal life—that he was gay and that his wife had moved out of the mansion—rather than the bruising redistricting fights, and journalists noted that some of the rumors were spread by opposition camps, including by staff members of Strayhorn, the comptroller.[97] But as the rumors continued to spread—the chair of the state

Democratic Party made a public reference to them at an event for presidential hopeful John Edwards, and protestors paraded in front of the governor's mansion carrying signs reading "IT'S OK TO BE GAY"—Perry was clearly bothered.

"I had never seen a rumor spread this quickly," recalled a bemused Herman, an *Austin American-Statesman* columnist. "People were hearing it from their barber and cab drivers."[98]

Perry flatly denied the allegations in an interview with Herman in March 2004, calling the rumors "a cancer on the political process that is deadly."[99]

But the rumors, and the tensions from the marathon special sessions of 2003, didn't distract Perry from calling a fourth special session that spring, ordering legislators back to overhaul the ailing public school finance system in light of the state supreme court's decision to hear a case challenging the current funding model.

Perry had a bold plan, tackling a practice conservatives had complained about since its introduction. He wanted to eliminate the Robin Hood share-the-wealth funding system developed in the 1990s, which redistributed property tax revenue from wealthy school districts to low-income districts. His plan to permanently retire Robin Hood involved reducing property taxes by $6 billion, instead setting (and increasing) business property taxes (which would then drop over subsequent years), and increasing so-called sin taxes on cigarettes, video lottery gambling, and adult entertainment. "I can't promise our work will be done in one session, or two, or three. But I can promise this, we won't fail simply because we refuse to try," said Perry, who had changed his mind from the 2003 session about the need for expanded revenue.[100]

Lawmakers were skeptical: Dunnam issued a statement calling Perry's proposal a "bait and switch tactic to distract from the real Republican agenda" of vouchers and other failed policy objectives.[101]

Unlike redistricting, Republicans did not unify behind a single solution. Some backed a state income tax, while others supported a state property tax in lieu of local property taxes. House leaders passed a payroll tax increase, and Dewhurst and others favored increasing the state sales tax. Many Republicans balked at expanding gambling. Perry floated the idea of private school vouchers, a third rail in education reform circles. Critics pointed out his close relationship—and a February trip to the Bahamas—with wealthy campaign donor and voucher proponent James Leininger, a physician and businessman from San Antonio.[102]

Leininger and homebuilder Bob Perry (no relation)—both prominent, wealthy backers of using public money for private schools—poured millions into defeating veteran Republican legislators like Delwin Jones, Charlie Geren, and Tommy Merritt in 2002. All three were reelected, but dividing lines inside the GOP were forming. In competitive races across the state, conservatives were beating incumbents deemed too moderate. In Houston, a talk-radio-show host and frequent Republican bomb thrower (so much so he was denied a speaking role at the 2006 GOP convention in San Antonio) would be elected to the state Senate. Dan Patrick would go on to be the most dominant lieutenant governor the state has seen.

Fueling speculation that she was interested in a 2006 run for Perry's job, Strayhorn claimed Perry's school finance plan could balloon the state's deficit by $10 billion over five years. She also disapproved of the "sleaze tax," accusing Perry of partnering with sexually explicit nightclubs to finance the educations of her five granddaughters. As Strayhorn's comments threatened to blow up the special session, Perry countered that her analysis was filled with "eye-popping miscalculations."[103]

The war of words was on, with the governor lamenting the "astonishing fact that the top number-cruncher in this state could be so wrong on the numbers." Strayhorn responded, "How dare the governor question the integrity of this agency? . . . I am telling the truth, and I will keep telling the truth."[104]

Unwilling to reenter the partisan fray, Republican committee heads worked cautiously to find consensus before acting. With no consensus, little got done. This was risky territory for Republicans—most plans meant raising taxes, or at the very least, restructuring taxes, which might give the appearance of tax increases.

Perry, like Bush before him, had miscalculated the appetite for reform and perhaps the difficulty of overhauling the state's complex school finance system so quickly. Exhausted, bitter, and wary, the legislature adjourned with few changes, and Robin Hood remained the law of the land.

—7—

THE 2005 SESSION AND 2006 ELECTION

"Governor 39 Percent"

Perry started his fifth year as governor—and his third decade in public office—brimming with his characteristic optimism about the state's future. Redistricting, tort reform, budget crises, and an unsuccessful effort to redesign the way Texas funded public education all had left political scars, but Perry started his third State of the State address on January 26, 2005, by focusing on better times to come.[1]

He had first taken the oath of office on the same spot in the House chamber twenty years earlier, and some of his old House classmates were in the audience as Perry promised better times to come. The state had added jobs at a clip of 162,000 over the past year, revenue was in the black, and Texas attracted nine of the twenty-four largest capital investment firms, including Texas Instruments and Countrywide Mortgage, achievements Perry credited to the Texas Enterprise Fund.

He struck conservative themes on his political tuning fork: fiscal responsibility, low taxes, and strategic investments. Looking back over the previous three sessions, he saw much progress. Administrative savings and regulatory reform kept the Wall Street crowd happy, sure. But Perry also had his eye on the growing number of religious and social conservatives in the Republican Party. In polling, two-thirds of Republicans wanted abortion outlawed or permanently limited.[2] The Texas

GOP's 2004 platform had reaffirmed the United States as a "Christian nation," and Perry heeded the message.

Calling the right to life "a fundamental right," he pledged to sign a bill strengthening parental consent for a minor to have an abortion; the bill required doctors to have written consent from parents or a court order before performing the procedure. (A prior law signed in 2000 required doctors to notify parents forty-eight hours before a minor under eighteen years old could have an abortion.) Ditto for a bill to ban human cloning. The 2005 State of the State address marked the first time Perry had mentioned abortion on a big stage, a sign of the changing cultural politics in the GOP and an expansion of his policy agenda.

While many of the policies he touched on were standard fare, Perry's explicit move into abortion politics was something more. Speaking in front of hundreds of antiabortion activists carrying American flags and signs reading "Parental Rights," Perry reiterated his support for legislation limiting abortion. The event, planned to coincide with the thirty-second anniversary of *Roe v. Wade*, the landmark abortion case, brought marchers to downtown Austin. The group headed towards the Capitol chanting, "Hey, hey, ho, ho, Roe v. Wade has got to go."

Perry also opposed embryonic stem cell research (which is conducted using stem cells harvested from early-stage embryos), drawing a contrast with some Republicans, including his potential rival for a US Senate seat, Kay Bailey Hutchison, who supported more research.

Perry had long opposed abortion, with exceptions for cases of rape or incest. Hearing the story of a woman conceived when her mother was raped convinced him to change his mind; he modified his position to oppose abortion in all cases.

The change of heart put him outside the mainstream of public opinion but squarely inside the conservative wing of the Republican Party.

The sour taste of his failure on school finance reform during the 2003 session and a special session in 2004 had Perry anxious to take another swing, despite the political risks. Former governors Mark White and Bill Clements both took major political hits when a bankrupt public school system forced them to sign off on higher taxes.

Perry sensed that the stone had been ground down enough to find success. "We need to act now," he said, unveiling a plan to give teachers a pay raise and cut property taxes by $7 billion over the next two years, paid for by increasing sales taxes to 6.95 percent from 6.25 percent and making certain services, including cosmetic surgery and automotive repairs, subject to the sales tax.[3] This was less than one third of the $11 billion cut lawmakers proposed but didn't pass in the special session.

Republicans had campaigned on lowering school property taxes, but Perry was well aware of teachers' demands for higher pay.[4] Complicating matters, a district judge in Travis County had ruled the state's system of public school finance unconstitutional the previous fall, giving the state a year to fix it.

Ultimately, the legislature would fail to find a resolution during the regular session. With a court deadline looming—and politics heating up—Perry called a special session in June 2005. That same day, Comptroller Carole Keeton Strayhorn announced she would challenge him in 2006.

Raising taxes was a nonstarter for many Republicans in the legislature, and for most voters, but *restructuring* them might fly politically. Some cover came from an unlikely source: Perry's political rival and Aggie classmate, John Sharp. For Perry, the fallout from the nasty 1998 campaign wasn't personal, making it easier to lean on Sharp for this job. Perry appointed him to chair a twenty-four-member commission made up of business leaders and other stakeholders to make recommendations on tax reform and school finance. Perry called on Sharp to help the state, recognizing he needed a high-profile Democrat to "give us a little bit of air cover so to speak so the Ds won't think it's some crazy idea. I give him a lot of credit for getting this done."[5] The future of public education, through the funding mechanism, was in their hands.

Suggestions the commission studied ranged from taxing junk food to a reverse payroll tax, which would mean that businesses could lower their tax burden by making new hires or opening new facilities. The consensus among members of the Sharp Commission was to reduce property taxes by raising the state franchise tax.[6] Perry was open to considering a broad-based business tax.[7]

GOP activists had other ideas, not only bitterly opposing revising the business tax plan to fund public schools but also pushing unsuccessfully for a plank in the state party platform calling for repeal of the business tax at the 2006 state convention. Hard-liners at the convention succeeded in getting their opposition to tax reforms debated on the convention floor, but Perry's allies were able to defeat them in a roll-call vote. Perry survived, but the vote spelled trouble with the right wing of the party. Tax critic Dan Patrick viewed Perry as holding a weak position: in a contested, four-way governor's race, Perry squeaked out a narrow victory at the convention: "That's a very shallow victory."[8]

Frustrations boiled over, exemplified by Perry's hot-mic moment following a remote interview with a Houston television station. Eleven seconds after the live interview ended, thinking the camera was off, Perry turned to his staff and mocked the reporter's quest for more details about the education plan. *"Adios, mofo,"* he joked.[9]

Public education was a topic as old as the republic—one of the chief complaints when Texas declared its independence from Mexico was the Mexican government's unwillingness to establish a school system. Over the course of the 2005 session, the House and Senate worked through more than a hundred amendments involving aid for bilingual students, improved teacher performance pay, caps on tax redistribution, and additional money for busing.

The pressure was on: state district judge John Dietz had ruled the state's $30 billion school finance system unconstitutional the prior fall and gave the state until October 2005 to fix it. Failing that, state money for schools would be frozen.[10] Dietz estimated that the state would need an extra $4.7 billion per year, out of a budget of just over $118 billion, to meet constitutional standards. The Texas Supreme Court was also set to hear oral arguments on an appeal involving the current funding model in July 2005.

Negotiations went down to the wire, culminating just days before legislators gaveled out for the session in late May. A tense, early-morning meeting between Dewhurst and Craddick found no agreement between the factions. "We're down," Perry said as he left a similarly unproductive afternoon meeting with the Speaker.[11]

Once tightly aligned, the two men had some fences to mend after three difficult and ultimately unproductive sessions focused on the very reforms they were under the gun to pass now. Craddick was miffed when Perry refused to publicly back a House proposal to slap a payroll tax on businesses in the second called session in May 2004, causing the bill's authors to scrap it and come up short of revenue. The bill went down in flames, 126–0.[12] Maybe it was a stunt—pitching a bill with no chance of passing—but the lopsided vote reflected the antipathy of legislators towards the way the governor approached his legislative role.[13] More than heavily engaged, he was heavy-handed. Republicans were angry that Perry had called the special session without Republican consensus, forcing awkward negotiations and opening the door to tough votes on outside-the-box revenue sources, such as expanded video gambling.[14]

The vote also reflected differences between the chambers—the House wanted to stick it to the Senate. The chambers differed on the total price tag, which would have been easy enough to negotiate. The sticking point was how much to cut local property taxes and how high to raise the sales tax. The Senate plan made all Texas businesses except sole proprietorships subject to a new franchise tax, while the House plan exempted general partnerships, publicly traded partnerships, and real estate investment trusts. The House proposal hiked sales taxes by one cent, while the Senate threatened to filibuster any increase of a penny or more.[15]

This issue of education funding was too important to play hide the pea, Dewhurst pleaded, saying the Senate was open to compromise.[16] "The problem with take it or leave it is sometimes you get nothing," Dewhurst lectured in response to Craddick's famously hard-line negotiating tactics.[17] Craddick chided Dewhurst for slow-walking his process. With a short deadline, "tensions are running high, and it's easy to point fingers out of desperation," Craddick said.[18]

In the end, they couldn't agree. Perry thought they had a deal at the last minute, but Craddick (who ruled the chamber with an iron fist and no velvet glove) and House negotiators indicated there was no steam there. Craddick, a member of the legislature since 1968—when Republicans were as rare a sight in Austin as fans of Oklahoma football—was unwilling to betray the conservative people and principles that had put his party in power. Across the Capitol, Dewhurst remained mindful of how much new taxation rank-and-file Republicans would swallow.

Neither chamber's leader could give much. But the clock was ticking. The state would defend the structure in court, but the funding was still a problem.

"Good. Bravo. Ten points for Perry," Judith Zaffirini (D-Laredo), vice chair of the Senate Finance Committee, sarcastically responded. "If it hasn't been resolved by now, then it's not going to be resolved in another special session," she said. "If we can't agree on a good bill, we should have no bill at all."[19]

School finance was consuming much of the legislative oxygen, with the failures of the special sessions in 2004 fresh in everyone's minds. But Perry also tackled a number of other issues, both in the legislature and outside it as he began wielding his gubernatorial power more confidently.

In March 2005, about halfway through the session and without fanfare, Perry recommended giving officials in coastal communities the authority to order hurricane evacuations, updating routes and traffic-control plans. Six months later, Hurricane Katrina devastated New Orleans, causing over 1,200 deaths and leaving millions homeless along the Gulf Coast.

"I was very proud of him," a beaming Rep. Senfronia Thompson remembers. "He was just like a governor who walked into the room, pulled up his sleeves, and said 'lemee help.' He did a monumental job helping people in that catastrophe."[20]

Perry opened Texas to thousands of evacuees and deployed first responders and the National Guard to aid in recovery efforts. A month later, Hurricane Rita hit the upper Texas coast, leading to more than one hundred deaths in the state, most of them caused by the evacuation. Coastal officials called for evacuations, resulting in the worst traffic gridlock the Gulf Coast had seen, as drivers idled in traffic for twenty hours or more. Cars ran out of gas, fights broke out along the highways, and dozens were killed or impaired by heat stroke. A bus carrying evacuees from a Bellaire nursing home caught fire, killing twenty-three.

Ed Emmett, a former House colleague who was elected Harris County Judge in 2007, recalls the ease with which his office worked with the governor's office. "It was always whatever I needed. He understood the county was an arm of the state, and he just said OK, if it was at all possible." He didn't play politics with it, but he was into the macho "I'm going to save people" mentality.[21]

Being governor frequently meant dealing with disasters, from hurricanes and tornadoes to wildfires, and Perry's rural upbringing gave him empathy for those affected and a resolve to harness the hero mentality.[22] But more than personal empathy, Texans needed a governor who could operate effectively in chaos.

Republicans were resurgent, but that didn't give Perry a free pass to operate without oversight. While his role as natural disaster cheerleader-in-chief largely drew praise, his use of the Texas Enterprise Fund sparked decidedly more scrutiny. Created by the legislature in 2003 with $295 million syphoned from the Rainy Day Fund, it was intended to award deal-closing grants to companies that were considering moving to or expanding in the state. In exchange, companies were expected to create new jobs at wages equal to or greater than the average wage in the county in which their businesses would operate.

Critics argued the fund was a boondoggle and that the money would be better spent on education, but Perry asked the legislature for, and received, an additional $300 million for the fund. "You just can't ask the legislature for a slush fund to give to people who contribute to your campaign," one critic said. Except Perry did. "That is how it works in Perry world. You give big contributions. You get big business deals."[23]

A 2005 audit by the *Austin American-Statesman* found that of the 123 companies that applied for the money, only 17 received it—proof, the governor said, that the fund was properly managed and worth the investment.[24] Perry extended his hand, asking for another $300 million for the Enterprise Fund and another $300 million to establish an Emerging Technology Fund from skeptical legislators. Both would be administered by his office. Both measures cleared the legislature.

Another Perry pet project, the Trans-Texas Corridor, was also under fire—farmers opposed it, water rights activists were concerned, and metro area officials were upset about possible new toll roads. Perry's $184 billion megahighway plan was new, and lawmakers were worried.

Even after limiting which roads could become toll roads (no new construction), some Republicans were still skeptical. Sen. Todd Staples

(R-Palestine), chairman of the Senate Committee on Transportation and Homeland Security, acknowledged that Texas was facing a mobility crisis. But, he warned, "We want change to occur in the most user-friendly manner as possible." Austin-based conspiracy theorist Alex Jones accused Perry of creating a "NAFTA highway" and creating a "one-world government."[25]

The 2005 session was decidedly conservative, and legislators, with Perry's backing, waded further into social issues, from a bill allowing parents to use corporal punishment to discipline their children to a ban on abortions after twenty-four weeks. Legislators also passed the bill requiring parental consent (not just notification) for unmarried girls younger than eighteen, a version of a bill that had failed in 1999, 2001, and 2003. Fetal sonograms were required at least twenty-four hours before the procedure could be performed.

Another bill asked voters to approve amending the state constitution to ban same-sex marriage, and Perry signed it in a ceremony at Calvary Christian Academy in Fort Worth. He defended the venue as "an appropriate place to come together and celebrate a victory for the values of the people of Texas," and a spokesman noted that he signed it not from the pulpit but in the academy gymnasium.[26]

The bill represented a change in the social politics of gay marriage. "We are making a horse race out of it for the first time in any state," said Glen Maxey, an openly gay former legislator who was directing the opposition group No Nonsense and who later wrote a book about Perry, *Head Figure Head*.[27] The new pushback against same-sex marriage was a more activist front from Republicans who opposed expanded rights for LGBTQ Texans.

For his part, Perry dug in, writing in an email to a supporter from the Texas Marriage Alliance, that "marriage is the union between a man and a woman [and] is a truth known to each one of us already, and any attempt to allow same-sex marriages is a detriment to the family unit and hurts our state and nation."[28]

The proposition overwhelmingly passed by more than three-to-one, serving as a dry run for Perry's reelection campaign. "I'm an opinionated person," Perry said. "I have a strong set of beliefs and values. And

I'm not afraid to stand up and say, 'Here's what I believe in.' If someone wants to say, 'Gosh, he just believes that for political purposes,' that's their reason, but they're wrong," he added.[29]

But the issue of gay marriage provided a preview of intraparty fighting to come. Conservatives and moderates disagreed over social and economic issues, adding language to bills to make them more conservative but poisoning the end broth.

Tina Benkiser, Republican state party chair, defended the schisms as a show of the party's strength. "This is a family, and families have discussions and sometimes they have disagreements."[30] But no amount of spin could hide the discord.

The party continued to build from the grassroots up, and Republicans were willing to go to far-flung and sparsely populated parts of the state in pursuit of growth. The party invested millions of dollars in targeting voters, crafting messages, holding local training sessions, and recruiting new candidates.

The latter effort was made easier by the party's recent successes. Benkiser recalls meeting with a politically frustrated man at a small breakfast club in Lubbock and telling him: "America is a two-party system, so pick one and get involved." That man, Charles Perry, ended up running to the ideological right and beating an incumbent Republican state senator.[31]

Despite the party's growing strength, governing was hard. Tax reform was a centerpiece of the Republican agenda, but no tax reform bill was passed in 2005.

And Perry's goal of school finance reform remained elusive, as well. "I'm not interested in assigning credit or blame, but [in] getting a good result for taxpayers and schoolchildren," he said as the final talks were taking place at the end of the regular session.[32]

In the end, he vetoed a $35.3 billion public education budget, calling for "real reform." The decision was announced just moments before Strayhorn said she would challenge Perry in the 2006 GOP primary.

Longtime legislative leaders like Craddick pointed out that no school funding bill had been adopted in Texas without a special session or a court order (or both) since 1948. Facing a legislative revolt over new taxes, a possibly contentious GOP primary, and a looming court ruling, the pressure in the governor's mansion to make something happen was intense.

After six attempts in two years, through two regular and four special sessions, school finance reform was no closer, seemingly doomed by the Republican antitax ethos. Without a new revenue source or agreement on how to reshape current revenues, no plan could take firm shape. Sniping almost from the start, the personalities of chamber leaders also stood in the way of agreement. The clashing personalities of Craddick and Dewhurst made reaching an agreement tougher. Tying property tax reform to school finance was a necessary evil but also a Gordian knot that lawmakers had been unable to unravel.

But the nature of governance is that no single issue, no matter how pressing, can command undivided attention. In Texas in 2005 that meant growing concern about drug-fueled violence on the state's southern border. Perry met with other border governors, including Bill Richardson of New Mexico and Arnold Schwarzenegger of California, and the three stood together against mistreatment of migrants—both documented and undocumented—and pledged to take more responsibility for border security. "One of the greatest challenges our nations face is cutting off the drug trade and ending the violence that it has brought to both sides of the border," Perry said.[33] But he also objected to congressional funding for seven hundred miles of border fencing, saying it would be ineffective. "If you build a 30-foot wall or fence, the 32-foot ladder business is going to get real good," he said.[34] Republicans would shift their positions on this in later years—but not Perry.

Was the border safe? In a post-9/11 world, border security was needed, Perry argued, saying the funds were needed to deter crime and terrorism. The headlines were filled with stories about immigrants smuggled into the US dying in extreme heat inside packed trailers. Violent assaults against Border Patrol agents increased 108 percent, blamed on smugglers and warring drug cartels.[35] A surge in drug-related violence just a short walk from the Texas border made local officials skittish but certainly played well politically. Did it work? Between 2005 and 2010, border apprehensions dropped 61 percent.[36] The governor boasted that these initiatives reduced all types of crimes by as much as 70 percent and resulted in the seizure of 3,600 pounds of marijuana.

But the operations didn't produce any terrorism-related arrests in the first six months, instead netting more undocumented immigrants than criminals or terrorists. "They dilute their power when they lose focus on criminals and start doing immigration stuff," said Sen. Juan Hino-josa (D-McAllen). "It defeats the whole purpose."[37]

Perry negotiated for state and federal funds for Operation Rio Grande to underwrite a wide-ranging series of border security operations. Operation Del Rio—described as a zone blitz—put a thousand Department of Public Safety officers into action to reduce crime and disrupt drug-smuggling operations. Operation Linebacker provided border sheriffs with $3.8 million to pay overtime for increased patrols, surveillance equipment, and specialized vehicles. Operation Jump Start, announced by President Bush in 2006, deployed six thousand National Guard troops in rotating shifts along the border to help stop illegal immigration. Immigration and border security was a federal responsibility, to be sure, but without permanent federal solutions, Texas would lead. "We couldn't wait on Washington, DC," Perry said.[38]

Perry's Operation Rio Grande was the origin of border security as a political talking point, a plus for a Republican in an election year. "The bad guys aren't going away after November 7 [election day]," he said. "And neither am I."[39]

Although some of the session's most extreme bills didn't pass—for example, denying state benefits to the children of undocumented immigrants, taxing money transfers to Mexico, or allowing US citizens to sue the federal government over the costs of border control—the Republican Party had certainly migrated to the right on immigration.

The issue evolved into questions about race. Perry refused to oppose the Texas Minutemen, one of several volunteer (or vigilante, depending on your point of view) groups who patrol the border. "I don't care who you are, you're under the same danger as I am," said one volunteer. "Right now, Baghdad's more secure than the border."

Those objecting were "brown supremacists."[40]

Fueling speculation about a run against Perry in the weeks after the 2005 session ended, the maverick Strayhorn teased her intentions with a rally near the Capitol, where she promised a "major announcement." Pundits expected a fiery race. "She's brash, outspoken, has millions in the bank, and she knows state government. And she won't be out-worked. She's the Energizer Bunny of Texas politics," said Republican pundit Bill Miller.[41]

Perry, a veteran campaigner who had never lost an election, suggested the pundits were mistaken. "I think you all are putting the cart way out in front of the horse."[42] Still, Strayhorn had received more votes than Perry in the 2002 election, when she was running for comptroller, posting 2.9 million votes to Perry's 2.6 million.

Her campaign would largely focus on Perry. "Now is time to replace this do-nothin' drugstore cowboy with one tough grandma," Strayhorn told hundreds of supporters at a block party near the Capitol. "I want my legacy to be that with every breath of air in Carole Keeton Strayhorn's lungs, she fought passionately for education, she fought passionately for paychecks and jobs, and she fought passionately for protecting our most precious resource, our children."[43]

A blast from Perry's past—Kay Bailey Hutchison (state treasurer from 1991 to 1993 and US senator for Texas from 1993 to 2013)—was also mulling a run for governor in summer 2005, and money poured into the campaigns. Perry joked years later that he would remind the senator that his 1990 campaign against Jim Hightower was so strong it hurt her "Hightower" opponent (Niki Van Hightower).[44] Perry reported almost $8 million in the bank, only modestly outpacing Hutchison at $6.7 million and Strayhorn at $5.7 million.[45]

The Republican Party had little room for dissenters. Hutchison in late 2005 announced she would run for a third term in the US Senate after several county Republican chairs urged her not to run against Perry. Strayhorn decided her chances would be better as an independent. Polling bore that out: December 2005 polls had Strayhorn trailing Perry 55 percent to 24 percent in a primary matchup.

With the campaign unfurling in the background, Perry continued to push for a transformative deal on public school finance.

"The final chapter of this book has yet to be written," he said. "Legislators' inability to strike an agreement on school finance will make for a long and uncomfortable summer when they go home and explain why they did not act on education reform and property tax relief."[46]

Perry, ever the optimist, was sure that political pressure, combined with an earful from constituents, meant agreement was just around the corner. But others were not so sure. In an interview with a Midland television station, Speaker Craddick said there was no deal and "no plan that we've agreed upon at all at this point." Perhaps waiting until after the Texas Supreme Court ruled would be the better option, he later said. Legislators needed something to aim at. And, he acknowledged, any school finance plan would also require legislators to revisit appraisal caps and local tax revenue limits. "They all go together."[47]

After four attempts in two years, Perry called the legislature back into session on June 21, 2005. A palatable mix of property tax cuts, sales tax increases, or taxes on bottled water or adult-oriented businesses (the "tassel tax") remained elusive. Lawmakers were frustrated. "I didn't call this meeting," said Jim Keffer, an Eastland Republican. "We are here and again, we've got to start somewhere."[48] Politics had seeped in, and Perry was looking for someone to blame.

Perry produced a plan that would increase the homestead exemption, end loopholes in the franchise tax, increase the sales tax to 6.95 percent, and add $1 to the cigarette tax, but was still $200 million short in promised property tax relief. Strayhorn, relishing the spotlight and a chance to twist the knife, claimed that Perry's "so-called plan" would increase taxes by $5.3 million in the next five years. "This is not a workable solution to the school finance problem our state faces," Strayhorn said.[49]

The Perry team cast Strayhorn's criticisms as crassly political. "Everyone had hoped Comptroller Strayhorn could put aside her political ambition and her well-established pattern of cheap political attacks to provide an honest analysis."[50]

Every legislative decision became a chance for the two to slight each other. Both Perry and Strayhorn may have started their political lives as Democrats, but the similarities ended there. Strayhorn was eleven years older and the daughter of a university dean. She had been married three times. Perry was proud of his rural roots and was the first member of his family to graduate from college. He was a baby boomer who'd married his high school sweetheart.

The House and Senate had plans similar to Perry's to raise school revenue, but the House wanted to increase the sales tax while the Senate preferred to expand the number of businesses that would be required to pay a newly restructured state business tax. House members also objected to higher alcohol taxes in the Senate plan.

Perry put his political capital on the line. He made an aggressive push to sell his plan—eleven cities in three days and $400,000 in statewide radio spots to encourage Texans to support it. "I hope Texans will be telling their legislators that Texas needs the three 'Rs' of education reform: results, resources, and relief."[51] This was a critical time: a financial crisis that was complicated by political divides. Perry had expanded the role of the governor, but the power wouldn't be worth anything if he couldn't get what he wanted.

Amid the chaos the Texas Supreme Court heard arguments on the state's school funding plan. Attorneys for hundreds of poorer districts argued the state had failed in its obligation to educate its children, while attorneys defending the plan for the state argued the legislature, not the courts, should repair Texas's troubled school finance system.

This was easier said than done. On the final day of the special session, stalled talks suggested there would be no compromise. A Democratic filibuster in the Senate started at 9:45 p.m., meaning the clock would run out at midnight without a final vote.

With no agreement, Perry again flexed his executive muscle and called a second special session for July 21, just two hours after the prior session ended. It was his sixth special session in his six years as governor, nearing the record of eight called by Bill Clements between 1987 and 1990, the most since gubernatorial terms were extended to four years in 1974.

Perry predicted that this time the session would be successful. "Lawmakers won't leave Austin until both priorities are addressed."[52] House and Senate leaders vowed they were committed to a solution, too. With just a ten-hour break between sessions, lawmakers went back to work.

There was trouble from the start. Republicans controlled the House, but a lack of unity led members to vote down their own multimillion-dollar funding bill and property tax relief measure, with Democrats goading them on. Teachers' groups viewed the salary increases and healthcare stipends as insignificant, and superintendents criticized the changing formulas for bilingual education and transportation. Some worried the new distribution system would leave them short-changed. The business community rallied against any new business tax, and tobacco companies lobbied against proposals from both chambers to slap a $1 (or more) tax per pack on cigarettes.

Craddick spent much of the session's final two weeks chatting with members and passing congratulatory resolutions. "The members are just basically worn out voting on these different proposals. I don't know where we go from here," he said.[53]

On the other side of the Capitol, the Senate trudged on, passing a $2.8 billion spending bill complete with a teacher pay raise. But because the funding depended on a tax swap, which rules required to originate in the House, the legislation fizzled. The special session ended with no deal.

Republicans made the Kool-Aid, but they weren't drinking it, said one Democrat. "We've gotten to the point where this is becoming folly," sputtered Coleman.[54] Everyone, it seemed, was waiting for guidance from the courts.

Adding legal insult to political injury, the Texas Supreme Court declared in November 2005 that the property tax system used to finance the state's public schools was unconstitutional and, ironically, unfair to both rich and poor districts. In effect, the legislature—unable to find a way to wean itself off overreliance on property taxes for school funding—had forced most districts to push the limit locally, resulting in a de facto state property tax, which violated the state constitution. Act by June 1, the court ordered, or no funding for schools and no back-to-school parties in the fall.

No more money was needed, but how the money was collected needed to be changed. The legislature would have to go back to the drawing board.

Perry's approval ratings had been their highest in three years before the session began, at 51 percent.[55] This was a significant rebound from a year before, when his "good job" rating fell below 50 percent. It slipped again after the contentious session, to 45 percent, a reflection of the session's failure to advance his number-one goal, school finance reform.

Meanwhile, 67 percent approved of the job Hutchison was doing in the US Senate; that rose to 78 percent among Republicans, 15 points higher than Perry's rating by members of his own party. Strayhorn had high marks as well—51 percent of those surveyed approved of her performance as comptroller, although a full third of those surveyed hadn't heard enough about her to have an opinion. (That was likely in part because she had remarried and changed her last name from Rylander to Strayhorn.) The lack of name recognition would be an opening for the Perry campaign to define Strayhorn before she could define herself, although Strayhorn's camp pledged that voters would soon know Strayhorn as "one tough grandma."[56]

Perry called a special session (again). The third called special session in a year started on April 17, 2006, and legislators limped to Austin for another round. This was the sixth attempt to restructure public school financing in Texas since 2003, through two regular and four special sessions.

Would this session be different? A state supreme court mandate to fix school financing by June 1, 2006, would certainly keep the pressure on, and Texas's leaders were optimistic that they had, in Thomas Edison's words, not failed six times but found six approaches that didn't work.

Perry was upbeat, repeating his standard refrain that legislators would have an opportunity to significantly reduce property taxes, reform the franchise tax, and ensure that schools had a reliable and constitutional stream of revenue. He kept the call narrow to avoid distracting fights over other issues. He hinted he had an ace in the hole: a secret plan devised by the Sharp team.

Strayhorn, too, responded in character, scoffing at the delay and pledging she would do better. "In a Strayhorn administration, the children and the teachers will come first. In the misplaced priorities of a Perry administration, the special interests come first."[57]

By mid-March Strayhorn had dropped out of the Republican primary to run against Perry as an independent, but her day job as comptroller required giving the governor good news: the state had a bigger budget surplus than expected, at $8.2 billion. It was tempting to use this fiscal sugar rush to fix the school funding issue and adjourn, but such a move led to worries about the long-term hole in education financing.

"Let's make it happen!" Perry exclaimed to a group of real estate agents expressing support for property tax relief high up in the Senate gallery, as the gavel thwacked to bring lawmakers to attention and then promptly snapped in half. "I hope that's not a reflection on the session,"

Dewhurst worried aloud.[58] Dewhurst generally (but flatly) backed Perry's business tax but also wanted broader reforms.

Perry's secret plan "broke the code" for modernizing the state's antiquated tax structure, cutting $6 billion in property taxes, replacing the hole with a new business tax, and relying heavily on the booming state surplus and a new forty-one-cent-a-pack cigarette tax.[59] No sales tax—the sticking point for both chambers in several sessions—would be needed, Sharp argued. Perry's "secret" plan was basically the Sharp plan, which most lawmakers backed without seeing all the details. A booming economy would save the day.[60] The new business tax was fairer and broader and offered fewer loopholes—but it was still a tax swap, conjuring memories of past tax shell games that had appeared to raise state revenues while ultimately leaving massive holes in the budget. Some Republicans, worried about sapping too much from the state's business community, initially balked, including a Republican from Dallas's posh Highland Park, who offered an amendment prohibiting future legislatures from raising the business tax in tough budget years. It went nowhere.

And the comptroller's last-minute budget update, which reported an $8.2 billion surplus, made some legislators reluctant to back a $6 billion tax swap, in addition to saying the tax savings plan was "hogwash" and that Texans might be able to buy one more Coca-Cola out of a vending machine each week.[61] Perry's plan also drew criticism from groups representing teachers, principals, and school districts, who complained that there wouldn't necessarily be more money for school improvements. This approach fixed the tax problem. If the state couldn't produce a more substantial plan now, with pressure so high, the groups asked, when would it?

Perry was resolute, determined not to set the picnic table with more than he knew the legislature would eat. Additional money for teacher pay raises and other priorities would have to wait until after the tax bills passed. The chambers moved quickly. The House moved first, approving Perry's plan without changes. The Senate added language for teacher raises and performance incentives. Dewhurst said the majority of senators wanted a long-term fix, not just a Band-Aid, and he poured campaign money into television commercials urging action on school improvements to keep the pressure on members.[62]

Agreement that something had to be done didn't mean there wasn't drama. Craddick prioritized a bill from Republican representative Warren Chisum of Pampa to give one-fourth of the surplus money to taxpayers. Senators refused to vote in a meltdown in a budget committee vote on an important use of the budget surplus. The House rejected an early Senate effort to redesign the business tax. Later, Republicans led by Florence Shapiro walked out of a committee hearing when the chair clipped her efforts to increase funds for schools. The committee chair ordered the chamber's sergeant-at-arms to round up the missing senators.

Here we go again, thought Perry.[63]

But in the end, Perry got what he needed and more. Sharp wrangled the business community to support the revised business tax his commission had devised, and Perry got antitax apostle Grover Norquist to bless the idea.[64] The final bill replaced some portion of school property taxes with $2 billion in state budget funds and allotted additional funds for schools and teachers, including a $2,000 pay raise for teachers and school librarians, nurses, and counselors. It also gave districts an extra $275 for every student—more than $6.8 million for a district with 25,000 students. More companies would pay the new business tax, generating $3.4 billion to offset the property tax caps. Texans would pay more for used cars and cigarettes through higher taxes.

All that took "a bit of courage" from a Republican, even in that era,[65] Perry included. He pointed to education reforms as the main difference he made in the state—"a comforting thought" to conclude his political career, he later noted.[66] Republicans pushed for extra school funding despite the governor's initial reluctance. He worried that lawmakers would use the "get outta Dodge" plan and spend one-time surplus revenue, completing the constitutional mandate and pushing harder questions off until after the November election. His worry was justified, as the governor calling expensive session after session with little result would make him look politically weak.

The Big 3 met the final passage with a massive sigh of relief. Tense meetings and acidic dueling press conferences were replaced by effusive praise, as Perry credited Dewhurst and Craddick with the cooperative spirit that led to success. The men began meeting weekly, a key part of their success. Bill Miller, the Republican political consultant, said their ability to pull together had been key. "They [otherwise] might have achieved success, but it would not have been beautiful," he said. "It would have been an ugly baby."[67]

Bipartisanship pulled the legislature together, but the cooperative spirit would not last long, and complaints about the hard-won plan mounted quickly. The 2006 election was just a few months away, after all. Democrats panned the bill as a tax swap bound to fail. Strayhorn claimed the plan didn't pay for itself and that Perry had in effect written a $23 billion hot check.[68]

In fact, journalist Paul Burka reported, the check wasn't just hot but *radioactive*—the gap between the projected revenue and cost of public education in the next four years would run up to $11.6 billion, more than 10 percent of the total budget. That was money the state was unlikely to have even in good economic times.[69] Strayhorn was right in principle if not correct on the specific number.

And not all Republicans backed the plan. Conservative activists like Steven Hotze, a wealthy archconservative physician from Houston, emailed a screed against it to his followers, urging them to oppose it. The years-long effort to structurally shore up school funding—a major accomplishment for Perry—ended up hurting him within his own party.

After seven years as governor, including two tough regular sessions in 2003 and 2005 and seven painfully difficult special sessions in three years, Perry was vulnerable heading into November. Bush was in the White House, his post-9/11 popularity diminished by the extended war in Iraq. Gas prices had spiked in the summer. Republican enthusiasm was tepid in Texas. The state was shifting, too, as large urban areas, including Dallas and Houston, began to trend blue.

Perry later confided to journalist Jay Root that he would have lost if Hutchison or another popular figure had run against him in the primary.[70]

Instead, his nemesis was fast-talking Carol Keeton Strayhorn, who came into the gubernatorial race after a lifetime steeped in politics. Her father, Page Keeton, was a longtime dean of the University of Texas School of Law and had instilled in his only daughter a passion for public service. She hosted her own television public affairs program called "The Rylander Report."

She was the first Republican woman elected to the state's Railroad Commission, which oversees oil and gas operations in Texas, and was elected comptroller in 1998. Like Perry, she was a former Democrat, and she had worked for Walter Mondale's failed campaign to unseat Ronald Reagan. But she also served in nonpartisan posts as mayor of Austin and on the Austin school board before switching parties and losing a Republican primary for railroad commissioner in 1992. She was a mother to four sons and grandmother to six girls. She was also newly married, having gotten hitched to Eddie Joe Strayhorn forty-five years after he first asked, when they were both eighteen. ("Eh, she was worth the wait," Eddie Joe said in a later campaign ad.)

Strayhorn even tried to use "Grandma" as a nickname on the ballot, arguing people knew her as "One Tough Grandma" rather than by her more recent married name. The secretary of state denied the request.[71]

More than a dozen years after switching to the Republican Party, Strayhorn announced in January 2006 that she would run for governor as an independent. "I am a Republican," she said with Eddie Joe and three of her granddaughters at her side. "But I know we must set partisan politics aside and do what's best for Texas. Texas belongs to no special interest group, no special political credo, no special individual."[72]

If she won, she would become the first independent Texas governor since Sam Houston. But she faced strong headwinds from the start.

"Transparent political opportunism," one GOP official responded. "Carole Strayhorn's decision to leave the GOP is a direct response to Governor Perry's strong leadership and support, and an admission that she would have been defeated in the upcoming GOP primary by those who know her best: Texas Republican voters."[73]

One of Strayhorn's chief talking points—a crumbling public education system and Perry's failure to fix it—was temporarily off the table after the legislature approved the reforms. But she pivoted to calling out Perry for higher taxes, bigger government, higher insurance rates, a broken and abandoned border, toll roads, and a rise in partisan divisions in Texas.[74]

Her funding (raising $1.5 million after her announcement and sitting on $7 million total) was certainly bipartisan and based on opposition to Perry: Democrats who had contributed to John Sharp in his run against Perry in 1998, business executives who worried about increasing business taxes, and trial lawyers who normally contribute to Democrats.[75] "There is something wrong when a governor calls a special session and then proposes the largest tax increase in Texas history, then turns around and takes checks from those who don't want to be taxed," Strayhorn said.[76]

Only in a Texas in political transition could this party friction fly. Infighting continued as the state Republican Party divided along tactical and ideological lines. Strayhorn's opposition to Perry's spending plans would hurt her among some Republicans but boost support from those worried about the sticker price of the school finance program, in addition to Perry's pork barrel economic development funds and a ballooning state budget. Members of Strayhorn's staff, including her chief fundraiser of twenty years, quit the campaign over her attacks on fellow Republicans.

Strayhorn wasn't the only competition. Chris Bell, a former Houston city council member and US congressman whose district had been demolished under the DeLay-led redistricting plans, announced his candidacy on August 14, 2005.

Bell, a former lawyer, news reporter, and talk-radio host with a studious manner and dry sense of humor, embraced the "Democrat" label in a field brimming with candidates: the Republican incumbent, two independents, and a libertarian. It was a hot day on the University of Texas at Austin campus as Bell spoke in front of a statue of Martin Luther King Jr. Lucky members of the audience found shade under nearby oak trees. Others fanned themselves with signs reading "GOT BELL?" (a play on popular Dell Computer advertising of the time) and "ANSWER THE BELL." He outlined the issues as he saw them: deregulating college tuition had been a failure, health insurance was too expensive, and too few children had health coverage.

Bell was not a newcomer to the rough-and-tumble of Texas politics. He left the Houston City Council for a seat in US Congress in 2003, only to lose his bid for a second term after redistricting forced him into the same district as longtime US representative Al Green, a fellow Democrat. Bell lodged an ethics complaint against DeLay over the redistricting.[77]

He argued that the state needed new blood, but while his name recognition was high in Houston, it was low everywhere else.[78]

Bell thought support for Perry was soft, hurt by angst in the Republican Party and open disparagement among Democrats.[79] His early fundraising lagged, partly because Strayhorn was raising money from such traditional Democratic donors as trial lawyers and teachers. It didn't help that the state Democratic Party was at a nadir—Texas was the ATM for the nation, and with Democratic money flowing out the door, especially to other races across the nation, the "Dream Team" in 2002 fizzled, and enthusiasm was low.

"When I got on the phone to start asking for money, it was just horrible," Bell remembers of those early days. Potential donors didn't see a path to victory. Ben Barnes, the former Democratic lieutenant governor who remained influential in swaying donations from trial lawyers, organized a group to support Strayhorn in the Republican primary, promising to throw his support to Bell if Strayhorn lost the primary. When Strayhorn instead decided to run as an independent, those donors stuck with her.

The GOP had held every statewide office since 1998, and no Democrat had occupied the governor's mansion since Ann Richards in 1990. It was an uphill fight, and Bell would not be the only pugilist.

Certainly Bell was not the most quotable of the candidates.

"I call for the unconditional surrender of Rick Perry," the man dressed in black told several hundred friends and supporters following a prayer from a rabbi, a song from Billy Joe Shaver, and a group of kids playing violins. This was the political origin story of Richard "Kinky" Friedman—a nickname he'd carried since his college days for his wiry black hair—who joined Strayhorn in running as an independent for Texas governor.

Puffing on his ubiquitous cigar in front of the Alamo, he disdainfully referred to the established Democratic and Republican parties as a choice "between paper and plastic" and vowed to wake the sleeping giant of Texas independence. "No one owns me," Friedman said. "I come with no strings attached. The only two things that influence me are my fellow Texans and my heart. And if you can elect somebody like that, an independent, a Texan, it might seem like a joke in some people's minds, but it will send shivers up the spine of every career politician in this country."[80]

Friedman was a showman, a longtime musician, author, and entertainer, and if he claimed politics wasn't totally foreign—he had twice been an overnight guest at the White House—the complex process of collecting signatures to run as an independent was something new.[81]

His band, the Texas Jewboys, became popular in the romping 1970s Austin music scene, even touring with Bob Dylan. He's written more than a dozen books, including popular mysteries with titles like *Kill Two Birds and Get Stoned*. Former US senator Dean Barkley, who engineered wrestler-actor Jesse Ventura's surprise 1999 victory as governor of Minnesota, joined the campaign.

Could a writer-musician-humorist win in Texas? Well, Barkley had helped Ventura use political dissatisfaction and clever advertising to win in Minnesota, so "Why the hell not?" as Friedman's campaign signs, bumper stickers, and posters asked. After all, Pappy O'Daniel had given Texans a (short-lived) tradition of singing cowboys in the governor's mansion.

"Humor is what I use to attack the windmill of politics as usual," he said. "Basically, that's my weapon." In fact, he argued that the real joke was the current crop of politicians. Not everyone laughed. The *Waco Tribune-Herald* ran a story headlined "Uncouth Hopeful Eyes Governorship." He offered "a governor who knows how to ride, to shoot straight, and to tell the truth, a governor as independent and as colorful as the state itself."[82]

Friedman's focus on issues ranged from the traditional (solid schools with highly paid teachers—"If you don't watch out, Guam is going to pass us in funding of public education") to legalized casino gambling and creating a Peace Corps for Texas. (Friedman spent two years in the Peace Corps in the 1960s.)

He supported gay marriage—"They have a right to be as miserable as the rest of us"—and reducing reliance on standardized testing.[83] He bragged he was the only candidate in favor of both prayer in schools and abolishing the death penalty. What other candidate could boast of a reality TV show airing on Country Music Television based on his campaign, or a golf and barbeque fundraiser hosted by Willie Nelson?

Both parties used Friedman's run to bash the rival party. Perry's campaign director, Luis Saenz, called the Friedman effort "no less a joke than what Democrats have put up in recent years." Jason Stanford, spokesman for the Bell campaign, said of Friedman's entry into the race: "Kinky is funny but Rick Perry is a joke."[84]

Friedman projected confidence, insisting that Texans were ready for a viable alternative to the two-party monopoly.[85]

The strategy, according to one supporter, was simple, if devastating for the Democrats: "The Democratic Party in Texas just really isn't there anymore. Nobody likes Rick Perry, [and] Kinky's the alternative that people seem to respond to. He's not going to lie to you. He's not going to play politics. He genuinely cares about the people of Texas, and that comes across."[86]

The ballot was filling up by the time Perry made it official in December 2005. He was running and, if elected to another four-year term, would hold the office of governor for ten years, making him the longest-serving governor in the state's history.

"I want the Texas of tomorrow to be a place where jobs and opportunity are even more abundant than today," he said, stressing his conservative credentials as he focused on job creation, property tax relief, and public school reform.[87]

The Perry campaign suspected he wouldn't get above 50 percent with all the "munchkins" running, as the campaign's consultant called Strayhorn and other lesser-known candidates. Getting above 50 percent would require millions of dollars the campaign didn't have (or didn't want to spend if they did have). Perry didn't care: don't spend a dollar to get to 52 percent if you don't need it—51 percent gets you the keys to the governor's mansion for another four years. But a four-way race complicated his ability to get even close to 50 percent, even as Bell and Perry tried to frame the race as a two-way race between them.

Perry was AWOL on the trail, so Bell, Strayhorn, and Friedman would often appear together. "Sometimes I felt like I ran away and joined the circus. It was just weird," recalls Bell.[88]

Even without Perry, Bell was often overshadowed by the two inde-pendent candidates, Strayhorn the political veteran and Friedman the showman. He, in contrast, was a poor campaigner, especially early on: too scripted, not as well versed on state issues. By the time he found his voice, it was too late.

The campaign was immediately ugly, with Perry and Strayhorn going straight for the jugular, a pattern for both candidates. Perry's allies cast Strayhorn as a "pseudo-Republican" backed by trial lawyers, including former Democratic lieutenant governor Ben Barnes.[89] Strayhorn allies cast Perry as ineffectual, unnecessarily divisive (in contrast with the bi-partisan manner in which Bush had operated as governor), and in the pocket of industry.

Bell attacked the Perry-engineered $2,000 teacher pay raise as too small and continued his assault on Texas's overreliance on high-stakes standardized testing. Teachers fumed over an incentive-based bonus plan many considered unworkable. Perry acknowledged that test-ing causes "pressure and stress" in schools,[90] but for the most part, he shook off the criticism as so much white noise.[91]

Many of the fights were a continuation of past grievances, with Strayhorn objecting to Perry rules governing how children qualified for health coverage under CHIP, and Perry accusing her of flip-flopping on CHIP after she recommended shortening the reenrollment period to save money, resulting in the removal of 160,000 children.

Strayhorn also veered into what was quickly becoming a Republican flashpoint, telling the Greater Houston Pachyderm Club that the state had an obligation to immigrants, legal or otherwise. "We can't turn them away from the hospital steps."[92]

Republicans were having none of it, especially in the middle of a na-tional debate about illegal immigration and border security. At their 2006 state convention, they called for a "physical barrier" along the en-tire US-Mexico border. A platform plank read "No amnesty! No how. No way." Amnesty was simply another word for surrender, supporters claimed as they gathered in San Antonio, met by two state legislators who derided their stance.

"Don't forget to tip the immigrant who's going to clean your room and serve your meal," said Rep. Trey Martinez Fischer of San Antonio.[93]

It had been less than a year since Perry had objected to federal plans for a border fence as ineffective. He was, however, in favor of a guest worker program. "Perry always recognized the importance of Mexico as an economic and security ally" as well as the shared history and culture, said Ray Sullivan, chief of staff. It was economic, but it was also political, running Spanish-language ads. "He did not go out of his way to demonize or antagonize Hispanic voters."[94] But the emergent harsh approach to immigration favored by many Republicans forced the governor to walk a fine line, acknowledging both the hard-liners and business leaders like homebuilder Bob Perry and Bo Pilgrim (cofounder of chicken processor Pilgrim's Pride), who needed immigrant labor and wanted true immigration reform. Delegates to the 2006 convention wanted more direct action to secure the border.

Perry's plan didn't address the larger issue of undocumented immigrants already living in Texas but backed $100 million in border security funding from the legislature. Strayhorn proposed doubling the size of the Texas Rangers and putting them in charge of homeland security efforts. Bell opposed amnesty but favored allowing immigrants to earn citizenship and advocated for strictly enforced laws forbidding companies to hire undocumented workers.[95]

Three opponents meant three opportunities to rev up the anti-Perry vote, and the Perry campaign was clearly concerned.

The Trans-Texas Corridor—the four-thousand-mile network of superhighways, toll roads, and high-speed rail lines that Perry had championed since his first term as governor—had always been controversial. The 2006 campaign pushed the controversy into overdrive.

Farmers and ranchers survived droughts, hailstorms, tornados, and grasshopper attacks, but they worried they might be beaten by what opponents called the "Trans-Texas Catastrophe," which threatened to take private land to build the new infrastructure. Strayhorn appeared at rallies against toll roads in Texas and blasted those "land grabbing highway henchmen" who were cramming the toll roads down Texans' throats, even though in 2001 she suggested converting underused road capacity to toll lanes.[96]

All three of Perry's opponents criticized at least parts of the plan, including a massive state contract with the Spanish company Cintra, S.A. (Concesiones de Infraestructuras de Transporte) for the first phase of building part of Interstate-35.

The fact that Dan Shelley, Perry's former legislative director, was a consultant and lobbyist for the Spanish company, coupled with Perry's acceptance of campaign funds from a San Antonio construction company that worked with Cintra to develop the plan, played into Strayhorn's long-standing contention that Perry was too cozy with lobbyists and high-dollar donors.

And the Trans-Texas Corridor wasn't the only example. When Strayhorn heard that Vought Aircraft—which had taken $35 million from the Texas Enterprise Fund by promising to expand in Dallas and create three thousand jobs—was cutting six hundred jobs, she pounced. "As the state's chief fiscal officer, I am gravely concerned," Strayhorn wrote while wearing her comptroller's hat. In campaign mode, she ratcheted up the rhetoric, calling the fund "wasted giveaways of Texans' tax dollars."[97]

Firing back, Perry's campaign pointed to a state auditor's report showing that the comptroller's office had settled 3,656 tax cases totaling $461 million within a year of Strayhorn receiving related campaign contributions.[98]

Friedman claimed he was against all politicians, telling high school students the Texas governor's post was "not a powerful job, more like a judge at a chili cookoff."[99]

Kinky was, well, Kinky. Saying the state needed a governor who wasn't afraid to offend, he quickly delivered. He was never without his cigar, although it was not always lit.

He was also scattered and unfocused. He called for same-day voter registration and legislation to make it easier for independent candidates to get on the ballot. He supported legalizing marijuana to keep nonviolent users out of prison. Got a gripe? Governor Kinky would set up a phone line for citizens to speak directly to the governor. Immigration? He called on the Mexican government to step up and pay their fair share.[100] He acknowledged he hadn't studied the details but said

Perry's school finance plan wouldn't improve public education and the tax swap just shifted taxes around. "What is Kinky Friedman's school finance plan?" a Perry spokesman responded. "This sounds like it could be his biggest joke."[101]

Friedman counted on his celebrity friends. Former pro wrestler Ventura joined him on the stump at colleges in an attempt to spark interest from young people who were otherwise unlikely to vote. Island-hopping musician Jimmy Buffett played two benefit concerts. In return Friedman joked that he would give Buffett the Gulf Coast city of Port Aransas. Longtime friend, supporter, and biodiesel proponent Willie Nelson would be appointed energy czar, because we "are running out of dinosaur wine." Musician Mojo Nixon changed the words to his "Elvis Is Everywhere" to feature Friedman:

> Every person out there has got a little bit of Kinky in them, everybody except one person that is the evil opposite of Kinky, the anti-Kinky. You know who I'm talking about? Let me tell you: Rick Perry has no Kinky in him. Kinky is wild, crazy and free. Kinky is a real Texas American nut job. Kinky is truly independent.[102]

Getting attention in a crowded race was tough, even for the Kinkster. The celebrities drew enthusiastic crowds, but his campaign officials worried these fans were novelty hunters, less willing to vote in November. Noting that only 29 percent of Texans had voted in 2002, Friedman saw plenty of room for new voters to get involved.

His outsider approach appealed to some voters, who liked the "not a politician" stance. "He doesn't have people in his back pocket or he's not in someone else's back pocket."[103]

Not all attention is good, of course. In Houston he rolled out a plan to give the city $100 million in state funding for more police protection amid a crime spike he blamed on "thugs and crackheads" who arrived from Louisiana after Hurricane Katrina. Anyone not working or caught breaking the law should be sent back to Louisiana, he claimed. And a tape resurfaced from two decades earlier, highlighting racist language he used in joking about sexual predators.

Critics, at least those who acknowledged he was in the race, blasted the statements as racist. Where did the tape come from? "It was clear someone did that to help me," remembers Bell. Regardless, Democrats were "done with him at that point."[104]

His opponents mostly ignored him, save for when Perry, to discredit Freidman's outsider bid, brought up a 1999 *Playboy Magazine* article wherein Jesse Ventura criticized organized religion. But these were just Kinky with the hide stripped off, unvarnished with no polish. "They've ignored us for a year and a half. They see that the polls are very threatening to them. This didn't just happen accidentally."[105] He was making fun of racists and sexists, a parody like his song "Get your Biscuits in the Oven and Your Buns in the Bed."

Taken together, the remarks pointed to a candidate with an unusual past who was out of place in the narrowly defined space where political campaigns live.

Perry had a comfortable lead in February, favored by 36 percent of voters eight months before the election. But 70 percent of voters said they could not name a single important accomplishment during his time as governor. When given a list of options, most ranked relief efforts for Hurricane Katrina as the top choice.[106] The campaign's strategy was to run out the clock—avoid newspaper editorial boards, meet with friendly audiences, and run television ads focused on broad issues: border security (without mentioning immigration), job creation, fiscal responsibility, property tax cuts, and improvements to public school finance, including increasing funding and teacher pay. Perry's "eggheads" (a group of academics working with the campaign who studied campaign dynamics) found these worked better than other, traditional forms of engagement. With four candidates in the race, maximining every opportunity mattered.

Perry's war chest made it possible for the ads to air in most of the state's media markets, with most viewers seeing an average of four ads a week. "The only thing he's good at is smiling in TV ads," a spokesman for Bell scoffed.[107]

But the ads were effective, highlighting Perry's personal appeal, camera-ready smile, Texas accent, and enough accomplishments to brag about.[108] With three opponents to split the moderate and Democratic vote and a comfortable lead in the polls, the campaign showed few signs of worry.

Strayhorn was determined to make it a two-person race. "Why am I running for governor? Here's why: I'm 67 years old. My future isn't in politics. It's my grandkids. And I want to protect their future from an Austin that doesn't listen, spends money we don't have."[109]

Perry agreed to one debate and only one debate, set for one month before the election. His campaign insisted there be no live audience, since Friedman and Strayhorn were both known for their witty applause lines.

He had a good night, fending off criticism, sticking to his campaign themes, and highlighting his record on property tax cuts, alternative energy, border security, and transportation. With lackluster fundraising and little statewide presence, Bell hoped the debate would be a turning point. He reminded voters that he was a Democrat, focusing on education, immigration reform, and government ethics. Strayhorn stuck to her script, describing herself as a challenge to the Austin establishment, bashing Perry for a paltry property tax cut but also forgetting the name of the president of Mexico. Friedman seemed uncharacteristically lost. When he did speak, he was on the defensive about the controversy over racially tinged remarks. Overall, the debate was light on substance. Observers faulted the format as uninformative and "game show–ish," especially a hokey knowledge-quiz speed round, which included a question about when the Battle of the Alamo took place.

But who was even watching? The debate took place on Friday night, a night reserved for high school football, and on the eve of the Red River Showdown, an annual game where archrivals the University of Texas and University of Oklahoma meet in Dallas to battle on the gridiron.

His opponents suggested the timing was by design. "The governor's strategy is to have as few people as possible actually see this debate," said Mark Sanders, a spokesman for Strayhorn.[110] The Belo Corporation, which at the time owned the *Dallas Morning News* and television stations in Dallas, Houston, San Antonio, and Austin, didn't allow competing stations in those markets to air the debate.

The debate finished in the top three programs for its time slot in Houston, Austin, and San Antonio. It finished behind *Deal or No Deal*, a prime-time game show, in Dallas.[111]

But it provided a bit of momentum for Bell, as people tuned in to see the Kinky Show but ended up liking what they heard from Bell. "Our server blew up that night," Bell remembers.[112]

He tried to capitalize on the momentum, reaching out to Friedman's campaign in October and asking him to drop out of the race in order to reach their common goal of beating Perry. "Suffice it to say, he didn't reach back."[113]

It was a Hail Mary pass, but Bell's only chance was to go one-on-one with Perry. Internal polling showed he was ahead of Strayhorn, but not by enough to win, so everyone stayed in the race.[114]

In fact, Perry's lead had grown slightly over the previous months, with 38 percent of Texans backing Perry in October polling, followed by 19 percent for Strayhorn, 15 percent for Bell, and 14 percent for Friedman. But there were worrisome signs for Perry. He was supported by only 60 percent of Republicans, and just over half of his own voters from 2002. Following an ad blitz over the next few weeks, that number increased to 70 percent.[115]

The numbers were understandable, considering he was in a four-way race that included another Republican, even if Strayhorn was running as an independent. But Perry clearly needed to shore up Republican support to keep his job.

Perry also began more openly talking of the ways in which faith and conservative values guided his politics, calling for easing barriers to partnerships between religious and community groups that help people in need. He also called for government to play an important role in promoting strong moral values and saving children from a "culture of godlessness" that existed on television. "It's a ridiculous notion to say you cannot legislate morality."[116]

The approach alienated moderate Republicans but attracted new "values voters." But conservatives were grumbling about the governor, too. Paul Bettencourt, the Republican Harris County tax assessor–collector, called the aftermath of the tax bill the "summer of conservative discontent" due to the new business taxes approved as part of school finance reform. "Clearly it's a problem for a grass roots party that believes themselves to be anti-tax," said Bettencourt, who was elected to the state Senate in 2014.[117] And social issues were becoming a more prominent part of the Republican brand. Convention delegates in 2006 added platform planks to outlaw abortion and repeal *Roe v. Wade*, oppose gay marriage and deny same-sex partner benefits, and make "American English" the official language. Fringe issues like withdrawing from the United Nations made it in, too.

In the October poll, Friedman did well among young male voters but trailed among women. Strayhorn was strong with women and independents, picking up both Republican and Democratic voters. Bell wasn't known at all—attracting only 39 percent of Democrats and 37 percent of Black voters.[118] Fully two-thirds of voters didn't know enough to have an opinion.

As Bell's strong debate performance boosted his fundraising, Perry returned to familiar ground, calling Bell a "former Washington liberal Democrat" with "very left-leaning beliefs."[119] He released an ad with a huge shark ominously swimming, as the theme from *Jaws* played in the background, intended to highlight how Bell would raise taxes and leave the border unprotected.

Bell's response to staff: an enthusiastic "Yes!" The direct attacks meant they had the Republican versus Democratic race they wanted.

Campaigning in old Yellow Dog Democrat territory in Longview, an area once firmly Democratic but increasingly Republican, Perry campaigned hard against Bell, citing Bell's votes while in Congress against using military troops to patrol the border and making it harder to deport undocumented immigrants. "He may have forgotten his Washington record, but Texans haven't."[120]

As Halloween neared, a Perry ad tried to spook voters about the potential for higher taxes: "Congressman Chris Bell, a Washington liberal Texans can't afford."

Bell struck back, hoping to lead the Democrats out of the wilderness and pledging to improve education, spend more money to fully fund CHIP, clean up campaign finance laws (including donation limits in state races, ironically announced the day he received a $1 million donation from Houston trial lawyer John O'Quinn), better fund infrastructure in border *colonias*, and make Texas a leader in stem cell research. "If you give me the bully pulpit and a veto pen, I will lead a new Texas revolution. This requires nothing more radical than common sense, but in our state Capitol, it requires nothing less than a revolution," Bell said in a speech at the Texas Democratic Party Convention in Fort Worth. He linked Perry and Strayhorn, "two sleeves of the same empty suit" and hoped to solidify Democratic support by making it clear that Strayhorn was a Republican.[121]

He urged party unity, speaking just a month after 2002 Democratic gubernatorial nominee Tony Sanchez announced his support for Strayhorn. "We've got to learn to win again."[122]

In retrospect, Bell thought he would have done better to focus on a few key issues. "We talked about just about everything, including video games. Really, video games?"[123] The Democratic brand was mushy. Bell was unapologetically in favor of abortion rights, same-sex unions, and tougher punishment for polluters. He professed his Episcopalian faith but drew a line between his private faith and his public beliefs.

The constitutional amendment banning gay marriage, recently passed by Texas voters, divided the party, too. Although he supported legal same-sex unions, Bell didn't support gay marriage, but he also thought the vote was unnecessary since gay marriage was already illegal.

Mainly, the Democrats were fighting for relevance.

The final days were a three-way blur of sharp attacks. Perry tried to shift the conversation to border security, gathering with a group of South Texas sheriffs in Austin to hail the progress of Operation Rio Grande. Perry left the event without taking questions. Perry campaigned in the Rio Grande Valley, picking up endorsements from local Democrats. "We've been bringing home the bacon. You don't bite the hand that feeds you," the mayor of Pharr said of his decision to endorse the Republican incumbent.[124] Bell took his "Bell on Wheels" bus tour through traditionally Democratic areas like East Texas, fighting the state's conservative shift that had made these areas harder to win.

Bell stepped up his attacks on Perry, accusing him of putting big business over children's health by cutting CHIP funding. Perry responded that CHIP was fully funded after the 2005 restoration of cuts. The national party offered some help, with former President Bill Clinton making radio ads and 2004 presidential nominee John Kerry campaigning for Bell in urban areas.

Bell was significantly outspent—Perry had ten times the money Bell had by the summer of 2006. The last-minute $1 million boost from O'Quinn, who would ultimately provide half of the $2 million raised by Bell, wasn't enough. Less funding meant carefully picking and choosing voter engagement, a major problem for a candidate who was not well known and who needed massive voter turnout to win. "You're not a serious statewide candidate until you appear on television," Bell acknowledged.[125]

But diagnosing the problem was easier than developing a persuasive agenda to solve it. The party was facing an identity crisis and struggling to connect to Texans. Bell flew to West Texas to hunt doves, where he didn't fire a shot. When he tried to, his borrowed shotgun still had the safety on.

So Bell, in effect, was fighting on two fronts. And if he faced long odds in the gubernatorial race, the effort to reinvigorate the demoralized Democratic base was even more daunting. "We have to learn to win again," he exhorted the small crowd at the Fort Bend County Democratic Party Labor Day picnic. "That means getting past our defeatist attitude. We have to learn to win again, because Texas needs us to lead again."[126] No money and low name identification didn't help either.

A party searching for relevance and a divided electoral field meant the campaign was over before it began. Perry won easily, if underwhelmingly, with 39 percent of the vote to Bell's 30 percent, while Strayhorn received 18 percent and Friedman 12 percent.

"Now it's time to get the remaining Democrats who may have Strayhorned or become a little bit Kinky," Bell joked on Election Day, drawing laughter and cheers.[127]

He fell short on his goal of unifying the party, as two-thirds of Democrats voted for him but just one-third of Hispanics and only a small majority of liberals. He wasn't the "Hollywood candidate, not the news-hook candidate," but with an uninspiring slate of Democratic statewide candidates, the operation rested on Bell's shoulders. "It was just hard to get folks motivated," he said.[128]

Friedman was the news-hook candidate, but not even his snappy one-liners and true outsider status were enough to motivate voters. His celebrity was more a hindrance than an accelerant for his campaign, as what worked as satire in the entertainment world fell flat in the political world.

In the end, Friedman won barely more independent voters than the traditional politicians in the race. He said early in the campaign that his race wouldn't be Kinky versus Perry but Kinky versus apathy. Apathy won, as only 29 percent of registered voters turned out to vote.

Friedman refused to concede. Three days later, Perry called him for what Friedman described as "a gracious little pep talk . . . [and] a random act of kindness."[129] He later backed Perry's 2012 presidential run. "So would I support Rick Perry for president? Hell, yes!"[130]

Strayhorn's campaign, on the other hand, had felt distinctly personal, reflecting the heated disagreements with Perry during earlier legislative sessions. But such personal politics was orthogonal to the rising mantra of party loyalty that was engulfing Texas. The cult of personality was no longer a driving force for Texas voters the way it might have been in the past. Texas voters—those who bothered to show up—were more partisan than ever before, with a stronger attachment to polarizing issues and a laser-like focus on their candidate's victory. Strayhorn's recently altered partisan alliances and shifting positions on issues such as abortion, vouchers, and toll roads also made it hard for voters to know where she was coming from.

She had the money to compete (raising $8 million by summer and buying a week of ads totaling about $1 million), but it was a drop in the bucket compared to Perry's war chest and built-in advantages. Moderates found no quarter from increasingly partisan voters. She only picked up one-fourth of those who disapproved of Perry, winning one in eight GOP voters.

Perry's victory put him back in the governor's mansion, his message about the state's sunny future drawing just enough voters to win, but the lukewarm win also earned him the derisive nickname "Governor 39 Percent." He carried 209 of Texas's 254 counties, down from 218 in 2002. Issues dogging the national GOP, from the war in Iraq to scandals involving Tom DeLay, lobbyist Jack Abramoff, and Rep.

Mark Foley (who was accused of sending sexually suggestive messages to teenage boys serving as congressional pages), tarnished the Republican brand even in ruby-red Texas. Bush was still popular in Texas, despite slumping numbers nationally, and appeared at a Dallas rally for Perry in the final days before the election.

"It was the perfect scenario for him because Democrats were peeled off," recalls Bell. Friedman, too—"You'd see a lot of 'W' (Bush) stickers with a 'K' sticker (Friedman's attempt to parody Bush's campaign swag), and those people were just kind of angry." Even so, "Everybody blamed Kinky, but [Strayhorn] was the one who caused more problems for us."[131]

Every other statewide Republican candidate won over weak challengers. Perry managed to keep the party unified in the face of the various factions that had begun to form: social conservatives, libertarians, chamber of commerce Republicans. He leaned heavily on ties to the Texas Association of Business, the state's largest business lobbying group, with whom Perry worked on liability lawsuit limits and new business taxes.

He captured three-fourths of the Republican vote. Exit polling suggested that the splintered independent race hurt Bell more than Perry.[132] Republicans got another assist from the Democratic Party's shift to the left in a state that Tina Benkiser, then the Republican state chair, described as still believing in "strong families, and strong economies, and independence and freedom."[133]

In a move that marked the start of another major shift in the state's politics, Houston-based talk-radio host Dan Patrick beat Libertarian Michael Kubosh, who was part-owner of Patrick's radio station. A fellow Democrat won Pete Laney's West Texas district, but elsewhere in rural Texas the partisan winds were blowing towards the Republicans. Demographics favored Democrats in exploding urban areas, including West Houston, where Hubert Vo, the first Vietnamese American to be elected to the legislature, fended off a challenge from former member Talmadge Heflin, the conservative Republican who'd lost the two years earlier.

The bar was admittedly low, but Texas Democrats ended 2006 with a sense that they not only held the line but had highlighted issues like social justice, equity, and education, issues which would become an increasing part of the party's identity in future years. A short two years later, Barack Obama helped reinvigorate the party, and Democratic primary turnout swelled, even in Texas. Obama lit a fuse—twenty thousand people showed up at Auditorium Shores in Austin to hear him speak. "That probably equaled the total number I appeared to speak in front of in 2006," Bell joked.[134]

—8—

THE 2007 AND 2009 SESSIONS AND THE 2010 ELECTION

No Mood for Compromise

After the cut and thrust of the 2006 election, Perry changed tactics. He struck a conciliatory tone and pledged to work with lawmakers from both parties to secure the border, create jobs, and improve schools. "We need less partisanship. We need less cynicism. We need more bridge building." Texas is better off when Republicans and Democrats work together, he added.[1]

But why bother with bipartisanship when you have majorities in both the House (eighty-one Republicans to sixty-nine Democrats) and Senate (twenty Republicans to eleven Democrats) and a booming economy at your back?[2]

Those words were barely spoken before he turned up the partisan heat, focusing on the widening gulf between Texas and the federal government. "I hope in two years we're not expending state dollars to defend our border, to secure our border," he said. "For God's sake, Washington needs to understand it's their responsibility. . . . I've never been one of those anti-government conservatives," he said. "I'm a limited government conservative."[3]

Being Texas governor was "the best job in the world," but, in reference to a possible White House run, Perry wouldn't commit to completing the four-year term. "That's kind of up to the good Lord. He may decide he wants me doing something different and I'm out of here tomorrow. Who knows?" Perry said.[4] For however long he was in office, he promised to be a "100 percent" governor, despite earning the support of only 39 percent of Texas voters.

The campaign's optimistic tone carried over to Perry's third inaugural celebration on January 9, 2007, as he ticked off reasons to be pleased about Texas: a record budget surplus, all-time-high job numbers, improving standardized test scores, and decreasing rates for home and medical insurance. For the first time in years, court rulings weren't hanging over the public school finance system and school property tax rates were on the way down. The Aggie basketball team was even ranked in the Top Ten. "Apparently, hell has frozen over," he joked.[5]

Reflecting his national ambition, this inaugural speech was broader and more international than his prior inaugural addresses, referencing the "Godless ideology" of fanatical terrorism, the AIDS crisis, genocide in Sudan, and border security. Immigration is a polarizing issue, to be sure, but Perry said, "I simply make one request based on the words of the prophet Isaiah: "Come now, and let us reason together." No unmanned walls, no amnesty, but a guest worker program possibly leading to citizenship.

Even as Republicans were surging in Texas, times were rough for the national party. Bush's approval rating was below 40 percent. The economy was sliding into recession. One Republican member of the Texas House switched parties to join the Democrats—the first party switch in a decade and the first time since 1993 a Republican representative had switched to the Democratic Party.

State Rep. Kirk England of Grand Prairie had been elected in 2006 by just 235 votes, and he decided Republican priorities no longer matched those of his district. Echoing growing concern among some Republicans, England worried that the party had migrated to the right, abandoning pocketbook issues he and his constituents cared about, such as affordable healthcare, public education, and health insurance for kids. He also blamed Perry and Craddick, saying he "came to the realization that the leadership didn't have the tolerance for an independent-minded Republican."[6]

An ebullient Perry showed no such concerns as he settled between paintings of two other gubernatorial giants, Jim Hogg and Sam Houston, for the 2007 State of the State address. Ramrod straight, Perry ticked off a list of factors in a "new era" of Texas prosperity: moving from the largest shortfall to the biggest budget surplus, a flush Rainy Day Fund, a drop in frivolous lawsuits, thriving hospitals staffed by top doctors, higher teacher pay, and lower school property taxes. But he acknowledged that the prosperity had not reached all Texans. "For the next four years, my goal is to spread opportunity far and wide for those willing to take personal responsibility for their lives and those they bring into this world," he said. Government couldn't solve every social ill, but it did have a role to play.[7]

Healthcare was a major national issue. If not broken, the system was certainly bent, and costs were on the rise. Texas was a prime example of the problem, with one in four people uninsured. Large cities strained to deliver care to their residents, with increasing demand at safety-net clinics and family support service providers.[8] Perry pitched several proposals, including a new initiative called Healthier Texas that would redirect hundreds of millions of federal dollars spent on uncompensated care to instead be used to purchase insurance for working Texans. In a preview of battles to come with the federal government, he called for reforming Medicaid to give the state more flexibility, saying Washington's "one size fits all" approach would bankrupt the states.

Indeed, Perry focused heavily on anti-Washington sentiment. "In the spirit of that mythical holiday, Festivus, let me begin the airing of grievances with Washington," he said, calling out environmental regulations and the federal response to illegal immigration as key concerns.[9]

The attacks on Washington were the biggest applause lines of the day, setting the stage for the next level of Perry's political career.

Despite the governor's paean to bipartisanship, the coming months were dominated by arguments, some of them within the Republican Party. While much of his State of the State address had been laden with audience-pleasing ideas, Perry also broached a topic that continues to reverberate through the Republican Party and American society at large.

He called for increased funding for cancer research—not too controversial—but also for the widespread use of a new vaccine against HPV, the human papillomavirus associated with sexually transmitted infections that can cause cervical and other cancers. It is recommended for adolescents before they become sexually active, and Perry acknowledged concerns. "But I refuse to look a young woman in the eye ten years from now who suffers from this form of cancer and tell her we could have stopped it, but we didn't. . . . If I err, I will err on the side of protecting life," he said to tepid applause in the chamber.[10]

And err he would, at least as far as many Republicans were concerned. The following month, he made a bold move few saw coming, issuing an executive order requiring girls aged fourteen and older in Texas public schools to be vaccinated against HPV, with a proviso allowing parents to opt out.

Armbrister, the Victoria Democrat who joined Perry's office as legislative director after leaving the state Senate, was bombarded with calls from angry—and blindsided—legislators the Sunday evening after the order was issued.

"I'm going to have to call you back," he told his former colleagues. The next morning, he strode up to Perry's media officers.

"You can do whatever you want, but I'd like a little heads-up so I can alert these members," he told them. "I've got some pretty pissed off members."[11]

Greg Davidson, the clerk in charge of distributing the order, came in twenty minutes later with a letter of resignation. He had forgotten to include Armbrister on the email alerting Perry's staff about the order.

But Armbrister wasn't out for blood. "Greg, are you shitting me? Go back to work. It's done."[12]

The legislature was far less sanguine about Perry's decision to act without consulting them. Republicans worried the mandate interfered with parental decisions, that the vaccine was too new, and that it would encourage premarital sex.

Many inside the governor's office were surprised at the reaction. They were "clueless about the backlash they were going to get," journalist R. G. Ratcliffe recalled.[13]

Chad Wilbanks, political director of the Republican Party of Texas, reacted with profanity: F**k!" He knew the political storm that would come from the party. "You can't do stuff like that."[14]

Dewhurst offered that the legislature would have accepted a program allowing parents to opt in for the vaccine, rather than requiring them to opt out.[15] Sen. Jane Nelson recalled being stopped at a softball game by constituents who were worried about the mandate.[16] Democrats pointed out that Toomey, Perry's former chief of staff, currently worked as a lobbyist for the pharmaceutical company that manufactured the vaccine. And current chief of staff Deirdre Delisi met with key aides about the vaccine the same day the manufacturer, Merck & Co., donated $6,000 to Perry's campaign.

Coincidence, Perry's staff said of the timing. As for the meeting, it was about providing the vaccine to young women on Medicaid, not a mandate.[17] "In the scheme of thing, it wasn't driven by Merck. It was not driven by the money."

Merck's vaccine, however, was the only one for HPV on the market, and the optics were undeniable. Van de Putte, the Democratic state senator from San Antonio, had planned to sponsor legislation that imposed a similar requirement, but the legislative well had been poisoned.

Perry at first doubled down—he had a picture of a little girl who contracted cervical cancer on his desk. "She touched me in a way that no issue ever has," the governor said privately. His wife, Anita, a registered nurse, influenced his thinking on why the vaccine was important.[18] Heather Burcham, a cervical cancer patient who was by then too ill to travel to Austin, sent a videotaped message supporting the mandate.

Perry—riding high on his earlier successes and his latest victory at the polls—was surprised at the resistance.[19] Nevertheless, it was a "clarion moment" for the governor. The mistake, he admitted, was how he addressed the issue, not the importance of the issue itself. His compassion to some degree blinded him to the politics. In hindsight, he agreed with his "conservative, libertarian friends" about the mandate but was happy that the episode raised awareness of the virus.[20]

Even so, he wasn't itching for a fight, and it was clear no bill converting his order into law would pass. Quite the opposite: both chambers overwhelmingly approved a bill preempting the executive order.

He could have vetoed it, but the legislature was likely to overturn the veto, something that happened rarely (the last time was 1979) but was a body blow to a governor, and Perry ultimately let the legislation become law without signing it.

The ruckus was about vaccines and parental controls, issues that would take on increased importance in the nation's conservative movement. But it also highlighted the explosive growth of grassroots conservatives in Texas.

"I haven't seen this kind of explosion in the grass roots in a number of years," said Kelly Shackelford, president of the Plano-based Free Market Foundation, whose group sent emails to more than 150,000 people. "It really struck a nerve."[21]

Perry's effort to preempt the legislative process didn't help his standing with the legislature, either.

"[The governor] just by executive order, destroyed that," said Republican state representative Warren Chisum. "So that's a real problem for the members of the Legislature right now. We just feel like we got dumped on."[22]

It went beyond hurt feelings. The antivaccine movement had taken root. "Look at the antivax movement now. It's crazy. There is a certain portion of the Republican base where there is just something about vaccines that just cuts across. I don't understand it, but it's there," Toomey reflected years after that first stirring.[23]

Perry may have shot from the hip—a political ready, fire, aim. Harvey Kronberg said, "If Perry has a weakness, it's that he didn't do his prefatory politics beforehand. There was no run up to it, there was just the announcement."[24]

He believed in doing it, but he did it on impulse. He didn't "think it through," said Ratcliffe.[25] This was a change from the more deliberate Perry who used his keen legislative sense to explore issues and build consensus. Electoral success and no backstop to his political power may have gone to his head.

Some of the most dramatic moments of the session didn't involve Perry but rather involved his fellow West Texan, Tom Craddick. The two men were close—Perry considered the diminutive Craddick a longtime friend and partner in conservative causes. Bruising legislative battles solidified their friendship. This was Craddick's third session to be elected Speaker, although the margin was just 94 votes, as Rep. Jim Pitts of Waxahachie mounted the first effort to depose an incumbent Speaker in decades.[26] Pitts's numbers might have been higher, but the chamber had voted against a secret ballot.

The problem wasn't that Craddick was too conservative, or at least it wasn't the only problem. Journalist Paul Burka described the clash for *Texas Monthly*:

Craddick is such a polarizing figure—not so much because of his political views but because of his Machiavelli-like enthusiasm for the tactics of reward and punishment—that the two warring factions in the House are not Republicans and Democrats but bipartisan alliances of pro-Craddicks and anti-Craddicks.[27]

Craddick would rather be feared than loved, and his pugilistic partisan style stifled the independence of members, in contrast to Laney, his predecessor, who had run the House in a bipartisan fashion.[28] He was quickly becoming the "Godfather of the House," too powerful to be crossed without punishment. He was increasingly willing to punish Democrats, despite the handful of "Craddick Ds" that saved his speakership, but Republicans were unhappy, too. After two bipartisan rebellions late in the session, Byron Cook, a reputed ally of the Speaker, urged him not to run for a fourth term. "Please don't put this body through eighteen months of hell. Your reelection will result in a bloody and brutal and, I believe, nonproductive eighty-first session."[29]

In the final week of the 80th (2007) session, unrest turned into a coup. In the middle of a terse exchange with Pitts, Craddick suddenly announced the House would recess, banged the gavel, and headed to his office. When he returned hours later, two House parliamentarians had resigned, replaced by two former members who were allies of the Speaker. Members were stunned. Like Moses coming down from Mount Sinai, he unveiled a series of rulings giving himself the authority to refuse to recognize members making privileged motions, contrary to long-established precedent. That meant members could not make a motion for him to vacate the chair. He blew up the parliamentary maneuver that, with majority approval, would have immediately pushed him out of the Speaker's role.

Effectively, Craddick made himself bulletproof, at least until the following session.

Democrats had seethed in frustration for the whole session. Led by Calendars chair Charlie Howard, a Craddick loyalist, Democratic bills suddenly didn't qualify for the Local and Consent calendar, a shortcut through the legislative process for bills that did not require funding and had drawn no objections. That is, bills from Democrats who didn't back Craddick. Republican bills proceeded as usual. Democrats retaliated by debating Republican bills to death (called "chubbing"), even employing a procedure that ended consideration of a Local and Consent bill after ten minutes of debate. Dozens of angry House members who wanted Craddick out of the Speaker's role walked out of the chamber, bringing work to a halt on a critical day.

The Senate got in on the act, too, as frustrations with rising partisanship and Dewhurst's impatience with running for higher office became apparent. Senators complained they were "being treated like an auxiliary campaign committee."[30]

An episode on the Senate floor involving Dan Patrick highlighted how the Republican Party was beginning to turn on itself. Patrick brought talk-radio dramatics to the Senate floor with a flair not seen in the clubbish Senate. Just months after being elected, he asked fellow senators to replace the two-thirds rule (which required a two-thirds majority to begin debate) with a simple majority, breaking with decades of tradition.

"Freshmen are usually seen and not heard," Patrick said. "The right thing is to have majority rule in the Senate."[31]

Colleagues privately urged him not to showboat, even as he arranged for $1 million cash as a prop for a news conference on the budget. He insisted on passing a resolution to have the words "In God We Trust" inscribed on the frieze above the lectern in the Senate. When his nemesis Fred Hill, a Republican from Richardson, announced his candidacy for House Speaker, Patrick sent a mass email referring to him as "Fred the Snake."[32]

This intraparty skirmishing took place as Republicans began jousting internally about another issue that was to attract outsize attention in later years: in-state tuition for undocumented immigrants.

Texas had been one of the first states to allow undocumented immigrants to pay in-state tuition rates at public colleges and universities (which are considerably lower than the tuition out-of-state students pay). Perry, who according to Ray Sullivan saw the need for more college-educated Texans, had signed the bill in 2001.

But the matter was far from resolved. Republican lawmakers had tried to end the policy on several occasions since 2001, arguing in part that the policy allowed the immigrants a break denied to US citizens from out of state, who had to pay more. The effort failed in 2007, 2011, and 2021, but the issue continues to be argued in the courts.

Perry was predisposed to back the bill, but getting other Republicans to agree would be a challenge. "His heart was there," recalled Van De Putte, who carried the bill in the Senate. Rick Noreiga, a Houston Democrat, maneuvered the bill through the House, but Senator Van De Putte had to get it through a more conservative Senate, specifically a committee led by archconservative senator Teel Bivins. "He [Perry] grew up in West Texas, where those farmhands, those people who were working, he said they were good hard-working people, they want to take care of their families, they go to church, they are faithful to their communities, they are law abiding, and they stay under the radar, Leticia." Perry relayed to Van De Putte that "mommas and daddies didn't have the right paperwork. Some of my best friends didn't have the right papers until they got into the military and were able to earn the right papers. He didn't come in from the outside. I think it's that he knew what our history was. He understood these kids didn't have a choice, they weren't breaking the law, they got here as little kids. How can you tell little ones 'stay in school, study hard, go by the rules, make good grades, and stay clean,' you're going to get a good job. How can you tell them that and then destroy their dreams?"[33]

The politics was another matter. Van De Putte lined up support from the Texas Association of Business, poultry magnate Bo Pilgrim, homebuilder and megadonor Dick Weekley, and dozens of Republican donors who were making phone calls to reluctant senators. She had twenty-one votes in the Senate, and Perry helped persuade other Republicans to join. Her ace in the hole: two-hundred Spanish-speaking evangelical churches, all pro-life. "Oh, these are going to be our voters," Perry told her. "They dress like George Strait. Its polka, beer, and sausage. Keep yourself clean. They like their guns, 'Don't you dare take away our guns.' They ranch and they hunt. And they go to church. It's the same culture." Legislative compromises such as how long the family had been in Texas (three years, paid enough taxes) and no criminal background ultimately sealed the deal.[34]

A bill from Leo Berman (R-Tyler) that would have denied citizenship to children born in the United States to undocumented immigrant parents died in committee. House members passed bills requiring divorcing couples to take a course in "forgiveness skills," requiring school districts to offer a Bible study class, and imposing criminal penalties for abortion. None of the bills passed the Senate.

In a jab at Perry, House Republicans passed (129–29) a bill proposing a constitutional amendment to trim the governor's veto powers by giving lawmakers more time to override the vetoes. The bill was left pending in a Senate committee.

Even beyond the debacle over the HPV vaccine, the session was mixed for Perry. With opposition mounting to the Trans-Texas Corridor, which Perry had championed since early in his governorship, he employed a mix of tough negotiation tactics and veto power to avoid most efforts to cut back the ambitious transportation project.

As rising opposition swept through the legislature, Perry vetoed several bills that could have stalled the project, including legislation ending privatization contracts for roads, a bill to rein in the costs of the project (which he said jeopardized federal transportation funding), and a bill to limit the use of eminent domain, partly because it could stall or stop highway construction.

But he realized he was unlikely to be able to sustain a veto of another bill, in which both the House and Senate agreed to a sweeping moratorium and more local control over toll projects authorized in the original legislation.

Perry tried to slow-walk the legislation, which was sparked by concerns the Texas Department of Transportation would redistribute to other counties local toll money collected in Harris County and other regions with established toll roads. A clerk in the governor's office was even sent home "sick" in order to delay the bill's official receipt.

In the end, Sen. Tommy Williams (R-The Woodlands), a close ally of the governor's, held firm, and two-thirds of members signed on to the legislation, meaning the Senate could override any veto.

The governor's office, already facing an embarrassing loss after capitulating on the HPV mandate, was forced to negotiate.[35]

Opponents of the megaproject were not happy. "I feel like he's let us down a little bit," said one Central Texas farmer. "He's got big 'ag' background, but since he's become a politician, he's kind of left ag out."[36]

No longer would the state wallow in a Godless state pledge of allegiance—the words "under God" were included by statute.[37] Texas students would have greater religious freedom on campuses because new legislation protected religious beliefs that were expressed in homework, artwork, or other assignments; students could not be penalized. Border security legislation, in addition to new funding, passed, setting up a Border Security Council appointed by the governor to allocate funds, and expanding law enforcement agency wiretapping capability. Flanked by border sheriffs, they reported they were "fed up," previewing the title of Perry's future book.[38]

The session was also the start of Rick Perry the criminal justice crusader, a shift, if not a complete 180, from his past positions. Legislation was passed moving drug users and probation violators out of prison to free up prison beds for violent offenders and in the process reducing the cost for building new prisons—a rare bill that was supported by both the ACLU on the left and the Texas Public Policy Foundation on the right. "Perry was a law-and-order guy," but you could talk to him about criminal justice issues, remembers persuasive House member Senfronia Thompson. "He saw the justice in it."[39] HIV testing in state prisons was expanded and became mandatory for new inmates. Perry did, however, veto a bill requiring informing former inmates about their eligibility to vote. He was back to his bipartisan roots, at least temporarily, while also getting policy wins and satisfying the base.

Perry's strength wasn't limited to his veto pen and the bully pulpit of the governor's office. He raked in more than $880,000 in campaign donations during the month after the session ended (campaign finance laws limit fundraising during the session), leaving him with a sizeable $1.4 million on hand, three years before the next election.

Longtime megadonors like Houston homebuilder Bob Perry and San Antonio supermarket mogul Charles Butt chipped in big checks that were unlimited in giving location and scope.

Perry was as prodigious a fundraiser as the state had seen to that point, raising more than $102 million during his terms as governor, and he used this money to cement his power base, supporting candidates and traveling the stump.[40] "He's got the power," one lobbyist said. "That is his draw."[41]

"Grab hold," Perry said in remarks to the legislature on its opening day in 2009. "You're in for the ride of your life."[42]

It was good advice.

Dark clouds were looming as early as October 2008, when the governor asked state agencies to trim their budgets for the remainder of the fiscal year, with a special focus on taxpayer-funded travel. That year saw an economic downturn that became known as the Great Recession. "Texas businesses and families are tightening their belts. They are cutting spending and exercising greater discipline," he told Houston business leaders. "State government should be no different."[43]

The most profound political change of the looming session would be the overthrow of Craddick and the ascendency of Joe Straus, a moderate and urbane Republican from San Antonio. The House was closely split, with seventy-six Republicans and seventy-four Democrats, creating an opportunity for a small, bipartisan group of members who were frustrated with Craddick's autocratic style on such issues as the new state business tax and the 2003 redistricting battle.

In a secret coup orchestrated by moderate Republicans and a few Democratic colleagues, Straus and allies ousted Craddick, whose imperious leadership style alienated members in both parties.

The ABC (Anybody But Craddick) coalition was a bipartisan group. "Regardless of how the Republican and Democrat numbers change in the Texas House, there is a majority desire for a new speaker," said Jim Keffer. "The sentiment for change is not personal. Members in the Texas House just want bipartisan leadership which is committed to restoring the rules of conduct and fairness."[44] Bipartisan steam was building to oust Craddick. Eleven Republican members—called the Polo Road Gang because they met in January 2009 at Rep. Byron Cook's house on Polo Road in Austin—decided to back the little-known Straus.[45]

The youthful Straus was a moderate Jewish Republican from a wealthy San Antonio family that built racetracks, a member of the country-club, business-minded wing of the party. He didn't toe the line on conservative issues, and he ran in different circles than the socially conservative crowd that backed Craddick. First elected to the House in 2004, he had never chaired a House committee; he was a lifelong Republican, a former precinct party chair who had managed the campaign of US representative Lamar Smith and had served in the US Customs Service (now part of US Customs and Border Protection) under Pres. Ronald Reagan and in the US Department of Commerce under Pres. George H. W. Bush.

His voting record showed an independent streak, supporting both the state's new business tax and Perry's order to mandate the HPV vaccine. He opposed a ban on gay foster parents. He authored legislation requiring school districts to set goals for reducing energy use and creating a sales tax holiday for energy-efficient appliances.[46]

He pledged to restore civility to the House chamber. "We will create an atmosphere where everyone's voice can and should be heard," he said. "A place where we respect each other's points of view, Democrat and Republican, urban and rural, liberal and conservative."[47]

He immediately followed through, giving more committee chair positions to Democrats who helped elect him (sixteen out of thirty-four committees) and appointing more African American and Hispanic legislators as chairs, in contrast to Craddick, who doled out committee assignments based upon each member's position on Craddick's political friend and foe depth chart. This also meant more power to committee chairs—Straus's lieutenants, such as Phil King and Tommy Merritt—who were "taking a lot more Tylenol and Advil than in previous sessions."[48]

Speaker Straus was seen as a defeat for the socially conservative wing of the Texas Republican Party,[49] deepening a division between moderates and conservatives over a dozen issues and complicating efforts at Republican unity.

Publicly, informed by his time in the House, Perry stayed out of the Speaker's race. "He knew enough not to get involved if he didn't have to."[50] And in those early days, the new configuration of the Big 3 didn't find much to disagree about, with Straus, who had only eleven days to prepare to lead the chamber, primarily sticking to the business of running the House. "But it is clear that [Straus] is not their kind of Republican, and vice versa," according to *Texas Monthly*.[51] Odd, because he and Perry shared many of the same donors, including Jim Leininger, a longtime voucher proponent, and Charles Butt, the heir to the HEB supermarket chain. Perry normally came down in support of the conservatives in the legislature, rather than leadership.[52]

Still, Perry made a point to acknowledge Craddick, the other half of the Twin Towers, as the session opened on January 13, 2009, but Craddick wasn't there to hear. He was stuck in Midland during an ice storm. He might have been better off staying there.[53]

The global economic meltdown meant Texas had three choices: it could crack open the Rainy Day Fund for every need or hunker down until the recession was over. Perry proposed a third way, dealing with the crisis Texas-style by following the lessons from the 2005 session, when the state had confronted a $10 billion shortfall. While some states grew more dependent on the federal government, Texas should go another way: "All across the country, states are hiking sales taxes, they're slashing education spending, preparing to pay state employees with IOUs, and begging Washington, DC, for a bailout. Because we took a different approach back then, we know it's better to control spending to make government less burdensome, as a way to free up the economic power of our citizens," Perry said. The recipe this time would be the same: "proven economic developments like the Texas Enterprise Fund, our Emerging Technology Fund, and film incentives, which target an industry that has brought more than $1.2 billion to our economy over the past 10 years."[54]

Who could argue with the fact that 70 percent of jobs created in the United States were in Texas, home to one out of every ten Americans and seven out of ten new American jobs, including at Cooper Tire, Caterpillar, and other companies lured to the state by Perry-driven incentives. Fiscal conservatism was also part of the Texas style—a robust Rainy Day Fund to be used only for one-time expenses, low taxes (Perry pointed to raising the small business exemption to $1 million), and peeling away "suffocating layers of regulation."

"Texas is strong because we aggressively play offense."

Playing offense, in Perry's view, also included a call for Texas to lead on energy innovation (despite the possibility of falling afoul of potential federal environmental regulations) through incentives for hybrid vehicles, solar power, biofuels, and wind energy. On the border, he called for funds to coordinate multiforce efforts, to pay for prosecutions of gang-related offenses, and to improve equipment and communication technology. He was interrupted by applause when he called for outlawing "sanctuary cities" that allowed local governments to "pick and choose" which laws to enforce. He said the state should track the citizenship status of those receiving state-funded services in order to quantify "the financial impact of Washington's failure to handle the immigration challenge."[55]

Taken together, Perry's approach represented a sharpening of his border security critique against the incoming Obama administration. This also put Perry and the Texas governor's office at the center of this national debate.

It certainly sounded like Perry was interested in running for president. Texas Democratic Party chair Boyd Richie likened the speech to the "state of Governor Perry's campaign" address, and Van de Putte, leader of the Senate Democratic Caucus and a longtime friend and occasional ally of Perry's, noted that his priorities "scapegoat immigrants, suppress voting rights, harm a woman's right to choose an abortion, and give teachers incentives that teachers don't support."[56]

Reacting against Obama's presidential win, eager to raise his national profile, reading the tea leaves of the ever more conservative Texas party, the governor's agenda lurched to the right: sanctuary cities, border security, abortion, voter identification laws. Changing party ideology demanded a response to Obama's election. But Sen. Kay Bailey Hutchison was a more immediate threat, since her political aspirations to be governor continued to percolate. While she supported some abortion rights, Perry's position put him firmly to her right. He asked for an additional one thousand troops at the border as violence mounted in northern Mexico.[57]

"Secede!" they shouted.

Conservative grumpiness swelled with the election of Barack Obama and the significant federal investment required to resuscitate a crippled economy. During an antitax rally in April 2009, Perry predicted the future, reminding some onlookers of his long-ago days as an Aggie yell leader as he revved the crowd against the federal government.[58]

Donning a "Don't Mess with Texas" button, Perry was anxious to take a cannon shot at Washington. At that surprisingly large event he vaguely threatened that if Washington "continues to thumb their nose at the American people, you know, who knows what might come out of that." He hedged by saying "we've got a great union" and there is "no reason to dissolve it," but the broader message was sent.[59]

He was one of the first major politicians to mix with the conservative activists known as the Tea Party, early to the show that would define Texas and national politics for a decade. Many political observers were shocked, but also a little impressed. "These people are nuts and we've got a governor associating with crackpots? He was completely comfortable with it," recalled political consultant Harold Cook. "And it was really smart to do so. We've witnessed what has happened to other Republicans who have been left behind."[60]

It wasn't so much that the Tea Party was a perfect fit for Perry's philosophy, but he had always been a quick political study, and he saw where the party was going.[61]

Indeed, Perry "saw the Tea Party coming really before any major politician," said journalist Jay Root. "And it saved him."[62]

Asked afterward about his secession comments, he demurred but did not apologize. But by the following week he was backpedaling, at least slightly, saying that he never advocated for secession and pointing out that his beef with Washington was about respecting states' rights under the 10th Amendment: "None of us want to see unconstrained government of the magnitude that the amendment's authors were so careful to legislate against," Perry wrote.[63] He later called the comment a "throwaway line."[64]

He was fed up.

Secession wasn't a realistic prospect, but after the election of Barack Obama political opportunity was ripe, and Perry was ready to embrace the new Republican primary base.[65]

He called these conservative activists "patriots" and praised them as "individuals who embrace concepts like lower taxes and smaller government and freedom for every individual. I'm talking about states' rights, about states' rights!"[66]

Tina Benkiser, the Republican state chair, recalled the crowd at that April rally in 2009 as a mix of libertarian and traditional conservatives, many new to politics. But there were also those who clearly believed there were no differences between establishment Republicans and Democrats.[67] They were frustrated. The Perry agenda could be neatly packaged as a Tea Party formula, attracting a new and earnest group of Republicans. Perry's attempts to coopt this group were successful, but doubts from members of the Tea Party about Perry's fealty to the cause remained. Video of that news conference made the rounds on the Internet (there were no television cameras there) and attracted favorable support from conservative commentators. Perry was one of the highest-ranking politicians to go all in with the Tea Party, becoming a leader of the movement at this point.[68]

Texas Democrats jumped on the issue, releasing statements disavowing secession and joking about Perry's political ambitions.

"We all knew he wanted to be president. I just didn't know it was president of the Republic of Texas," Rep. Jim Dunnam joked.[69]

But Democrats missed the point. The Tea Party had moved from the fringe to the mainstream. The Tea Party was just "a nominal piece of paper" until he recognized them, noted consultant Bill Miller. "He's the guy put the life into the Tea Party. They were just a sidebar circus show until he started paying attention to them and giving them life and showing them respect. . . . It's like they were taken off life support and given pure oxygen."[70]

Insiders rolled their eyes, Perry noted. They put the video on YouTube themselves, hoping to embarrass the governor; in a week it got a quarter of a million hits. Longtime journalist Jay Root wrote after Perry's twenty-point, come-from-behind win against Hutchison, "Before most Americans had even heard the phrase 'tea party,' Perry was leading one in downtown Austin."[71]

Senator Hutchison, considering running for governor against Perry at the time, said privately to her consultants, "I just won the governorship of the state of Texas today." "That was one of the biggest misconceptions that she had about the Texas political environment," Perry recalled.[72]

The good news for Texas budget writers was that the arrival of federal stimulus dollars, courtesy of the American Recovery and Reinvestment Act of 2009, saved the state's biennial budget from a sea of red. Without the injection of cash from the Obama administration, lawmakers would have had to confront the grim news from Comptroller Susan Combs: the Texas economy had shrunk so much there would be $9 billion less to spend over the next two years, despite the money lawmakers socked away in 2007 for education and tax cuts.

And Texans needed the money. Session after session of property tax cuts, coupled with minimal school spending from general revenue, had created a structural budget deficit that would require ongoing spending cuts or consistent new revenue. As the economy slowed, the business taxes approved in 2005 weren't sufficient to cover the property tax cuts that completed the deal. The national recession had dampened consumer spending, and sales tax revenues suffered. Meanwhile, the budget would have to address the financial fallout from Hurricane Ike's devastating hit to the Gulf Coast in September 2008.

Perry was an outspoken critic of President Obama's $787 billion federal stimulus bill, although he accepted roughly $17 billion on behalf of the Lone Star State. However, as unemployment in Texas spiked to 7 percent by the spring of 2009, Perry drew a line in the sand and rejected $550 million in funding for unemployment insurance, claiming it came with too many strings attached. Texas's unemployment fund was running dry and would be empty by October. Perry labeled it "excessive spending," claiming employers would eventually be worse off by having to pay more. He argued that the state would have to change the definition of employment to include part-time employees and other low-wage workers and that permanently changing state law for one-time funds didn't make sense.

"The federal government is trying to come in the back door and expand government without any debate," said Perry, who announced his decision at a makeshift podium in a Houston paint store as an example of how small businesses would be hurt.

Democrats, perhaps predictably, saw it differently. Rejecting the money, Sen. Kirk Watson (D-Austin) said, "demonstrates the height of denial about the challenges confronting this state and its people."[73]

Perry was undeterred. "This is exactly how addicts get hooked on drugs," he said as he rejected the offer.[74]

Texans backed him, more or less—emails, faxes, letters, and phone calls to the governor's office favored his decision by two to one. "I applaud your courage, sir, in your stance on the economic 'spendulus,'" one Llano correspondent wrote in a handwritten note. Or not. "May the fleas of 1,000 camels infest your linen closet," a dissatisfied Texan wrote.[75]

Legislators disagreed as well. Moments after he announced he would reject the federal money, legislators did an end run, passing legislation to expand benefits to people seeking part-time work and those who quit their jobs for compelling reasons, such as family violence or the illness of a child.

The chambers responded. The final $178 billion budget was a 149–0 victory in the House. (The Speaker traditionally does not vote.) It relied heavily on $11 billion from the federal stimulus package—state spending decreased by about 3 percent.

"The budget gap we face this session could very well pale in comparison" to the shortfall the state is likely to face in two years, Pitts said. "The gap is not artificial nor is it manufactured," Jim Pitts said. "It is very real."[76] The final budget was $182 billion and used $12 billion in stimulus funds. Washington made up 96 percent of the budget shortfall.[77]

It was easy enough to hold news conferences railing against federal regulations. Countering the enthusiasm surrounding Obama as a candidate and as president presented more complex political problems for the governor.

"Obama" became a one-word dog whistle to signal distrust of big government and racial animosity towards the nation's first African American president. This was an easy sell to the emerging populist strain of the Republican Party, the same way prairie populists had fought against the banks, railroads, and big business in the late 1800s.

And, Root said, it was "Perry's natural habitat."[78]

Texas Monthly—echoing a frustrated Republican senator—referred to the 81st session of the Texas legislature by comparing it to *Seinfeld*: a show about nothing "other than an endless succession of dying bills, forlorn hopes, and bitter recriminations in the closing days."[79]

The 2009 session was much more bipartisan and harmonious than sessions of the recent past, although that harmony obscured the intraparty split that would define Texas Republican politics throughout Straus's terms as Speaker. Some of the most contentious issues, such as stem cell research, abortion, and immigration, stayed on the side-lines, and other controversial Conservative causes stalled. There was even a life-affirming moment when Rep. John Zerwas, a physician and Republican from Richmond, saved colleague Edmund Kuempel's life when Kuempel suffered a massive heart attack in a Capitol elevator, performing CPR until EMS arrived.[80]

Or, put differently, the session was less conservative than the prior session. It wasn't for a lack of trying, as conservatives unsuccessfully pushed legislation eliminating scholarships for undocumented students, drug testing for those receiving financial assistance from the state, and restrictions on teaching evolution. Rep. Bob Deuell, a Republican from Greenville, signaled the alarm: "If we're to remain a viable party, we need to start looking at medical facts and dealing with reality and not dealing with black helicopters and other myths that are put out there by right-wing extremists."[81] (Deuell lost his seat to Bob Hall, who was backed by the conservative group Empower Texans, in the 2014 Republican primary—Republicans losing primaries in this manner called the process "getting Deuelled.")

The most conservative wing of the party gained another antagonist in Joe Straus, and their animosity would fuel Republican primary races and right-wing talking points for years to come.

These litmus-test issues would fracture the GOP.[82]

It may have been a relatively quiet session in many respects, but the same can't be said of Perry's relationship with the legislature during the months of the 81st session.

"When you're the governor for that long, you start making enemies. Inevitably you get crossways with people," said one former legislative staffer.[83]

The governor was called to defend a $50 million grant from the Emerging Technology Fund to Texas A&M for a National Center for Therapeutics Manufacturing, intended to develop new vaccines quickly and inexpensively.[84]

Even legislators who weren't opposed to the fund in theory worried about spending money there at the same time that other needs—including the state's woefully underfunded unemployment insurance fund—were pressing.[85] After all the fighting, Perry acted more quickly than lawmakers eager to crush the Trans-Texas Corridor by ending the program himself, even as large construction projects moved forward. "I think the concept of the Trans-Texas Corridor is frankly one that got misunderstood," Perry said, but more than misunderstood messaging, lawmakers were frustrated by controversial toll roads and the prospect of rural Texas landowners giving up their property.[86] "I'm not sure what we could have done different," wondered a perplexed Ray Sullivan, chief of staff to the governor. "I'm not sure in rural parts of the state where they don't always see the benefits of economic development . . . we could have convinced property owners and rural voters that this was a good idea." Perry never threw in the towel, but he couldn't fight the legislature much longer.[87]

Or the public. Perry recalls that in 2015, in tiny Round Top, Texas, population 90, he spotted a pickup truck parked downtown with a sticker on the back window that read "TTC" with a circle and a slash through it. The episode forced the state to think about transportation and mobility, but Perry has the scars on his back to prove the bad politics.[88]

One episode almost ended in a literal floor fight when an irate Perry hurdled the rails dividing the Senate floor from the space open to staff and visitors to physically confront Sen. Eddie Lucio III (D-Brownsville). Lucio had promised to vote with Perry on a bill and did not. Perry "did one of those cowboy things [and] jumps over the railing to start going at Lucio. I'm thinking 'not good.' This West Texas cowboy here is going to beat the shit out of my Valley boy," said Van de Putte, who was on the senate floor.

Other members intervened to pull Perry away and off the floor. A "shaking, red faced" Perry calmed down and showed remorse over losing his usual control, thankful for being restrained.[89]

If Perry was frustrated with the legislature, the feeling was mutual. The House cut the governor's office budget by $23 million, taking money earmarked for salaries, rent, and travel expenses and moving it to mental health services and counseling for veterans. The money was restored during negotiations, but the effort spoke volumes about the troubled relationship between Perry and Republicans in the legislature. The House also threatened to hold $136 million from the Texas Enterprise Fund hostage if the state refused to expand unemployment insurance, thus making the state eligible for $555 million in federal stimulus money. Perry refused on the grounds that there were too many strings attached. He eventually persuaded enough members to see it his way, and he got his enterprise funds.

Perry had a few wins. Eyeing the next hurricane season, he signed into law bills to restructure the Texas Windstorm Insurance Association, depleted after millions of dollars in claims after Hurricanes Ike and Dolly. It is the provider of last resort for property owners unable to purchase windstorm insurance on the private market. A number of insurance companies had quit doing business along the Gulf Coast following Hurricanes Katrina and Rita in 2005.

The pot of funds insured up to $2.5 billion in losses. This was on top of $425 million approved for other disaster-related expenses, including money for the University of Texas Medical Branch, which had suffered catastrophic damage during Hurricane Ike.[90]

But the bill almost didn't pass, jeopardizing a state headed into hurricane season.

The package came down to negotiations between the chambers, and Perry made it clear that he expected results, going so far as to order lunch for the negotiators to avoid a break.

"We thought, oh shit, they're not letting us out," said Van de Putte, who was part of the Senate negotiating team. "He would get very impatient with House-Senate negotiations. He was a legislator, so he understood. Perry understood the legislative process, he understood leadership."[91]

When the negotiations continued without success, Perry met with the entire committee or just the conference committee chairs. He was not pleased.

"I'm not calling 181 people back (for a special session) just because you can't get your act together," a red-faced Perry fumed.

The pressure worked, and the bill passed.

He also got his proposed tax break for small businesses that earned less than $1 million annually.[92] The bipartisan-backed bill was "probably the only tax cut bill in the United States," said Republican Sen. Dan Patrick of Houston, who sponsored the bill in the Senate.[93]

But Perry's attention was elsewhere. A bitter 2010 primary battle was ahead of him, and he prepared as he had in the past—by moving right.

He helped fellow Republicans raise money for their campaigns, building support in the process. He raised money for his own campaign, too, putting $7 million in the bank to begin 2009. The Republican Party of Texas's fundraising efforts were anemic, running the GOP into significant debt to the tune of more than half a million dollars by 2010.[94] Perry's revving of the fundraising machine bailed out the party, recalls Chad Wilbanks, former political director of the state party.[95] Perry also presented conservative right-wing radio host Rush Limbaugh with an Honorary Texan Award. On a national tour for his book *On My Honor: Why the American Values of the Boy Scouts are Worth Fighting For*, Perry attacked the American Civil Liberties Union in what he characterized as a moral struggle for the country's future. Bumper stickers with the R (Republican) insignia from past campaign materials and "Again in '10" started popping up around Austin.

Hutchison didn't directly say she was running for governor, either, but her actions did—she transferred $1 million from her Senate campaign account to a state account. She had openly flirted with the idea as early as 2008, when she was the most popular elected official in the state. Arriving in Austin for a campaign event, a reporter greeted her by joking, "Governor, good to see you." She responded, "I like the sound of that."[96]

She brushed away concerns that a run would be divisive for the Republican Party and dismissed questions about whether Perry should run for a fourth term. "Whatever. I'm just going to do what I'm going to do."[97]

Ironically, the two *were* the Republican Party back in the early 1990s. Both were handpicked by Rove and emerged successful in the 1990 election, Perry as agriculture commissioner and Hutchison as state treasurer, giving Republicans a needed foothold on statewide offices. Rove and David Weeks were the consultants for both campaigns in 1990, the last time Democrats won a majority of statewide offices. "If you're talking about the changing power in Texas, that was the cycle when Republicans started winning," recalled Weeks.[98] But almost two decades later, there was tension under the big tent of the GOP.

Hutchison made her move in August 2009, returning to La Marque High School in Houston, where she had been head cheerleader and coronation queen, for the formal announcement. She was Texan hewn out of an old rock, as famous Texas writer Frank Dobie used to say— her great-grandfather, Charles S. Taylor, signed the Texas Declaration of Independence. Hutchison joined the US Senate in 1993 after a special election to fill a seat left empty when Lloyd Bentsen resigned to become treasury secretary in the Clinton administration, and she had since been reelected three times. Only two Texans—Sam Houston and Price Daniel—had been able to make the leap from the Senate to the governor's mansion.

Hutchison's first campaign trip took her on a nineteen-city tour with the theme "Texas Can Do Better." Day one included a visit to Austin, where she had graduated from UT and was one of only seven women in her class at UT Law School, and then she moved on to Houston, where she had worked as a television reporter and which she had represented in the Texas Legislature at a time when only three other women were elected.[99]

Internal polling in the Perry campaign had Hutchison starting 19 points ahead. Of Perry's chances, "this is going to be tough," said one former House friend.[100] But when asked about her accomplishments, most voters pointed to the 1993 homemaker IRA—sixteen years earlier. At that point the Perry campaign realized they could paint her whatever color they wanted. She didn't have a reason for running, Dave Carney, Perry's campaign brain, said. The Perry camp took this polling presentation around the state to try to dissuade her from running, but it didn't work. It did, however, hurt her ability to organize the grassroots.[101]

Hutchison criticized the lack of consensus and trust in Austin, blaming Perry for setting the tone. "I think that's why we need new leadership. I think people are looking for positive, happy warriors. And I'm a positive, happy warrior," she said.[102] Hutchison's campaign immediately underestimated Perry, calling him "flyboy."[103] The dislike ran in both directions. Hutchison had always wanted to be governor, and Perry was in the way. She didn't trust Perry, a former Democrat whom she considered more lucky than smart.

And she drew on an argument Carole Strayhorn had tried to make stick four years earlier, accusing Perry's administration of fostering a culture of cronyism and corruption during his nine years in office. She also knocked him for being politically inconsistent. "I'm saying he wasn't there in the beginning," she said, referring to Perry's 1989 party switch. "He's a Republican of convenience. I'm a Republican of conviction."[104]

Perry had other looming problems. An uncomfortably high number of Texans (19 percent) said the term "corrupt" applied to Perry "extremely well," compared to 17 percent who said "not at all well."[105] Years of attacks on Perry's comingling of business and politics caught up to him in 2010. The governor's rough campaign style caught up to him as well, as newspapers bashed his "bully tactics" and "strong-arm style."

The *Austin American-Statesman* went so far as to write that "the governor is turning into a caricature in order to please a rowdy constituency that feeds on secessionist fantasies and fairy tales about tax cuts."[106] Even so, the Perry campaign was confident, perhaps overconfident. Hutchison's fundraising potential was strong, but otherwise she "wasn't a threat." The main goal was to avoid a runoff.[107]

Perry's team labeled her "Key Bailout," a play on her maiden name, Bailey, and a reference to her vote in favor of the $700 billion federal financial bailout package at the height of the Great Recession. They got some Future Farmers of America students from Lampasas to bring a pig in a cage in the back of a pickup truck to a Hutchison event on the University of Texas's campus at the Alumni Center. The Perry campaign had fake Monopoly money printed to hand out at Hutchison campaign events. It was "designed to get press but also designed to get under the opposition team's skin," recalls one campaign staff member.[108] Team Perry liked these aggressive tactics.

Hutchison's years in Washington, DC, played into Perry's bruising political strategy, as he blasted the federal government for increased spending, lack of action on border security, and slow hurricane response, branding her an out-of-touch Texan who had been in Washington too long.

The race was an important battle in the war for the GOP in Texas. The tug-of-war between the moderate and conservative forces was on display. In some ways this was the final race to determine which faction would prevail in Texas. As they had in the 2002 and 2006 campaigns, Perry's team went personal. Among the targets? They raised allegations of conflicts of interest against Hutchison's husband, Ray Hutchison—

former legislator and state GOP chair and a prominent bond attorney—over his work representing cities and public agencies that benefitted from hundreds of millions of dollars his wife helped secure from her perch in the Senate.[109] Democrats anticipated carnage.[110]

"There will be blood," said consultant Mark McKinnon, who had worked for both Republicans and Democrats. It was in part a clash of cultures—Hutchison came from the more polite world of the US Senate, while the Perry team was accustomed to brawling campaigns. Hutchison would have been an extremely popular general election candidate, the kind that Republicans found success with in the 1990s. But the primary came first, and Perry was an extremely popular primary election candidate who knew how to excite the conservative base. He also shrewdly coopted the party establishment, asking Benkiser to resign as state party chair and join his campaign, which she did, serving as a bridge between the campaign and important constituencies, such as women, moderates, and the Tea Party.

Early polls gave Perry an edge: he held 33 percent to Hutchison's 21 percent, but with 45 percent of voters still undecided, the race was up for grabs.

Individual property rights were among the most contentious issues. Both candidates claimed they would protect landowners from abuses of eminent domain. Perry was pushing a state constitutional amendment to safeguard such rights, but not everyone believed him after his 2007 veto of a similar bill. (He said that bill would have created a legal cause of action that would have benefited trial lawyers.)[111]

Hutchison seized on one of Perry's pet projects, the Trans-Texas Corridor, arguing that the massive toll road network it envisioned threatened to whittle away rural Texas by seizing rural land. The $175 billion program had been largely abandoned by that point—legislators would officially cancel it in 2011—and Perry deflected the criticism by pointing to population growth and the resulting highway congestion. On the ground, campaign staff reported talking with voters who said they would never vote for Perry because of TTC.[112] The Texas Farm Bureau—which had backed Perry for agriculture commissioner in 1990—endorsed Hutchison in the primary but refused to endorse a candidate in the general election for the first time since 1988.

Other issues also flared. In response to a 2007 mass shooting at Virginia Tech that killed thirty-two people, Perry backed allowing concealed carry without restrictions. (Current law made secured airport areas, hospitals, courthouses, bars, churches, and schools off limits for weapons.) He signed "castle doctrine" legislation, which said the use of force against anyone "unlawfully" entering your house, building, or vehicle was presumed to be justified. Perry had a concealed-carry license. Hutchison did not.

Border security and immigration were reliable issues—Perry ordered DPS helicopters to the border to "block any spillover of Mexican border violence."[113] It's a "federal responsibility but a Texas problem," his office noted, as President Obama temporarily deployed fifteen hundred National Guard troops to the border, short of the number Perry asked for in 2008.

But he stopped short of endorsing a law similar to one passed in Arizona that required local and state law enforcement officers to question people about their immigration status if they suspected the person was in the country illegally. "Texas has a rich history with Mexico, our largest trading partner, and we share more than 1,200 miles of border, more than any other state," Perry said on the topic. "The focus must remain on border security and the federal government's failure to adequately protect our borders."[114]

On immigration, Perry still followed the thinking of an earlier era, but times were changing. Half of Texans and almost 80 percent of Republicans supported a law like Arizona's.[115]

He also highlighted support for the state's "Choose Life" license plates, with the profits dedicated to providing housing, food, and other needs for pregnant women considering adoption over abortion. "If there's been a more pro-life governor in Texas history, I'd be hard-pressed to name who that was," he said.[116]

Hutchison's position was conservative but not conservative enough for the party's antiabortion wing. She supported abortion rights but also favored existing restrictions and said she wanted to reduce the number of abortions. While Hutchison met with supporters for a private strategy session in 2009, Perry rallied his base at an antiabortion demonstration at the Capitol. Gesturing in the direction of Hutchison's gathering on the other side of downtown Austin, he urged the crowd to shout its convictions, to "let them know that Texas is here, and Texas is pro-life."[117] Abortion offered a clear battle line, and Perry read Texans perfectly.

Perry's ongoing challenge to federal government served as a convenient proxy in his fight against Hutchison, even when she had opposed the very policies he was protesting. He bashed Washington-style healthcare fixes after the Affordable Care Act was signed into law in March 2010. "They want more control of your health care, and they want it now."[118] He ultimately rejected joining a temporary high-risk insurance pool funded by the federal government because of a lack of program rules or reliable federal funding.

As a senator Hutchison had voted against the ACA, but that wasn't enough to overcome the political stench of the Washington establishment. Moreover, she defended the stimulus program, even if it wasn't popular with many Republican voters.

At the same time, she suggested that many of the mandates were ill advised, and she was overheard saying at a campaign stop, "It's the people in Washington that are the problem." Maybe so, but she was one of them now.[119]

Her disavowal of Washington didn't stop her from tapping its heavyweights for help. Former vice president Dick Cheney belittled Perry, saying, "We westerners know the difference between a real talker and the real deal. When it comes to being conservative, Kay Bailey Hutchison is the real deal."[120]

She was endorsed by former president George H. W. Bush, a reversal from the 1990 race for agriculture commissioner but a signal of the blooming Republican civil war.

"The Washington establishment likes to stick together," the Perry campaign responded.[121] (That sentiment didn't stop Perry from accepting the elder Bush's endorsement in the general election.) John Cornyn, by then the state's junior US senator, didn't endorse Hutchison, but he did pan Perry's anti-Washington criticism as "unfair."[122]

Meanwhile Perry picked up the support of former Alaska governor Sarah Palin, the 2008 GOP vice presidential nominee. "He sticks to his guns," she wrote in a January endorsement letter, "and you know now how I feel about guns!"[123] Palin and rock musician Ted Nugent campaigned with Perry on Super Bowl Sunday, with Nugent delivering an ear-splitting version of the national anthem in the 8,500-seat arena in the Houston suburb of Cypress.

The national economy was still lagging, but Texas had begun to recover. At least, in Comptroller Combs's view, there was a path to recovery but no rocket ship.[124]

Hutchison couldn't exactly campaign against the state's recovery, but she could certainly question how much credit Perry should receive. "It's not because he's handing out $5 million checks to [encourage] companies to move here," she said, criticizing Perry's use of the Texas Enterprise Fund to lure companies to relocate or expand in the state, even as she admitted the idea was "legitimate" for "maybe making the last pitch."[125]

And her campaign was ready to pounce with video of Perry joking during a luncheon speech to the East Houston Chamber of Commerce. What recession? "We're in one?"[126]

Sure, Texas was better off than many places, but Texans were still suffering, and the video made the governor look out of touch. The Hutchison campaign was able to milk a rare, undisciplined moment.

The battle was clearly about more than Perry versus Hutchison. Texas was in the grip of Tea Party furor and had been ground zero for grassroots conservatism for more than a decade. Most activists, including new Republican Party state chair Cathie Adams, backed Perry.[127] But even he wasn't conservative enough for many activists, since business taxes had gone up on his watch while a voter identification law had stalled and, in activists' views at least, the high cost of illegal immigration had been ignored.

Dissent came in the form of a third Republican candidate, Debra Medina. Medina was a Wharton nurse who ran a medical billing company; she was a Tea Party activist who took a hard line on immigration, gun rights, and property rights—the *Guardian* dubbed her "a Texan Sarah Palin."[128] She entered politics with her pastor's encouragement in the early 1990s, attending the Wharton County Republican convention in 1992 and watching in horror as deacons from her small Southern Baptist church defeated the pro-life plank of the convention.

"It just about killed me," she said. "I thought, holy shit. It was mind-boggling to me that my own deacons could take that position. They didn't feel that it [abortion] should be in a Republican Party platform."[129]

Democrats were still in charge in the state House, and GOP leaders were concerned they would lose voters if they moved too far right on the issue.

Like Perry, Medina ran on an anti-Washington message, but her positions were more extreme. She favored unilaterally withdrawing from international trade treaties with Mexico. She favored using state resources to deport undocumented immigrants and ignoring federal mandates and environmental regulations. She opposed any new taxes, tolls, or fees. She didn't rule out seceding from the United States. She was riding a wave of conservative anger, fed by the belief that the federal government was doing too much and spending too much money doing it.[130]

But Medina was also at war with the Texas Republican Party, which she accused of systematically shutting out "liberty leaning" activists like herself in favor of easily controlled grassroots volunteers who guaranteed predetermined outcomes. Medina was not easily controlled and was proud of it, representing a group of aggressive activists who were angry that their elected leaders ran on conservative talking points but governed in a more moderate way. She and her group worked to block Republicans against the pro-life platform by taking control of local party apparatus. They even took the Republican Party to court for violating its own rules by not allowing some social conservatives to attend county or state conventions.[131] The rift with the establishment widened.

Perry and Hutchison were both awful, in her assessment.

Perry was a false Tea Party prophet, in her view, talking small government while spending big. Tea Party activists disapproved of the Trans-Texas Corridor, and they wanted constitutional carry, which allowed people to openly carry a gun without being licensed, something mainstream Republicans had yet to pick up.

"[Our] country is going bankrupt and it's Republicans who are leading us there," Medina made clear.[132]

Ultimately, Medina was the only name that activists could agree on, and she began months of traveling the state.[133] Although her crowds were growing, radio stations didn't want to talk with her, television stations ignored her. But then came the debates. The second debate was key, generating significant interest. Website traffic exploded; the Medina campaign generated more traffic than a national advertising campaign. The campaign raised more money in the twenty-four hours after the debate than in the other weeks of the campaign combined.[134]

Some of her comments on the campaign trail were startling, as she argued the government shouldn't license or regulate firearms or require children to go to school. In an interview on the conservative Glenn Beck radio show, she refused to dismiss theories that the government was involved in the September 11, 2001, terrorist attacks.[135] "That turned me plumb off her," said an Amarillo-area rancher who had been considering voting for her.[136]

Medina later tried to walk back the comments, but it was hard to unring that dinner bell. "They just fled," Medina later said of voters inclined to support her.[137]

Perry feared she would pull enough conservative support to deny him a majority of votes in the first round. She didn't, but the 19 percent of votes she did garner provided ample evidence that angry Republicans were on the rise.

Other Republicans were getting primaried, too—seventeen of the seventy-seven Republicans in the state House had at least one primary opponent. Channeling anger at the federal government's "giveaway" stimulus programs, Texas groups like Empower Texans and Young Republicans of Texas sought fresh conservative blood to challenge Republican incumbents, people like accountant Charles Perry, who successfully challenged thirty-year House veteran Delwin Jones in West Texas, and David Simpson, who was also successful in his challenge to longtime representative Tommy Merritt in Longview. Simpson said voters in the deep East Texas district were upset about politicians "ignoring the Constitution, destroying our freedom, grabbing all this power. People are angry . . . they're frightened, they think they're going to lose their country."[138]

Jones, among the first generation of Republicans elected to the Texas House, had aligned with Straus but pointed to his votes against business taxes in 2006. "If that's moderate, then I guess I'm a moderate," Jones said.[139]

Perry did not take the race for granted, crisscrossing the state in custom-made ostrich-skin boots emblazoned with the Texas battle slogan, "Come and Take It." He looked sharp, touting his conservative record and experience as the state's chief executive like an evangelist. "When a company's been running right and making a profit, I don't think they want to can the CEO," he said. A woman at one campaign stop expressed fear that Texas education officials would "take God out of our history books"; Perry promised it wouldn't happen on his watch and gave her a big hug.[140]

As he had in past campaigns, Perry went aggressive early, with a January 2010 ad focused on Hutchison's support for federal spending.

"Voting with Washington since 1993," one ad ended, calling out Hutchison for hypocrisy for her support for federal spending while showcasing her biggest weakness—her time in Washington. The Perry campaign also reminded voters Hutchison was a contender for "Porker of the Year" by a conservative antigovernment spending group.[141]

Hutchison's campaign responded with a letter from Perry to West Virginia Democratic US Rep. Joe Manchin urging passage of a stimulus.

The old Perry campaign luck emerged in 2010, as well. A social media director for the Perry campaign had been in Waco and seen Hutchison deliver her (now infamous) 2008 remarks about refusing to deliver a blank check even to Ronald Reagan, given the day before she voted for a massive federal bailout of the financial industry. It was a "fortuitous thing" that he recorded it, kept it, and was able to find it. The Perry campaign hired him.[142]

Hutchison hit Perry on the state's new business tax, which she called a "tragic mistake." She challenged him on requiring the state to use the federal "E-Verify" program to ensure state workers' legal status. She chastised him on the "hired cronies" who pushed for the HPV vaccine mandate and on the Trans-Texas Corridor, which had proven politically unpopular. Responding to an angry Gainesville landowner threatened by the corridor, Hutchison replied, "Well, you *should* be angry," and insisted it wouldn't really be dead until she was governor.[143]

This aggressive populist rhetoric had worked in Texas in the past, but it fell flat coming from the studious and "senatorial" Hutchison, who lacked Perry's "colorful bombast." Or Medina's crazed fervor.[144]

Perry described his election and fight against the overreach of the federal government as a "struggle for the heart and soul of our nation." He hammered home the point that Washington is a different place than newly conservative Texas. Elections are different from governing. Hutchison's friendship with New York senator and former first lady Hillary Clinton became an issue for her—at an event at a museum devoted to women's history in Washington, Clinton was captured on video saying she was "delighted that Kay is my partner on so many fronts." The Hutchison camp, meanwhile, uncovered a letter from Perry, then agriculture commissioner, to Clinton as first lady in 1993, commending the healthcare reform efforts she was leading for the White House.[145]

Republican voters liked Hutchison, but the state's anti-Washington mood, her backing of embryonic stem cell research (which angered evangelical conservatives), and her support for the 1973 US Supreme Court decision legalizing abortion all hurt her. (Of likely Republican voters, 48 percent reported they would not vote for a candidate who supported *Roe v. Wade*.)[146]

She was every bit as conservative as Perry on a number of other issues, including opposing gay marriage and supporting gun rights, but her soft-edged brand of conservatism didn't attract the type of primary voter she needed to win. And Hutchison lacked Perry's easy ability to assimilate into the political surroundings. Where he could slip from pinstriped suit into jeans and cowboy boots without missing a beat, observers saw something unnatural about her efforts to don a "denim blouse, flouncy skirt and monogrammed cowgirl boots to blend in with the studiously quaint backdrops of hay and tractors and quarter horses."[147]

Still, Perry had problems of his own. Fewer than half of those surveyed in February 2010 approved of his performance as governor, even as his constituency in a state shifting ever more conservative propped him up. He was popular with men, older voters, and wealthier Texans. But the base of the party was changing. While he had the traditional

GOP constituency, he also was able to win the new base of the party by virtue of being a culture warrior; he didn't cede that vote to Medina.

"Perry was sufficiently a culture warrior, and she wasn't," said Harvey Kronberg. "He was a rare politician who could blend a middle-finger salute to the establishment while being the establishment."[148]

Fired-up Republican activists "in no mood for compromises" at the GOP convention in Dallas in summer 2010 threw out Chair Cathie Adams in favor of Houston businessman Steve Munisteri. The members bucked Perry, calling for a plank in the platform making it illegal for undocumented immigrants to "intentionally or knowingly" live in Texas and for legislation similar to Arizona's law that required local police to verify legal residency when making arrests. Keynote speaker Mississippi governor Haley Barbour waived Republicans away from purity tests. "It's a big party and we need everybody who is on our side."[149]

Delegates paid little mind as they considered a resolution pressing House Republicans to remove and replace Joe Straus as Speaker.[150]

Perry won the Republican primary with just over half the vote, avoiding a runoff by beating one challenger to his ideological right as well as a moderate with whom he'd built the Texas Republican Party starting in the early 1990s. "I think the message is pretty clear: Conservatism has never been stronger than it is today," Perry said after claiming the primary victory. "We're taking our country back, one vote at a time, one election at a time."[151]

Once again a strong campaign organization had shielded him from the most damaging attacks—he exploited the moment well, framed his opponents well, and stayed on message. Hutchison had tried to make the case that Perry overstayed his political welcome, but she was never able to clearly articulate why he didn't deserve another term, ending the primary with just over 30 percent of the vote. Medina received almost 19 percent.

Perry nationalized the race—jabbing at high-spending, border-ignoring Washington, DC—and crafted his candidacy around the budding Tea Party movement, while preventing the race from becoming a referendum on his politics or policies.

Conservative columnist Fred Barnes called Perry's win over Hutchison "a signal."[152] A signal of the far-right politics to come, and it was here to stay.

On the Democratic side, former Houston mayor Bill White easily dispatched six challengers, earning 76 percent of the vote as he prepared to take on Perry.

White brought a lengthy resume to the task—a native of San Antonio, he attended Harvard University and law school at the University of Texas, worked in the oil and gas industry, and served as state Democratic Party chair. He ran for mayor of Houston after serving as deputy energy secretary in the Clinton administration, governing Houston more like a city manager than a visionary ideologue.

He came out swinging, calling the governor's anti-Washington message a distraction from his own failed record. "Perry is more interested in the angry headline," White said, but he contended that rage politics didn't address the issues.[153]

In White, Perry faced a candidate offering the clearest contrast of his political life. Perry was a back-slapping, political animal, while White came across as pragmatic, serious, and studious. The White campaign's efforts to shape his image early were a struggle: image-makers could not find a picture angle to make him look good.

White himself described the race as the "show horse" versus the "workhorse," and he made it clear whom he considered the show horse. His image was that of a micromanager, studying the issues, measured in his messaging, and the antithesis of television friendly—journalists called his voice "drone-like" and noted that even his name was bland.[154]

He was the kind of Democrat the party had been waiting for: a lifelong Democrat, a wunderkind technocrat like Bill Clinton with the policy sensibilities of Barack Obama, a bipartisan, big-city mayor with political experience, and a candidate who could raise big money. (He had raised more than $10 million by the campaign's end.)

The party's exile from statewide offices had given the GOP an aura of invincibility, and Democrats were worried about fundraising after the 2008 death of Fred Baron, a wealthy Dallas trial lawyer and holder of the purse strings on the party's funds. Democrats had shown modest success of late—coming within two seats of flipping the Texas House in 2006, gaining seats in the state Senate, and benefitting from the move of urban counties towards the Democrats in 2008. But a state-wide win eluded them, despite committed megadonors, allied organizations such as Annie's List, and a plan to build on successes.[155]

And in 2010 there was no Barack Obama on the ballot to rally Democrats.

Perry's strategy was simple: nail down support from economic conservatives, embrace social issues to cement his standing with social conservatives, and tickle religious conservatives with talk about the great spiritual battle under way for the state and the nation.[156] As journalist Jay Root put it:

> On the campaign trail, Perry was the consummate Texas country boy. He skewered federal bureaucrats and political insiders with a deep Paint Creek drawl that he can turn on and off at will. He made "stimulus" sound like a dirty word. This isn't Bush's compassionate conservatism. His is a full-throttle, blue-collar, pro-gun, states' rights, red-meat conservatism.[157]

Former opponents grudgingly admitted Perry knew how to win elections. "Whip up the right, and you don't have to worry about anything else," Strayhorn's former communications director said.[158] Carney, who was so closely aligned with Perry that he functioned as his alter ego, recognized this trend in Republican Party politics, and Perry made himself "the Christian candidate."[159]

It wasn't the "rise of the Christian conservatives," but they were becoming more central to Republican Party politics. At the state party convention, Perry was a "revival preacher," talking about issues of importance to Evangelicals.[160] He joined Glenn Beck in Tyler for a "Taking Back America" town hall, complete with American flags and Christian rock music. "If you care about America, if you care about taking this country back, you find you a Tea Party. Get involved," Perry said to wild applause from about five thousand people waiving American and Gadsden flags.[161]

He visited megachurches, reminding supporters and cynics alike that retail politics still worked, even in a massive state like Texas. Never mind the critics who scoffed that only Rick Perry could "turn a day about the Lord into a day about Rick Perry."[162]

Fundraisers for the governor were often protein-heavy events (chicken-fried venison, wild boar, and stuffed pheasant at one fundraiser featuring country singer Pat Green), where the number of people in attendance was limited and the guest list secret.[163] He laid on the politics as thick as the gravy. Perry issued a proclamation declaring a "day of prayer" after the Deepwater Horizon disaster, which killed eleven workers and spewed tens of millions of gallons of crude oil into the Gulf of Mexico. The campaign sponsored Bobby Labonte's car at NASCAR races at the Texas Motor Speedway—the hood of the car read "GOVERNOR PERRY" and the sides were emblazoned with the name of the campaign website: RickPerry.org.

Guns and gun control became an issue. White resigned his position with a New York–based gun control group, Mayors Against Illegal Guns, saying he opposed new restrictions on firearms. He had joined the group in 2006 after a major spike in gun deaths; gun sales spiked in 2008 on fears that Barack Obama and a Democratic Congress would swiftly limit firearms.[164] (They did not.)

White said he planned to apply for a concealed carry permit, but Perry went one better. He often bragged about jogging while carrying a laser-sighted pistol, and in April 2010 he told the Associated Press that he had shot and killed a coyote that threatened his daughter's young dog, Rory, during a jog. (The dog was the offspring of a black lab given to Perry's son as a graduation gift by John Sharp. Perry was out that early morning on a golf course before church on a Sunday and took long enough dealing with the situation that his security detail worried where he was.)[165]

It was Rick Perry to a T. As David Carney described it,"There is zero chance that was not 1,000 percent Rick Perry, including running on the golf course, where he wasn't supposed to be, including wearing those silly running shorts, including shooting the coyote with one bullet, and throwing it in the brush for other coyotes to eat it. That's just the way he is."[166]

The event inspired the manufacture of a special-issue Ruger .380 caliber handgun ("for sale to Texans only"), a replica of the weapon Perry used to defend his dog. It was marketed as the Coyote Special, complete with the words "A True Texan" emblazoned on the side. Perry was endorsed by the National Rifle Association in September. "Everyone knows Rick Perry is pro-gun. The coyote population knows he's pro-gun," said the NRA's chief lobbyist.[167]

The coyote shooting made a great story, but White focused on a darker narrative, one that had been pushed by previous Perry opponents to little avail. Describing the three-term governor as a career politician who "looks out for his friends and benefactors," White pledged high-wage jobs, better public schools, and results on border security.[168] "He does more image and I do more reality," he said of Perry.[169]

White's multipoint education plan called for expanding prekindergarten, improving technical education through two-year colleges, and making college education more affordable. He called for term limits on Texas governors, despite appointing a commission as mayor to study extending term durations for the mayor and city council. He called for hiring a thousand new local law enforcement officers and 250 state troopers and promised to "revamp" the Texas Department of Public Safety in an attempt to draw attention to what he saw as the governor's failure at the border.[170]

"Welcome to the debate," Perry said, pointing out that he had called for a similar increase and that the state had already spent considerable money on the problem. "His campaign is very high on criticism and very light on any new ideas," Perry said.[171]

These were all practical solutions, but they failed to animate the race. Many of White's proposals were similar to Perry's own programs and didn't effectively set him apart from Perry.

Perry linked White to Obama at every turn, continuing the anti-Washington screed that had proven effective against Hutchison. He contended that White, a lawyer, was in cahoots with other trial lawyers who were bleeding Texas dry. Houston was also part of the problem, in Perry's view—the city's finances were a mess, and it was too friendly to undocumented immigrants, making it hard for the state to address the problem.[172] As mayor, White had turned Houston into a "sanctuary city" for undocumented immigrants, leading to the murder of a Houston police officer by an immigrant who had been deported multiple times. With a week to go before early voting began, Perry was on the air with an ad featuring the widow of the slain officer, calling White's approach in Houston a failure.[173]

In truth, the city did have a "hands off" policy towards undocumented immigrants, asking about immigration status only after arrest, but it also participated in the federal Secure Communities program, which checks the fingerprints of people arrested against federal databases to identify those with criminal histories who might be subject to deportation.[174]

And while Perry's detractors had long accused him of cronyism, White came under fire for his involvement in a billing dispute involving a company he recommended to help the region's recovery from Hurricane Rita.

White had served on the board of the company's parent company, and as mayor he appointed four of the seven seats to the governing board of the Coastal Water Authority, a state-level intergovernmental agency created by the legislature in 1967. At White's recommendation, the company provided power generators to the authority, which later complained that some of the generators did not work and that it would have been cheaper to lease them. White acknowledged making an initial call about the dispute, but records showed he was more involved in facilitating City Hall's assistance with billing issues and later invested in the company. He denied that the company received special treatment. Perry's team pounced, saying the mayor used his position to line up lucrative private business deals.[175]

The tactic was a common refrain in Perry's campaigns, beginning with his run for agriculture commissioner. Expose opponents' questionable financial dealings. Cling tight to social issues, and label opponents too liberal for Texas. Surprise dramatic mudslinging drop towards the campaign's end. Tout positive economy and job growth. Repeat.

White attacked Perry for raising campaign funds from tech firms who benefited from state money—longtime Perry donor David Nance's startup company, Convergent Life Sciences, received a $4.5 million award despite rejection by a regional screening board—and appointing big donors to political positions. The nonprofit Texans for Public Justice reported that more than $17 million of the $83 million Perry had raised since becoming governor came from people (or their spouses) he'd appointed to state boards, commissions, and agencies, transforming his appointment powers "into a well-oiled patronage machine."[176] White seized on the report, promising to make bipartisan appointments and limit appointees or their families to contributing no more than $10,000 per election cycle.

Late in the race White's campaign distributed the results of an external investigation of a 2009 whistleblower memo that described ethical lapses and insider deals at the $100 billion Teacher Retirement System of Texas and alleged special treatment for investment firm executives who made big contributions to Perry. The investigation found "no improprieties."[177] Ads called out Perry for a fancy Austin fundraiser where twenty-nine of the thirty hosts were lobbyists, many of whom were former Perry staff members from the "revolving door" Perry used to conduct state business.

None of the attacks stuck to Perry.

Perry tried another tack late that summer: unless the wealthy White released his income tax returns by September 15, Perry wouldn't agree to a debate. "Bill White's staunch opposition to transparency is unbecoming of someone seeking to be elected the chief executive of the greatest state in the nation," Perry said. "There is a very simple solution to this situation. Release your taxes, Mr. White, and we can move forward with debate preparations."[178]

He hinted darkly at serious repercussions if White were to be elected governor without disclosing his financial records, only to have potentially damaging details emerge once in office.[179]

Candidates are not required to publicly disclose their tax returns under state ethics laws, but it was standard practice for most. White released his returns for the years he served as mayor of Houston but not for the years when he served as deputy energy secretary or chair of the Texas Democratic Party. Perry provided tax returns dating back to 1991.

White's campaign countered that Perry was simply reluctant to answer tough questions about his record and noted that Perry had placed assets in a blind trust, which he said shielded them from scrutiny.[180]

The debate, sponsored by the state's five largest newspapers and an

Austin television station, was set for October, regardless of who planned to attend.

White claimed Perry's threats amounted to a lack of respect for Texas voters. But there was more at play. White needed the momentum he hoped the debate could provide, much as it had for Bell four years earlier, as polling in early fall showed Perry with a lead of five to seven points and strong support among conservatives, women, and rural Texans. White had an edge in urban areas like Austin and among moderates and independents.[181]

Despite millions of dollars in ad spending, the race was essentially unchanged since February, and the lack of movement had begun to hurt White's fundraising. After outraising Perry for much of the summer and fall, even if he didn't come close to the spending Sanchez unleashed in 2002, he was down to $3 million on hand in the final month of the race, while Perry reported $10 million. Perry also had more large donors, including six-figure donations from prominent GOP donors Harold Simmons of Dallas, Houston Astros owner Drayton McLane, and homebuilder Bob Perry.[182]

The debate seemed the last chance to turn that around. Influential Democratic supporters, including Houston attorney Steve Mostyn's group Back to Basics Political Action Committee, ran a newspaper campaign using a black-and-white photo of Perry emblazoned with "COWARD," in an effort to goad Perry into debating.[183] Perry also broke with another tradition and refused to meet with the editorial boards of major Texas newspapers, which overwhelmingly supported White. Perry's decision in 2010, reaching back to similar decisions in 2006, set a precedent many Republicans running for state office in Texas followed.

White didn't release the requested returns, and Perry stood by his ultimatum: he was a no-show at the only statewide, televised debate. Even so, he was the star attraction as White and two third-party candidates clubbed him in absentia. Libertarian Kathie Glass called Perry a phony conservative with a failed record. Green Party candidate Deb Shafto said she couldn't think of anything good Perry had done as governor.

White came prepared with a salvo about unleashed cronyism, Perry's "political machine," and a decade of mismanagement at the helm of Texas.[184]

Perry gave no sign he was concerned, slipping into cruise control for the final days of the campaign. He even took the Saturday before Election Day off to watch his beloved Aggies play football.

His optimism was well placed—he received 55 percent of the vote to White's 42 percent. That, Perry proclaimed afterward, was a clear signal that voters rejected big government and "wanted their freedoms back. The work is in front of us now. I think the American people said 'Listen, we're spending too much money on things that we don't want.'"[185]

He won two-to-one among voters angry with the federal government and those worried about the direction of the economy.[186] Just as he had with Hutchison during the Republican primary, he managed to successfully connect White with not just Washington, DC, but also the unpopular president, running ads calling White an "Obama-style individual."

The rhetoric certainly helped fuel sales of Perry's new book, *Fed Up! Our Fight to Save America from Washington.* The book was ghost-written by conservative wunderkind Chip Roy, who himself would go on to win a seat in Congress.

The questions that had swirled in the background for several years grew louder. Would Perry run for president? He demurred, without really saying no. "Anyone running for the presidency is not going to go take on these issues with the power that I do," he said.[187]

White may have polled a dozen points higher than Bell had four years earlier, but the result was the same. Democrats were in the wilderness, even if they presented a stronger and more well-funded candidate. Republicans cemented their supremacy in Texas.

Anger at the Obama administration shaped every race. White's scattershot approach to strategy didn't help, as he moved from one listless attack line to another.[188]

Issues cut against him, too, as he was seen as too willing to support "cap and trade" efforts to reduce carbon emissions in a state built on the energy industry; neither would he rule out higher debt or tax increases to relieve highway congestion. He drew support both from former president Bill Clinton and from President Obama, but the latter, especially, proved complicated. White decided not to meet with Obama during the president's Texas trip, fearing it would add fuel to Perry's anti-Washington crusade. That angered Black Democrats, who responded with lukewarm support.[189]

One of his opponents in the Democratic primary, hair-care magnate Farouk Shami, endorsed Perry, saying he hadn't liked his dealings with White and the Democratic Party. Besides, he joked in a reference to his best-known product line, Perry had "good hair because he uses CHI."[190]

In the end the Republican tide was simply too strong. The slow gravitation of voters towards the GOP in the former Democratic strongholds of East Texas and rural West Texas hit the gas in 2008 and 2010, driven by anger at Washington and an African American president who shaped racial identity and shifted support. "Straight Republican," a retired Midland oil worker said to describe how he had just voted. "I don't like Obama. He's a socialist."[191]

Democrats lost twenty-four state House seats, including those of longtime incumbents who hadn't been considered vulnerable, in addition to losing their House caucus leader. A new, more confrontational strain of Republican was morphing from the Democrats' disaster.

Other statewide Republican incumbents, including Dewhurst, Abbott, and Agriculture Commissioner Todd Staples, won easily. With Perry at the top of the ticket, Republicans rolled up two-to-one margins among white voters (who made up two-thirds of the Texas electorate), wealthy voters, evangelical Christians (one-third of the electorate), and voters who wanted tougher immigration laws. Perry received almost 40 percent of the Latino vote.[192]

White won by only twenty thousand votes in his adopted hometown of Houston.

Many conservative Republicans had run on social rather than economic issues, a slight but important shift in how the Republican Party would approach legislation. Some had run under the Tea Party banner, angered by Obamacare. Others cited the failure in the House of a bill, sponsored by Dan Patrick in the Senate, that would have required a doctor to describe the details of a sonogram before a woman could have an abortion. Mainstream, moderate Republicans lost to more conservative primary challengers, significantly reshaping the Republican caucus in ways that would manifest in a more conservative session in 2011.

Perry was poised to take advantage. A strong incumbent with a large war chest, spending $42 million to White's $25 million, he used his perch to "brush off bad news."[193] He repositioned himself as a Tea Party–loving conservative in a state where anti-Washington sentiment was high, the economy was strong, and Republicans had the baked-in advantages of incumbency and healthy campaign funds.

A quarter of the electorate described themselves as being part of the Tea Party movement.[194] Only two in five Texans rated President Obama favorably.[195] This was a turning point for Texas. Democratic legislative leader Jim Dunnam remembers that his Republican colleagues were talking about "this force in their own primary they didn't know what to do about. They even said these people are crazy. They lost control of their own party."[196]

Talk of secession, constitutionalism, and federalism percolated throughout the state, "music to the ears of every Tea Party member," said one observer.[197] The executive director of the Democratic Governors Association considered Perry's record and cast him as an embodiment of the "radicalization of the GOP."[198]

The win continued Perry's twenty-five-year streak of electoral success, and his stock was still rising, thanks to anti-Washington sentiment and an antitax conservative vision sweeping the nation.

The race would be his last in Texas but not his last campaign.

—9—
THE 2011 SESSION AND
THE 2012 PRESIDENTIAL ELECTION

"I can't . . . Oops"

The glow of winning a record-setting fourth term wore off quickly. By 2011 the state faced a $15 billion hole in its upcoming budget cycle, including a drop of $7.8 billion in revenue, even with the federal stimulus money. That number was closer to $27 billion if the state maintained status quo spending. A wicked combination of lower consumer spending (which resulted in lower sales tax revenue), lower property tax values, higher enrollment in public schools and healthcare programs, and a spike in healthcare costs all contributed to the state's grim economic outlook. This was a mix of lingering effects of the Great Recession and Texas's booming population growth.

The vaunted 2006 tax swap—replacing property taxes with a new business tax—did not generate the expected funds and created a structural shortfall in the budget. Perry asked state agencies to plan for 10 percent cuts in the upcoming 2012–2013 budget.

Perry downplayed the state's financial predicament. "I don't think it's the end of the world," he said. "I don't think it's apocalyptic."[1]

The economic calamity came at a time when fiscally conservative Republicans ruled the statehouse with dominant majorities (including two Democratic members who switched to the Republican Party just after the 2010 elections). Tea Party Republicans pressed to cut programs and eliminate taxes, and one of Perry's overriding philosophies was "Don't spend all the money."

"There are no excuses now," said Rep. Dan Patrick, a Tea Party conservative before the phrase was coined. "It's a perfect storm, in a positive way, for conservatism." Perry played along. "It's only a budget hole when somebody has wished that they had more money," he quipped.[2] He repeated his promise to oppose tax increases but left open the door to possible hikes in fees or using the state's Rainy Day Fund.

Lt. Gov. David Dewhurst struck the same tuning fork: "Unlike Washington, the Texas Legislature prioritizes spending based on available revenue, not from an infinite wish list of earmarks and automatic spending increases." Democrats disagreed, but their political hole was even deeper than the state's fiscal hole. If the 99 Republican members in the House, a record, wanted "to slash and burn, that's what they will do," Rep. Garnet Coleman acknowledged.[3]

Despite darkening economic skies, Perry was in a good position. Fifty-one percent of Texans approved of his job performance (including 73 percent of Republicans), and two-thirds thought he should run for president. Even the so-called moderate Joe Straus kept his job as House Speaker after a leadership challenge. He was ultimately reelected by a 132–15 vote, including 49 Democratic votes, a rare display of bipartisanship in an increasingly divided Capitol.

"Division, threats of retribution, attacks on people's religious beliefs, and distortions of people's records have no place in this House," Straus said after winning the post, referring to attacks by some conservatives on his Jewish faith. "The men and women who are remembered beyond their years are not those who sow the seeds of discord, but those who plant for a future they may never see."[4]

The opposition Straus faced from die-hard conservatives was a harbinger of battles to come. A sign below the staircase leading to the House chamber summed up the mood: "We Are Watching You." A pair of tiny green binoculars hung from the poster board.

Perry's agenda was big—rumors of a presidential run animated what he called a "Texas Century." Following the swearing in by Wallace B.

Jefferson, chief justice of the state supreme court, whom Perry had appointed, Perry delivered his inaugural address on January 18, 2011, on a sunny but windy day at the Capitol.[5] "You know, for 154 years they kept an Aggie out of the governor's office," he said. "You know there are some people out there are wondering if I'm ever going to leave."[6]

He pointed to the sacrifice in battle of so many Texans, channeling his presidential voice in asking those who served their nation to stand or wave—heroes who paid the price of freedom with their own blood with a sacrifice that "no man or woman should ever endure."

"Sacrifice" would be the watchword of his term. "Tough economic times require strong leadership and tough choices for everyone," he said. "If we cannot exercise fiscal discipline in governing Texas, I doubt it can be achieved anywhere, least of all in Washington."

His optimistic message was the same in the State of the State address to the legislature on February 8, kicking off what he labeled an "historic legislative session."[7]

Sacrifices must be made, but other states were in even more dire budget straits, he said. "Now, the mainstream media and big government interest groups are doing their best to convince us that we're facing a budget Armageddon. Texans don't believe it, and they shouldn't, because it's not true."

Belt tightening and streamlining state government would move Texas through tough economic times and leave the state "more competitive than ever."

It was a recounting of Perry's greatest hits. Washington was failing, and Texas led the way. Individual liberty and small government. Fiscal discipline through reduced spending and not raising taxes. There is no such thing as government money; it's the people's money in government's hands.

Pulling a line from his book *Fed Up!*, he pounced on immigration, saying Texas would not compound the failure of the federal government to fight illegal immigration. "We must keep taking the fight to vicious Mexican drug cartels, and the gangs that operate in our state on their behalf, as we support the men and women of law enforcement who remain on the front lines of this struggle."

"Some will say we're just spoiling for a fight," he said, concluding his critique of the federal government, "and I'll admit that Texans rarely walk away from a tussle. But we'll also never walk away from our freedom."

It was never a question that Texas under Perry would not expand Medicaid, which provides healthcare for low-income residents through the Affordable Care Act, better known as Obamacare. Both the politics of federalized healthcare and the dislike of President Obama made Perry's decision to reject expansion politically easy. Aiding the governor's office were market-hugging think tanks, such as the Foundation for Government Accountability and the Texas Public Policy Foundation, which argued that expanding Medicaid to cover more people would drive up costs for both the state and the federal government while taking away from the state's flexibility to implement its own reforms and doing nothing to reduce the number of uninsured Texans.

Perry concluded his State of the State with a laundry list of conservative desires: voter ID, a crackdown on illegal immigration, a requirement for doctors to conduct and discuss a sonogram of the fetus before providing an abortion, and a call for an amendment to the US Constitution requiring Congress to balance the federal budget.

His emergency (top) items included ending the practice of "sanctuary cities" for undocumented immigrants and protecting private property, and he called for public universities to offer four-year degrees for $10,000 and expand college opportunities for military veterans.

Republicans, fresh off massive wins, wanted a live kill—and Perry delivered.

Rep. Lon Burnam (D-Fort Worth) claimed Republicans "want to shortchange hardworking, overtaxed Texans by cutting basic services to make up the shortfall they created."[8]

But with only 55 seats in the House, there just wasn't much Democrats could do to stop them.

Legislation couldn't solve every problem, and Perry turned to a higher power as extreme drought and burning wildfires scorched more than 1.8 million acres, destroyed nearly four hundred homes, and killed two firefighters battling the blazes. In April 2011 the governor asked Texans to pray for rain. The drought grew worse over the next four months, with no significant rainfall until the fall.

Perry's embrace of his role as the state's prayer-promoter-in-chief indirectly led to an embarrassing revelation of the ways in which his money didn't always match his mouth—an investigation found that through 2009, he had given one-half of one percent of his earnings to churches and religious organizations, or about $14,000.[9] He did donate his 2008 pay raise to charity, and his spokesperson made the larger point that tithing is only one aspect of a person's faith.

One month after Texans had been asked to pray for rain, and a month further into the deadly drought, legislators were locked in tense negotiations over the budget. Susan Combs, the state comptroller, offered a mild reprieve in mid-May, announcing the state had an additional $1.2 billion to spend over the next two years. "The recovery from the recession is under way."[10]

That was good news, but it wasn't enough to spare lawmakers the complex political and financial work of plugging the hole to fully fund public education.

Initial budget drafts cut $14 billion from the budget overall, including $5 billion from public schools; the cuts also eliminated funding for four community colleges and state financial aid for incoming college students. Medicaid reimbursement rates had been slashed, as well. As the governor celebrated his record-setting inauguration, the Democrats fumed. "No financial aid for kids to go to college. No pre-kindergarten for kids to learn their numbers and their letters. Health and human services slashed," said Rep. Pete Gallego (D-Alpine). "No Texan can be proud of this."[11]

After weeks of negotiation, Perry and House leaders agreed to use about one-third, $3.2 billion, of the state's reserve to plug the *current* budget hole—but not for the hole in the 2012–2013 budget, which had to be approved during the current session. Legislators would have to find another way to fund the budget for the coming biennium. Perry promised that no sacred cows would be spared from the budget, but protecting the Rainy Day Fund would be a badge of honor for Republicans.

"I remain steadfastly committed to protecting the remaining balance of the Rainy Day Fund and will not sign a 2012–2013 state budget that uses the Rainy Day Fund," Perry proclaimed.[12]

The Senate disagreed. The chamber's proposed 2012–2013 budget was $12 billion higher than the House plan and counted on drawing extra money from the Rainy Day Fund, just as legislators had agreed for the 2011–2012 budget. Any spending beyond the $3.2 billion for the prior biennium's budget from the RDF would not pass the House and would rile conservatives in the Senate.[13]

The House wasn't the only impediment to that plan. Patrick, who had been elected to the Senate with strong Tea Party backing, argued for preserving the Rainy Day Fund. Texans for Fiscal Responsibility felt the same, putting Steve Ogden, chair of the Senate Finance Committee, in a tight spot.

"The question I ask my colleagues is 'What do we have it for?'" he asked. "If you're not going to use the Rainy Day Fund when it's raining, we might as well get rid of it." But without twenty-one votes—Patrick's efforts to abolish the two-thirds rule had so far been unsuccessful—the Senate couldn't move forward. It would have to make more cuts.[14]

At that point, Ogden said, "You're down to a mess."[15]

Closed-door meetings between Dewhurst and Perry yielded no results. Dewhurst, considering a run for US Senate in 2012, wasn't eager to anger conservatives inside the chamber or outside. So the Senate went nuclear.

Senate leadership used a loophole in Senate rules that allows them to take up House bills without a two-thirds agreement, a welcome move for Patrick, who in the 2009 session spearheaded a nasty fight to kill the two-thirds "blocker bill" rule altogether. "I stand on the shoulders of our founding fathers," Patrick said. "The majority should not be blocked by one-third of our body."[16]

Old-timers like John Whitmire—first elected to the Senate from a central Houston district in 1983—opposed the move, saying Senate rules allow the legislature to collectively "cool things down, to be cautious."[17] But with a looming budget disaster, exploding deadlines, and a conservative majority watching closely, the Senate bypassed tradition and passed the budget on a party line vote 19–12. Democrats were resigned. "No longer will any minority party in the Senate have a say in the budget bill," Van de Putte said.[18] This was certainly prophetic, as the two-thirds rule would be whittled down to a five-ninths rule requiring eighteen instead of twenty Senators to support moving legislation forward. Republicans won enough seats to hit that number, leaving Democrats with little say in the upper chamber.

Ultimately, the financial squeeze on Texans came not through the front door but the back. No new taxes, sure, but the state hiked fees, repealed tax exemptions, reduced college financial aid, and instituted toll roads to make the budget work. The business tax did not receive the review some Republicans hoped. Even tinkering with taxes was a political loser for Republicans.

In addition to cuts to public education, the budget reduced funding for colleges, nursing homes, highway maintenance, state parks, and Medicaid reimbursements, which had reimbursement rates cut by $5 billion.

"Medicaid MasterCard," Democrats complained, comparing the deficit spending to that of Washington, DC, the subject of so many Republican complaints. Republicans were pleased if not jubilant, with Jim Pitts proclaiming it the second session in a row to cut state spending by more than a billion dollars. "That has never happened in this state's history."[19]

The Republican Caucus budget talking points emphasized that although they might be portrayed as heartless, cruel, and without compassion, the "ultimate form of compassion is honesty and truthfulness" about the woeful state of Texas's finances.[20]

For all the talk about not kicking the can down the road, lawmakers spent a lot of time kicking. The budget was balanced through accounting maneuvers and delayed payments (e.g., delaying a $2.3 billion payment to public schools by one day, pushing it to the next budget cycle).

It did follow through on Perry's core promises to avoid raising taxes and to take a minimum from the Rainy Day Fund.

Even with all of that, the 2011 session was the calm before the storm—a special session was coming to deal with redistricting, school finance, and other tense issues—allowing Perry to claim victory. He signed bills aimed at limiting frivolous lawsuits by levying fees on plaintiffs, allowing meritless suits to be dismissed earlier in the process, and requiring unsuccessful plaintiffs to pay their opponents' court costs and attorney fees.

Perry also signed a bill authorizing state restitution to people who had been wrongly imprisoned, sparked by Anthony Graves, who spent eighteen years in prison, including a dozen on death row, wrongly convicted of murder. The state paid Graves $1.4 million.

Republicans finally got several conservative wish-list bills that had eluded them two years earlier, including the abortion sonogram bill, sponsored by Rep. Sid Miller of Stephenville, requiring abortion providers to conduct and describe the results of a sonogram before an abortion.[21]

Voter ID finally passed, too, requiring voters to present a valid state or federal photo identification card.[22] The Obama Department of Justice challenged the law, arguing that it was discriminatory and designed to suppress the minority vote in violation of the Voting Rights Act. A federal court ultimately backed Texas in 2018, allowing the law to stand.

A special session was imminent, but Perry was on the move, with travel to New Orleans, New York City, and North Carolina, spreading the gospel of Rick Perry.

Democrats reacted with disdain. "He went from just paying partial attention to the Legislature to paying zero attention as he's kicking off his presidential non-campaign," said Rep. Jessica Farrar, leader of the House Democrats. "I do hope he can find some time in his busy schedule to do what he's paid to do, which is to sign this budget."[23]

The session was less live combat and more like a military drill—lawmakers barely broke a sweat in swiftly moving to pass education reforms. Why worry? Republicans had significant majorities and the governor's pull to seal the deal.

Perry added retooling the Texas Windstorm Insurance Association to the agenda, as promised. It passed. A bill addressing aggressive patdowns during airport security screenings made intentional, inappropriate touching during screening a criminal offense after a similar measure had failed during the regular session, prompting Patrick to accuse Dewhurst of killing the measure.[24] The new version provided security officials with a defense if they claimed a reasonable suspicion sparked the search, prompting a small group of conservative activists to call out "Traitor!" to members below.[25]

Republican infighting spoiled efforts to give police more power to inquire about a detainee's citizenship status. Democrats smirked as Perry and Republican lawmakers angrily pointed fingers. Dewhurst blamed the House, calling out House Republican leader Larry Phillips of Friendswood for going to the Bahamas on vacation when Dewhurst skipped his annual trip to Normandy in order to be in Austin for the special session. The House blamed the Senate. Perry blamed Sen. Robert Duncan, who was the lead negotiator on the budget bill who refused to add the immigration provision, prompting the Senate Republican Caucus to tell Perry to "back off."[26]

A measure to strip local law enforcement agencies of the ability to make immigration violations a lower priority failed, as did a requirement to check an applicant's immigration status before issuing a driver's license. An unusual coalition of Democrats and business groups typically allied with Perry joined forces to stop the latter bill (for the present) amid worries it would hurt business and increase the harassment of Latinos. But Republican Tommy Williams from the Woodlands successfully added it to the school finance bill, making it law.[27]

Even with the driver's license law tacked on, the school funding bill passed with little fanfare, as did an additional $2 million for armored patrol boats to police the Rio Grande and $40 million to battle wildfires caused by a punishing drought across the state. Legislators again refused to tap the Rainy Day Fund or kill the business tax. The $4 billion in cuts to school finance formulas, along with an additional $1.4 billion in cuts to education programs, were so deep, many teachers and school trustees feared the state would never recover. "Right now, we're driving a '72 Ford Pinto, not a Cadillac," a school administrator from Pflugerville testified.[28]

Legislators privatized more Medicaid services, as Perry had requested, and banned organizations that receive state funding from partnering with family planning groups that also provide abortion.

It took six months, but Republicans accomplished most of what they wanted and all of what they needed. Perry could brag that he balanced the budget without raising taxes in the midst of painful economic times by doing what Texas families were doing, living within their means.

Democrats could only sputter helplessly. "This is like a bad movie that just won't end," Sylvester Turner said.[29] Without sufficient numbers in the House (even with an accommodating Speaker) and with the erosion of the two-thirds rule (although it had yet to be removed), Republicans held the upper hand.

Perry liked to say that being governor of Texas was "the best job in America," but his appetite for bigger horizons was growing. His charismatic smile and custom-made "Come and Take It" boots were on full display for an April *Newsweek* cover story, fanning the political flames. "Give 'em a little leg?" Perry said obligingly to the photographer against the backdrop of the gleaming Capitol dome.[30]

In New York in June 2011 for the annual Lincoln Dinner, a fundraising event for the New York GOP, he filled in as the keynote speaker for Donald Trump, who had recently passed on running for president in 2012. "I find it ironic to be filling in for Donald Trump tonight," Perry said. "He's known for saying 'You're fired.' We're known for saying 'You're hired.' That's what we do in Texas."

His speech hit the usual themes. "Washington isn't supposed to be the all-powerful, all-knowing, all-spending Oz, pulling the levers behind the curtain while limiting the freedom of our citizens. Instead, the states are supposed to lead the way."[31]

By the end of the 2011 session, he acknowledged that he was "going through a thoughtful process" to discern his political future. "I'm basically asking people, 'Do you think there's room in this presidential election for a full-throated, unapologetic fiscal conservative? And if you do think there's room, are you going to help?'"[32]

Speaking to donors in Colorado, the crowd chuckled when he slipped a little, starting his answer to one question, "As the president . . ."

Make that "As the governor of the state of Texas," he quickly corrected.[33]

A "Draft Perry 2012" website went live in late May, sponsored by several California state lawmakers. Conservative radio show host Rush Limbaugh cast Perry as the opposite of Washington elites. "And he's got great hair," Limbaugh said. "You are not going to be elected president unless you've got at least a 10-inch part in your hair."[34] Anita, his wife, privately urged him to run.[35]

But Perry was very reluctant to run, feeling the pressure of those around him and trying to deflect pleas. "I never really wanted to be president," he recalled later. A vision was relayed to him from a Christian witness (a woman named Kathy Sweat) of him and his grandson (he had no grandson at the time) in the Oval Office. As a "Christian who believes that there are people who have special gifts," meeting the woman and hearing the vision and affected him. "On the balance scale, it weighed down on the side that said you need to run."[36] (Perry's son Griffin later had a son who eventually did make it to the Oval Office for a picture with President Donald Trump in 2019.)

A month before making it official, Perry underwent back surgery that included a spinal fusion and nerve decompression to treat a recurring injury. The procedure used an experimental injection of his own stem cells, not embryonic stem cells, which he and other conservatives opposed on religious grounds. The non–FDA approved therapy was intended to boost tissue repair. In the meantime, he had to wear a back brace and trade his boots for orthopedic shoes.[37]

The timing, not the procedure, was a disaster for the nascent campaign. The doctors performing the procedure had said he would be as good as new after a short four weeks, just in time for a formal announcement. In reality, it took much longer to recover, and it was "debilitating for him," especially during a grueling campaign.[38]

But political campaigns are demanding taskmasters, and Perry couldn't wait long for what most people considered to be inevitable. On Aug. 10, 2011, he announced he would seek the Republican presidential nomination at the RedState gathering of conservative activists in Charleston, South Carolina, a key early battleground state.

"We cannot and must not endure four more years of rising unemployment, rising taxes, rising debt, and rising energy dependence on nations that intend us harm," he bridled. As a Washington outsider, he pledged to restore fiscal responsibility at home and US exceptionalism abroad, saying his goal as president would be to make Washington "as inconsequential in your lives as I can." He railed against the EPA, Obamacare, and federal bailouts, contending they frayed the fabric of individual freedom and hurt the nation's businesses.[39]

He was an instant contender, making splashy appearances in South Carolina and New Hampshire and leaving local activists gushing.[40]

But his focus was on the Iowa Straw Poll, where he hoped to make a strong showing over more established candidates. Since the Republican establishment hadn't yet rallied around a single candidate, Perry had a chance to unite a diverse Republican coalition: the Tea Party, evangelical Christians, and fiscal conservatives. He was more strongly connected to the party establishment than was Newt Gingrich, as libertarian as Ron Paul, as staunch a social conservative as Michelle Bachmann, and as attractive to evangelical Christians as Tim Pawlenty. With all those candidates, there was still an appetite for somebody else.[41] Perry might fit the bill.

For all Perry's advantages—a strong record as governor, prodigious fundraising capacity, political buzz—he had a rocky relationship with the conservative wing of the party. The emerging Tea Party faction challenged his record on immigration and public healthcare; and, by the way, he used to be a Democrat who had supported Al Gore's 1988 presidential bid. "It's real easy to walk into church on Sunday morning and sing from the hymnal. I saw a guy that talked like a Tea Party candidate but didn't govern like one," said Debra Medina, the Texas activist who had challenged Perry in the 2010 Republican gubernatorial primary. "I still don't think he governs like the conservative he professes to be."[42]

Fellow Texan and presidential rival Ron Paul, a libertarian congressman from the Houston area, ran the first negative ad against Perry, contrasting Paul's 1980 support of Ronald Reagan to Perry's role eight years later as Gore's first presidential chair in Texas.

There were considerably more fronts in a presidential campaign than in a state campaign for governor. A whisper campaign grew to modest opposition as emails from allied organizations warned their followers, "We should be aware there is more to him than meets the eye."[43]

Anyone damning Perry as a moderate could find ample ammunition in an era where conservative activists were gaining power. As governor he'd signed laws offering in-state tuition to undocumented immigrants. He blasted the idea of a border wall as "idiocy." He backed tax hikes on businesses in supposedly business-friendly Texas. He had issued an executive order requiring an anticancer vaccine. He argued that Arizona's controversial immigration law was not right for Texas, although he later supported Arizona's right to pass such laws under the Tenth Amendment.

Democrats criticized him, too. Former president Bill Clinton called Perry a "good looking rascal" and brushed aside the governor's policies as "crazy."[44]

Perry had always had an uneasy working relationship with the most conservative wing of the party, but his political skills helped Texas Republicans earn major policy successes and political majorities. Yet he was about to discover that what worked in Texas might not work in New Hampshire or with a national Republican Party that was drifting to the right.

There was a fine line between being tough on illegal immigration and not offending the business lobby. As a cunning politician in a state where Latinos made up more than one-third of the population, Perry had been able to snag about one-third of the Latino vote. But he had to balance that against conservatives who wanted unprecedented crackdowns at the border.

Perry also needed the warp and weft of a campaign operation: hiring staff, collecting phone numbers from supporters in order to raise more money. Sen. Fred Thompson of Tennessee offered a cautionary tale. He'd been a strong candidate for president in 2008 but had entered the race late, which hampered his efforts. That was a risk for Perry in a race where some candidates had been running for literally years. The three-term Texas governor had never run a national campaign, although he had allies across the country through the Republican Governors Association.

The race was already crowded when Perry announced and included the frontrunner, former Massachusetts governor Mitt Romney, who had also run in 2008 and had a national fundraising network; Ron Paul; Pawlenty, the governor of Minnesota; former Utah governor Jon Huntsman; Gingrich, the former US House Speaker; Bachmann, a congresswoman from Minnesota; former Pennsylvania senator Rick Santorum; and former Godfather's Pizza CEO Herman Cain.

In a flash, he was in Iowa at a business roundtable, then to New Hampshire to headline the Politics and Eggs breakfast in Manchester, then back to South Carolina. His chief consultant was New Hampshire–based Dave Carney, who had spent the past fourteen years as an advisor to Perry and had left the Gingrich campaign earlier that summer.

Supporters flocked to Perry as he set up operations in Iowa, New Hampshire, and South Carolina. His boasts on Fox News about the Texas Miracle and the state's resilient economy helped establish him as a national voice.[45]

Fed Up!—Perry's 2010 diatribe against federal overreach and an impassioned defense of states' rights—provided the ideological anchor for his run. Washington was out of step with America's heartland, according to Perry, who said Americans were in a fight to "retake the reins of our government from a Washington establishment that has abused our trust." He called it "a battle for the soul of America."[46]

He had also described Social Security as a failure and a Ponzi scheme. And he criticized cuts to NASA's space shuttle program, which he said would leave American astronauts with no alternative but to hitchhike into space. He so favored states' rights that he was "fine" with New York state's approval of gay marriage. "That is their call. If you believe in the Tenth Amendment, stay out of their business."[47]

Within days of entering the race, Perry showed just how fed up he was with Washington by threatening the life of the Federal Reserve chair, Ben Bernanke. With characteristic Perry zeal, he contended that Bernanke's efforts to boost a sagging economy by purchasing treasury bonds to free up lending amounted to "treason." At an event in Iowa with his family by his side, Perry offered a blunt assessment. "If this guy prints more money between now and the election, I don't know what you all would do to him in Iowa, but we would treat him pretty ugly down in Texas. I mean, printing more money to play politics at this particular time in America history, is almost treacherous, treasonous in my view."[48] Since the punishment for treason is death, Perry's remarks were a direct threat on Bernanke's life.

Nervous laughter from the crowd followed. In fact, as an independent entity, the Federal Reserve kept out of partisan politics as much as possible and had recently announced it would keep interest rates flat through the election, in part to not influence the process.

President Obama's White House press secretary Jay Carney cautioned Perry that his "words have greater impact" because he was running for president. Even Karl Rove, who took credit for poaching Perry from the Democrats in the 1980s, said the comments were over the top and not a "presidential statement."[49]

Perry spokesman Ray Sullivan offered context but no apology: "The governor was passionate and energized by a full day of campaigning," he said. "It was his way to talk about his views on the budget and the country's fiscal problems."[50]

The episode suggested two things about Perry's campaign—it would be no-holds-barred, and it would be less disciplined than his tightly structured gubernatorial campaigns, where his team knew every angle.

The Tea Party might complain that Perry wasn't conservative enough, but his rugged brand of right-wing politics played well enough with many Republican primary voters. Selling that brand to moderates was a challenge.

Within days of announcing his bid for the nomination, and at a time when the evidence for human-influenced climate change was well accepted by most climate researchers, Perry said he did not believe the science behind global warming and accused scientists of manipulating data to get funding.[51]

More controversy followed. He opposed court rulings that found the Boy Scouts of America discriminated against gay scouts and leaders, citing his goal of minimal separation between church and state. He backed a ban on gay marriage, opposed a repeal of the "Don't Ask, Don't Tell" rule that effectively closeted gays in the military, and, taking a cue from the Texas Board of Education, suggested adding a discussion of creationism to the teaching of evolution. He claimed in *Fed Up!* that Social Security was unconstitutional and a "crumbling monument to the failure of the New Deal," without offering any plan for reform, which alarmed many seniors.

That would come back to haunt him during the debates, when Romney, like a dog with a bone, seized on his statements about Social Security and wouldn't let go.

Perry often said he felt "called" to run for president, raising concern among those who felt it an unseemly mingling of religion and politics but shoring up support among conservative evangelical voters.

Just days before his announcement, he had hosted a day of prayer at Houston's Reliant Stadium, signaling that he wouldn't be shy about promoting Christianity on the campaign trail.

Cynics dubbed the event "Prayerpalooza."

"Father, our heart breaks for America," Perry preached to the crowd of thirty thousand. "We see discord at home. We see fear in the marketplace. We see anger in the halls of government, and, as a nation, we have forgotten who made us, who protects us, who blesses us."

Perry prayed for parents, pastors, generals, and the president whose policies he often pilloried.[52]

The Freedom from Religion Foundation, an organization of atheists and agnostics, sued, arguing Perry's involvement violated the establishment clause of the Constitution, which separates religion from governing. A federal judge later threw out the lawsuit, finding that the group did not have standing to sue.

As Perry officially entered the race a few days later, he was suddenly more than the "jobs governor." He was one of the nation's millions of evangelical Christians.

His political ads reinforced this approach. In his first national ad, America's jobs governor strode confidently into Americans' living rooms, promising Texas-style fiscal discipline, hard work, patriotism, and faith.

A second ad, "Strong," went further, claiming there was "something wrong in this country when gays can serve openly in the military but our kids can't openly celebrate Christmas or pray in school." Perry promised to end Obama's "war on religion" and "fight against liberal attacks on our religious heritage." Memes about the antigay comments flooded the Internet. One pointed out that Perry's jacket in the ad was the same as that worn by a character in *Brokeback Mountain*, which featured two gay cowboys.[53]

Polls showed Perry neck and neck with Bachman for second place, both short of Romney, who led the pack. The day Perry announced, Romney made his infamous "corporations are people" comment to a heckler at the Iowa State Fair, puncturing Romney's attempt to shake his aloof and elitist image. The comment was in the context of remarks outlining options for reducing the deficit and overhauling entitlement programs but was an awkward way to reframe what the Supreme Court ruled. Campaign aides recall Romney was shaken by Perry's entrance into the race, complicating the field.[54]

Romney's image as the bridge between the party's social and economic wings was tested by Perry's entrance into the race, most directly by their dueling arguments that they would be the best candidate to create jobs. Romney felt that left Perry exposed on another point—Perry had never worked in the private sector, save on his family farm, and was lacking the business experience Romney said a president would need.

On that score, only Herman Cain could compete with Romney's twenty-five years in the private sector. Perry's response was to encourage voters to "look at [Romney's] four years in Massachusetts and my ten years in Texas."[55] Huntsman got in on the act—Massachusetts ranked forty-seventh in job growth, while Utah ranked first. Perry's ads either focused on his jobs record, energy initiatives, and tax plan or went negative against Romney.

Perry's tax plan would allow people to choose between their current tax rate or a flat tax of 20 percent: so simple, he said, that taxpayers could fill out their tax returns on a postcard. The plan would eliminate taxes on Social Security benefits and inheritances.

"I'm going to talk about the economy; don't get any ideas that I'm going to run away from my faith or my beliefs," he said.[56]

Perry hit the presidential campaign trail running, but the other GOP contenders weren't his only foes. His recovery from the controversial back surgery had gone far more slowly than he anticipated, taking a toll on the focus and work ethic he had long relied on to fuel his successful style of retail politics.

In their chronicle of the 2012 campaign, *Inside the Circus: Romney, Santorum, and the GOP Race* (2012), journalists Mike Allen of *Politico* and Evan Thomas of *Newsweek* wrote that Perry's performance on the stump may have been affected by his heavy use of painkillers to manage severe back pain. One campaign manager reported hearing Perry loudly singing "I've Been Working on the Railroad" in the men's room before a campaign event.

The Perry campaign corroborated the use of painkillers but denied it was a factor in the campaign.

"The third one, I can't. Sorry. Oops."

The flub during a debate in November 2011 will forever echo in presidential campaign history, a funeral dirge for Perry's 2012 ambitions.[57]

His history as a debater was mixed. His style was direct, but even when he was using notes, he stumbled over words. He seemed uncomfortable with the format and generally stuck to his talking points rather than engaging with the moderators or other candidates. And he hadn't shared a debate stage with more than two opponents since 2006, when the wild field of independent and Democratic opponents fought to deliver the best one-liners and Perry largely stayed out of the way. His last debate had been against Hutchison and Medina in 2010. Sheltered by political forces in Texas, he had fallen out of practice in the art of sparring on a stage.

But with so many Republican contenders, the debates were a critical forum.

Romney tried to capitalize on Perry's comments on Social Security, demanding to know if Perry believed Social Security should be ended as a federal program.

"I think we need to have a conversation . . ." Perry began.

"We're having that conversation right now, governor," Romney snapped. "We're running for president."

The two continued sparring, as Perry stumbled through his contention that Romney opposed Social Security. In Iowa he accused Romney of favoring a mandate requiring individuals to purchase health insurance. Romney promptly suggested a $10,000 bet.

"I'm not in the betting business," Perry responded.[58]

In Orlando Perry reiterated his support for the Texas law allowing undocumented immigrants to pay in-state tuition, saying of those who disagreed, "I don't think you have a heart." Romney pounced, saying the position was a "magnet" that draws people to the United States.[59]

Ron Paul argued that undocumented immigrants should receive no benefits. Santorum claimed Perry was "soft on illegal immigration." Perry doubled down, claiming a border fence was impractical even as he pledged to stop illegal immigration and make America more secure.

Perry represented a border state, but he was in danger of "being out-flanked on a top issue for Republican voters," one journalist said years later.[60]

Other observers blamed his campaign staff for not adequately preparing their candidate for a question they must have known was coming.[61] Watching from a hotel in Austin, the campaign staff knew they immediately needed to walk it back, realizing it was a no-no for Republican voters. "That was a killer," remembered a stunned Ray Sullivan.[62]

After struggling through the first three debates, with two more scheduled over the next nine days, Perry's aides suggested he get more sleep.[63]

Then there was the infamous "Oops" moment during the CNBC debate in Michigan. Perry was full of steam, promoting his ideas to slash and burn the federal government's footprint.

> *Perry:* It's three agencies of government when I get there that
> are gone. Commerce, Education, and the, uh, uh, what's the
> third one there? Let's see.
> *Ron Paul:* Five.
> *Mitt Romney:* EPA?
> *Perry:* EPA. There you go.
> *Maria Bartiromo (Moderator):* Let's talk deficit.
> *John Harwood (Moderator):* Seriously. Is EPA the one you are
> talking about?
> *Perry:* No, sir.
> *Harwood:* You can't name the third one?
> *Perry:* The third agency of government? I would do away with
> Education, uh, the, uh, Commerce, and, let's see. I can't. The
> third one, I can't. Sorry. Oops.

"Rick Perry Stumbles Badly in Republican Presidential Debate," read a *Washington Post* headline on November 10, 2011.

"It turns out George Bush was actually the smart Texas governor," comedian Jimmy Fallon quipped.

Perry's hopes to revive his ailing campaign with a mistake-free performance didn't materialize, to put it mildly. His staff called it a "human moment" and authentic.[64]

"Yeah, I stepped in it, man," Perry said. "Yeah, it was embarrassing.

Of course it was. But here's what's more important: People understand that our principles, our conservative principles, are what matter, not a litany of agencies that I think we need to get rid of."[65]

He tried to use the blunder to draw a contrast with President Obama's star power on *Fox & Friends* the next morning. "If anybody's looking for the slickest politician or the smoothest debater, I readily admit I'm not that person," he said. "But my conservative values have led one of the most influential states in the nation."[66]

On the *Today Show* that same day Perry acknowledged that his back was still bothering him following the surgery earlier in the year and tried to pivot. "One error is not going to make or break a campaign," he said. "We're going to continue talking about the challenges facing this country."

There had been a lot of cyclical ups and downs during the campaign, so it wasn't out of the question that Perry could rebound. His campaign staff, however, recall the moment more direly.

"We're screwed," one staff member recalls thinking after the debate.[67]

It was more than just one error. After a rambling speech to the Cornerstone Action Dinner in New Hampshire, an overly giddy Perry was compelled to state for the record that he was not drunk.

Critics pointed at Dave Carney, the gruff but forceful consultant who had worked for Perry since his 1998 run for lieutenant governor. The "wandering answers and unfocused jabs" made the campaign look adrift.[68] The strategy that had proven successful in Texas—generally avoiding the media and downplaying debates—may have caught up to them. In a crowded primary field, not debating was not an option.

"I was not prepared, particularly, for the rigors of a national campaign. Physically, having had major back surgery weeks before was a huge mistake. I had this superman mentality," Perry remembers of the pain and recovery. He was taking every kind of painkiller to quell the pain, and other medications to sleep and focus: "As doped up as I was, I was impressed I did as well as I did for as long as I did."[69]

"He was just not ready for it," a former campaign aide said. "In hindsight, you wished he would have gone back and said we can't do this right now. We need time." For all Perry's knowledge and skills in the Texas political arena, national politics was a different animal. The national debate stage was out of his comfort zone.[70]

The campaign announced raising $17 million in early October, a healthy sum for a long-distance primary slog, but the boost was overshadowed by controversy after media outlets reported that Perry's family hunting camp had once been called "Niggerhead." The campaign responded that the family painted over the rock on which the racially offensive name had been emblazoned almost immediately after leasing the property in 1983.[71]

Herman Cain, the only African American in the Republican field, criticized Perry as insensitive. Several Black Republicans and Democrats in Texas came to Perry's defense, including Wallace Jefferson, the first Black chief justice of the Texas Supreme Court, who said "to imply that the governor condoned either the use of that word or that sentiment, I find false." Former state senator Ron Wilson, who is Black, said Perry "doesn't have a racist bone in his body."[72]

It was as though his "moment had passed," according to one journalist.[73] Perry finished a distant fifth in the trend-setting Iowa caucuses, with just over 10 percent of the vote, followed by a less than 1 percent in New Hampshire, where he had largely skipped campaigning to focus on South Carolina. But polling in South Carolina didn't look promising, either.

Five months after he entered the race as an instant front-runner, Perry formally suspended his campaign on January 19, 2012. Expectations were high with surging poll numbers, but things changed quickly. "It was about the best three hours of my life," Perry joked years later.[74] Between entering the race with a highly anticipated announcement at the opulent Francis Marion Hotel in Charleston, South Carolina, and its end at a St. Louis Holiday Inn, Perry had been unable to break ground with a full combat load on board. Everything that could go wrong did go wrong.

"It was a perfectly horrible campaign; it was a complete catastrophe," said Root, who wrote a book about the race called *Oops: A Diary from the 2012 Campaign Trail*.[75]

Where Perry had been able to straddle the Tea Party–establishment divide in Texas, the national gulf was harder to navigate.

"It felt like there were two Republican parties," said a campaign staffer.[76]

Perry had been one of the first mainstream Republicans to fully embrace the group, appearing at rallies and demanding that Washington retreat from state affairs. But fellow Texan Ron Paul practically invented the modern Tea Party, serving as its woebegone ambassador.

Perry's stance on illegal immigration—a circumstance that some groups claimed provided $14 billion to Texas's gross state product—left him vulnerable to accusations that he was insufficiently conservative, despite several joint campaign appearances with Joe Arpaio, the sheriff of Mariposa County, Arizona, known for his strident opposition to illegal immigration. Undocumented immigrants in Texas were eligible for not only in-state college tuition but also drug treatment and mental health services, accommodations the most conservative Republicans simply would not abide.

Perry repeated that his goal was to turn immigrants into "taxpayers, not tax wasters," but his focus on business undercut his message on illegal immigration.[77]

His relatively late entrance into the race didn't help. One pundit commented that Perry's best day "was his first day in the race."[78] Relationships with party activists are formed early. Perry benefited from the implosion of some candidates—a shakeup of Gingrich's campaign allowed Perry to pick up seasoned staff and helped with fundraising—but he never fully caught on. Asked later what lessons he learned, his advice was succinct: "Get in early."[79]

The sour end of the George W. Bush administration in 2008, with Bush's dismal approval ratings helping lead Democrats back to power, proved another hurdle, leaving the party wary of another Texan. Perry subtly worked to distance himself from Bush and attacked two of Bush's high-voltage domestic achievements, the Medicare drug benefit and No Child Left Behind.

No Child Left Behind is "a cool name, but it's a monstrous intrusion into our affairs," Perry said of Bush's signature education law. "I like George, but that's not good public policy."[80]

In the end, however, Perry couldn't capture the lightning in the bottle that had defined his extraordinary electoral run Texas.[81]

He was better at retail politics than debates and speeches, but the "debate of the week" campaign schedule meant he didn't have time to fully employ those retail skills. Mistakes were magnified in the presidential campaign fishbowl. Many of his gaffes were innocuous and could possibly be explained by his use of painkillers to treat recurring back pain, but they added up. What seemed like typical Perry swagger became a liability as he appeared underprepared for the job of president.

In an interview with the editorial board at the influential *Des Moines Register*, he argued against the 1950s Supreme Court decision banning school prayer, saying the ruling was made by "eight unelected and, frankly, unaccountable judges." He labeled the two newest Supreme Court justices, Sonia Sotomayor and Elena Kagan, "activist" judges, and he and referred to Sotomayor as "Montemayor."[82]

He also challenged House Minority Leader Nancy Pelosi to a debate about overhauling Congress, arguing that Congress should follow the example of Texas with part-time legislators who had to "go back home" and "have a real job." Pelosi said she was too busy.

"Monday, I'm going to be in Portland in the morning. I'm going to be visiting some of our labs in California in the afternoon. That's two. I can't remember what the third thing is."[83]

Oops.

–10–

THE 2013 SESSION, INDICTMENT, AND THE 2016 PRESIDENTIAL RACE

"Answer to No One"

At least things back home were looking up. The Texas economy was booming, promising that the 2013 legislative session would be less brutal, and certainly it would take some of the sting out of Perry's bruising presidential primary loss.

The state was flush with an $8 billion surplus, giving Perry and his party some breathing room. Standing before the assembled members of the 83rd legislature, a puffed-up Rick Perry declared that the state of Texas was "stronger than ever" as the state shifted from recession to recovery. But even with a rosier fiscal picture, Republicans were not in the mood to increase spending or to reverse the historic cuts of the previous session. Some legislators saw news of the surplus as the "equivalent of ringing the dinner bell," Perry said.[1]

Instead, the battle would be over how much smaller to make the budget. Dale Craymer, president of the Texas Taxpayers and Research Association, summed it up. "It's just going to be a fight for the icing."[2]

Perry's muted State of the State address in 2013 belied what would be a fractious session. He didn't even mention abortion, voter ID, sanctuary cities, or redistricting, but a new and aggressive group of Republican legislators were pressing for a "fetal pain" bill banning abortion after twenty weeks, drug testing for recipients of unemployment benefits, and concealed handguns in classrooms.

Democrats girded for battle. "Expand Medicaid Now," protestors from the progressive Texas Organizing Project (TOP) shouted as they were escorted by DPS troopers from the House gallery during Perry's address, while Republicans responded with a standing ovation for the governor.[3]

While establishment Republicans were uneasy about the internal rifts over hot-button social issues, groups affected by the earlier budget cuts were frustrated and angry. Education advocates wanted the $5.4 billion cut from public education restored. Frustrated Texans stuck on Interstate 35 and other roads wanted more infrastructure investment for roads and water projects, especially in areas affected by drought.

"The session could be very difficult," Jim Pitts, chair of the Ways and Means Committee, said in a masterpiece of understatement.[4]

Perry said he would wait until summer to decide on running for another term, but his decision not to announce any emergency items for the session fueled speculation that he would not run again. Apparently worried about a challenge from his right flank, he announced on a Dallas television station that he and Greg Abbott, the popular Republican attorney general, had a gentlemen's agreement that they would not run against each other. Abbott, known for describing his days at the office as "suing the federal government, then going home," never confirmed the deal.[5] "People should never discount Rick Perry. He has been counted out before, but he always gets up off the mat," said Sen. Dan Patrick.[6]

As far as what would come after the governor's mansion, Perry said only that the 2016 presidential race "is a pretty good piece down the road."[7]

As the state's most famous yell leader, Perry led Team Texas in recruiting companies from all over the globe to move to or expand in Texas. He addressed the American Chamber of Commerce in Japan. He led the Texas delegation to Beijing before attending the World Economic Forum in Tianjin, China. He traveled to Missouri, Connecticut, New York, Maryland—all states led by Democratic governors—to advertise the Texas economy. A public-private marketing partnership ran ads in

California urging industry leaders to "come check out Texas." "It is not about Texas. This is a national conversation," he said.[8]

Back home, lawmakers were considering a measure requiring elected officials to reimburse taxpayers for security costs accrued for "unofficial" travel. (The security bill for Perry's presidential bid cost the state $3.7 million.)

Lawmakers approved requiring politically active nonprofit organizations to publicly disclose major donors—"dark money" contributions that are made in secret to avoid campaign finance disclosure laws. Tea Party–aligned groups objected, claiming the law would allow powerful politicians to threaten and intimidate their donors. Perry vetoed the dark money bill. The bill requiring reimbursement of security costs didn't make it out of committee after Perry had a "come-to-Jesus" meeting with its author.

The deal-closing Texas Enterprise Fund had been a target from the beginning, but in 2013, conservatives and liberals alike took aim. Sen. Wendy Davis, who later ran to replace Perry as governor, sponsored legislation to direct the state auditor to review the fund recipients' applications and success at job creation. In September 2014, the office of the auditor found that some companies, including Citgo and Cabela's, received money from the fund without submitting an application, which allowed them to avoid an "objective scoring tool" that was supposed to be a required part of the process. Companies that did not reach their job-creation goals were not penalized, nor did they pay the fines levied, totaling tens of millions of dollars.

The governor's office claimed more than 66,000 jobs had been created due to the fund, but auditors said this claim could not be verified because of "weaknesses" in monitoring by Perry's office.[9] Investigators were able to verify only that 73 percent of jobs promised were actually created.[10] The audit found that one company wasn't even operating in Texas but in California.

The fund lost money investing in several startups, costing the state as much as $6 million. The report was the death knell of Perry's signature economic development program, as Republicans, uneasy about giving public dollars to private companies, called for the fund to be scrapped.

Perry defended the fund but acknowledged that its future was the legislature's call.[11]

The Enterprise Fund survived, but days after taking office in 2015, Governor Abbott signed legislation dismantling the Emerging Technology Fund.

Turmoil surrounding the state's $3 billion cancer moonshot agency, the Cancer Prevention and Research Institute of Texas, or CPRIT, also reverberated throughout the session after allegations that an $11 million grant directed to a private company in Dallas had bypassed the scientific review process.

Executive Director Bill Gimson, a Perry appointee, stepped down as a result of the turmoil, eight months after the resignation of the chief science officer, Nobel laureate Dr. Alfred G. Gilman, in protest of a different grant,[12] and a month after chief commercialization officer Jerry Cobbs resigned. Cobbs had included an $11 million grant to Damascus Pharmaceuticals in a funding request without the required review and was later indicted on a felony count of securing execution of a document by deception.

Perry called for an embarrassing suspension on new grants until confidence in the once-celebrated agency could be restored.

More scandal erupted at the state's Health and Human Services Commission after details emerged about the agency's 2012 awarding of a $20 million contract to Austin software company 21st Century Technologies, Inc., without following proper procedures. Ultimately, Perry asked both the inspector general and the deputy inspector general to resign.

Completing a record-setting run of gubernatorial appointments, Perry appointed his former chief of staff, Jeff Boyd, to an open seat on the Texas Supreme Court. He'd made a similar move in 2004 when he appointed his serving general counsel, David Medina, to the same court. Other close advisors over the years were tapped to be chancellor of the Texas A&M University System, secretary of state, Texas Department of Transportation, and the Transportation Commission.[13]

The tiny community of West was a bucolic reminder of the state's rural past, a tight-knit town of 2,800 residents who nurtured the town's Czech heritage through their kolache shops and restaurants serving authentic Czech-Texas meals.

But the town's history was forever changed at 7 p.m. April 17, 2013, as a thunderous explosion and fire erupted at the West Fertilizer Company, killing fifteen people and injuring 160 residents and first responders.

Heat from the fire destabilized tons of explosive fertilizer made of ammonium nitrate, and the resulting blast was so big it registered as a small earthquake, blowing out windows, knocking people blocks away off their feet, and leaving a massive ninety-three-foot crater in the ground.

"It was like the whole earth shook," said one resident.[14]

It was a tragedy, but West also served as one more focal point for the continuing animosity Perry demonstrated for President Obama and his administration.

State officials sent personnel from the Texas Commission for Environmental Quality, the emergency management department, and the state's top urban search-and-rescue team. The US Chemical Safety Board and the American Red Cross dispatched crews to Central Texas.

President Obama attended a memorial service for the victims, but two months later, the Federal Emergency Management Agency (FEMA) denied the state's appeal for help, stating in bureaucratic terms that the explosion was "not of the severity and magnitude that warrants a major disaster declaration."

Perry reminded Obama that he had stood in front of the grieving community and told them they would not be forgotten. "He said his administration would stand with them, ready to help," Perry said. That help, the governor insisted, needed to come from FEMA.[15]

There was a palpable tension between the two leaders as Obama made several trips to Texas that year, including to attend the unveiling of the George W. Bush Presidential Library in Dallas and to visit a suburban Austin high school and tech company.

Perry was cordial but unimpressed. If the president wanted to talk jobs, "he certainly came to the right place for that."[16]

By the following year, when Obama returned to Texas to confront a humanitarian crisis caused by the influx of undocumented minors over the Texas border, things came to a head.

Tens of thousands of children were pouring across the border from Honduras, Guatemala, and El Salvador, driven by gang violence and poverty. Perry called out Washington for "lip service and empty promises," saying he would not stand by "while our citizens are under assault and little children from Central America are detained in squalor."[17]

He sent a thousand National Guard troops to the border to assist federal officers in support roles, prompting objections by Democrats about the militarization of the border and, as Perry made a quick trip to Iowa, of his "continuing his routine of photo-op to further his presidential aspirations" rather than seeking long-term border solutions.[18]

Photographers captured a dramatically frowning Perry in contrast with an ebullient Barack Obama chuckling in response to a comment by Dallas mayor Mike Rawlings. When the president stepped off Air Force One in Austin, Perry refused to greet him on the tarmac, saying a quick handshake would not allow for thoughtful discussion about border issues.[19] Perry instead offered to meet for a substantive discussion, later suggesting on Fox News that President Obama didn't care about border security and that he must either be "inept" or hiding "some ulterior motive."[20]

Perry and fellow Republicans threw more obstacles in the path of the president's healthcare reforms, adopting more stringent training requirements for people hired to help Texans sign up for the health insurance coverage than those imposed by the federal government.

Attorney General Abbott took an equally pugnacious approach to the federal government. Since 2004, thirty-one lawsuits had been initiated by Abbott's attorney general's office, including three against the Bush administration and twenty-eight against the Obama administration—and costing $4 million in taxpayer money—on issues ranging from voter ID and redistricting to the environment.

"If we lose our liberty to an overreaching federal government, we will lose absolutely everything, and that's why I will continue pushing back against Washington, DC," said Abbott, positioning himself to succeed Perry.[21]

Bragging points, perhaps, but the state's record against the federal government would have gotten a football coach fired. By 2013 Texas had won fewer than 25 percent of the cases it brought.[22]

Unemployment was at a four-year low as the legislature convened, and sales tax receipts were skyrocketing, thanks in large part to a new oil boom and fracking frenzy. The state had extra cash, but what this meant depended on one's political persuasion. Perry saw a surplus, so he called to cut business taxes by $1.8 billion, or 5 percent, addressing what had festered as a thorn in his side since 2006, when the inelegant tax swap found the state functionally raising taxes on businesses. Democrats saw a chance to restore billions of dollars in services lawmakers had cut since 2007.

The final budget had something for everyone to dislike. Perry got most of his tax cuts, though hundreds of millions of dollars less than he wanted. The 15 percent increase in spending put Texas back on solid economic ground, but population growth and inflation meant it was still too little to take care of the state's neediest population.

Republicans wanted a smaller budget and less reliance on the Rainy Day Fund. Democrats complained that the state restored only $2.8 billion, or about half, of the public education funding it had ripped away in 2011.

Fiscal worrywarts got $530 million to shore up the faltering Teacher Retirement System. "We've come a long way, baby, since last session," said Tommy Williams, the Senate's chief budget writer.[23]

But if the finances had changed, the politics remained the same. Republicans were forced to take a hard vote on tapping the Rainy Day Fund, which added $1.9 billion to reverse school payment delay.[24] Internal memoranda from the governor's office showed that Perry's team was sensitive to the belief espoused by the conservative advocacy group Empower Texans that the budget should increase by less than the combined rate of population and inflation growth, with an email from John Opperman to Perry's chief of staff highlighting an "MQS" editorial (Michael Quinn Sullivan, Empower Texans CEO) emphasizing those limits.[25]

The budget, Perry's office bragged, would be under that number.

The drama of the 2011 session over with and the bipartisan surge to finish the budget out of the way, the 2013 session was tamer. That was about to change. Abortion politics played a big part in that.

In a further tightening of abortion policies, Sen. Larry Taylor, a Galveston Republican, filed legislation requiring doctors who provide abortions to have admitting privileges at a nearby hospital, which he said would facilitate access to additional care if needed. "It will prevent hit-and-run abortions in Texas," said MerryLynn Gerstenschlager, vice president of the conservative Texas Eagle Forum. "If the doctor is not competent to obtain hospital privileges, then he is not competent to perform abortions."[26]

Opposition groups, including NARAL-Texas, said the law would give hospital administrators the power to decide where abortions could be performed; many hospitals, especially in rural areas, are affiliated with religious organizations, potentially making it difficult for doctors in those areas to gain privileges.[27]

Perry also announced his support for legislation banning abortion after twenty weeks, the point at which antiabortion activists said a fetus could feel pain. At a Rally for Life outside the Capitol marking the fortieth year since the *Roe v. Wade* decision, Perry noted that his opposition to abortion derived from a "Biblical source" and he would work to make "abortions as rare as possible."[28] Although Dewhurst and Perry didn't always see eye to eye, there was no daylight between them on this, as Dewhurst looked to sharpen his image with conservatives (who backed Ted Cruz for Senate over him in 2012) and Perry saw an opportunity to curry favor with Christian conservatives.

Sen. Wendy Davis said both proposals were an attempt to chip away at women's rights. "Because these so-called small government advocates won't acknowledge that a woman's right to choose is the law of the land, they're reduced to expanding government into women's health care decisions," she said.[29]

As the battle waged on the chamber floor, Perry was honored by Texas Right to Life with a lifetime achievement award in September.

More red meat: Perry was surrounded by bell-ringing Santa Claus impersonators and cheerleaders (from Kountze High School in Hardin County) dressed in "I cheer for Jesus" T-shirts as he signed a bill protecting Christmas and other holiday celebrations in Texas public schools from legal challenges. The "Merry Christmas" bill removed the potential legal consequences of saying "Merry Christmas" in schools and protected other traditional holiday symbols (like a menorah or nativity scenes) as long as more than one religion and a secular symbol (such as Santa Claus) are included. Dwayne Bohac, a Houston Republican, sponsored the bill after discovering his son's school had erected a "holiday tree" because school officials feared that mentioning Christmas would invite litigation. "This is not a governor that shirks away from the tough issues," Bohac said. "And this should not be a tough issue, which is what's even amazing about all this. But this is just political correctness that's run amok."[30]

The legislature also prohibited state officials from double-dipping into state pensions, a response to the stir Perry caused when financial disclosures revealed he was drawing his state salary while collecting pensions from both the Air Force and his previous public service. Perry's proposal for a $10,000 college degree? University presidents expressed support, even interest, but most agreed with UT President Bill Powers that it couldn't be done at every university.

This was a session where Perry's veto had weight, and his history of wielding the veto like a sledgehammer was in the mind of most legislators, ensuring that the governor's implicit threats to use the big red stamp were impactful. He axed twenty-eight laws, including proposals to prevent wage discrimination against women, bipartisan legislation to tighten ethics laws by requiring public officials to divulge more about their personal financial holdings, and banning of the sale of sugary drinks at many public schools, an initiative supported by First Lady Michelle Obama. Only small modifications were made to the wobbly budget, patched together with a mix of cuts and new fees, Perry judging correctly that any major shifts would jeopardize the temporary peace.

Perry followed through on his threat to strip funding from the state's Public Integrity Unit, housed in the Travis County District Attorney's Office, fulfilling a promise that he would do so unless there were leadership changes within the unit. It was the opening salvo in a political and legal liability that dogged him for years.

The district attorney in question, Rosemary Lehmberg, had been stopped on suspicion of drunk driving by Travis County deputies at eleven p.m., April 12, 2013, at the height of the legislative session. Officers said she was belligerent and abusive and could not produce identification; Lehmberg also refused a breath test and was taken to the Travis County Jail. She continued her tirade against officers, kicking and spitting at them until she was physically restrained as officers waited for a warrant to draw her blood. Results showed her blood alcohol was .239, almost three times the legal limit.

Lehmberg's office, as the district attorney's office in the county encompassing the state capital, also was responsible for the Public Integrity Unit, which received state funds to investigate and prosecute illegal actions by public officials, in addition to state insurance and tax fraud cases. Perry threatened to kill these funds by line-item veto. The unit had thirty employees and more than four hundred active cases.[31]

Outraged by Lehmberg's behavior, Perry called for her to resign immediately.

"It feels partisan, and it's misguided as far as I'm concerned," Lehmberg told reporters after meeting with Travis County Commissioners. Regardless of the funds, the district attorney would still be responsible for prosecuting cases.[32] Lehmberg was sentenced to forty-five days in jail, along with a $4,000 fine, and her driver's license was suspended for 180 days.

Even with all that was accomplished, there was still unfinished legislative business, ensuring there would be at least one special session. As it turned out, there were three.

Fresh off a 2012 Senate primary race runoff loss to Ted Cruz and anticipating a tougher 2014 primary to retain his post as lieutenant governor, Dewhurst wanted to revive conservative efforts that failed in the regular session: tighten abortion restrictions, fund school vouchers, loosen gun restrictions, and enforce a harder cap on state spending, all efforts Democrats were able to block in the regular session. Democrats knew a special session would mean trouble for their agenda, especially in the Senate, where the two-thirds rule did not apply, and fewer bills meant fewer opportunities to jam up the flow.

Instead, they tried to slow-talk the special. "Many of the red-meat issues that the governor might add to the call are out of step with mainstream Texas," Democratic state Rep. Rafael Anchía of Dallas said. "I think it hurts Republicans if those issues are brought forward in furtherance of the governor's political ambitions."[33]

No such luck. Perry ended weeks of speculation and called a special session on redistricting the day after the 2013 regular session gaveled to a close. Lawmakers quickly approved the maps on a strict party line vote. Any harmony from the regular session was gone. Frustrated Democrats fought to increase minority representation in some North Texas districts. Republicans fought with Democrats about changes they argued would not be defended by Abbott in court. Republicans fought with Republicans as Pat Fallon of Frisco accused Bennett Ratliff of moving a potential challenger out of Ratliff's district, sparing the moderate Ratliff from a primary challenge.[34]

The maps would be litigated further until, in 2018, the US Supreme Court ruled that one district restricted minority voting rights, which the legislature promptly addressed.

Transportation funding, mandatory life sentences for teens convicted of murder, and abortion restrictions were also on the agenda since no major abortion bills passed in the regular session. Abortion got all the attention. "I'm still hoping that our current special session is short and relatively painless," Straus said. "But I'll have to admit that with each passing day I'm a little more doubtful about that."[35]

Anita Perry's selection of stylish black Jean Lafont eyeglass frames for her husband was a buzzworthy choice. The *Christian Science Monitor* pondered the "political optics" of the move.[36] A *Los Angeles Times* columnist speculated that the glasses made Perry more politically "palatable to moderates and young people."[37] The *New Republic* quoted consultants who mentioned that "a little visual gravitas might not hurt" and that it was easier to "fail a vision test than to pass an IQ test."

Donald Trump unartfully tweeted that Perry only began wearing glasses so people would think he was smart. In some ways, Perry hadn't come very far from the days in which outsize attention was paid to his hair and his blue jeans.

The glasses were not, it turns out, part of the governor's campaign strategy. The glasses were also apparently not "hipster" since, as a writer for the *Washington Post* noted, they were worn by a middle-aged dad from Paint Creek, Texas.[38] He had been wearing them since 2013, although he later chose not to wear them in his official portrait, which hangs in the rotunda of the Texas Capitol.

The national attention paid to the governor's sartorial choices underscored an important element in his career—image was assumed to be more important than substance. When he unveiled his official portrait, the question among the press corps wasn't what he would say but whether he would be wearing the glasses.[39]

The legal fallout from Perry's veto of Public Integrity Unit funding continued. Texans for Public Justice filed a complaint contending Perry had potentially committed one or more criminal offenses by pressuring Lehmberg to step down. (She had refused.) In particular, because he was the one who would appoint her replacement, coercing her to resign was wrong. Several top Perry aides testified before a grand jury empaneled in Austin.[40] Perry was initially unfazed, insisting the veto was made in accordance with the veto power afforded to every governor under the Texas Constitution. Democrats didn't miss a chance to hit Perry over corruption issues, a theme they had played upon for years without success. "Texans deserve real leadership, and this is unbecoming of our governor," Texas Democratic Party chair Gilberto Hinojosa said in a statement. He demanded that Perry immediately resign.[41]

In a surprise development, Perry was indicted in August 2014 on two felony counts—abuse of official capacity and coercion of a public servant. The special prosecutor leading the case, Michael McCrum, argued Perry had tried to force a Democratic district attorney to resign because he didn't approve of the "historical and current management decisions" within the public corruption unit she ran.[42] He faced 109 years in prison if convicted. Perry called the prosecution a witch hunt and a political ploy, the action of liberal Austin residents who constituted the grand jury. "Even before Trump and the weaponization of the legal system against him, I went through it in Travis County," Perry angrily related years later. "Been there, done that, and got the T-shirt to prove it" he said of his famous mug shot emblazoned on T-shirts.[43]

He was in rare company—Gov. James E. "Pa" Ferguson was indicted in 1917 and removed from office after being convicted of ten charges by the Texas Senate.

Perry lawyered up. Using campaign funds, he hired a top-flight legal team, including Mark Fabiani, Tony Buzbee (a donor and celebrated trial lawyer from Houston),[44] Ben Ginsberg, Bobby Burchfield, Tom Phillips (former Texas Supreme Court justice), and David Botsford.

The pugnacious Buzbee dismissed the case as "banana republic politics." The crux of Perry's defense was that as governor, he had every legal right to veto the funding. "The veto in question was made in accordance with the veto authority afforded to every governor under the Texas Constitution," said a spokeswoman.[45] He pleaded not guilty to both counts.

The indictment required a political defense, too. "Across the board you're seeing people weigh in and reflecting that this is way outside of the norm. This is not the way that we settle differences, political differences in this country," Perry said on *Fox News Sunday*, days after the indictment became public. "You don't do it with indictments. We settle our political differences at the ballot box."[46]

Republicans rallied to his side. His booking in Austin was more a pep rally than a criminal justice issue, with dozens of supporters packing the area outside the courthouse door, some holding signs reading "STOP DEMOCRAT GAMES" and "RICK IS RIGHT."

"I'm going to fight this injustice with every fiber of my being. And we will prevail," Perry said before walking inside the building, setting off the metal detector but not breaking stride.[47]

"The party was in the midst of a changing of the guard," Texas GOP chair Steve Munisteri said. "But this particular situation has brought the focus back to Gov. Perry and kind of reminded everyone why we like him."[48] He was fingerprinted at the Travis County Courthouse and photographed sporting a confident grin, more glamour shot than mug shot.[49] He left the rally, heading for Sandy's Hamburgers in downtown Austin, photographed holding an ice cream cone as his lawyers stood in the background with their own cones.

"That's not a consultant telling him to do that. That's him," remembers former *Austin American-Statesman* journalist Jonathan Tilove.[50]

The gloves were off. Perry's political action committee, RickPAC, released internet footage of Lehmberg's unruly behavior to build public support for the governor. His office had to walk back a disparaging Tweet posted from his official account, which they claimed was unauthorized and was later deleted. "I don't always drive drunk at 3x the legal blood alcohol limit," the tweet read, "but when I do, I indict Gov. Perry for calling me out about it. I am the most drunk Democrat in Texas."[51]

The legal case fizzled. In July 2015 one of the felony indictments was tossed by the Third Court of Appeals in Austin, which sided with the argument of Perry's dazzling legal team that the coercion charge violated the now former governor's free speech rights. In 2016 the Texas Court of Criminal Appeals, dominated by Republican judges, held 6–2 that Perry's veto power couldn't be restricted by the courts and that the prosecution of an official for using the veto violates the separation of powers.

"Come at the king, you best not miss," Republican judge David Newell wrote in his concurring opinion, quoting a popular line from the HBO series *The Wire*.[52]

"I've always known the actions I took were not only lawful and legal, they were right," said a defiant Perry, speaking at the headquarters of an influential Texas conservative think tank, which had previously christened its balcony overlooking downtown as the "Gov. Rick Perry Liberty Balcony."[53] With a voided criminal indictment from the court, a judge dismissed the case on April 6, 2016.

The final bill for Perry's all-star legal team was $2.6 million.[54] The political impact would linger, affecting Perry's second run at the presidency in 2016.

Abortion was a late addition to the legislature's to-do list for the May 2013 special session, but it was now central to the Republican Party base, coming to define the party's conservative wing. Rep. Brandon Creighton, a Conroe Republican who chaired the House Republican Caucus, issued a statement promoting a tougher round of laws as legislators prepared for a special session: "We are a conservative majority and we were elected to support conservative pro-life, pro-family legislation."[55]

The wing of the party that cared about abortion was the same bloc that helped Republicans win primaries—750,000 votes statewide from these committed voters was as good as a ticket into office in Republican-filled Texas. Simone Ward, women's outreach director for the Democratic National Committee, noted that Republicans had promised to tone down their rhetoric and reach out to women voters after the national losses of 2012. "But when it comes to women's health, the Grand Old Party is the just the same old extreme party it's always been."[56]

After back-to-back presidential losses, the party's most loyal constituents wanted to double-down on the issue.

The special session had turned deeply partisan, tackling two of the most contentious issues the body had faced since Perry took office: redistricting and abortion. Out of this frustration was born an idea—to stall. House Democrats held out as long as they could, using procedural delay after point of order to slow down the bill and give their Senate colleagues a chance to filibuster in the closing days of the session. The record for the longest filibuster in Texas history is held by Sen. Bill Meier (D-Hurst), who in 1977 talked for forty-three hours against a bill that eventually passed anyway. He sipped water, ate lemon slices, and relieved himself in an "astronaut bag" attached to his leg under his pants.[57] Most filibusters, however, last about an hour and are used either to make a political point or to draw attention to an issue.[58]

This one would be different.

Donning the pink tennis shoes that would become famous, Wendy Davis—a Fort Worth Democrat and a former teenage mother who'd graduated from Harvard Law—took to the Senate floor at 11:18 a.m., June 26, 2013, with the hope of running out the clock on an omnibus abortion bill that would ban all abortions after twenty weeks, require doctors performing abortions to have admitting privileges at a nearby hospital, and mandate that all abortion clinics meet the standards of hospitals or surgical centers of similar grade. The special session was to end at midnight.

The gallery was packed with thousands of protesters—most young and female—calling out, "Go Wendy!" and engaging in what they called a "people's filibuster." Chaos erupted, with a male protester who backed the bill removed by security after shouting, "Abortion is genocide!"[59]

Republican senator Donna Campbell called the pro-Davis protesters a distraction, especially since time in the special session was running out. Every minute mattered until the midnight deadline. "I want them out of here!"

Van de Putte had rushed back to Austin after burying her father that morning, only to be frustrated when her attempts to be recognized failed. "At what point must a female senator raise her hand or her voice to be recognized over the male colleagues in the room?"[60]

Davis got her first warning at 5:30 p.m. for talking off topic when she brought up funding cuts to women's health services. Her second strike came when a colleague provided her with a back brace. Her third came when she mentioned Texas's mandatory pre-abortion ultrasound law, which was ruled off-topic. The jockeying about the rules on the third strike between legislative staff, the members, and the presiding officers, in addition to the deafening crowd noise from the packed gallery, pushed the clock past the midnight deadline, ending the filibuster after thirteen hours.[61]

Or did it? As Republican officials huddled at the dais, Democrats waived their cell phones to show the clock read 12:03 a.m. After a meeting lasting more than an hour between angry Democrats and frustrated Republicans, the official record held that the bill passed before the midnight deadline, but there wasn't time for Dewhurst to sign it and send it to Perry before the clock struck midnight.

The bill failed.

The chaos surrounding the normally staid Capitol complex landed at the feet of the lieutenant governor. Accusing Dewhurst of a lack of leadership, Dan Patrick was the most pointed in his criticism of the lieutenant governor, who stood helplessly with his hands in his pockets as the Senate gallery exploded.[62] Land Commissioner Jerry Patterson, who had announced he was running against Dewhurst in the Republican primary, said Dewhurst "has lost his grip on the reins of the Senate, and his horse has run wild." Dewhurst wasn't at the dais for much of the action, and reports placed him sipping wine and eating steak at a local steakhouse. "No steak," he reported when he returned.[63]

Both sides tried to profit from the clash, sending out fundraising appeals and flooding social media with calls to action. "Something special is happening in Austin tonight," President Obama tweeted during the filibuster, and other messages of support from national Democrats followed. Davis was famous. Photos of her pink Mizuno running shoes were everywhere, spiking sales, and the hashtag #StandWithWendy was trending. The episode also fueled speculation that Perry would seek the White House again.

He wasted no time in calling a second special session, putting abortion at the top of the to-do list. The "mob rule" and a "raw abuse of power," as Perry labeled it, dissipated, with additional state troopers posted to the Capitol to quell any demonstrations. "If there are any demonstrations, we are going to clear the gallery," Dewhurst said. "I hope we don't get to that point, but if we do, we do."[64]

Opponents packed the Capitol Rotunda holding "WANTED" posters of several prominent Republican lawmakers, chanting "Whose choice? Our choice!" Supporters of the bill competed for chant time, praying, singing "Amazing Grace," and holding up crosses with signs reading "WE CHOOSE LIFE!"[65]

The chambers passed the bill quickly, sending a bill to Perry that made Texas's abortion law one of the toughest in the nation: it requires doctors to have admitting privileges at nearby hospitals, allows abortions only in certified surgical centers, and bans abortions after twenty weeks.

For all the fighting, it was eventually overturned by the US Supreme Court, which held in a 5–4 opinion that the admitting privileges and surgical clinic requirements would force more clinics to close and place an undue burden on a woman's right to choose. But politically, the fracas "lit a fuse," according to Cecile Richards (daughter of former governor Ann Richards), who was then president of the National Planned Parenthood Federation of America and one of a few Texas Democrats with royal political blood.[66]

Some conservatives privately worried that while social conservatives were energized by the battle, it may have alienated moderate voters, making it harder to compromise.[67]

Strategists met with focus groups in which the GOP was described as "narrow-minded" and an "out of touch party" of "stiff old men," and those looking at the results had misgivings that the GOP would find it hard to expand the big tent.[68]

The speculation about Perry's political future in Texas finally ended. America's longest serving governor called it quits.

Gone was the Rick Perry who ruled with an "iron hand," a combination of friendship and fear. Lawmakers had put more money into education, even after Perry had suggested it was unnecessary. He had been forced to shift his position on spending from the Rainy Day Fund. The Senate considered a bill aimed at Perry that would have added term limits to the state constitution and required officeholders to resign in order to run for another office if they had fewer than thirteen months left on their terms, clearly directed at Perry's failed 2012 and possible 2016 presidential runs.

They had considered requiring security for political travel to be paid for by the campaign, not the taxpayers. Audits of the Texas Enterprise Fund initiated by the legislature led to embarrassing revelations of mismanagement. Harsh critics like Tea Party–backed Kevin Eltife of Tyler claimed nothing had changed since Perry was elected. "What have we solved in the last 10 years? What can I really stand up and say I'm proud of?"[69]

Perry's party was changing—again—one reason for the political mudslide. Conservative social issues were front and center and had hit a turning point. Abbott, speaking to conservative activists, rallied for gun rights and limited federal government intervention, and he highlighted his fight against removal of the Ten Commandments from a monument on the state Capitol grounds. He used his office to issue an opinion that local school districts violated the state constitution if they offered domestic partner benefits to employees in same-sex relationships.[70]

But the newly empowered grassroots wanted more than talk. JoAnn Fleming, chair of the Tea Party Advisory Committee, found Abbott short on substance: "We appreciate that he's suing the federal government," she said, "but we need to hear more than 'Washington, DC, is run by a bunch of crooks.'" Debra Medina, who ran against Perry from his ideological right in 2010, noted that Abbott seemed more conservative than Perry but lamented that both had spent their adult lives in public office. "That's not good for the rest of us."[71]

For all their victories, storm clouds were bearing down on Republicans. Demographic changes were shifting the Texas political landscape. "Republicans have at most one two-term governor left in them," a Republican pollster said. "From 2022 on, everything is up for grabs."[72]

"Thank you." Perry began his last speech as governor behind the podium in the House Chamber, addressing legislators as the 84th session began. "I appreciate this one final opportunity to speak to you in the chamber where it all began for me 30 years ago. I have come here to reflect on what we have done together and to say farewell, but most of all, to tell you it has been the highest of honors to serve as your governor for the last 14 years."[73]

Drawing on the tumultuous landscape during his time as governor—recessions, drought, hurricanes, wildfires, a humanitarian crisis at the border, and the disintegration of the Space Shuttle Columbia—he listed a dozen accomplishments, as much a preview of his coming presidential run as a review of his legacy in Texas. He praised the state's diverse economy, unbridled job creation, efforts at tort reform, expansion of water and transportation projects, and energy independence, noting that New York state had banned fracking. "Our formula for success is simple: keep taxes low, implement smart regulations, provide an educated workforce, and stop lawsuit abuse at the courthouse." Criminal justice reform to alter how the state approached nonviolent drug offenders—diversion programs—hadn't made Texas soft on crime, he said. "It's made us smart on crime."

"I leave you with this," he concluded. "Be true to Texas, always, and she will be true to you. Good luck, Godspeed, God bless you, and through you, may God bless Texas."

With little fanfare, he celebrated his last day in office a week later with a vanilla ice cream cone in front of Sandy's, the same ice cream parlor he had visited after he was booked following his indictment less than eight months earlier. He skipped Abbott's inauguration.

Battleground Texas emerged from the ashes of Davis's filibuster, led by a political action committee guided by veterans of the Obama campaign with a mission to fight back against Republican dominance and the Republican agenda in 2015. The group raised $1 million in its first month—eight of ten donors were from Texas—and signed up ten thousand volunteers.[74] Texas Democrats badly needed this shot in the arm. The Democratic Party was faltering at the local level, with barely half of county party offices functioning, contributing to "miserable" turnout and mediocre fundraising.[75]

But things were changing. Women, young people, and Texans of color had jammed the Capitol for legislative hearings and the abortion filibuster in 2013.

Perry scoffed, calling the idea of a Democrat winning Texas "the biggest pipedream I have ever heard."[76] The University of Texas would don archrival A&M's maroon-and-white before Texas goes blue, he joked.

Other Republicans saw change coming. Cornyn's "Keep It Red" ground campaign amassed more than thirteen thousand supporters to walk blocks and flood social media with Republican messaging. FreedomWorks, the deep-pocketed conservative group responsible for Ted Cruz's 2012 Senate victory unveiled its "Come & Take It Texas" drive.

George P. Bush, nephew of former President George W. Bush, taunted the group as he campaigned for state land commissioner: "If anybody from Battleground Texas tells you they're about to turn Texas blue, we're going to say?" he called.

"No way!" the crowds responded.[77]

Perry's final speech to legislators in January 2015 admonished his fellow Republicans to not place purity ahead of unity. "Ronald Reagan knew that someone who agreed with him 80 percent of the time was not his enemy, but his friend. There is room for different voices, for disagreement," he said.[78]

But the rightward drift of the party largely prevented common goals, as delegates to the state Republican convention clashed over immigration, gay rights, and medical marijuana. Reformers, primarily business types with one eye on the *Wall Street Journal* and one eye on the Bible, wanted a guest-worker program for migrant labor. Hardliners called this "amnesty" and demanded harsher punishment and heftier fines for businesses that did not comply with stricter laws.

Tea Party activists who had seized control of the convention inserted a harder line on immigration into the party platform, rejecting the "Texas Solution" to model immigration reform.

"There is language that allows us to slide toward amnesty," delegate Jack M. Finger of San Antonio said of the defeated "Texas Solution" plan. "Guest worker, visa permit, all that puts us on a road to make our citizenship meaningless." Newly elected senator Ted Cruz whipped up the base, telling them that in Texas, gun control was "hitting what you aim at," but neither he nor Abbott was the convention's headliner.[79] That was Sen. Dan Patrick, the Tea Party insurgent from Houston who was running for lieutenant governor.

Gone was the business-friendly moderate approach to immigration, let alone support for in-state tuition for undocumented students, which Perry continued to defend. A more militant philosophy had taken root.

Yet Texas's future, and the political stability of both parties, lay with the growing Latino population. Patrick brushed aside concerns, saying Latinos wanted a secure border, too. Democrats called the proposals dehumanizing, duplicative, and harmful to the state.

Were Republicans moving too far to the right? Rock legend Ted Nugent didn't think so. Texas is the "last bastion of rugged individualism, of true independence" and must be protected, he said, introducing Abbott at an event.[80]

"What I do know is Ted Nugent stands for the Constitution. He stands against the federal government overreaching and doing what they're doing to harm Texans," said Abbott. Nugent also called President Obama a "subhuman mongrel" and suggested immigrants be treated like "indentured servants," prompting calls for an apology and concerns that the Republican Party had lurched too far to the right. Abbott and Perry objected to the language ("not the kind of language I would endorse in any way," said Abbott), but the sentiment seemed to stick.[81]

Republican-led Texas had banned abortion at twenty weeks, required the strictest voter ID laws, and approved some of the most open gun laws in the country. Some Republicans referred to illegal immigration as an "invasion." Others called abortion "genocide." Abbott backed letting parents opt out of required vaccines for religious reasons. Several Republicans, including Perry, floated the idea of repealing the Seventeenth Amendment, which let the voters, rather than state legislatures, pick members of the US Senate.

Democrats hadn't won a statewide election in twenty years, and their losing streak continued in dramatic fashion. The hype of Texas as a "battleground" fell to the reality of Republican dominance. Perry called Texas the Democrats' "political burial ground."[82]

And in 2014, it certainly seemed like he was right. Democrats offered the first all-female ticket in Texas history—Wendy Davis for governor and Leticia Van de Putte for lieutenant governor—and spent tens of millions of dollars, to no avail. Abbott won the governor's mansion with 60 percent of the vote, a margin of over one million Texans, including 68 percent of the suburban vote and 72 percent of small-town Texas. Patrick won lieutenant governor with 58 percent of the vote.

Six out of nine statewide elected positions changed hands. None went to Democrats. Democrats were realistic but hopeful. Whites, who traditionally supported Republicans, made up less than 50 percent of the state's population, and city dwellers outnumbered rural Texans more than two to one. Even among women, Abbott won 54 percent of the votes (62 percent among married women). Building the turnout needed meant some candidates would have to run knowing they were likely to lose.[83]

The Tea Party was fully steeped. Patrick easily defeated the more moderate Dewhurst in the primary for lieutenant governor. Ken Paxton bested moderate Republican Dan Branch, a former state representative from Dallas, for attorney general. Davis's Fort Worth swing district was won by Tea Party newcomer Konnie Burton.

But as the insurgency cheered, moderates continued to worry. Bill Hammond, the Republican president of the influential Texas Association of Business, was openly concerned that the rightward move would ultimately be bad for business. More than ever, he said, solid Republican candidates were losing primary campaigns to more conservative candidates. "It's absolutely a concern more and more for us."[84]

It was bittersweet for Perry, who congratulated Abbott, said other states were jealous of Texas, and predicted that things were "going to get even better" under Abbott.[85]

Inside a hot and humid aircraft hangar in Addison, Texas, and flanked by family, friends, decorated combat veterans, conservative radio host Mark Davis, Taya Kyle (widow of slain sniper and Navy SEAL Chris Kyle), and a plane bearing a "Perry for President" logo, Rick Perry mounted his second bid for the White House in June 2015.

Country-rap rocker Colt Ford blared "Answer to No One" as a triumphant Perry entered the hangar:

Shotgun toter / Republican voter / Rick Perry supporter, let's protect our border. To hell with anyone who don't believe in the USA / Rick Perry all the way.[86]

Perry had the all-American resume: son of a World War II tail gunner, humble farmer in a small-town Texas where his mother bathed him in a no. 2 washtub and sewed his clothes until he went to college, six-man football player, Eagle Scout, Corps of Cadets at Texas A&M University, Air Force officer, farmer. His values of dignity, responsibility to community, unbreakable bonds to family, and duty to country all had been honed in Paint Creek.

"*Run, Rick, Run*," the sweating crowd chanted.

Pledging to end an era of failed leadership and leaning on his success in Texas, he swiped at President Obama's oversight of the "so-called recovery" and regulatory oppression that he claimed had slammed the door on economic growth, leading to increased government debt and stagnating wages. "Weakness at home has led to weakness abroad," he said as he tackled the administration's failure in Iraq, a flawed nuclear deal with Iran, and an insecure border with Mexico.

Washington, DC, was "arrogant," with policies that had smothered the uniqueness of individual communities. "We need to return power to the states and freedom to the individual." He also took aim at the growing Republican field, saying "leadership is not a speech on the Senate floor. It is not what you have said but what you have done."[87]

First stop? Iowa. Specifically, the "roast and ride," a pig roast hosted by Tea Party senator Joni Ernst, with current and prospective GOP presidential candidates in attendance, included Wisconsin governor Scott Walker, Senators Marco Rubio of Florida and Lindsey Graham of South Carolina, former Arkansas governor Mike Huckabee, retired neurosurgeon Ben Carson, and former tech executive Carly Fiorina. The crowded field and long memories of his 2012 run put him behind the eight ball.[88]

Would he be ready? In January 2016 the sixty-five-year-old Texan and the nation's longest serving governor responded in the affirmative. "I got 14 years of preparation as governor running the most successful state in the nation," he said. "I spent the last 23 months in deep preparation on monetary, domestic, foreign policy. I'm ready."[89]

This would be a more serious campaign than 2012. But the stink of the 2012 race lingered in the minds of many activists. It wasn't just the sloppy campaign and missteps on the campaign trail but also the policy positions that found even the conservative Perry chasing a rightward-drifting party. Not to mention that the Texas governor was currently under indictment back home, a problem that could be explained but still a nagging issue for many in a crowded field that would balloon to seventeen candidates.

The Perry camp had heard these concerns before. They argued that the issues Perry stood for were more explosive in 2016 than 2012: the border, a sluggish economic recovery, foreign policy failures. Perry was best when he was one-on-one with people—this time an unrushed campaign could take a longer view and play to Perry's strengths.

Being visible and, frankly, confronting the disaster of 2012 was a good strategy, said longtime Iowa governor Terry Branstad. Perry speaks Texan, which plays well in rural America, using expressions like "the horse is out of the barn" and joking that the economic surge in Texas meant "a lot of new pickup trucks." Perry spent forty minutes talking about cattle with the chairman of western Iowa's Plymouth County Republican Party.

An image makeover showcased his new glasses and traded his signature boots, which hurt his back anyway, for black dress shoes. But rebuilding is harder than building, and second chances are rare in a political world that is shifting all the time.

Policywise, it was 2012 all over again: the border wall wouldn't work; birthright citizenship should be removed; same-sex marriage should be not be legalized (although Perry said he "probably would" attend the same-sex marriage of a—hypothetical—family member).[90] Overall, Perry came off as a better candidate, and the media took notice. His confidence, vision, and experience boosting the Texas economy all showed that. However, he would need to separate himself from the rest of the field.

Making a stand meant taking on fellow Republicans. Perry called Rand Paul's isolationist foreign policy views "dangerous." Paul ridiculed Perry's fashion statements as he critiqued his stances on the issues. "Apparently his new glasses haven't altered his perception of the world, or allowed him to see it any more clearly," Paul wrote in an op-ed.[91] With sixty thousand foreign children streaming across the Texas border, Paul was "surprised" Perry had time to attack his opponents' foreign policy ideas. Perry, shifting to the right, stressed the years-long increase in state law enforcement at the Texas border, designed to slow unauthorized immigration from Central America.[92] Perry also called for Republicans to more seriously engage in the discussion about systematic racial injustice, especially its impact on poverty rates.[93]

The most intense infighting was between candidate Donald Trump and everyone else, with Trump jabbing especially hard at Perry. The outspoken Trump had referred to Mexican immigrants as rapists and drug dealers in his announcement for president, a view denounced by virtually every other Republican candidate. Perry, who had relied on the Hispanic vote in Texas for his sizeable victories in 2002 and 2006, said the remarks did not reflect the Republican Party. Fellow Texan Ted Cruz, now in the US Senate, called Trump "terrific" and "brash" and said he "speaks the truth."[94]

Trump infamously called Arizona senator John McCain, the 2008 Republican presidential nominee and a Navy pilot who'd spent five and a half years in a Vietnamese POW camp, "a dummy." "I like people who weren't captured," Trump said, suggesting McCain was only considered a hero because he had been captured after his plane was shot down.[95]

It was, Perry said, "a new low in American politics" and showed Trump was unfit to be commander-in-chief.[96]

Perry had had enough. In his harshest statement about Trump to date, a month after he announced Perry accused Trump of being "born into privilege" and demonizing Mexican Americans for political sport. "A really hard-hitting speech," he remembers years later.[97]

"Let no one be mistaken, Donald Trump's candidacy is a cancer on conservatism, and it must be clearly diagnosed, excised, and discarded," Perry said during a speech in Washington, DC. "It cannot be pacified or ignored, for it will destroy a set of principles that has lifted more people out of poverty than any force in the history of the civilized world, and that is the cause of conservatism." Trump was leading the polls at the time, but Perry decried his "barking carnival act" that is a "toxic mix of demagoguery and mean-spiritedness" that will lead the Republican Party to "perdition if pursued."[98]

It was a move designed to create political distance between Perry and Trump and position Perry to snag more Republican support when Trump imploded. But Trump fought on, especially on his favorite battleground, the social media site Twitter.

He responded to Perry's takedown with a tweet saying Perry had "failed on the border" and should "be forced to take an IQ test before being allowed the enter GOP debate." Perry's team responded with a video called "Meet Gov. Rick Perry's Biggest Supporter," a compilation of past videos and laudatory tweets from Trump: "Texas is lucky to have him—@GovernorPerry is a great guy"; and "Rick Perry—a good man, a great family and a patriot."[99]

"I gotta figure out whether I could draw blood on this guy or not," he said years later. "I subsequently found out I couldn't. If that speech didn't draw blood, then why waste your time?"

Ultimately, nothing could slow Trump's rise as he hogged the airwaves and dominated headlines. All the candidates, and the Republican Party more generally, had to adjust to Trumpism and the bombastic personality, name-calling, and inchoate policy positions that his brand entailed. Graham called Trump a "jackass"; Trump responded by making public Graham's personal cellphone number. Carson questioned the real estate mogul's "fear of the Lord," to which Trump responded that "you don't hit a person on faith" and further claimed that Carson lacked the energy for the tough negotiation skills a president would require. Jeb Bush, not wanting to alienate Trump supporters, called the rhetoric "ugly" and "mean-spirited."[100]

By August the cupboard was bare. Perry's poll numbers were slumping. The campaign stopped paying staffers. Unforced errors, such as the use of a Russian warship in a video touting the former governor's military background, made defeat seem inevitable.[101] In September Perry became the first candidate in a very crowded field to drop out, four months after he began the race. The Texas governor had never lost an election until he started running for president.

"We have a tremendous field of candidates—probably the greatest group of men and women," Perry said. "I step aside knowing our party is in good hands, as long as we listen to the grassroots, listen to that cause of conservatism. If we do that, then our party will be in good hands."[102]

What happened?

Perry raised barely $1 million in the first month after announcing. He blamed the August 2015 indictments for his sluggish fundraising, but polling showed he was trailing badly even before he set foot on primary soil. A Perry-backed super PAC, the Opportunity and Freedom PAC (run by the nephew of longtime friend Haley Barbour), was established to raise money on Perry's behalf.[103] It raised about $17 million in the same period, funded primarily by Dallas businessmen Kelcy Warren and Darwin Deason, who gave a total of $11 million. Even with a super PAC backing him, it wasn't enough.[104]

"Mr. Perry, he's gone. Good luck. He was very nasty to me," Trump offered in benediction.[105]

The nastiness of the 2016 Republican primary became a hallmark of politics from that moment on. Perry ran in Texas. "Trump changed the game," reflected Chad Wilbanks. "Perry did a good job staying away from that," but politics had become very mean-spirited.[106] Or maybe Rick Perry was getting a taste of his own medicine.

Perhaps the final straw for the insurgent voters who would largely determine the winner of the Republican primary was Perry's thorny criticism of Trump. For better or for worse, Trump harnessed a growing anger and populism within the Republican Party—an energy Perry himself had saddled and ridden to victory in his runs for governor years before. Perry, and most of the other GOP candidates, thought Trump's campaign was the final arc of the party's accommodation of populist anger. But the arc had not completed its curve.

His heart wasn't in it either. Some observers believed he was doing it because it was expected and to prove the first campaign was a fluke.[107]

Perry endorsed fellow Texan Cruz, saying Americans deserved a president who would keep our military strong. It was a bland endorsement—Cruz hadn't served in the military, and military readiness wasn't a key plank of the Cruz campaign—but it allowed Perry to skirt the obvious tension with Trump.

—II—

AN UNDERESTIMATED
POLITICAL REBIRTH

After the 2016 Republican primary, Rick Perry exited the political stage, but he quickly found another way to turn his retail political skills into an attention-grabbing moment. Acknowledging that his dance experience was "almost nil"—he had danced publicly only four times in the past fifteen years, performing a perfunctory waltz at each of his gubernatorial inaugurations—he nevertheless agreed to join Season 23 of ABC's *Dancing with the Stars*.

He had fallen in front of four million people, he cheerfully noted, and now would have the opportunity to fall in front of ten million. CNN journalist Jake Tapper joked that Perry would do a Texas two-step because in the past, Perry had trouble making it to three.

Perry took heat for trying to reclaim a rapidly fading limelight following fourteen years as governor and two failed presidential runs. But he was willing to accept the quips and criticism if his time on the show helped raise public consciousness about one of his key issues—military veterans and the challenges they faced when they came home after deployment to a war zone. He pitched *Advance the Colors* TV, an online resource for returning veterans. He had a more personal reason, too—his daughter, Sydney, was getting married, and he didn't want to embarrass her during the father-daughter dance.

Preshow training found Perry expressing himself without a podium, rolling his hips and twirling his dance partner. "People are going to think, what a dumbass," he said in a moment of self-awareness, but he hoped the show would help him get into the best shape of his life since leaving the Air Force.

His first dance, on week one of the broadcast, was a cha-cha set to "God Blessed Texas" and performed in front of a replica of the Texas State Fair, atop a projected Texas-shaped Lone Star flag. Perry emerged from behind "Rick's Corn Dog" stand, grabbing a corn dog and handing it off before beginning. Show rules meant no teams were eliminated in the first week, allowing Perry to return for the first elimination round (week two) on September 19. He performed a quick-step to the theme from the 1960s television show *Green Acres*, whimsically swinging his arms and bouncing across the stage. Predance footage included Perry in a political parody ad making light of his dryland cotton farm: "More like brown acres," he said.

Perry held a rhinestone-encrusted pitchfork as he and his partner, a professional dancer, awaited the judges' decision.[1] "You gotta be sh***-ing me! Holy mackerel!" Perry shouted upon hearing that they had done well enough in the combined scoring from the show's judges and viewers to advance.

The second round (week three) commenced as former rival Donald Trump and Democratic nominee Hillary Clinton took the stage for the first presidential debate on September 26. Perry and his partner danced a paso doble face-off against rapper Vanilla Ice and his partner.

Perry and his partner ended up with twenty points out of a possible forty—the lowest score of the night. Asked by the show's host how the competition compared with a presidential debate, Perry replied: "Presidential debate ain't even in the class. Oh, man, come on, this is crazy good. This is as good as it gets."

Same question, posed to one of the judges: "I don't know what part of it was crazy good," he said. "It was pedestrian."

While one judge called him fun to watch and "perky and efficient," Team Perry was off the show after three weeks. The national media broke down every excruciating step in GIF form, linking his failures on the dance floor to the failures of his presidential runs.[2]

But Perry saw his turn on *Dancing with the Stars* as both a personal win, helping him prep for his daughter's wedding, and the beginning of a rapprochement with his 2016 foe.

"I was probably more helpful to Donald last night being here than sitting in the audience at the debate, because people got to see a Republican that they may have thought was some stuffed shirt—you know, right-wing, crazy whack job or however they would like to identify us—and over the course of the last month, people got to see a person I think that they came to enjoy being around and liked," he said. "[They] saw a real different individual than may have been caricatured in the media over the course of the last 14 years."[3]

Perry was back for the finale (which aired on November 22, after the election), dancing alongside new friend Vanilla Ice to a Christmas-themed "Ice, Ice, Baby." "It remains to be seen whether Perry will go down in history for his governorship, failed presidential campaigns or his Cha Cha," a writer for CNN mused.[4]

Reality TV proved just the beginning of Perry's political rebirth. On November 21 he visited the president-elect at Trump Tower in New York to discuss a possible role in the Trump cabinet, which he likened to *The Apprentice*, Trump's own reality tv show.[5] The next day he was in Los Angeles for the *Dancing with the Stars* finale, sporting a gold chain and some new moves with Vanilla Ice.

"What was more surreal, performing with Vanilla Ice here tonight or your big meeting in New York yesterday?" Erin Andrews asked. "Uh, can I take 'no comment' on that one at the moment?" Perry answered.[6]

President-elect Trump, the same Donald Trump with whom Perry had clashed during the 2016 primary fight and whom he had called a "cancer on conservatism," met with Perry to mend fences. Perry made the pitch to be the secretary of defense, a passion of his. He had a track record of running "big things." As a veteran, "I can help you there," he told Trump. But Trump had other ideas. In a suite at the Army-Navy football game in early December with Oliver North, Steve Bannon, and Rudy Giuliani, the former New York City mayor asked Perry if he had any interest in heading up the Department of Energy. "Look, I want to help this guy be successful," Perry responded. The offer leaked, and in mid-December the president-elect nominated Perry to serve as secretary of energy. If approved by the Senate, Perry would be leading that third agency he so infamously was unable to name (and that he had slated for elimination) at that fateful debate during the 2012 GOP nomination battle.[7]

Perry's embrace of Trump was his greatest political 180 since he switched parties in 1989. But much like that move nearly three decades earlier, Perry had recognized that times were changing. To survive in the newly Trump-focused Republican Party, "you jump on board or you get run over."[8] Perry was one of the first to acquiesce to the influence of Donald Trump.

Perry later compared Trump to Bill Clements, the irascible governor when Perry was first in the House. Both were "rambunctious" and "blunt" and ruthless and successful. But personal relationships were key, and neither was comfortable with that part of politics. What was it like working for Donald Trump? "This guy was bigger than life," Perry later laughed. "He was fascinatingly complex. A different person than I've ever dealt with before in my life." "Nobody is Donald Trump's peer. He's got a good opinion of himself, I'll leave it at that." He reminded Perry on a regular basis that Perry said some nasty things about him. "Yes, sir, I did, but you gave as good as you took. We didn't get all tied up in that stuff."[9]

Energy wasn't a sexy post. It was a wonky agency, primarily in charge of the upkeep of the nation's nuclear arsenal, hunting weapons-grade plutonium and uranium loose in in the world, overseeing a network of research labs, and awarding grants and loans to encourage innovation in energy, cyber defense for energy infrastructure, and the development of new technologies. His immediate predecessors, Ernest Moniz and Stephen Chu, were, respectively, a nuclear physicist on leave from the faculty at MIT and a Nobel laureate in physics.

The new president's transition period was bumpy. The Trump campaign hadn't planned for the rapid staffing needed (Trump's victory had seemed implausible, even to his campaign staff), and delays in filling critical spots would keep the chute closed for too long. DOE employees were ready for a transition on day one, but nothing happened.

Perry was an early pick for secretary of energy, so the vetting went more smoothly. Not to say there weren't a few bumps en route to Senate confirmation. Perry's corporate board service with two energy firms linked to Texas billionaire and GOP megadonor Kelcy Warren, who had donated funds to both Trump's and Perry's campaigns, came up as a possible conflict of interest. One of the firms, Energy Transfer Partners, was building the Dakota Access Pipeline, a $3.8 billion project to carry oil from North Dakota to Illinois. The project sparked national protests that led to more than five hundred arrests and injured a North Dakota police officer and a protester. Trump himself owned almost $250,000 in Phillips 66 stock, and Phillips held a one-quarter share of Dakota Access—a small amount for the billionaire president and a modest conflict considering the president's reluctance to divest himself of his businesses more broadly.

Perry's climate change skepticism would come up, too, along with his promotion of coal. He had signed a 2005 executive order fast-tracking the construction of coal-fueled power plants in Texas. (The projects ultimately fizzled amid legal challenges from environmental groups.) Perry's long association with "crony capitalism" was an issue, too. The DOE was due to decide the fate of plans by Waste Control Specialists, founded by deceased Texas billionaire and top Perry donor Harold Simmons, to accept nuclear waste at their West Texas facility.[10]

Other actions Perry undertook as governor also undercut his confirmation. Climate change was a growing political issue, and even if red-state governments didn't do much to combat it, studying it was another matter. As governor, Perry had vetoed bills requiring agencies to create climate-change-vulnerability assessments in 2009, 2011, and 2013.[11]

Environmentalists and several members of Congress were skeptical. "It is deeply unsettling that our current secretary of energy, a renowned nuclear physicist, could be succeeded by a contestant on *Dancing with the Stars*," Frank Pallone, the top Democrat on the House Energy and Commerce Committee, said, calling for Perry to be rejected.

Michael Brune, the executive director of the Sierra Club, called Perry's nomination "an insult to our functioning democracy . . . the perfect way to ensure the agency fails at everything it is charged to do."[12]

Perry promised an "all of the above" approach to energy production, similar to his approach in Texas. Wind power expanded during his tenure in office, but so did coal production. It was a "nuanced energy legacy," and Texas was the nation's number one producer of both natural gas and wind energy when Perry left the governor's mansion. He had pushed back against EPA over-regulation and other issues while over-seeing a massive deregulation of the electric sector. He'd signed a bill in 2003 that made permanent a tax break for "high-cost" natural gas, saving drillers billions of dollars in payments over the years, but he also signed legislation requiring renewable energy benchmarks, kickstarting the state's major wind developments.[13]

At his confirmation hearing in January 2017, he expressed regret for saying DOE should be eliminated. "My past statements made over five years ago about abolishing the Department of Energy do not reflect my current thinking," he said. "In fact, after being briefed on so many of the vital functions of the Department of Energy, I regret recommend-ing its elimination." He brushed aside questions about the causes of cli-mate change and redirected the discussion to addressing climate change "in a thoughtful way" that didn't compromise economic growth, en-ergy affordability, or American jobs.

It was a pointed moment of contrition for a politician with such a long history in the public arena, but it was leavened with humor, even if it came at Perry's expense. When it was Sen. Al Franken's (D-Minnesota) turn to question Perry, he reminded Perry that they had previously met in Franken's office.

"Did you enjoy meeting me?" the senator asked.

"I hope you are as much fun on the dais as you were on your couch," Perry said, causing the room to erupt into laughter.

Perry quickly asked for permission to rephrase and added, "I think we've found our *Saturday Night Live* soundbite."[14]

Perry's time as governor had often been tumultuous, lurching between economic crises and explosive political issues, usually with him at the center or at least taking the heat. But in Trump's cabinet, his no-drama approach kept him out of the headlines until near the end, in contrast to fellow cabinet members like Health and Human Services secretary Tom Price, who billed the government for at least $400,000 in travel expenses for traveling by private jet; EPA chief Scott Pruitt, who took advantage of a sweetheart housing deal involving an energy lobbyist; or Housing and Urban Development secretary Ben Carson, who pur-chased a $31,000 dining set for his office with federal funds.[15]

He was the steady hand at DOE, giving boilerplate speeches about American energy and market innovation.[16]

But there was certainly some drama, if most of it relatively tame. A bear hug with coal magnate Robert Murray sent a clear message about the administration's approach to coal, an energy source that is reviled by environmentalists for its carbon-intensive profile.[17] He got into trouble for adding his wife, Anita, to the delegation for an official trip to Italy. And he reddened faces inside DOE by having posters displayed warning against leaks to the media, with depictions of an American flag dissolving into a puddle of computer code, captioned "Every leak makes us weak."[18]

The Trump administration, mostly the West Wing, was leakier than a broken faucet, and embarrassing details of the president's daily schedule or of phone calls with foreign leaders emerged. Critics worried the posters violated whistleblower laws that encouraged employees to report waste, fraud, and abuse; ultimately, the DOE took the posters down.

Perry drew ridicule, too, telling audiences after a 2017 trip to South Africa that more fossil fuels would reduce sexual assault.[19]

Perry had been in Africa for a regional energy summit, promoting a "global clean-coal alliance." Speaking to Chuck Todd after his return, he said fossil fuels would be required to electrify African villages. Quoting a young girl he spoke with at the summit, he said she'd told him electrification was important not only to spare villagers from lung-damaging smoke from the fires used in lieu of electricity but also because better lighting could improve public safety.

"When the lights are on, when you have light that shines, the righteousness, if you will, on those types of acts," he said. "So from the standpoint of how you really affect people's lives, fossil fuels is going to play a role in that." A 2009 study from South Africa seemed to back him up, finding that more lighting in public spaces would be a "quick gain" in reducing sexual assault.[20]

Trump cast himself as a big booster of the nation's coal industry, and Perry's support went far beyond that bear hug with Murray. At a House Energy and Commerce Committee hearing in October 2017, Perry proposed to guarantee financial payments to struggling coal and nuclear plants that were losing market share to natural gas and renewable energy, dismissing concerns that his plan would cost consumers several billion dollars a year. "What's the cost of freedom? What does it cost to build a system to keep America free?" he asked, contending that the power grid's vulnerabilities posed a threat to national security.[21]

Free-market advocates and environmentalists agreed with Perry's hands-off approach, if not his rhetoric—propping up some industries was antimarket, and helping old energy creators would hurt the environment. A DOE report stated that rules should not favor one source of energy over another, and Perry, despite his earlier efforts to prop up coal, seemed content to allow the market to decide which form of electricity generation would win out. Perry acquiesced. Political expediency won out.

The findings disappointed operators of coal-fired and nuclear power plants who hoped for the declaration to force grid operators to buy their electricity, even when it was not the cheapest.[22]

Perry, used to getting his way (for the most part) with lawmakers in Texas, took a less confrontational approach to Congress. After being rebuked by Congress for eliminating a breakthrough program known as the Advanced Research Projects Agency–Energy and slashing the budgets for his own department's national research labs, he vowed to make Congress "proud" of the programs if Congress decided to continue to fund them.

"If you see fit—this committee sees fit, Congress sees fit—to fund particular line items, I give you my solemn oath that it will be administered and managed as transparently and as successfully as possible," Perry said, receiving praise from members and, surprisingly, no condemnation from the White House.[23]

The old Perry charm was on full display as he quickly smoothed over concerns from Rep. Debbie Wasserman Schultz (D-Florida) about a proposed 86 percent cut to DOE's renewable energy budget.

After Perry half-heartedly defended proposed cuts, she accused the Texas governor of doing a "Texas two-step" in his answer. "Well, I was just trying to waltz with you," the former *Dancing with the Stars* participant said with a sly smile. The joke brought a chuckle from the room, including from Wasserman Schultz, who commented that she dances "backward, in high heels, like Ginger Rogers."[24]

But that conciliatory approach to Congress, and his promise to take an "all of the above" approach to energy, was at least partially a façade. Watchdog groups claimed that DOE delayed clean energy grants, slow-walked hiring, undercut staffing levels in the nation's clean energy programs, and underfunded one program for so long that the Government Accountability Office, a government watchdog agency, told the department to release the money or risk violating federal law.[25]

If the perceived indifference, if not outright antagonism, toward clean energy was in keeping with Trump's vocal support for fossil fuels, Perry was more of an outlier within the administration when it came to the causes of climate change.

EPA head Scott Pruitt said in 2017 that he did not believe carbon dioxide was a primary contributor to climate change, prompting Perry to publicly disagree, acknowledging in a television interview that carbon and human activity did play a role.

"The climate is changing. Are we part of the reason? Yeah," he said on CNBC. He did not quantify whether carbon dioxide and other greenhouse gasses produced from burning fossil fuels were the main problem, but he promoted the development of zero-emissions technology, claiming the Trump administration had made great strides in finding cleaner energy solutions.[26] His statements contradicted efforts, not always successful, to roadblock clean energy programs.

If serving in Trump's cabinet was in some ways the perfect job for Perry—providing opportunities to travel the globe promoting the free market and American exceptionalism—it also brought up some nagging concerns from his past.

Perry had long been dogged by accusations of cronyism, of doing favors for friends and donors, although none of the charges ever really stuck. When some of those old practices began to emerge in the final year of his term as energy secretary, however, Congress took notice.

It involved Ukraine, an Eastern European country that, at the time, few Americans paid much attention to.

In his role as Trump's energy ambassador, Perry promoted his goal for Ukraine to become the "Texas of Europe," according to the *Texas Tribune*, and he worked to open the country's oil and gas industry to outside investors.

He said, "Look, I'm a new guy, I'm a deal-maker, I'm a Texan," recalled Yuriy Vitrenko, then Ukraine's chief energy negotiator. "We're ready to do deals."[27]

When Perry traveled to Ukraine in May 2019, representing the Trump administration at the inauguration of President Volodymyr Zelensky, he encouraged the new president to add new members to the board of Naftogaz, the Ukrainian state-owned natural gas company. Michael Bleyzer, "a silver-maned Ukrainian American" oil and gas investor and major Perry donor from Houston, was among the names he recommended. Bleyzer had previously served on the advisory board of Perry's Emerging Technology Fund, and he was a frequent presence at the US embassy in Kyiv, playing the role "both as a private businessman in search of oil and gas deals in Ukraine, and as an informal advisor to Perry."[28]

Bleyzer's links to Perry went back more than a decade and included cutting the Perry campaign a $30,000 check in 2010. His business partner, Alex Cranberg, also had long ties to Perry, who had appointed Cranberg to the University of Texas at Austin board of regents. A week after Zelensky's inauguration, Bleyzer and Cranberg were awarded a contract to drill on government-controlled land in Ukraine, despite offering a bid that was several million dollars less than the only other bidder, according to the *Texas Observer*.[29]

Promoting the merits of US liquefied natural gas to markets in Ukraine and elsewhere came naturally to Perry, who spent the first twenty-six years of his political career in a state defined by oil and gas. (He called liquid natural gas "freedom gas," or, in one press release, "molecules of freedom.") His moves positioned him as the third of the Trump administration's "three amigos" leading US diplomatic efforts in Ukraine. (The other two were Kurt Volker, US special representative for Ukraine, and Gordon Sondland, a businessman whom Trump had named US ambassador to the European Union.)

Nothing in Perry's background suggested he was destined for high-level diplomacy, but he proved masterful at cutting deals in Ukraine. Perhaps too much so.

A six-month investigation by reporters from *Time*, WNYC, and ProPublica found two deals worth an estimated $20 billion that "seemed set to benefit Energy Transfer [whose CEO is Kelcy Warren], the Texas company on whose board Perry served immediately before and after his stint in Washington." A spokesperson for Perry said there was no contact between the secretary and Energy Transfer and that Perry was not a target of an investigation by federal prosecutors. But the deals became central to Ukraine's role in the impeachment of President Trump.[30] Perry later refused to comply with House Democrats' subpoena for documents related to his meeting with Zelensky, the Ukraine president, heightening scrutiny of his actions.[31]

At the same time that Perry was negotiating with the Ukrainian government to encourage it to open up to outside investment, Trump counselor Rudy Giuliani was pushing the same government to investigate the son of Trump's political rival, Joe Biden.[32] Perry claimed he was not directly involved with Trump's attempts to coerce Ukraine into investigating Hunter Biden and said he had not been in communication with Giuliani on the matter.

Instead, Perry claimed the Ukrainian government had requested his advice on energy experts who could help modernize their industry, and he said he applied no pressure on the government regarding Biden. Still, indications were that Perry generally urged Ukraine's president to root out corruption, indicating he was more deeply involved in Trump's efforts to pressure officials in Kyiv than disclosed. Through a DOE spokesperson, Perry admitted to calling for a "modernization and reform of Kiev's business and energy sector," but claimed he did not comment on a call to expand the Naftogaz board or to address corruption. In conversations overheard during a bilateral meeting with Zelensky and Trump in New York in September, Perry's message was clear: "You've got to take steps on your anti-corruption efforts."[33]

Perry portrayed himself as a dealmaker in Ukraine, but that didn't spare him from Congress's focus. Congressional investigators subpoenaed information about Perry's travels to Eastern Europe, records related to his meetings on Ukraine at the White House, and details of conversations between acting White House chief of staff Mick Mulvaney and Perry, along with records involving other current and former DOE employees.[34]

Later reporting revealed that Perry himself stood to benefit from some of the deals he orchestrated in Ukraine—his stock investments in Energy Transfer Partners were valued at around $800,000.

However, Perry was not a target of federal prosecutors investigating the deals. While ethics experts said Perry's advocacy for unvetted companies might be unethical and "skirt criminal statutes," Perry said through a spokesperson that he "never connected or facilitated discussions" between Energy Transfer and Ukraine's state energy firm.[35]

Calling his time as energy secretary the "coolest job" he'd ever had, Perry, the second-longest-serving Trump cabinet member, announced in October 2019 that he would step down at the end of the year.

In an emotional video montage showing Perry visiting DOE labs, speaking at nuclear power plants, and standing in front of tankers hauling natural gas, interspersed with Trump campaign footage, Perry bade DOE staffers goodbye. "From my first day on the job in March 2017, you welcomed me with open arms, even though you didn't know what to expect from this born-and-bred Texan who just arrived in Washington, DC."

He cited progress towards reducing the nation's energy-related carbon emissions, moving towards energy independence and becoming a net exporter of natural gas, bolstering nuclear security, and delivering electricity to over one billion "mired in energy poverty." "I thank President Trump for giving me the opportunity of a lifetime. I am so glad that I said yes."

After resigning, he said, "I'll return to my favorite place in the world: Texas."[36]

— 12 —
LEGACY AND IMPACT

Texas had changed in the years Perry was away. Its population had swelled by four million new residents from 2010 to 2020, driven by urban and non-White Hispanic growth.[1] During Perry's last year in DC, Texas added almost four hundred thousand people, more than any other state.[2] The state's median income for every racial group grew during the decade, although the growth was highest for White and Asian residents.[3]

Yet many of Texas's policy needs had also gone unmet, and the gulf between the haves and the have-nots widened. Adjusted for inflation, spending for public school students was lower than when Perry took office. Texas teacher pay lagged behind the rest of the nation's. Drought plagued most Texas counties, and failure to prepare the state's water infrastructure compounded the problem. The state's foster care system was broken and under the conservatorship of the federal government.

The state's political evolution had also gained speed. During Perry's time in office, Democrats slid from consistent statewide wins and comfortable margins in both chambers to experiencing Republican domination in every executive office and facing a supermajority in both legislative houses. Tea Party–backed candidates swept nearly every office, including all statewide offices. Between 1994 and 2020, Republicans won 139 straight statewide contests, including the presidential elections.

But political dynasties don't last—they can't. The political revolution Perry helped to create and nurture had turned against him. While many of the actions Perry had pioneered during his lengthy time in office—bruising political campaigns, prodigious fundraising, aggressive wielding of the governor's veto pen, and a slavish devotion to tax cuts—were now taken for granted as standard Texas political practice, he was now seen as the "establishment" pitted against the insurgent Republican Party. By the time he was floating a run for president in 2012, the *New Republic* was heaping scorn on his plans to cover the state in toll roads by seizing rural land through eminent domain, his heavy executive hand in mandating the HPV vaccine for public school students, and the 2006 tax swap that critics claimed hurt small businesses and didn't generate enough revenue anyway.[4]

The new Texas Republican Party began to dismantle key parts of Perry's legacy almost immediately after he left office: it killed a signature Perry program to lure top employers to Texas; sapped the state's pride—the Rainy Day Fund—to return money to taxpayers; and defunded an in-state tuition program for undocumented students.

The long-simmering grassroots surge boiled over as Perry departed the stage. "The young conservatives have completely moved on, but I think even some of the old guard are pretty tired of him," said one Austin-area Tea Party activist. The Republican Party that under Perry's leadership had avoided fiery immigration rhetoric and deferred to big business took a backseat to an increasingly nativist party.[5]

The party leaders had changed, too, with Gov. Greg Abbott's pragmatic blandness a sharp contrast to Perry's decade of swagger and confrontation. The new governor wasted no time in abolishing the decade-old Emerging Technology Fund and instructing lawmakers to reform the Texas Enterprise Fund, which had handed out more than a half billion in taxpayer dollars to Fortune 500 companies and other businesses that expanded or uprooted and moved to Texas. State auditors found that the program lacked transparency and that the state had failed to adequately track its performance. The legislature replaced the Emerging Technology Fund with a new university fund to recruit top academics to the state.[6]

"With all the controversy around those, at least the perception of cronyism, I think acting quickly like that and distancing himself from the controversies from the prior administration is a brilliant move," said Lyle Larson, a moderate Republican and former legislator from San Antonio, referring to criticism that the funds rewarded Perry donors and allies. "You don't carry that baggage with you. You dispose of it."[7]

Other Republicans were more critical, especially the new breed of Tea Party Republicans who cried foul about the use of state funds to promote business development.

Perry had been a frenetic force with a passion for closing deals.[8] Critics found it hypocritical to argue for limited government on one hand while stuffing incentives into the pockets of big business with the other. The right-leaning Texas Public Policy Foundation called the "deal closing" fund a slush fund for corporate welfare. "We don't need to pay people to come to the state of Texas," said JoAnn Fleming, executive director of Grassroots America, a leading Tea Party group.[9]

Abbott called it "crony capitalism" and suggested Texas shouldn't pick "winners and losers." Perry campaign staff realized that their "thumb on the scale" would rankle purist Republicans, but they also felt it wasn't practical to think this way in a modern economy when other states and nations were offering these incentives.[10] This model had, after all, been used for decades to prop up the "Texas Miracle."

Republicans weren't complaining about strong economic growth—just the means to get there. They may have had a point. Even with the funds closed or minimized, Texas still led the nation in luring companies from California, the state Texas Republicans love to hate.[11]

Perry reads political tea leaves better than any politician in Texas history. Most of his political career was spent in a state politically in flux. In a state witnessing this much political churn, politicians must be adaptable to succeed. And Texas politics is not a spectator sport—you have to move your feet. With Perry, this adaptability was more "evolution than revolution," a slow process that unfolded over the course of his career.[12] His political flexibility was his strength. As Christopher Hooks pointed out, Perry "could be pro-immigrant, a border hawk, a warrior for Christ, whatever you needed."[13]

"He could be different people, but it always seemed a bit outrageous but not surprising. I had the feeling it was all just calculation," Jonathan Tilove remarked. He was in "tune with how the tempers changed."[14] One national journalist called him a perfect cipher, scathing criticism that for many hit home: "A man whose only discernible passion is his extreme willingness to be whatever someone will pay him to be, or vote for him to be."[15]

His number one objective "was to win."[16]

Perry "made a calculated decision to become the head of the Party it has now become," according to a former Texas congressman. This meant leading the charge on some conservative issues against the way his "mama and papa taught him."[17]

Perry "built the Republican Party for him and Kay [Hutchison]" starting in the early 1990s. He spent a lot of time focusing on making appointments that would be helpful, doing events for the party, and raising money. His endorsement in the 2000s was tantamount to "winning a primary in Texas."[18] A former Republican National Committeeperson said Perry "made a huge contribution to the growth of the party in Texas," including his support for Republicans running against Democrats in the Texas House, which helped turn the chamber red in the 2002 election and paved the way for 2003 congressional redistricting so onerous to Democratic lawmakers that they fled the state in an effort to stop it.[19] Perry was intimately involved in making phone calls, attending events, connecting donors to the party, and encouraging local Democrats to switch parties, recalls Chad Wilbanks, former political director of the Republican Party. "His contribution was unmatched."[20]

He changed the party for himself, too. The Tea Party became a major influence in primaries. "To this day those seeds have matured into huge oak trees."[21] Advancing popular policies and winning elections was a big step, according to former state party chair Tina Benkiser. "He was great about attending fundraisers and attending events when asked. He made the grassroots feel welcome at the table."[22] The party had its own leadership, sure, but Perry was the real party leader, Wilbanks said. It was "What can we do to help make you more successful, Governor?" but the governor knew that he needed the party. "That's how he was able to put his stamp on that."[23]

When Perry entered political life, Republicans held a few hundred local county offices. By the time he left, that number was over three thousand.[24] The Party had energy but no direction. Perry gave it a steering wheel.

Others were less sure. "I think it's been more about what's good for Rick Perry as opposed to what's good for conservatism and the party," said Tom Pauken, a Perry critic who served in the Reagan White House and whom Perry appointed to the Texas Workforce Commission. The party did well despite Perry, not because of Perry: "Rick does a good job of taking care of the financial folks that helped him."[25]

"I see him more as a politics of personality and politics of loyalty rather than a strong policy-driven approach from a conservative perspective," Pauken said. "It's more kind of an LBJ-style of Republicanism."[26] Legislators missed that collaborative approach to lawmaking, an instinct some said was lacking in the officeholders after Perry.[27]

Some of the political changes were shaped by external events. Observers argue the election of Barack Obama changed Perry—but Obama's election really fast-forwarded the changes in the Texas GOP. (Perry included, who "understood the implications for Texas politics long before anyone else.")[28] Perry "jumped in front of the parade," said a former campaign manager.[29] Then he rode it for as long as he could before it bucked him.

Much as he had with the Tea Party almost a decade earlier, at the end of his career, he saw Trump as the future of the Republican Party. "This was totally different than the Rick Perry I had a conference with in 1985," said Stenholm, a former Democratic congressman and a neighbor of the Perry family in West Texas. "He understood [that] rural America needed more [help] to keep doctors and hospitals in these areas and [he] provided leadership on healthcare issues. He is more today in the Trumplican or Ted Cruz part of the party than he ever was."[30]

He was a "product of the old days" in Texas politics, when getting things done meant working with opposition members.[31] He understood Texas and the Texas politics of that era. Perry said: "I get it about the things that both sides of the aisle have to do to kinda make the base happy from time to time. But at the end of the day in the State of Texas we still can get along and not just personally try to destroy everybody."[32]

But the Republican Party evolved to a place where, even as ambitious as Perry was, he would never have gone. "Perry at least had a regulator on him. Having been through the politics on it, his instincts wouldn't let him go to certain places."[33]

In a different political era, Perry would have been a conservative Democrat in the mold of Preston Smith or Allen Shivers. He would have been at home in the 1950s Democratic Party, where most were culturally conservative and not afraid of government extending a helping hand. A more polished Bill Clements. A calmer Ross Perot.

Could Perry have survived as a conservative Democrat? According to Charlie Stenholm, "If he was the Rick Perry I knew," he could have survived.[34]

But it was the rightward drift of the Republican Party, with its insistence on purity and fealty to conservative causes, that drove the biggest change in his political career. The party has had majorities in the legislature for decades and has won more than a hundred statewide offices. The winning ironically begat a civil war, as Republicans jockeyed for position in a state where they had no meaningful opposition except themselves. It wasn't so much that Perry pivoted to accommodate the party's hard right turn, Leticia Van de Putte said, as that he "'leaned' into the new philosophy."[35]

But the party in which Rick Perry won those ten races was not today's Republican Party. "By today's standards, on some issues, he could be considered pretty progressive," said Democratic consultant Harold Cook of the rapid changes in the Republican Party.[36] Perry held the disparate wings of the party together for as long as was possible.

The Texas Republican Party had become a blend of economic libertarianism and social and cultural conservatism, evoking right-wing populism. The voters who helped George W. Bush and Rick Perry dominate Texas were now called "unicorns" by anti-Trump Republicans: Republicans who were politically moderate, didn't regularly watch Fox News, rejected conspiracy theories, and were highly educated.[37]

Christopher Hooks, writing for the *New York Times*, argued the Texas Republican Party was an unusual but comfortable mix of "good-ol'-boy rural conservatives, big-city chambers of commerce, fire-breathing evangelical warriors, white-shoe professionals, white-pride populists, and a surprising number of nonwhite voters."[38] Winning elections was the tie that bound the party together.

But over time, that more inclusive approach to party splintered and became a hostage-taking approach to politics that shattered legislative norms and used every tool to maintain power.[39] Said one longtime Republican congressional aide, the party was now about "owning the libs and pissing off the media."[40] Candidates were recruited to run *against* someone rather than run *for* an office.

This Republican Party was more "chaotic, divided, and unsteady" than the pre-Obama version.[41] Local Republican Party organizations censured politicians they deemed insufficiently conservative—such as frequent target Speaker Joe Straus, whom two thirds of Republicans in his home county and his lifelong party voted to admonish in 2017. "The party apparatus has drifted so far to the extreme that it's essentially a joke," he told the *New York Times*, comparing the party to a "clown show." "I think Republican leaders are too often following these groups rather than trying to lead them," he said.[42]

Perry may be the most prominent "Never Trumper" to convert to Trumpism, referring to Trump after the campaign ended as the "chosen one."[43] From the outside, the about-face was a head-scratcher, but Perry's career has been built on sensing the direction the party was moving in and following obediently. The creature Perry helped birth when *Dallas* was still prime-time television eventually consumed him. According to one Republican consultant, "Trump didn't hijack the Republican Party. He is the logical conclusion of what the party became over the past 50 or so years, a natural product of the seeds of race-baiting, self-deception and anger that now dominate it."[44]

Perry entered politics at a time when governing with opposition parties was possible and partisans worked together to solve problems in Texas. Partisan labels were shed at the door. According to one observer, "He was governor long enough to see that not everybody on the other side was an ogre."[45]

That shifted. If the election of Barak Obama had changed the Republican Party, driving it further right and deeper into intransigence, Trump and Trumpism were change on steroids, transforming the Republican Party both in Texas and nationally in four years as much as Perry changed the state party in thirty. "Pugnacious" became the GOP watchword.

The toll on Texas clout was high. The party that had dominated

Texas politics since the early 2000s no longer recognized itself. "Boy, I wish [George W.] Bush were here now," one former member said. But contemporary observations suggest that even George W. Bush couldn't get elected in today's Texas Republican Party.[46] Could Perry? "Oh yeah, if you've got enough money," Perry chirped years later. Although he flirted with running for president in 2024 ("not ruling anything out" as of June 2023), he privately admitted with a faint air of resignation that those days are over. "It's a bit less" about relationships and working together, Perry lamented. "I miss the circus; I just don't miss the clowns. It's performance art. Performance art that matters."[47]

Between 2018 and 2020, a "Texodus" sent ten veteran Texas Republican members of Congress heading for the exit. The "serious" people either were thrown out the window or headed for the door.[48] Polling revealed that almost half of Texans had a worse opinion of the state GOP than they had before Donald Trump was elected president.[49]

This is a consequence of a one-party state—there are no brakes on ideological extremism.

But writing a political obituary for Perry doesn't square with the political pull he maintains in Texas. "They always love you better after you're gone," he reflected from retirement.[50] He was hired in 2023 to be the spokesperson for the Texas Sports Betting Alliance, whose mission was to legalize sports betting in Texas. His efforts to help other Republicans have succeeded when they have run up against the new politics of the GOP. In a 2021 special election for the congressional seat left vacant by the death of US Rep. Ron Wright, Perry backed Waxahachie Republican state Rep. Jake Ellzey, who favored a path to citizenship for undocumented immigrants and opposed a border wall and school choice; Ellzey beat Wright's widow, Susan Wright, who had been endorsed by Trump.[51] Wright's campaign blasted Ellzey as an "opportunistic ladder-climbing RINO" (Republican In Name Only). Senator Ted Cruz came out against Ellzey, and the conservative antitax Club for Growth ran ads against Ellzey. "For the Club for Growth to have actively tried to destroy this guy's reputation, you've gotta be sh***ing me," said Perry.[52]

Perry also backed close family friend Morgan Luttrell—a disabled veteran Perry took in who slept on the third floor of the governor's mansion on an air mattress—who won the 2022 Republican primary in a bid to replace outgoing Rep. Kevin Brady in a district north of Houston. Luttrell was the cause of another Perry conversion—this time on the efficacy of psychedelic drugs to help veterans with mental health problems. In 2021 Perry backed legislation that would allow clinical studies on the use of psilocybin (found in "magic mushrooms") as an alternative treatment. Perry also stumped on the back of a pickup for his former scheduler Stan Gerdes, running for city council in Smithville (population 4,047). Gerdes was elected to the Texas House years later. Perry's endorsement still matters, especially in a primary race, his former chief of staff said. "People still love Rick Perry. That endorsement still works. Right now, he's still golden."[53]

The question is, did Perry change the Republican Party or did the party change him?

"The party changed out from under him, the party moved on," according to Joe Holley.[54] "'Phony' is such an ugly word. Let's stick with 'pragmatic.' I'm not sure that's an evil thing."[55]

"Reagan, Dole, McCain, Romney, Bush. They're like strangers in their party now," surmised former Democratic leader Jim Dunnam. "Rick Perry got caught up into that."[56]

Matthew Dowd was struck by the major changes to both Perry and the party he helped built in a relatively short period. "If Rick Perry the state representative of 1986 would show up today and see the Republican Party today, he would want nothing to do with it."[57]

The "Texas Miracle"—the supposed unique mix of Texas moxie, low economic regulations, and minimal taxes—was the gold in Perry's belt buckle while he was in office and running for president. Republicans have been taking bows for the economic prosperity birthed by the expansive Texas economy, contributing to the party's string of political successes since 2000.[58] Perry points to that, especially education policy tweaks to help create a skilled workforce—along with not overtaxing or overregulating—as keys to his legacy.[59]

There has been much to celebrate: Texas created one-third of the nation's new jobs between 2003 and 2013, or, as Perry put it, gained "lots of pickup trucks on highways." The basic governing philosophy was to keep taxes low and regulations lower. This legacy may very well have happened without Perry. But he was ruthless about cutting government services to avoid tax increases, especially when state revenues dipped dramatically in 2011, which kept the state's economy stable without scaring businesses away from Texas.

This economic development "put Texas on the map," and Perry's former chief of staff said the governor was the closer. "His magic with people. He dealt with CEOs and people from all over who wanted to come here. His ability to look people in the eye and tell funny stories, he did the economic development deals."[60]

But the economic miracle didn't reach every Texan. Most of the growth was concentrated in urban areas, favoring highly educated workers in professional jobs.[61] The number of low-skill, low-pay positions jumped, prompting some to claim that "McJobs" had created an illusion of growth.[62]

Median family income in Texas has not increased much, in part because population growth has provided a steady supply of new workers, allowing employers to keep salaries low.[63] Indeed, 11 percent of Texans live below the poverty line. Although the number of uninsured Texans has fallen in recent years, 62 percent of Hispanics and 19 percent of women still lacked healthcare coverage in 2016, one year after Perry left office.[64] Texas also ranked fifth nationally in income inequality in 2016. The gap between the rich and poor is huge—the richest 5 percent of households earned on average over $217,000 per year, while the poorest 20 percent earned on average just over $23,000.[65] Urban areas have particularly high rates of inequality.

Race is a factor, too—poverty rates for African Americans and Hispanics are three times higher than for Anglos, and Hispanics earn approximately 75 percent of what Anglos make. By 2017, 48 percent of Hispanics reported they were left behind by changes in the economy (compared to 27 percent of whites who agreed).[66]

As one observer put it, "Rick Perry is like the rooster who thinks his crowing caused the sun to come up."[67]

Perry was a tireless promoter of Texas exceptionalism, but he was also the original Washington-hater-in-chief. His skirmishes began during his time as agriculture commissioner, from fighting a proposed tax increase on natural gas to arguing against regulations under the Endangered Species Act. But the conflicts escalated as Perry ascended to the governor's mansion, in part in reaction to a stronger federal government and in reaction to the election of Barack Obama, who was viscerally disdained by many Texas Republicans.

He fought regulation, via lawsuits against the EPA, and blocked the expansion of Medicaid through the Affordable Care Act. He barred the state from competing for grants under the Obama administration's education initiatives. He argued that the federal government was doing too little to secure the border.

His successors have continued the tradition.

Perry also emerged as an unlikely champion of criminal justice reform, especially considering his early mixed record on such matters. But during his time in office, Texas became a national leader in reforms affecting nonviolent offenders and reducing the prison population.

Texas prisons were stuffed with thousands of small-time drug offenders and nonviolent criminals when Perry became governor in 2000. His Democratic predecessors, including Ann Richards, had bragged about adding prison beds and cutting the circumstances under which prisoners were eligible for parole. In response, the prison population had quintupled over the prior twenty years. As governor, Perry signed a dozen bills freeing those wrongfully convicted and expanded drug courts, keeping nonviolent offenders out of jail. The plans—often spearheaded by the legislature rather than the governor—allowed the state to close three prisons.

The bipartisan consensus on criminal justice issues was largely abandoned after Perry left office, and the next generation of Republican leadership, responding to rising crime rates and a conservative national trend, spiked bail reform efforts.

Beyond policy, Perry recreated the role of Texas governor. Traditionally considered a relatively weak position, with most power residing with the legislature, the governor's office under Rick Perry became a seat of power.

As one consultant put it, "He's made the state into his personal fiefdom."[68]

Paul Burka of *Texas Monthly* has followed Texas politics for decades, watching the ways in which governors have imposed their personalities on the office to make it stronger: "The fundamentals of governing are candor, competence, loyalty, and leadership. This is true during booms and busts, for Republicans and Democrats, in times of ideological fervor and in times of pragmatism. Personality transcends policy."[69]

Governors must earn the power they wield. But the structure of Texas's government makes it possible. The legislature meets only every two years, an anachronism for governing a state as large and diverse as Texas but a boon to its governors, who have significant power to run the state in the legislature's absence. Texas governors don't have to worry about legislative overrides to their vetoes—the state constitution sets the veto deadline after the legislative session ends. Most governors have taken advantage of that tactic.

Governors are also empowered to manage the state's fiscal affairs when the legislature is out of session, and Perry made aggressive use of the legislature's time away to engineer state government to fit his agenda.

Finally, and important in a state that experienced rapid changes in the decades following 1980, meeting in session only every two years allows for a fresh start every session, as lawmakers return to Austin *tabula rasa*. Governors can more easily adapt their politics to reflect changes in the state.

Perry was in office for so long, and made so many appointments to boards, commissions, state agencies, and judicial positions, that he had a "de facto cabinet," according to one observer.[70] The legislature allowed the governor to concentrate appointments and reach deep into agencies to populate them. Perry appointed 113 judges or justices, nearly a quarter of the state judiciary.[71] The left-leaning *Texas Observer* reported that of the four thousand jobs that he filled during his gubernatorial terms, more than a quarter went to political donors. Between 2001 and 2010, those appointees gave Perry more than $17 million, about 20 percent of his total fundraising haul, according to Texans for Public Justice.[72] Many other appointees were former staffers who had worked with or for the governor, giving him tighter control over state agencies through these loyalties. Appointments went beyond political favoritism. Many went to individuals who could shape state agencies in Perry's political image. Take the case of Wallace Hall Jr., appointed by Perry to the University of Texas Board of Regents to push for market-based reforms in higher education, positioning students as "customers" and emphasizing teaching and faculty productivity. Texas A&M University, Perry's alma mater, later adopted some of the reforms, which were largely funded by businessman and Perry donor Jeff Sandefer.

The proposed reforms caused intense angst in the state's higher education community, fueling conservative tropes about lazy professors and elitist institutions. But they weren't Hall's only efforts at shaking up UT. He requested eight hundred thousand records related to student admissions, many of which were confidential. (While Hall was demanding more transparency from UT, it turned out that he had failed to disclose several lawsuits against him in his application to serve on the board, prompting an impeachment investigation.)[73]

Perry was loyal to those loyal to him. When House member John Frullo drew a primary opponent in 2016, Perry flew up on his own to endorse him. "Over an Aggie," recalled a shocked Republican consultant. "I don't forget my friends," Perry said.[74]

But it worked both ways: "Cross him and he'll squash you like a bug," said a longtime observer.[75]

Stenholm, a fellow red-dirt farmer and congressman who had talked with a young Rick Perry about Texas politics for hours and backed him in his first run for the House, found that out the hard way.

"Rick is the governor who called three special sessions on redistricting to get rid of me and others," he said. "They took my farm and my home out of my district."[76]

In the 2020 Republican primary, Perry cut video ads in a little-watched judicial race for a Court of Appeals seat in Waco, endorsing Gina Parker over incumbent Judge Bert Richardson. Richardson, in 2015, was the trial judge who refused to dismiss the criminal indictment against Perry.

You were either a friend or you were not. He "had a very long memory," according to one longtime observer.[77] Republican consultants Mark Sanders and John Deaver worked for Perry opponents, and "that was it. They could never find work again in Texas."[78]

Throughout his career, Perry rewarded friends and punished enemies. Matt Taibbi wrote: "Favors are the one consistent thread running through Perry's political career. Throughout his time as governor, whenever his ideology or his religion comes into conflict with the need to give a handout to a major campaign donor, ideology and religion lose every single time."[79]

Mark Griffin was appointed by Perry to the Texas Tech Board of Regents in 2005. He resigned in 2009 after publicly supporting Hutchison's gubernatorial campaign. Griffin then ran for state representative, and Perry helped beat him.[80]

The governor's office functioned as a farm team for the state's lobbying corps, dubbed "Rick's Revolvers" by the crusading left-leaning group Texans for Public Justice, which reported that 5 percent of the governor's office staff had been or later became lobbyists. Clients—including ExxonMobil, Lockheed Martin, Apple, and dozens of local Texas cities—paid these revolvers between $53 million and $100 million between 2001 and 2012.[81]

Five of Perry's seven chiefs of staff were lobbyists.[82] His appointments provided powerful fodder for the charges of cronyism that dogged him throughout his time in politics. "Rick Perry has managed to set a scary new low in the annals of opportunism, turning Texas into a swamp of political incest and backroom dealing on a scale not often seen this side of the Congo or Sierra Leone," read one scathing review, published as Perry entered the national stage to run for president.[83]

He denied the charges.

He pushed to create a mega regulatory agency, the Texas Residential Construction Commission, and appointed his top campaign donor, Houston homebuilder Bob Perry, to sit on the agency's board. His 2007 executive order to require HPV vaccines would have benefited the drug manufacturer Merck, whose lead lobbyist was a former Perry chief of staff.[84] "To this day I don't really know if he was motivated by that [political money] or just susceptible to it," Cook, the longtime Democratic operative, said. "And there is a big difference."[85]

Crony capitalist or not, Perry became a millionaire while in office, a far leap from his humble roots in Paint Creek. He earned $150,000 as governor, but his outside investments proved more lucrative. Perry's personal investments were not large but fit a pay-to-play pattern, benefiting those who helped him. He held stock in thirty-seven companies and invested in three that received taxpayer money from the Texas Enterprise Fund, one of which was founded by a longtime donor, James Leininger.[86] Perry also held shares in at least three other companies that made hefty campaign contributions to the Republican Governor's Association, which Perry chaired in 2010 and 2011.[87]

He made several advantageous real estate deals, including the 1995 sale of a 9.3-acre tract of land to computer magnate Michael Dell (giving Dell badly needed access to an adjacent municipal sewage district) while serving as agriculture commissioner; Dell paid nearly four times what Perry had paid for the land two years earlier. The deal was brokered by Perry's friend and future chief of staff Mike Toomey.[88]

Luck, responded critics. Perry bought land during real estate troughs and sold at the peaks. His opponents were more cynical, pointing to Perry's power and political connections as leverage he used in cashing out. Another example? He bought land in 2001 from longtime friend Troy Frasier, who represented the area's development district in the state Senate.[89] Perry later sold the land at a profit of more than $800,000.

No charges were filed in connection with any of these dealings, and Perry brushed aside the scrutiny. "I've been in politics long enough to know that this is just a part of doing business," he told the *Fort Worth Star-Telegram* in 1998. "I know full well, as my wife knows, that our private lives, particularly on the financial side, becomes fair game."[90] Perry was adept at playing the game "the way it had always been played" in Texas.[91] Guard the wealthy and the powerful. Protect your friends.

"I don't know if he's either corrupt or just part of a system that is so brazen at trading favors that I don't know where to draw the line," said one former journalist.[92]

Representing the interests of energy, the incredibly wealthy, and big donors was never a strong indictment of Perry—it seemed too "technical" and not a clear crossing of the line that defined many scandal-ridden governors. He was "playing the game to win the game of politics," talking to lobbyists to accrue power and influence but never "doing something bigger and larger that was closely associated with what he believed."[93]

As governor, Perry also made substantial use of the "governor's gift"—the veto. He vetoed the most bills in one session in Texas history, and because of his longevity in office, the highest total in Texas history. Edmund J. Davis—the Reconstruction-era governor despised for his aggressive tactics—had the most vetoes on average per session, at 47.5. Governor John Connally had 170 total (28.3 per year), and Bill Clements, the first Republican governor of the state since the end of the Civil War, had 184 total (23 per year). Lawmakers say they never cowed legislatively in the face of Perry's aggressive use of the veto pen, but the threat of the veto hung over every bill.

After Governor Abbott line-item vetoed funding for the entire legislative branch in 2021, headlines screamed "How Greg Abbott Became the Most Powerful Governor in Texas History." If that was true, Perry jumped so Abbott could fly. (The funding was later restored.)

Perry changed the way Texas is governed, but he also changed the way campaigns are conducted. His vigorous fundraising paved the way for that of his successor—Abbott's relentless fundraising has produced a multimillion-dollar war chest, the fifth largest ever reported and the most of any governor in US history.[94] As governor, he has raised $105 million for his campaign account, and as of 2022, he flew past Perry to raise the all-time record for a Texas governor: $274 million since 1995. It took Perry nearly eleven years as governor to raise $100M; Abbott reached that milestone in half that time. Another Perry legacy? West Texas developer George McMahan told a local television station in 2018 that if you made a large enough donation to Abbott, you were eligible for an appointment. The Abbott campaign returned McMahan's money.

Perry also pioneered the rough, partisan campaigns that have become the norm in Texas. "Running against Perry is like running against God," Sharp said. "Everything breaks his way! Either he's the luckiest guy in the world or the Lord is taking care of him."[95]

Sure, intraparty warfare is as common as bluebonnets after a wet spring, but Perry's emergence as a political force in the 1990s brought fractious campaigns between Republicans and Democrats and ushered in a new muddy era in Texas political campaigns. After the bruising 1998 campaign for lieutenant governor against Sharp, who had been a close friend, Perry found the perfect analogy. "In the Capitol, I'm for everybody. On Thanksgiving Day, I'm gonna be for the Aggies."[96]

The growth of angry attack politics has real-world impacts beyond fraying decades of friendship. Smashmouth campaigns, where candidates will go to extremes to court their base, have led to a spread of misinformation and occasional violence.

It is, however, hard to argue with success: Perry won ten straight elections. "The guy just knows how to win," said one longtime Democratic operative.[97] Or at least he did, until he left Texas to run for president.

Returning to Texas from Washington after his time at the Department of Energy, Perry retired, but he did not retreat from public life. Sure, the state's most influential governor in history spent time as many retirees do: visiting with locals in the quaint, one-stoplight country town of Round Top, going to Aggie football games, babysitting his grandkids along with several dogs, and road-tripping across the country in his dream car (a 1970s classic Chevy Chevelle). He also helped spread the word about lost dogs who showed up at his ranch through his Instagram account and shared photos of himself dining on his favorite butterscotch-chip pie.[98]

But politics was never far removed from his mind. For a politician who never lost an election in Texas, "it all just happened mostly by the grace of God. But I was paying attention, too."[99]

But he also remains a consummate and cagey deal maker, holding an hourlong press conference (an infomercial, according to some) at the Texas Capitol in 2021, in the midst of the Covid pandemic, in an effort to convince state leaders to buy "catch and kill" air filtration devices from a company in which he acknowledged being an investor.

As for the size of that investment, Perry just grinned: "Well, that's none of your business. I'm not a public official anymore."[100]

ACKNOWLEDGMENTS

My fascination with Texas governors goes way back to my childhood in the Dallas suburbs. I quickly realized that two positions were the two most important in the state: the governor and the quarterback of the Dallas Cowboys. Since this was the mid-1980s, Danny White was the struggling quarterback of America's Team and Mark White was the (also struggling) governor. I reasoned that because of their last names and importance to the state, they must be related.

This was my introduction to executive politics in Texas—a fascination that continued through the genesis, design, research, and writing of this book. Governors, even the obscure ones, have tremendous power to influence state politics, and I chose to write this full-length treatment of one of the most consequential the state has known.

There were many ways that this book might not have come into being, but I'm glad it did. Fate brought me back to Texas, and a casual conversation with journalist Erica Grieder over tacos in East Austin set in motion a book project that was finally born during the pandemic. I'm grateful to Erica for her inquisitiveness about the topic and for connecting me with her contacts at the University of Texas Press.

I'm also grateful to the many people who helped me track down sources or let me bounce ideas off them or just gab about Texas politics during the 1980s to 2000s era. Although I've lost track of everyone who contributed, a short but incomplete list includes Jeremy Wallace, John Moritz, Mike Ward, John Austin, Bob Garrett, Bob Moore, Chris Fox, Madlin Mekelberg, Zach Despart, Ron Lewis, Harvey Kronberg, Peggy Fikac, Christy Hoppe, James Barragan, Elly Dearman, Jasper Scherer, Cayla Harris, Chad Wilbanks, Reena Diamonte, Jay Leeson, and Patrick Svitek. During the writing of this book, I was saddened by the loss of Texas political stalwarts Harold Cook, Jay Leeson, Chris Lippincott, and Congressman Charlie Stenholm, all of whom provided valuable insight. Although I was unaware Chris was sick, one of the last messages he sent me was, "The ball could roll off the table for any one of us any time." I've taken that to heart. Hector Gutierrez Jr. has been a great friend and supportive mentor and perhaps an even more erstwhile Aggie than the former governor himself. James Russell is an amazing friend who put me in touch with several critical people for the book but, more than that, was encouraging and daily ready with a hilarious story. I truly value his friendship and his political sensibility. Jason Smith, our community and government outreach guru at the University of Houston, was instrumental in connecting me with several key Perry staff. To the dozens of sources who talked to me for the book, thank you for helping me preserve this slice of Texas political history. I am especially grateful to Governor Perry, who was generous with his time and shared a lot about his life.

I owe a special thanks to Jeannie Kever, who taught a prose-averse academic how to write. This was a book that needed levity and lift—something I certainly did not know how to do. Her edits made this project sing, and it wouldn't be half as good without her gentle lessons. Patience was required to see this project through, and Casey Kittrell at UT Press had enough to fill the Brazos twice. From the beginning, he was enthusiastic about the project, even when I provided several inadequate early attempts. UT Press was my first and only choice for this book, and Casey's creativity and care make me certain of my decision every day. Christina Vargas at UT Press greatly assisted in securing the pictures—including the oversized poster—that liven up the book.

Finally, the only person who has heard all the stories in the book (and more) is my wife, Tracy, who was willing to move to Texas all those years ago and listen to yet another anecdote about Texas politics. I appreciate her patience throughout this yarn—the longest to date. Special thanks to my dad, who accompanied me on a research visit to Wichita Falls, where we got a view of the World's Littlest Skyscraper, a reminder that details matter. To my boys, who were my stay-at-home work colleagues during the pandemic writing process, thank you for all the laughs and for reminding me not to take Texas politics too seriously.

Brandon Rottinghaus
Houston, Texas

AUTHOR INTERVIEWS

Armbrister, Ken, August 26, 2021
Arnold, Jim, August 5, 2021
Austin, John, October 25, 2018
Bell, Chris, August 6, 2021
Benkiser, Tina, November 1, 2021
Carney, David, August 8, 2021
Cook, Harold, August 31, 2021
Danberg, Debra, August 24, 2021
Dowd, Matthew, August 9, 2021
Dunnam, Jim, August 15, 2022
Emmett, Ed, August 3, 2022
Gutierrez, Hector, August 16, 2021
Herman, Ken, August 10, 2021
Holley, Joe, July 26, 2021
Hoppe, Christy, August 27, 2021
Johnson, Cliff, July 28, 2022
Kronberg, Harvey, September 14, 2021
Lewis, Ron, August 5, 2021
McClellan, Jon, August 31, 2021
McNeely, Dave, August 27, 2021
Medina, Debra, August 19, 2021
Miller, Bill, September 10, 2021
Pauken, Tom, August 2, 2023
Perry, Rick, July 31 and August 4, 2023
Ratcliffe, R. G., July 26, 2021
Ratliff, Bill, August 17, 2021
Root, Jay, August 17, 2021
Scharrer, Gary, August 27, 2021
Selby, Gardner, August 19, 2021
Slater, Wayne, August 20, 2021
Smith, Jason, August 16, 2021

Stenholm, Charlie, August 3, 2021
Sullivan, Ray, August 2, 2022
Thompson, Senfronia, August 25, 2022
Tilove, Jonathan, July 26, 2021
Toomey, Mike, January 12, 2022
Van de Putte, Leticia, November 12, 2021
Wayne, Reb, September 3, 2021
Weeks, David, August 17, 2021
Wilbanks, Chad, August 1, 2022

NOTES

Chapter 1: A Political Rebirth at the Dawn of the Modern Texas Republican Party

1. Interview with Leticia Van de Putte, November 12, 2021.
2. Peggy Fikac, "Perry the Master of the Bold Move," *San Antonio Express-News* (hereafter cited as *SAEN*), January 9, 2015.
3. Jay Root, "Savvy Conservatism, Country Charm Led Perry to Win," AP, March 4, 2010.
4. Interview with Joe Holley, July 26, 2021.
5. Interview with Dave McNeely, August 27, 2021.
6. Interview with Rick Perry, July 31, 2023.
7. Patricia Kilday Hart, "It's Rick Perry's Party Now," *Texas Monthly*, October 2000.
8. Interview with Tina Benkiser, November 1, 2021.
9. Interview with Ron Lewis, August 5, 2021.
10. Interview with Jay Root, August 17, 2021.
11. Interview with Jonathan Tilove, July 26, 2021.
12. Interview with R. G. Ratcliffe, July 26, 2021.
13. Interview with David Carney, August 8, 2021.
14. Root interview.
15. Interview with Debra Medina, August 19, 2021.
16. Tilove interview.
17. Holley interview.
18. Interview with David Weeks, August 17, 2021.
19. Weeks interview.
20. Perry interview, July 31, 2023.
21. Carney interview.
22. Gov. Rick Perry at a 2011 Roast for Rep. Senfronia Thompson, YouTube, https://www.youtube.com/watch?v=LpPCxAMFV9k.
23. Interview with John Austin, October 25, 2018.
24. Van de Putte interview.
25. Ratcliffe interview, July 26, 2021
26. Van de Putte interview.
27. Robert Draper, "It's Just a Texas-Governor Thing," *New York Times* (hereafter cited as *NYT*), December 2, 2009.
28. Dave Mann, "Whatever Rick Perry's Record Is, It's Not Conservative," *New Republic*, August 18, 2011.
29. Interview with Tom Pauken, August 2, 2023.
30. Interview with Wayne Slater, August 20, 2021.
31. Interview with Ken Herman, August 10, 2021.
32. Interview with Jim Arnold, August 5, 2021.
33. Jay Root, "Rick Perry: The Democrat Years," *Texas Tribune*, July 14, 2011, https://www.texastribune.org/2011/07/14/rick-perry-democrat-years.

34. McNeely interview.

35. Fred Gantt Jr., *The Chief Executive in Texas: A Study in Gubernatorial Leadership* (Austin: University of Texas Press, 1964), 43.

36. Gantt, *Chief Executive in Texas*, 6.

37. Brian McCall, *The Power of the Texas Governor: Connally to Bush* (Austin: University of Texas Press, 2009), 5.

38. Perry interview, July 31, 2023.

39. AP, "Baldwin Thinks Texas Is for the Dogs," October 9, 2003.

40. Van de Putte interview.

41. David O'Donald Cullen, "From 'Turn Texas Loose' to the Tea Party: Origins of the Texas Right," in *The Texas Right: The Radical Roots of Lone Star Conservatism*, eds. David O'Donald Cullen and Kyle G. Wilkinson (College Station: Texas A&M University Press, 2014).

42. Pauken interview.

43. Perry interview, July 31, 2023.

44. Interview with Mike Toomey, January 12, 2022.

45. Interview with Matthew Dowd, August 9, 2021.

46. Herman interview.

47. Dowd interview.

48. Interview with Jon McClellan, August 31, 2021.

49. Steve Kornacki, *The Red and the Blue: The 1990s and the Birth of Political Tribalism* (New York: Ecco, 2018), 5.

50. Holley interview.

51. Perry interview, July 31, 2023.

52. Lewis interview.

53. Root interview.

54. Interview with Bill Miller, September 10, 2021.

55. Fikac, "Perry the Master of the Bold Move."

56. Tilove interview.

57. Interview with Cliff Johnson, July 28, 2022.

58. Carney interview.

59. Hart, "Perry's Party Now."

60. Lewis interview.

Chapter 2 The House Years, 1984–1990

1. Staff writer, "Where Rick Perry Comes From: How the Texas Plains Shaped a Future Presidential Candidate," *Dallas Morning News* (cited hereafter as *DMN*), October 8, 2011.

2. Perry interview, July 31, 2023.

3. Matt Curry, "Perry Mobilizes Evangelicals as Gov's Race Heats Up," AP, June 10, 2005.

4. Interview with Gary Scharrer, August 27, 2021.

5. Weeks interview.

6. Interview with Harvey Kronberg, September 14, 2021.

7. A combination of his years of military service, state service, and age exceeded the state-required eighty years, so he qualified by state law for the annuity. Gary Scharrer and Richard Dunham, "Perry's Retirement, Pay Boost Spark Charges of Hypocrisy," *Times Union*, December 16, 2011.

8. Paul Weber, "Texas' New Governor Not the Same Kind of Cowboy," AP, November 5, 2014.

9. "Iowa Community Indicators Program," Iowa State University, https://www.icip .iastate.edu/tables/population/urban-pct-states.

10. "Rick Perry, Part 1," Kent Hance, *Best Storyteller in Texas* podcast, November 22, 2021, https://beststorytellerintexas.libsyn.com/rick-perry-part-1two-outta-three-aint-bad.

11. Interview with Hector Gutierrez, August 16, 2021.

12. Chris Hooks, "Aggie Years Launched Perry—and a Rivalry," *Texas Tribune*, August 2, 2011.

13. Kelley Shannon, "Perry Seeks Reelection on Carefully Cultivated Record in Office," AP, October 26, 2006.

14. Perry interview, July 31, 2023.

15. Interview with Debra Danberg, August 24, 2021.

16. Biographical details about Perry's prepolitical life are taken from Rick Perry, *On My Honor: Why the American Values of the Boy Scouts Are Worth Fighting For* (New York: Stroud & Hall, 2008).

17. Hance, "Rick Perry, Part 1."

18. Perry, *On My Honor*, 21; and Perry interview July 31, 2023.

19. Kronberg interview.

20. Hance, "Rick Perry, Part 1."

21. Saul Elbein, "The Boy from Haskell," *Texas Observer*, September 21, 2011, https:// www.texasobserver.org/the-boy-from-haskell.

22. Elbein, "Boy from Haskell."

23. Interview with Reb Wayne, September 3, 2021.

24. James Salzer, "Perry Warms Up Quickly to Legislative Duties," *Abilene Reporter-News*, May 19, 1985. See also Hance, "Rick Perry, Part 1."

25. *Wichita Falls Times Record News* (hereafter cited as *WFTRN*), January 12, 1984.

26. Interview with Charlie Stenholm, August 3, 2021.

27. Rick Perlstein, *Reaganland: America's Right Turn, 1976–1980* (New York: Simon & Schuster, 2020).

28. Perlstein, *Reaganland*, 33.

29. Johnson interview.

30. Interview with Ken Armbrister, August 26, 2021.

31. Average growth in Republican-held districts was 52 percent, compared to 20 percent in Democratic-controlled districts. Adam Clymer, "Republicans Dividing and Conquering in Redistricting of Texas," *NYT*, July 23, 1981.

32. Sam Kinch Jr., "No Contests," *DMN*, December 12, 1984.

33. Charles Worth Ward, "Candidate Forum Helps Voters See Races," *WFTRN*, March 31, 1984.

34. Lewis interview.

35. Hance, "Rick Perry, Part 1."

36. Johnson interview.

37. Perry interview, July 31, 2023.

38. Interview with Harold Cook, August 31, 2021.

39. Johnson interview.

40. Perry interview, July 31, 2023.

41. Johnson interview.

42. Lewis interview.

43. Johnson interview.

44. Johnson interview.

45. Interview with Ed Emmett, August 3, 2022.

46. Herman interview.

47. Van de Putte interview.

48. Wayne Slater, "At the End, 'Silly Session' Set In and Speaker Began to Sing," *DMN*, June 2, 1985.

49. Salzer, "Perry Warms Up Quickly."

50. Lewis interview.

51. Staff, "When Perry Turned Republican, He Left Some Helpful Democrats Behind," *DMN*, November 5, 2011, https://www.dallasnews.com/news/politics/2011/11/06/when-perry-turned-republican-he-left-some-helpful-democrats-behind.

52. Grace Wyler, "GROSS: You'll Never Guess What Rick Perry's Nickname Used to Be," *Business Insider*, December 2, 2011, https://www.businessinsider.com/rick-perry-nickname-crotch-2011-12.

53. Salzer, "Perry Warms Up Quickly."

54. Gutierrez interview.

55. Salzer, "Perry Warms Up Quickly."

56. Perry interview, July 31, 2023.

57. Lewis interview.

58. Paul Reyes, "White Set to Call Special Session over State Deficit," *Houston Chronicle*, June 28, 1986.

59. Reyes, "White Set to Call Special Session."

60. Harte-Hanks Bureau, "State Lawmakers Mull Possibility of Special Session," *WFTRN*, July 8, 1986.

61. Toomey interview.

62. Interview with Harold Cook, August 31, 2021.

63. Clay Robison, "Speaker Has GOP Rival after All," *Houston Chronicle*, February 16, 1986.

64. Paul Reyes and Anne Marie Kilday, "Gambit for White, Lewis Is Balancing the Budget," *Houston Chronicle*, August 10, 1986.

65. Robert Reinhold, "Texas: Clements Is Elected Governor," *NYT*, November 5, 1986.

66. Jay Rosser, "House Votes to Overturn Blue Law," *WFTRN*, May 2, 1985.

67. Cindy Horswell, "District 21: 2 Dems and a Bubba," *Houston Chronicle*, April 30, 1986.

68. Dana Palmer, "Personal Wealth for Lawmakers May Be in Voters' Imagination," *WFTRN*, June 6, 1988.

69. Dana Palmer, "Spending Varies among Representatives," *WFTRN*, June 6, 1988.

70. James Salzer, "Frequent Flier Perry Joins Flight Committee," *Abilene Reporter News*, October 28, 1987.

71. Salzer, "Frequent Flier Perry."

72. Clay Robison and Jan Rich, "Tougher Budget Battles Await 1987 Legislature," *Houston Chronicle*, December 14, 1986.

73. Clay Robison, "It's 2:45 am and a Zany-Time in the Capitol," *Houston Chronicle*, April 19, 1987.

74. Carolyn Barta, *Bill Clements, Texian to His Toenails* (Austin: Eakin Press, 1996), 351.

75. Barta, *Bill Clements*, 351.

76. Johnson interview.

77. AP, "Legislators Ready to Fight Cuts in Texas Agriculture Programs," *WFTRN*, March 2, 1987.

78. Lewis interview.

79. Toomey interview.

80. Janet Warren, "House OKs Measure to Let Voters Decide State Tax Issue," *WFTRN*, April 22, 1987.

81. Anne Marie Kilday and R. G. Ratcliffe, "Legislators Hopeful Special Session Won't Be Needed," *Houston Chronicle*, May 6, 1987.

82. McNeely interview.

83. Perry interview, July 31, 2023.

84. Toomey interview.

85. Paul Burka and Alison Cook, "1985: The Ten Best and (Groan) the Ten Worst Legislators," *Texas Monthly*, July 1985.

86. Toomey interview.

87. Wayne interview.

88. Jay Root, "Rick Perry: The Democrat Years," *Texas Tribune*, July 14, 2011.

89. The group was composed of Representatives Perry, Johnson, Toomey, Lewis, Richard Smith, Ric Williamson, McKinney, Jim Tallis, and Chris Harris.

90. "When Perry Turned Republican."

91. Johnson interview.

92. Scharrer interview.

93. Cook interview.

94. Lewis interview.

95. Danberg interview.

96. Lewis interview.

97. Perry interview, July 31, 2023. Perry recalled that the group thought they were "hot stuff," but then they realized that it was the "Speaker's committee" and it didn't make a difference how many votes they had.

98. Miller interview.

99. Interview with Bill Ratliff, August 17, 2021.

100. Interview with Christy Hoppe, August 27, 2021.

101. Sam Attlesey, "Beeper Bunch Keeps Ear to Budget Work," *DMN*, March 27, 1987.

102. Lewis interview.

103. Johnson interview, July 28, 2022.

104. Hance, "Rick Perry, Part 1."

105. Wyler, "GROSS."

106. Paul Burka, Kaye Northcott, Emily Yoffe, and Ellen Williams, "1987: The Best and Worst Legislators," *Texas Monthly*, July 1987.

107. Root, "Rick Perry: Democrat Years."

108. Anne Marie Kilday and Clay Robison, "Clements' Tax Turnabout Angers GOP Lawmakers," *Houston Chronicle*, May 8, 1987.

109. Scott Rothschild, "House Fails to Pass Tax Bill Three Times," *WFTRN*, July 21, 1987.

110. Robison and Rich, "Tougher Budget Battles Await."

111. Clay Robison, "Partisan Pall over the Capitol," *Houston Chronicle*, July 26, 1987.

112. Anne Marie Kilday and R. G. Ratcliffe, "Clements Signs Record Increase in State Taxes," *Houston Chronicle*, July 22, 1987; Barta, *Bill Clements*, 339.

113. UPI, "GOP Expects Tax Bill Backlash to Hurt Party's Candidates," *Houston Chronicle*, July 21, 1987.

114. Lewis interview.

115. Danberg interview.

116. Rena Pederson, "The Demos' Personality Split," *DMN*, October 13, 1989.

117. Dowd interview.

118. Harte-Hanks Bureau, "Legislators Graded by Group on Conservative Vote Record," *WFTRN*, June 19, 1987.

119. Barta, *Bill Clements*, 363.

120. Clay Robison, "Taxes, Prisons Take Legislative Center Stage in Austin," *Houston Chronicle*, January 8, 1989.

121. Johnson interview.

122. Hart, "Perry's Party Now."

123. AP, "Clements Said to Back Bail Changes," November 16, 1989.

124. Elbein, "Boy from Haskell."

125. Robert Cullick, "Pro-Choice Rally at State Capitol Draws Thousands," *Houston Chronicle*, November 13, 1989.

126. R. G. Ratcliffe, "Stage Set for Abortion Fight at GOP Meeting," *Houston Chronicle*, June 29, 1990.

127. R. G. Ratcliffe, "Clements Expects to Call Session on Abortion by Spring," *Houston Chronicle*, July 7, 1989.

128. Cullick, "Pro-Choice Rally."

129. Dana Palmer, "Bill Raising Texas Sales Tax Awaits Action by Governor," *WFTRN*, May 26, 1990.

130. Dana Palmer and Greg Perliski, "8 Votes Short," *WFTRN*, May 30, 1990.

131. Hance, "Rick Perry, Part 1."

132. Danberg interview.

133. Danberg interview.

134. Hoppe interview.

135. Perry interview, July 31, 2023.

136. Lewis interview.

137. Mary Beth Rogers, *Turning Texas Blue* (New York: St. Martins, 2016).

138. "Honor Roll—Here are the Best Legislators of the 71st Legislative Session," *DMN*, June 4.

139. Bruce Hight, "State Vote Sought on Workers' Comp," *Austin American-Statesman*, July 18, 1989.

140. Mark Toohey and Claire Osborn, "Big Bucks Were Spent to Influence Legislation, Records Show," *Houston Chronicle*, July 23, 1989.

141. Legislative Reference Library of Texas online, 71st Legislature, 6th C.S., HR63, https://lrl.texas.gov.

142. Cook interview.

143. AP, "Students Learn Naked Truth about Drug Abuse," *WFTRN*, January 28, 1986.

144. Mike Ward and Laylan Copelin, "Gifts Commonplace for Key State Officials," *Austin American-Statesman*, July 13, 1989.

145. Mike Ward and Bruce Hight, "Legislator Says Free Travel Didn't Derail His Ethics," *Austin American-Statesman*, July 13, 1989.

146. Texas Republican Party, "28 More Democrat Officials Join the Republican Party," https://www.texasgop.org/wp-content/uploads/2013/11/Party-Switchers-1.pptx.

147. Dowd interview.

148. Bill Hanna, "Perry Makes Switch to GOP," *Abilene Reporter-News*, September 30, 1989.

149. Johnson interview.

150. Danberg interview.

151. Toomey interview.

152. Dave McNeely, "Republican Party Gloats over Defection of State Lawmaker," *Austin American-Statesman*, October 1, 1989.

153. Root, "Rick Perry: Democrat Years."

154. Johnson interview.

155. Lewis interview.

156. Holley interview.

157. Lewis interview.

158. Interview with Gardner Selby, August 19, 2021.

159. Miller interview.

160. Dana Palmer, "Haskell State Representative Announces Switch to GOP," *WFTRN*, September 30, 1989.

Chapter 3: Republican Agricultural Commissioner, 1991–1998

1. Ratliff interview.

2. Slater interview.

3. Bill Hanna, "Rep. Perry Will Enter GOP Race for Ag Post," *Abilene Record-News*, December 5, 1989.

4. Lewis interview.

5. Armbrister interview.

6. Wade Goodwyn, "5 Things You Should Know about Rick Perry," *National Public Radio*, June 4, 2015.

7. Dana Palmer, "Rick Perry Enters Race for State Ag Post," *WFTRN*, December 7, 1989.

8. Miller interview.

9. Miller interview.

10. Toomey interview.

11. Weeks interview.

12. Tilove interview.

13. Perry interview, July 31, 2023.

14. Weeks interview. Perry gave Weeks significant credit for his 1990 win (Perry interview, July 31, 2023).

15. Keith Schneider, "The 1990 Elections; Farm Chief's Foe Has Last Laugh," *NYT*, November 8, 1990.

16. Richard Woodbury, "Don't Mess Around with Jim," *Time*, April 3, 1989.

17. Palmer, "Perry Enters Race."

18. AP, "Critic Says Adviser May Have Helped Ag Commissioner Win," August 18, 1991.

19. R. G. Ratcliffe, "Panel Creation Pares Power of Hightower," *Houston Chronicle*, May 11, 1989.

20. R. G. Ratcliffe, "Hightower May Have Won Legislative Battle," *Houston Chronicle*, April 10, 1989.

21. Debbie Graves, "Farm Board Lines up 6 to Face Hightower," *Austin American-Statesman*, December 30, 1989.

22. Perry interview, July 31, 2023.

23. "Not Always a Red State: A History of Texas' Political Transformation," *Reform Austin*, November 13, 2020, https://www.reformaustin.org/elections/not-always-a-red-state-a-history-of-texas-political-transformation.

24. Weeks interview.

25. Arnold interview.

26. Holley interview.

27. Kronberg interview.

28. Arnold interview.

29. Weeks interview.

30. Johnson interview.

31. Interview with Senfronia Thompson, August 26, 2022.

32. Schneider, "The 1990 Elections."

33. Arlette Saenz, "Rick Perry Accused of Running 'Race-Baiting' Ads in 1990," *ABC News*, October 4, 2011.

34. "When Perry Turned Republican."

35. Wayne interview.

36. Joe Brown, "Win No Surprise to Agriculture Commissioner," *WFTRN*, November 11, 1990.

37. Wayne interview.

38. AP, "Candidates for Statewide Races File," *WFTRN*, 1990.

39. "Williams Nervous," *WFTRN*, October 26, 1990.

40. Scott Rothschild, "Parmer Charges Gramm with Ethics Violation," *WFTRN*, October 24, 1990.

41. Candace Beaver, "Texans Feel at Home Splitting Their Votes," *WFTRN*, May 29, 1990.

42. Jake Silverstein, "The Great Campaigner," *Texas Monthly*, September 2011, https://www.texasmonthly.com/news-politics/the-great-campaigner-2.

43. Sam Attlesey, "Texas GOP Counting on Gramm's Coattails in 1990," *DMN*, December 17, 1989.

44. Chip Brown, "GOP Rallies Support in West Texas Stops," *WFTRN*, September 2, 1990.

45. Michael Holmes, "Richards to Go Gunning for Votes," *WFTRN*, September 1, 1990.

46. Candace Beaver, "Poll Shows Big Difference in Opinions on Bush, Clements," *WFTRN*, September 4, 1990.

47. Hoppe interview.

48. Kronberg interview.

49. Editorial, "We Endorse Richards, Gramm and Sarpalius," *WFTRN*, October 20, 1990.

50. Texas Department of Agriculture Records, Texas State Archives (hereafter cited as TDA Records, TSA), 2002/084-56, Press Releases September–December 1990, "Hightower Calls for Curing Our Critically Ill Health Care System," October 25, 1990.

51. Hoppe interview.

52. Interview with Ray Sullivan, August 2, 2022.

53. Hoppe interview.

54. Weeks interview.

55. Schneider, "The 1990 Elections."

56. Weeks interview.

57. Wayne interview.

58. Pauken interview.

59. Tilove interview.

60. Cook interview.

61. Perry interview, July 31, 2023.

62. Rick Perry, "Your Opinions: 4-H Club memories," letter to the editor, *WFTRN* October 14, 1992.

63. Editorial, "Agriculture Still among Leading State Industries," *WFTRN*, June 22, 1992.

64. Herman interview.

65. Steve Ray, "Study Examines Feasibility of Marketing Bluebonnets," *WFTRN*, October 29, 1994.

66. Richard Mize, "Armyworms May Be on the March towards Wheat Crop," *WFTRN*, September 1, 1993.

67. TDA Records, TSA, 1.1.019, 1/25/91–3/31/92, COM-91-1, WA30, "Persistence and Knowledge Needed to Manage Fire Ants," Editorial, July 28, 1991.

68. TDA Records, TSA, 1.1.019, 1/25/91–3/31/92, COM-91-1, WA30, "Bees with an Attitude Bear Watching," August 11, 1991.

69. Jim Davis, "TDA Chief Cuts 52 Jobs," *WFTRN*, June 22, 1991.

70. AP, "Idea to Move Agriculture Agency Draws Fire," *WFTRN*, February 27, 1993.

71. "Perry Wants Agency Moved from Austin," *WFTRN*, February 26, 1993.

72. Michael Holmes, "Texas Ag Commissioner Plowing Cyberspace," *WFTRN*, August 3, 1995.

73. TDA Records, TSA, 1.1.019, 1/25/91–3/31/92, COM-91-1, WA30, "TDA Examining Turning Over Gas Pump Inspections to Private Sector," November 12, 1991.

74. Dana Palmer, "Ag Commissioner Unveils Program to Aid Economy," *WFTRN*, June 4, 1991.

75. Van de Putte interview.

76. TDA Records, TSA, 1.1.019, 1/25/91–3/31/92, COM-91-1, WA30, "Raising 'Ag Literacy' in Texas," June 1991.

77. TDA Records, TSA, 1.1.019, 1/25/91–3/31/92, COM-91-1, WA30, "PROJECT TEACH: Perry Calls on School Districts to Review Bid Specs," February 27, 1992.

78. Peggy Fikac, "Got All Your Milk?," *WFTRN*, July 18, 1997.

79. Perry interview, July 31, 2023.

80. TDA Records, TSA, 1.1.019, 1/25/91–3/31/92, Box 1995/103-1, "Perry Cites Property Rights, Government Overregulation as Issues Facing Agriculture," April 9, 1994.

81. TDA Records, TSA, 1.1.019, 1/25/91–3/31/92, Box 1995/103-1, "Perry Tells Extension Agents Private Property Rights Must Be Protected," August 2, 1994.

82. "Rules Will Have Domino Effect," *WFTRN*, November 14, 1992.

83. Richard Mize, "Railroad's Demise Doesn't Deter Munday Chemical Maker," *WFTRN*, October 16, 1995.

84. Richard Mize, "Perry: Pesticide Plan Has Flaws," *WFTRN*, September 22, 1993.

85. TDA Records, TSA, 1.1.019, 1/25/91–3/31/92, COM-91-1, WA30, "BULLET TRAIN: Perry Applauds Efforts of Statewide Group Opposed to Bullet Train," July 3, 1992.

86. TDA Records, TSA, 2000/173-5, "We Must Challenge the Assumption that Government Best Protects Our Natural Resources," September 1992.

87. TDA Records, TSA, 2000/173-6, "Perry Criticizes Government Overregulation," January 20, 1994.

88. TDA Records, TSA, 2000/173-7, "Perry Cites Property Rights, Government Overregulation as Issues Facing Agriculture," April 8, 1994.

89. TDA Records, TSA, 2000/173-6, "BTU Energy Tax," May 31, 1993.

90. Richard Mize, "Perry Optimistic on Boll Weevil Eradication Bill," *WFTRN*, March 14, 1992.

91. Richard Mize, "Perry Backs Haywood on Carriker Money Shift," *WFTRN*, August 26, 1992.

92. AP, "Richards Betting on Cowboys, Again," January 28, 1994.

93. TDA Records, TSA, 1.1.019, 1/25/91–3/31/92, COM-91-1, WA30, "Great American Meatout," March 19, 1992.

94. TDA Records, TSA, 1.1.019, 1/25/91–3/31/92, COM-91-1, WA30, "'Make It Texas' Initiative Aimed at Creating Jobs through Commodity Processing," June 1991.

95. Opinion, "San Antonio Packaging Plant Ready for NAFTA," *WFTRN*, December 22, 1992.

96. Interview with Jim Arnold, August 5, 2021.

97. Kirsten Dietz, "Poll: Incumbents in Control of Races," *WFTRN*, 1994.

98. Weeks interview.

99. Herman interview.

100. Kronberg interview.

101. James A. Dyer, Jan E. Leighley, and Arnold Vedlitz, "Party Identification and Public Opinion in Texas: Establishing a Competitive Two-Party System, 1984–1994," in *Texas Politics: A Reader*, eds. Anthony Champagne and Edward J. Harpham (New York: Norton, 1998).

102. Kirsten Dietz, "Poll: Texans See Selves as Moderate, Conservative," *WFTRN*, October 29, 1994.

103. AP, "Bush Moves towards Gubernatorial Bid," *WFTRN*, September 16, 1993.

104. Jeff Claassen, "Four Seeking Republican AG selection," *WFTRN*, March 6, 1994.

105. Kirsten Dietz, "Hispanic Democrats Knock Perry," *WFTRN*, September 2, 1992.

106. TDA Records, TSA, 1.1.019, 1/25/91–3/31/92, COM-91-1, WA30, "Tort Reform," August 17, 1992.

107. Carroll Wilson, "Watch Out Ashby! A Wichitan Read Your Article," *WFTRN*, September 3, 1992.

108. Michael Holmes, "Waterfield Resigns after Racial Slur Allegations," *WFTRN*, August 1, 1991.

109. Richard Mize, "Perry Already Getting Ready for 1994," *WFTRN*, July 26, 1991.

110. Peggy Fikac, "Perry at the Top in Reimbursements," AP, 1993.

111. Herman interview.

112. AP, "Perry Says He Won't Run for Governor Yet," *WFTRN*, July 13, 1993.

Chapter 4: Lieutenant Governor, 1998–2001

1. Perry interview, July 31, 2023.

2. Perry interview, July 31, 2023.

3. Dowd interview.

4. Sullivan interview.

5. Miller interview.

6. Kronberg interview.

7. AP, "Republicans Hope Bush's Coattails Are Lengthy," October 31, 1998.

8. Wayne Thorburn, *The Republican Party of Texas: A Political History* (Austin: University of Texas Press, 2021), 279.

9. Richard L. Berke, "Religious Conservative Conquer G.O.P. in Texas," *NYT*, June 12, 1994.

10. Ratcliffe interview.

11. Berke, "Religious Conservatives Conquer G.O.P."

12. Pauken interview.

13. Pauken interview.

14. Arnold interview.

15. Dave McNeely, "GOP Gubernatorial Hopefuls Divided on Abortion," *DMN*, December 7, 1989.

16. Sullivan interview.

17. AP, "Analysis of Lieutenant Governor Candidate's TV Commercials," October 14, 1998.

18. Silverstein, "The Great Campaigner."

19. AP, "Republicans Hope Bush's Coattails."

20. Arnold interview.

21. AP, "Poll: Republicans Leading Most Statewide Races," September 6, 1998.

22. Sullivan interview.

23. AP, "Bush Leads Mauro by 45 Points in Latest Texas Poll," October 22, 1998.

24. AP, "Perry Says Sharp, Not He, Voted for Criminal Release Bill," October 19, 1998.

25. Wayne King, "New Police Chief Battles Crime Boom in Houston" *NYT*, January 14, 1983.

26. UPI, "Busted Oil Boom Blamed for High Murder Rate," September 12, 1983.

27. Mark White for Governor Ad—Executions, YouTube, https://www.youtube.com/watch?v=SuIocL3a1Uc.

28. AP, "Perry Says Sharp."

29. AP, "Perry Unveils Plan to Crack Down on Drug Pushers," October 2, 1998.

30. Anthony Wilson, "Exceeding Expectations," *Abilene Reporter-News*, April 18, 1999.

31. AP, "Lieutenant Governor Candidates Spar over Education, Partisan Politics," September 26, 1998.

32. Jim Vertuno, "Perry Received $1.1 Million Campaign Loan," AP, January 15, 1999.

33. AP, "Lieutenant Governor Hopeful Takes Aim Using Voucher Issue," September 29, 1998.

34. Gutierrez interview.

35. Perry interview, August 4, 2023.

36. Bob Bruce, "Just Friends," *Abilene Reporter-News*, November 20, 1988.

37. Bruce, "Just Friends."

38. McClellan interview.

39. Sullivan interview.

40. AP, "Perry Camp Unveils Ad Featuring President Bush, Decries Sharp," October 9, 1998.

41. Campaign ads, "Rick Perry Lt Governor Race," accessed August 18, 2023, https://www.youtube.com/watch?v=3CKGg4g3418.

42. AP, "Analysis of Lieutenant Governor Candidates' Television Commercial," October 9, 1998.

43. AP, "Perry Camp Unveils Ad Featuring Bush."

44. AP, "Lieutenant Governor Candidates Spar."

45. AP, "Sharp Says Perry Running Negative Ad: Perry Denies It," October 30, 1998.

46. Arnold interview.

47. Slater interview.

48. Arnold interview.

49. Thorburn, *Republican Party of Texas*, 291.

50. Hart, "Perry's Party Now.".

51. AP, "Perry, Sharp Battle It Out for No. 2 Post," November 3, 1998.

52. AP, "Perry Complains about Sharp Newspaper Insert," October 15, 1998.

53. Thorburn, *Republican Party of Texas*, 279.

54. Miller interview.

55. Interview with Chad Wilbanks, August 1, 2022.

56. Sullivan interview.

57. Arnold interview.

58. Dowd interview.

59. AP, "Exit Polling Shows Bush Improved over '94 in Many Categories," November 4, 1998.

60. Karl Rove, *Courage and Consequence* (New York: Simon and Schuster, 2010).

61. Thorburn, *Republican Party of Texas*, 285.

62. AP, "Exit Polling Sheds Light on Bush's Appeal to Hispanics," November 4, 1998.

63. Kronberg interview.

64. AP, "Exit Polling Shows Bush Improved."

65. Arnold interview.

66. Lewis interview.

67. Several interviewees made this point to the author.

68. Rick Lyman, "Bush Blends Optimism and Challenge in Texas Inaugural," *NYT*, January 20, 1999.

69. Inaugural Address of Rick Perry, January 20, 1999, Texas Inaugural Committee Bush-Perry inaugural records, Archives and Information Services Division, Texas State Library and Archives Commission.

70. Anthony Wilson, "Exceeding Expectations," *Abilene Reporter-News*, April 18, 1999.

71. Hoppe interview.

72. Peggy Fikac, "First-Ever Republican Lieutenant Governor Discussed Future," AP, December 27, 1998.

73. Hoppe interview.

74. Ratliff interview.

75. Ratliff interview.

76. Hoppe interview.

77. Gutierrez interview.

78. Peggy Fikac, "Senate Republican Leaders Don't Expect Major Rule Changes or Partisan Fights," AP, November 4, 1998.

79. Kronberg interview.

80. Will Weissert, "Rick Perry–George W. Bush Dispute Still Burns," AP, September 19, 2011.

81. Renae Merle, "Speaker Pete Sees No Problem with Working in Divided House," AP, January 5, 1999.

82. Merle, "Speaker Pete Sees No Problem."

83. Perry interview, July 31, 2023.

84. Ratliff interview.

85. Kronberg interview.

86. Van de Putte interview.

87. AP, "Report: Lobbyists Claim They Had to Meet Fund-Raising Quotas for Perry," December 8, 1998.

88. Root interview.

89. AP, "Perry Touts Work of Senate," March 31, 1999.

90. Peggy Fikac, "Perry Didn't Get Everything, but Senators Say He Got Respect," AP, May 31, 1999.

91. Armbrister interview.

92. Fikac, "Perry Didn't Get Everything."

93. Fikac, "Perry Didn't Get Everything."

94. Staff, "Very Bad Wizard—Troy Fraser," *Texas Monthly*, July 1999.

95. Thompson interview.

96. AP, "Governor of Texas Signs a Hate Crimes Bill," May 12, 2001.

97. Fikac, "Perry Didn't Get Everything."

98. Madeline Baro, "Lt. Governor Perry Visits South Texas to Discuss Education," AP, June 4, 1999.

99. "Summary of Enactments, 76th Legislature, Regular Session 1999," Texas Legislative Council, https://tlc.texas.gov/docs/sessions/76soe.pdf.

100. Interview with Chris Bell, August 6, 2021.

101. Dowd interview.

102. Kelley Shannon, "Texas GOP Leaders Confident Bush Will Weather Difficulties," AP, September 14, 2000.

103. Connie Mabin, "Bush Celebrates Texas-Sized Victory," AP, March 14, 2000.

104. AP, "Perry Ready to Play Defense for State of Texas," July 31, 2000.

105. Mary Lee Grant, "Republican Delegation Dominated by Conservatives, Right Wing Christians," AP, June 18, 2000.

106. Chris Williams, "Perry Snipes at Backers with Treason Comment," AP, March 10, 2000.

107. Jim Vertuno, "Frustrated Perry Waits to See If He'll Be Texas' Next Governor," AP, November 14, 2000.

108. AP, "Some Concerned Perry Won't Be Able to Bridge Parties," November 1, 2000.

109. "Some Concerned Perry Won't Be Able."

110. Stenholm interview.

111. Stenholm interview.

Chapter 5: Governor, 2001–2002

1. Michael Graczyk, "Aggie Rick Perry Makes First Aggieland Appearance as Texas Governor," AP, May 4, 2001.

2. Graczyk, "Aggie Rick Perry."

3. Graczyk, "Aggie Rick Perry."

4. AP, "Candidates Reveal Lighter Side in Newspaper Survey," October 27, 2002.

5. Barbara Belejack, "Editorial: El Educación del Gobinador," *Texas Observer*, July 20, 2001, https://www.texasobserver.org/332-editorial-la-educaci%EF%BF%BD%EF%BF%BD_%EF%BF%BD%EF%BF%BD___n-del-gobernador.

6. Van de Putte interview.

7. Federal Reserve Bank of Dallas, *Southwest Economy*, issue 2 (March/April 2001), https://www.dallasfed.org/~/media/documents/research/swe/2001/swe0102a.pdf.

8. AP, "State Predicts Economy Will Grow during 2002–2003 Budget Cycle," November 30, 2000.

9. Juan A. Lozano, "Perry Promotes Texas Economy, Education System to Business Leaders," AP, February 27, 2002.

10. Hart, "Perry's Party Now."

11. Ratcliffe interview.

12. Connie Mabin, "Texas Session: Bush Aftermath Monopolizing Agenda," AP, April 21, 2001.

13. Robert Draper, "It's Just a Texas-Governor Thing," *NYT*, December 2, 2009.

14. Perry, Texas State of the State address, January 24, 2001, C-SPAN, https://www.c-span.org/video/?162370-1/texas-state-state-address.

15. Burka and Hart, "Best and Worst Texas Legislators [2001]."

16. Kelley Shannon, "Lawmakers Head into New, Somewhat Uncertain Session," AP, December 26, 2000.

17. Kronberg interview.

18. Toomey interview.

19. Ross Ramsey and Jay Root, "In Perry's Texas, the Man Behind the Curtain," *Texas Tribune*, October 14, 2011.

20. Toomey interview.

21. Van de Putte interview.

22. Johnson interview.

23. Ratcliffe interview.

24. Gutierrez interview.

25. Johnson interview.

26. Van de Putte interview.

27. Toomey interview.

28. Perry interview, July 31, 2023.

29. Thompson interview.

30. Benkiser interview.

31. Van de Putte interview.

32. All quotes are from author's interview with Ken Armbrister.

33. Armbrister interview.

34. Selby interview..

35. Armbrister interview.

36. Toomey interview.

37. Gilbert Garcia, "Greg Abbott's Leadership Deficiencies Show in Property Tax Conflict," *SAEN*, June 3, 2023.

38. Tilove interview.

39. Armbrister interview.

40. Van de Putte interview.

41. Cook interview.

42. Selby interview.

43. Slater interview.

44. Hoppe interview.

45. Kronberg interview.

46. Armbrister interview.

47. Kelley Shannon, "Governor Pushes Selected Programs, Embraces Some Centrist Issues," AP, May 30, 2001.

48. Lewis interview.

49. Lisa Falkenberg, "Plans to Consider Hate Crimes Bill Halted," AP, April 18, 2001.

50. Root interview.

51. Van de Putte interview.

52. Thompson interview.

53. Selby interview.

54. Kelley Shannon, "Governor Signs Hate Crimes Bill into Law," AP, May 11, 2011.

55. Lewis interview.

56. Perry, State of the State address, January 2001. The texts of Perry's official speeches as lieutenant governor and governor are listed (in reverse chronological order) at Legislative Reference Library of Texas online, https://lrl.texas.gov/legeLeaders/governors/searchproc.cfm?governorID=44&govDocTypeID=6.

57. Kelley Shannon, "Perry Signs Bill Giving Inmates Access to State-Funded DNA Testing," AP, April 5, 2001.

58. Simon Maloy, "David Gregory's Humiliating Rick Perry Interview: How 'Meet the Press' Botched a Death Penalty Segment," *Salon*, May 5, 2014, https://www.salon.com/2014/05/05/david_gregorys_humiliating_rick_perry_interview_how_meet_the_press_botched_a_death_penalty_segment.

59. Natalie Gott, "Governor Vetoes Bill Banning the Execution of Mentally Retarded Killers," AP, June 17, 2001.

60. AP, "Highlights Wednesday from the Texas Legislature," April 18, 2001.

61. "Major Issues of the 77th Legislature Regular Session," House Research Organization, https://hro.house.texas.gov/pdf/focus/major77.pdf.

62. Elise Hu, "Too Busy for a Review," *Texas Tribune*, September 30, 2009.

63. Tim Murphy, "Rick Perry's Death Penalty Problem," *Mother Jones*, July 8, 2011.

64. Van de Putte interview.

65. AP, "Governor Pushes Higher Education Grant and Loan Programs," May 6, 2002.

66. Lisa Falkenberg, "Lawmakers Sent Charter School Measure to Perry," AP, May 27, 2001.

67. Dunnam interview.

68. Jim Vertuno, "Ratliff Working on State Property Tax Plan: Perry Says Options Open," AP, March 22, 2002.

69. Slater interview.

70. Sullivan interview.

71. Cook interview.

72. Wayne interview.

73. Michael Graczyk, "Governor Pushes Transportation Proposals Facing Voters," AP, October 17, 2001.

74. Sullivan interview.

75. Armbrister interview.

76. Miller interview.

77. Cook interview.

78. Deborah Sontag, "Perry Survived, Even as His Big Plan for Texas Failed," *NYT*, December 10, 2011, https://www.nytimes.com/2011/12/10/us/politics/perry-survived-failure-of-his-grand-transportation-plan.html.

79. Kelley Shannon, "Governor Unveils Statewide Road, Rail Plan," AP, January 28, 2002.

80. Armbrister interview.

81. Kronberg interview.

82. Armbrister interview.

83. Emmett interview.

84. Carney interview.

85. Perry interview, August 4, 2023.

86. Johnson interview.

87. Perry interview, August 4, 2023.

88. Kronberg interview.

89. Herman interview.

90. Katrina Trinko, "The Vetoes of Rick Perry," *National Review*, September 6, 2011, http://www.nationalreview.com/article/276264.

91. Trinko, "Vetoes of Rick Perry."

92. Miller interview.

93. Perry interview, July 31, 2023.

94. Perry interview, July 31, 2023.

95. Miller interview.

96. Sullivan interview.

97. Slater interview.

98. Ratliff interview.

99. Fikac, "Perry the Master of the Bold Move."

100. Sullivan interview.

101. Thompson interview.

102. Kelley Shannon, "Governor Pushes Selected Programs, Embraces Some Centrist Issues," AP, May 30, 2001.

103. Armbrister interview.

104. AP, "Perry Addresses Southwest Voter Registration Project," June 22, 2001.

105. AP, "Perry's Veto of Bill Sparks Ill Will among Doctors," June 23, 2001.

106. Chris Roberts, "Some Say Perry's Vetoes Will Hurt Border Residents," AP, July 15, 2001.

107. Perry interview, July 31, 2023.

108. Kelley Shannon, "Legislature about to Adjourn after Law-Making Flurry," AP, May 26, 2001.

109. Ratliff interview.

110. Jim Yardley, "Once-Heralded Bipartisanship Fades in Texas House," *NYT*, December 30, 2001.

111. Ratcliffe interview.

112. Van de Putte interview.

113. Betsy Blaney, "Perry Kicks Off Campaign at Childhood Paint Creek School," AP, January 8, 2002.

114. April Castro, "Perry Outlines Election Goals during Kickoff Run through State," AP, January 9, 2002.

115. Center for Public Policy Survey, Hobby School of Public Affairs, University of Houston, June 2020.

116. Michelle Cottle, "Identity Crisis, *New Republic*, February 18, 2002, https://newrepublic.com/article/66133/identity-crisis.

117. Natalie Gott, "From Packing Produce to Oil and Gas Wealth, Texas Democrat Aims for Governorship," AP, March 12, 2002.

118. AP, "Laredo Businessman Preparing to Begin Campaign," August 29, 2001.

119. Gregory Curtis, "Who Killed the Texas Democratic Party?," *Texas Monthly*, January 1998, https://www.texasmonthly.com/politics/who-killed-the-texas-democratic -party.

120. Kristen Hayes, "Democrat Dan Morales Endorses Republican Rick Perry," AP, October 8, 2002.

121. Kelley Shannon, "Democratic Candidates Square Off in Historic Debates," AP, March 1, 2002.

122. Ross Ramsey, "An Unreliable Narrator with a Story to Tell," *Texas Tribune*, September 30, 2013, https://www.texastribune.org/2013/09/30/unreliable-narrator-story -tell.

123. AP, "Moderation Seen as Winning Ticket for Democrats," December 4, 2001.

124. "Moderation Seen as Winning Ticket."

125. Natalie Gott, "Who Coined the 'Dream Team' Term for Democrats?," AP, October 13, 2002.

126. Kelley Shannon, "Sanchez Looks to Broaden Voter Base after Bitter Primary," AP, March 14, 2002.

127. Betsy Blaney, "Abortion Protesters Attend Sanchez Rally in Amarillo," AP, August 9, 2002.

128. Natalie Gott, "Sanchez: Republicans 'Very Partisan'," AP, October 24, 2001.

129. Kelley Shannon, "Sanchez Says Perry Mishandling Corporate Relocations," AP, September 19, 2002.

130. Kelley Shannon, "As Gramm Bows Out, State's Political Landscape Quakes," AP, September 4, 2002.

131. AP, "Highlights of a Texas Poll on Statewide Campaigns," June 16, 2002.

132. AP, "Newspaper Poll: Perry Holds Lead over Sanchez," April 7, 2002.

133. Natalie Gott, "Cornyn Says Hispanic Vote up for Grabs," AP, September 13, 2002; Connie Mabin, "Sanchez Kicks Off TV Campaign with English, Spanish Ads," AP, January 14, 2002.

134. "Newspaper Poll: Perry Holds Lead over Sanchez."

135. Connie Mabin, "GOP Hopes to Come Full Circle, Democrats Still Fighting," AP, February 15, 2002.

136. AP, "Candidate Says Hispanic Heritage Works Against Him in Some Regions," October 9, 2002.

137. Jim Vertuno, "Ratliff Says Top GOP Leaders Not Critical Enough of Ads," AP, March 6, 2002.

138. Dowd interview.

139. Gott, "From Packing Produce."

140. Kelley Shannon, "Abbott Says He Opposed Abortion in Rape, Incest Cases," AP, June 24, 2002.

141. Jim Vertuno, "First Perry Ads Start in Statewide Rotation," AP, May 17, 2002.

142. AP, "Sanchez Catches Criticism for Encouraging Enron Deal," July 19, 2002.

143. AP, "Documents Question Management of Sanchez's Thrift," October 1, 2002.

144. Matt Slagle, "Sanchez Renews Attack on Perry during Longview Visit," AP, July 10, 2002.

145. Lisa Falkenberg, "Perry Accuses Sanchez of Laundering Money for Camarena's

Killers in New Ad," *My Plainview*, October 24, 2002, https://www.myplainview.com/news/article/Perry-accuses-Sanchez-of-laundering-money-for-8829854.php.

146. Wilbanks interview.

147. Falkenberg, "Perry Accuses Sanchez of Laundering Money."

148. Blaney, "Abortion Protesters Attend Sanchez Rally."

149. Mark Babineck, "Perry Criticizes Sanchez over Working to Diffuse Height Differential," AP, October 4, 2002.

150. Kelley Shannon, "Newspapers Chide Candidates, but More Endorse Perry," AP, November 1, 2002.

151. Betsy Blaney, "Survey: Sanchez Apparently Suffered More Backlash from Negative Ads," AP, November 26, 2002.

152. Lisa Falkenberg, "Perry, Sanchez Accuse Each Other of Pushing Vague Agendas," AP, March 18, 2002.

153. Susan Parrott, "Perry Says Robin Hood Is Unfair System, Must Be Reformed," AP, March 15, 2002.

154. Connie Mabin, "Perry, Sanchez Face Off before School Administrators," AP, June 25, 2002.

155. Mabin, "Perry, Sanchez Face Off."

156. Kelley Shannon, "Sanchez, Perry Campaigns Spar over Bipartisanship," AP, May 7, 2002.

157. David Koenig, "Hispanics Boost Democrats in South Texas, but Not Enough," AP, November 6, 2002.

158. Carney interview.

159. Herman interview.

160. Carney interview.

161. Holley interview.

162. Carney interview.

163. Stenholm interview.

Chapter 6: First Full Term, 2003–2006

1. Paraphrased text and quotes from the address can be found at Legislative Reference Library of Texas, Perry speeches, Inaugural address, January 21, 2003, https://lrl.texas.gov/legeLeaders/governors/searchproc.cfm?governorID=44&govDocTypeID=6.

2. Legislative Reference Library of Texas, Perry speeches, State of the State, February 11, 2003, https://lrl.texas.gov/legeLeaders/governors/searchproc.cfm?governorID=44&govDocTypeID=6.

3. Perry interview, July 31, 2023.

4. Connie Mabin, "$9.9 Billion in the Hole, Budget Session's Top Issue," AP, January 14, 2003.

5. Mabin, "$9.9 Billion in the Hole."

6. Paul Burke, "The Best and Worst Legislators," *Texas Monthly*, July 2003.

7. Kelley Shannon, "Legislature Will Convene with New Leaders, Money Worries," AP, December 31, 2002.

8. Toomey interview.

9. Armbrister interview.

10. Van de Putte interview.

11. Staff, "The Bobby Riggs Award," *Texas Monthly*, July 2003, https://www.texasmonthly.com/politics/the-bobby-riggs-award/

12. Connie Mabin, "Budget Debate Expected to Be Lengthy, Heated," AP, April 13, 2003.

13. Mabin, "Budget Debate."

14. Mabin, "Budget Debate."

15. Natalie Gott, "Majority of Senators for $5.8 Billion in 'Non-Tax Revenue' Ideas," AP, March 25, 2003.

16. Paul J. Weber, "Dewhurst Downplays State Budget Freeze on Business Funds," *Lubbock Avalanche Journal*, January 15, 2013.

17. AP, "Dewhurst a No-Show at Breakfast with State Leaders," March 27, 2002.

18. Toomey interview.

19. Natalie Gott and Connie Mabin, "Tale of Two Leaders: Dewhurst, Craddick Mark Their First Terms," AP, June 2, 2003.

20. April Castro, "Craddick's Competitive Leadership Style Taking Shape," AP, April 20, 2003.

21. Gott and Mabin, "Tale of Two Leaders."

22. Kelley Shannon, "Republican Leaders Declare Legislative Session a Success," AP, June 3, 2003.

23. Kelley Shannon, "Governor Tries to Guide Negotiations, Make Mark on Session," AP, May 31, 2003.

24. "Fiscal Size-Up, 2004–2005 Biennium," Legislative Budget Board, https://www.lbb.state.tx.us/Documents/Publications/Fiscal_SizeUp/Fiscal_SizeUp_2004-05.pdf.

25. April Castro, "Comptroller Rejects Two-Year, $185.9 Million State Budget," AP, June 19, 2003.

26. Castro, "Comptroller Rejects Budget."

27. Connie Mabin, "Comptroller Supports Raising Cigarette Tax to Help Balance Budget," AP, May 19, 2003.

28. Toomey interview.

29. AP, "Reaction to Texas Comptroller," June 19, 2003.

30. Toomey interview.

31. Toomey interview.

32. AP, "Comptroller, GOP Leaders Clash over Duties," *MyPlainview*, September 18, 2003, https://www.myplainview.com/news/article/Comptroller-GOP-leaders-clash-over-duties-8950984.php.

33. Pam Easton, "Texas Governor Says Comptroller Looking to Protect Turf," AP, October 15, 2003.

34. Shannon, "Republican Leaders Declare Success."

35. Alex Hanford, "How the Texas Legislature Reached a Dangerous Stalemate on Vaccines," *Texas Observer*, June 21, 2017, https://www.texasobserver.org/texas-legislature-vaccines-dangerous-stalemate.

36. Kelley Shannon, "Governor Signs 'Defense of Marriage Act' into Law," AP, May 27, 2003.

37. R. G. Ratcliffe interview.

38. Ratcliffe interview.

39. April Castro, "Senator Introduced Plan to Limit Lawsuits in Texas," AP, April 30, 2003.

40. Mark Babineck, "Governor Signs Tort Reform Bill," AP, June 11, 2003.

41. AP, "Perry Gets New Power over Economic Development," June 16, 2003.

42. Perry interview, August 4, 2023.

43. The delegation broke down to seventeen Democrats and fifteen Republicans.

44. April Castro, "Delay to Texas Legislature: Redraw Congressional Maps," AP, April 24, 2003.

45. Staff, "Pest," *Texas Monthly*, July 2003, https://www.texasmonthly.com/politics /pest.

46. Shannon, "Republican Leaders Declare Success."

47. Dunnam interview.

48. Thompson interview.

49. Ratliff interview.

50. The House cannot operate without at least two-thirds of the membership (one hundred members) present on the floor under House rules.

51. Clay Robinson, "Legislator: Perry Sent DPS to Neonatal Unit," *Houston Chronicle*, June 2, 2003.

52. Connie Mabin, "Texas House Democrats Break Quorum," AP, May 12, 2003.

53. Mabin, "House Democrats Break Quorum."

54. Connie Mabin, "Troopers Sent to Find Lawmakers Who Skip Out on Legislative Session," AP, May 12, 2003.

55. Dunnam interview.

56. Mabin, "Troopers Sent to Find Lawmakers."

57. April Castro, "Rebel Democrats Refuse to Break Ranks, Return to Texas," AP, May 13, 2003.

58. Castro, "Rebel Democrats Refuse."

59. The plane belonging to Pete Laney was found within forty minutes.

60. Angela K. Brown, "Missing Lawmakers Discovered in Oklahoma," AP, May 13, 2003.

61. "Editorial Opinion on the House Standoff," *Lufkin Daily News*, May 14, 2003.

62. Kelley Shannon, "Republican Say They're Working, Chastise Democrats," AP, May 14, 2003.

63. Connie Mabin, "Redistricting Bill at Center of Showdown Running Out of Time," AP, May 15, 2003.

64. April Castro, "Killer Ds Return to Austin, Get Back to Work," AP, May 16, 2003.

65. Dunnam interview.

66. Dunnam interview.

67. Items included the reorganization of legislative support agencies and offices, the abolition of the Office of State-Federal Relations and the transfer of its functions to the governor's office, legislation permitting the governor to designate the presiding officers for executive branch agencies, changes in the qualifications for members of the Texas Parks and Wildlife Commission, and clarification of the governor's budget authority.

68. Scott Gold, "Texas Republicans Take New Shot at Redistricting," *Los Angeles Times*, June 19, 2003.

69. Gold, "Texas Republicans Take New Shot."

70. Gold, "Texas Republicans Take New Shot."

71. AP, "Hearing Shows Contentious Redistricting Issue to Return," June 10, 2003.

72. Natalie Gott, "Bill Sponsor All but Says Redistricting Is Dead This Session," AP, July 25, 2003.

73. April Castro, "Lawmakers Go through Motions, but Anticipate New Special Session," AP, July 22, 2003.

74. Natalie Gott, "Focus on Senate for Special Session," AP, June 22, 2003.

75. Gott, "Focus on Senate."

76. Gott, "Focus on Senate."

77. Natalie Gott, "Democratic Lawmakers Flee Texas in Effort to Thwart Congressional Redistricting," AP, July 28, 2003.

78. Natalie Gott, "Lawmakers Adjourn without Redistricting Bill," AP, August 26, 2003.

79. Kelley Shannon, "Dewhurst Says He Prefers a Break after Session's End Tuesday," AP, August 22, 2003.

80. Armbrister interview.

81. Natalie Gott, "Democrats Sharpen Their Rhetoric against Dewhurst, Perry," AP, August 8, 2003.

82. Ratliff interview.

83. Kelley Shannon, "Governor Breaks Silence on Senate Democrat Walkout," AP, July 31, 2003.

84. Natalie Gott, "Democratic Senator Criticizes Governor," AP, August 3, 2003.

85. Van de Putte interview.

86. AP, "Nelson Calls Senate Democrats Heroes," August 9, 2003.

87. Natalie Gott, "Texas Lieutenant Governor Says He Might Turn to Legal Action to Get Democrats Home," AP, August 5, 2003.

88. Natalie Gott, "Perry: As Long as There Is Work to Be Done, Lawmakers Can Expect to Be in Austin," AP, August 13, 2003.

89. T. A. Badger, "Democrats Cancel Trip to Laredo Court Hearing, Fearing Trap," AP, August 27, 2003.

90. April Castro, "DOJ Approves GOP Redistricting Map, Fed Trial Continues," AP, December 19, 2003.

91. AP, "Baldwin Offers Dog Biscuits to Perry," October 7, 2003.

92. Wayne J. Thorburn, *Red State: An Insider's Story of How the GOP Came to Dominate Texas Politics* (Austin: University of Texas Press, 2014), 185.

93. April Castro, "Ratliff 'Distraught' over Redistricting, Contemplates Resignation," AP, August 19, 2003.

94. Van de Putte interview.

95. Department of Energy Exit interview.

96. AP, "Poll: Perry's Support Drops," March 6, 2004.

97. Ratcliffe interview.

98. Herman interview.

99. Keach Hagey, "Texas Tales of Perry Go National," *Politico*, September 18, 2011, https://www.politico.com/story/2011/09/texas-tales-of-perry-go-national-063755

100. April Castro, "Governor Rick Perry Calls Special Session," AP, April 13, 2004.

101. Castro, "Perry Calls Special Session."

102. Kelley Shannon, "Perry Says He'd Like to See Voucher Bill," AP, April 21, 2004.

103. Shannon, "Perry Says He'd Like to See Voucher Bill."

104. Shannon, "Perry Says He'd Like to See Voucher Bill."

Chapter 7: The 2005 Session and 2006 Election

1. Legislative Reference Library of Texas online, Perry's speeches, State of the State, January 26, 2005, https://lrl.texas.gov/legeLeaders/governors/searchproc.cfm?governorID=44&govDocTypeID=6.

2. University of Texas/Texas Tribune Poll, July 2008, https://www.texastribune.org/series/ut-tt-polls.

3. April Castro and Jim Vertuno, "Perry to Introduce School Funding plan," AP, June 20, 2005.

4. Castro and Vertuno, "Perry to Introduce School Funding Plan."

5. Perry interview, August 4, 2023.

6. T. A. Badger, "Broader Franchise Tax Promoted to Relieve Property Burden," AP, March 6, 2006.

7. April Castro, "Legislature Moving Forward on School Finance," AP, January 5, 2005.

8. Thorburn, *Republican Party in Texas*, 321–322.

9. Catherine Alvarado, "Rick Perry's 6 Most Viral Moments," *Austin American-Statesman*, October 12, 2016.

10. Dietz argued that because so many districts were at the maximum taxing level, the system amounted to a statewide property tax, which was banned by the state's constitution. Schools would also need about $1,100 more per student to provide an "adequate" education as required.

11. April Castro, "School Finance Negotiations down to the Wire," AP, May 27, 2005.

12. April Castro, "Perry, Craddick Mend Fences, Discuss 'Host of Things,'" AP, May 10, 2004.

13. Selby interview.

14. April Castro, "House School Finance Debate Falls Apart, Stripped Bill Passes." *My Plainview*, May 4, 2004.

15. Castro, "Negotiators down to the Wire."

16. Kelley Shannon, "Education Funding Taking Center Stage as Legislature Convenes," AP, January 11, 2005.

17. April Castro, "School Funding Hopes Dashed as Session Nears End," AP, May 28, 2005.

18. April Castro "Craddick Offers Terse Words in Response to Dewhurst," AP, May 25, 2005.

19. AP, "Special Session Unlikely If School Funding Overhaul Fails," May 20, 2005.

20. Thompson interview.

21. Emmett interview.

22. Carney interview.

23. AP, "Perry Aides Defend Enterprise Fund Management," February 21, 2005.

24. "Perry Aides Defend Enterprise Fund."

25. Jim Vertuno, "Lawmakers Taking Critical Look at Trans Texas Corridor," AP, February 9, 2005.

26. AP, "Perry to Sign Abortion, Gay Marriage Bills at Church School," June 3, 2005.

27. Kelley Shannon, "Texans to Decide on Gay Marriage Ban," AP, November 3, 2005.

28. AP, "Perry Sends Email in Support of Same-Sex Marriage Amendment," August 24, 2005.

29. Kelley Shannon, "Perry Speaks Out on Gay marriage Ban Victory," AP, November 10, 2005.

30. Benkiser interview.

31. Benkiser interview.

32. Kelley Shannon, "With No School Funding Plan, Texas Lawmakers Wrap Up Session," AP, May 30, 2005.

33. Olga R. Rodriguez, "U.S. Governors Pledge to Help Mexican Counterparts Fight Wave of Violence," AP, July 16, 2005.

34. Lynn Brezosky, "Texas Governor Signs Compromise Border Security Bill," AP, June 6, 2007.

35. Marisa Trevino, "Border Control Aims at Wrong Bad Guys," *USA Today*, February 24, 2006.

36. "Apprehensions by the U.S. Border Patrol: 2005–2010," Department of Homeland Security, Office of Immigration Statistics, https://www.dhs.gov/xlibrary/assets/statistics/publications/ois-apprehensions-fs-2005-2010.pdf.

37. AP, "Report: Operation Catches More Immigrants than Criminals," November 20, 2006.

38. Elizabeth White, "Texas Governor Applauds Border Security Operation," AP, June 27, 2006.

39. White, "Governor Applauds Border Security."

40. Lynn Brezosky, "Citizens' Patrols Not So Welcome in Texas," AP, June 1, 2005.

41. Miller interview.

42. Jim Vertuno, "Strayhorn Creates Buzz, Questions over Hutchison's Future," AP, June 16, 2005.

43. Natalie Gott, "Strayhorn Announces Candidacy for Governor," AP, June 18, 2005.

44. Perry interview, July 31, 2023.

45. For past campaign finance reports of Texas candidates, see Texas Ethics Commission, View a Campaign Finance Report, https://www.ethics.state.tx.us/search/Quick ViewReport.php. Perry's finances are filed under Texans for Rick Perry (Filer 00015741).

46. AP, "Lawmakers Still Have Work to Do," May 31, 2005.

47. April Castro, "Perry Vetoes Education Spending, Calls Lawmakers back to Austin," AP, June 18, 2005.

48. April Castro, "Lawmakers No Closer to Agreement on School Tax Bill," AP, June 22, 2005.

49. April Castro, "Governor's School Funding Plan on the Hot Seat," AP, June 27, 2005.

50. Castro, "School Funding Plan on the Hot Seat."

51. Castro, "Lawmakers No Closer."

52. Jim Vertuno, "Governors Call Special Session with Political Risk," AP, July 22, 2005.

53. Kelley Shannon, "House Rejects School Finance, Tax Measures," AP, July 26, 2005.

54. Shannon, "House Rejects School Finance."

55. AP, "Perry's Approval Rating at Highest Level in Three Years," February 18, 2005.

56. AP, "Poll Shows Perry's Approval Slipping," May 12, 2005.

57. April Castro, "Governor Calls Special Session to Address School Finance," AP, March 17, 2006.

58. Kelley Shannon, "Signs, Slogans, High Stakes Political Stakes Greet Lawmakers," AP, April 17, 2006.

59. The funds primarily come from a restructuring that taxed a percentage of a company's gross receipts with deductions for employee compensation or the cost of goods sold. The law excepted sole proprietorships, general partnerships, and businesses whose gross receipts totaled $300,000 or less. The property tax rate would go from a maximum of $1.50 for every $100 of property value to a maximum by state law of $1.30.

60. A year after the tax was in effect, it generated $4.2 billion in revenue. April Castro, "State's Business Tax Raised $4.2 Billion So Far," AP, June 25, 2008.

61. Why the difference? The governor's office reported that their numbers were based on an average Texas house value of $180,000, while the comptroller's office based their numbers on an average value of $118,000 before deducting the $15,000 homestead exemption.

62. Kelley Shannon, "Growing Voice at Capitol Asks Where Money Is for Schools," AP, April 20, 2006.

63. Toomey interview.

64. Chris Hooks, "Aggie Years Launched Perry—and a Rivalry," *Texas Tribune*, August 2, 2011.

65. Ratcliffe interview.

66. Perry interview, August 4, 2023.

67. April Castro, "Leaders Work Past Tensions for School Finance Solution," AP, May 20, 2006.

68. Kelley Shannon, "With Legislature Adjourned, Campaign Spin Heightens," AP, May 17, 2006.

69. Paul Burka, "Capture the Flag," *Texas Monthly*, July 2006.

70. Root interview.

71. To include a nickname on the ballot, election rules require the nickname to have been commonly used for at least three years. Strayhorn's campaign saw a double standard. Friedman's nickname "Kinky" had been used for forty years. "Rick" Perry's real name is James Richard Perry. "Grandma" was determined to be a slogan, not a nickname. Jason Stanford, campaign manager for Bell's campaign, called the move a "high water mark for absurdity in Texas politics." "Grandma" is not a nickname: "I don't consider 'dad' a nickname when I go home. It's not something my kids just thought up." See "'Grandma,' 'Kinky' Vie for Spots on Texas Ballot," AP, June 8, 2006, https://www.nbcnews.com/id/wbna13210337.

72. Ami Smith, "She's Her Own Grandma," *Austin Chronicle*, July 28, 2006, https://www.austinchronicle.com/news/2006-07-28/390533.

73. April Castro, "Strayhorn Running for Governor as Independent," AP, January 2, 2006.

74. Castro, "Strayhorn Running for Governor."

75. AP, "Strayhorn Gets Support from Donors Who Oppose Perry," May 9, 2004.

76. Kelley Shannon, "Millions of Dollars Donated for Governor's Race in Short Stretch," AP, July 15, 2005.

77. AP, "Bell Kicks Off Gubernatorial Campaign," August 14, 2005.

78. Wendy Benjaminson, "Democrat Chris Bell Announces Bid for Governor," AP, July 28, 2005.

79. Bell interview.

80. Michael Graczyk, "Mystery Author, Entertainer Friedman Announces Candidacy," AP, February 3, 2005.

81. State law required 45,540 valid signatures on petitions to place a candidate on the ballot as an independent (an equivalent of 1 percent of turnout in past gubernatorial elections).

82. Kinky Friedman, *Texas Hold 'Em* (New York: St. Martin's Press, 2005).

83. Graczyk, "Friedman Announces candidacy."

84. Graczyk, "Friedman Announces Candidacy."

85. AP, "Former Ventura Aide Joins Friedman Campaign for Texas Governor," April 29, 2005.

86. April Castro, "Willie Hosts Friedman Fundraiser," AP, October 30, 2005.

87. April Castro, "Perry Launches Re-election Campaign," AP, December 19, 2005.

88. Bell interview.

89. Kelley Shannon, "Governor's Race to Be Big Show Next Year in Texas Politics," AP, December 25, 2005.

90. Kelley Shannon, "Perry Praises Teachers, Bashes Bell, Defends Standardized Testing," AP, June 29, 2006.

91. Kelley Shannon, "Wackiness Rules, More than Usual, in Texas Politics," AP, August 4, 2006.

92. Wendy Benjaminson, "Strayhorn Says State Has Responsibility to Immigrants," AP, August 16, 2005.

93. Kelley Shannon, "Republicans Voice Strong Opposition to Illegal Immigration," AP, June 2, 2006.

94. Sullivan interview.

95. Liz Austin Peterson, "Border Is a Tricky Issue for Gubernatorial Candidates," AP, September 28, 2006.

96. AP, "Strayhorn Attacks Perry on Toll Roads," August 23, 2004.

97. Jim Vertuno, "Strayhorn Rips Perry over Enterprise Fund," AP, April 6, 2006.

98. Vertuno, "Strayhorn Rips Perry."

99. Michael Graczyk, "Unconventional Friedman Makes Conventional Campaign Stop," AP, May 11, 2005.

100. Pam Easton, "Kinky Friedman Tells Journalists He'll Offend If Elected Governor," AP, April 9, 2006.

101. Jim Vertuno, "Kinky Friedman Unveils Plans for Political Reform," AP, June 5, 2006.

102. Michael Graczyk, "Friedman Attracts Crowds but Wonders If They'll Respond as Voters," AP, September 28, 2006.

103. Graczyk, "Friedman Attracts Crowds."

104. Bell interview.

105. Kelley Shannon, "Another Racially Charged Friedman Remark Emerges," AP, September 22, 2006.

106. AP, "Perry Has Big Lead in Governor's Race." February 19, 2006.

107. Kelley Shannon, "Perry Launches New Ad Campaign Centered on School Funding," AP, May 22, 2006.

108. Bell interview.

109. Lyn Brezosky, "Strayhorn Calls for Teacher Raises, Tuition Freeze, TAKS Changes," AP, August 29, 2006.

110. Jeff Carlton, "Texas Governor Debate Might Be Missed among Football Hoopla," AP, September 29, 2006.

111. Carlton, "Texas Governor Debate Might Be Missed."

112. Bell interview.

113. Bell interview.

114. Bell interview.

115. AP, "Perry Has Large Lead among Likely Voters, New Poll Says," October 29, 2006.

116. April Castro, "Bell Campaigns while Perry, Strayhorn Spar in the Last Days of Race," AP, November 3, 2006.

117. Michael Graczyk, "Gov. Perry Getting Unexpected Heat from Segment of GOP Right," AP, September 6, 2006.

118. AP, "Poll Shows Perry Leading Governor's Race, Opposition Divided," October 5, 2006.

119. Kelley Shannon, "Challengers Look to Break from the Pack, Catch Perry in Final Weeks," AP, October 13, 2006.

120. Kelley Shannon, "Perry Criticizes Bell, Liberals as He Campaigns in East Texas," AP, October 25, 2006.

121. Angela K. Brown, "Democratic Governor Nominee Bell Vows to Lead 'Revolution,'" AP, June 10, 2006.

122. Brown, "Democratic Governor Nominee Bell."

123. Bell interview.

124. Lynn Brezosky, "Perry Campaigns in Rio Grande Valley," AP, October 16, 2006.

125. Bell interview.

126. Juan A. Lozano, "Democrats Confident They Can Win in November," AP, September 4, 2006.

127. Kelley Shannon, "Gubernatorial Candidate in Final Campaign Rush," AP, November 7, 2006.

128. Bell interview.

129. Kinky Freidman, "Rick Perry's Got My Vote," *Daily Beast*, August 24, 2011, https://www.thedailybeast.com/kinky-friedman-rick-perrys-got-my-vote.

130. Freidman, "Perry's Got my Vote."

131. Bell interview.

132. AmericaVotes 2006, CNN, https://www.cnn.com/ELECTION/2006/pages/results/states/TX/G/00/epolls.0.html.

133. Benkiser interview.

134. Bell interview.

Chapter 8: The 2007 and 2009 Sessions and the 2010 Election

1. Legislative Reference Library of Texas online, Perry speeches, inaugural address, January 16, 2007, https://lrl.texas.gov/legeLeaders/governors/searchproc.cfm?governorID=44&govDocTypeID=6.

2. The legislative totals in the House would change over the course of the session—one representative left the Republican Party to join the Democratic Party, another Republican resigned and was replaced by a Democrat in a special election, and one Republican died, bringing the final composition to 78–71.

3. Kelley Shannon, "Perry Promotes Bipartisanship, Declines to Commit to Full Term," AP, November 8, 2006.

4. Shannon, "Perry Promotes Bipartisanship."

5. Perry, inaugural address, January 16, 2007.

6. Ross Ramsey, "England's New Flag," *Texas Tribune*, September 24, 2007, https://www.texastribune.org/2007/09/24/englands-new-flag.

7. Legislative Reference Library of Texas online, Perry speeches, State of the State address, February 6, 2007, 1/https://lrl.texas.gov/legeLeaders/governors/searchproc.cfm?governorID=44&govDocTypeID=6.

8. Todd Ackerman, "Study: Houston among Cities Feeling Health Care Pinch," *Houston Chronicle*, June 29, 2008.

9. Perry, State of the State address, February 6, 2007.

10. Perry, State of the State address, February 6, 2007.

11. Armbrister interview.

12. Armbrister interview.

13. Ratcliffe interview.

14. Wilbanks interview.

15. Kelley Shannon, "Major Legislative Proposals Moving towards Finish Line," AP, May 13, 2007.

16. Kronberg interview.

17. Liz Austin Peterson, "Perry's Staff Discussed Vaccine on Day Merk Donated to Campaign," AP, February 20, 2007.

18. Toomey interview.

19. Hoppe interview.

20. Perry interview, July 31, 2023.

21. Wayne Carter, "Majority of Senators Ask Gov. Rick Perry to Withdraw Vaccine Mandate, *DMN*, February 7, 2007, https://www.dallasnews.com/news/politics/2007/02/07/majority-of-senators-ask-texas-gov-rick-perry-to-with-draw-hpv-vaccine-order.

22. Wayne Carter, "Majority of Senators Ask Texas Governor Rick Perry to Withdraw HPV Vaccine Order," *DMN*, February 7, 2007.

23. Toomey interview.

24. Kronberg interview.

25. Ratcliffe interview.

26. Thayer Evans, "Texas Speaker Wins Challenge and Keeps Post," *NYT*, January 10, 2007.

27. Paul Burka and Patricia Hart, "The Best and Worst Legislators," *Texas Monthly*, July 2007.

28. Burka and Hart, "Best and Worst Legislators [2007]."

29. April Castro, "Powerful Texas Republican Facing Coup Attempt in State House," AP, May 23, 2007.

30. Burka and Hart, "Best and Worst Legislators [2007]."

31. Jim Vertuno, "Texas Legislature Convenes 80th Session," AP, January 10, 2007.

32. Burka and Hart, "Best and Worst Legislators [2007]."

33. Van de Putte interview.

34. Van de Putte interview.

35. Interview with Jason Smith, August 16, 2021; Senate Bill 792.

36. Betsy Blaney, "Farmers Upset over Perry Veto of Eminent Domain Bill," AP, June 19, 2007.

37. The new pledge read: "Honor the Texas flag; I pledge allegiance to thee, Texas, one state under God, one and indivisible."

38. Lynn Brezosky, "Texas Governor Signs Compromise Border Security Bill," AP, June 6, 2007.

39. Thompson interview.

40. Matea Gold and Melanie Mason, "Governor Rick Perry's Big Donors Fare Well in Texas," *Los Angeles Times*, March 18, 2014.

41. Kelley Shannon, "As He Keeps Raising Money, Perry Keeps Power Intact," AP, July 29, 2007.

42. Jim Vertuno, "The 81st Texas Legislature Convenes 2009 Session," AP, January 13, 2009.

43. Monica Rhor, "Perry Asks State Agencies to Cut Spending," AP, October 15, 2008.

44. Betsey Blaney and April Castro, "Craddick Campaigning on Two Fronts," AP, November 1, 2008.

45. Ross Ramsey, "Keffer, A Straus Lieutenant, Won't Seek Reelection," *Texas Tribune*, June 16, 2015.

46. April Castro, "Straus's Record Shows Moderate, Independent Side," AP, January 7, 2009.

47. Vertuno, "81st Texas Legislature Convenes."

48. April Castro, "Leadership Style of New Speaker Taking Shape," AP, April 26, 2009.

49. James C. McKinley Jr., "Texas Rebellion Gives a Centrist a Lift," *NYT*, January 28, 2009.

50. McClellan interview.

51. Paul Burka and Patricia Hart, "The Best and Worst Legislators," *Texas Monthly*, July 2009.

52. McClellan interview.

53. The quotes and paraphrases from Perry's address to the senate on the opening day of the 81st legislature are from Legislative Reference Library of Texas online, Perry speeches, address to the senate, January 13, 2009, https://lrl.texas.gov/legeLeaders/governors/searchproc.cfm?governorID=44&govDocTypeID=6.

54. Perry, address to the senate, January 13, 2009.

55. Perry, address to the senate, January 13, 2009.

56. Kelley Shannon, "Perry Delivers Speech to Legislature," AP, January 27, 2009.

57. Alicia A. Caldwell, "Perry Wants More Troops on Border," AP, February 24, 2009.

58. Selby interview.

59. Dana Milbank, "Editorial: Rick Perry's Birther Parade," *Washington Post*, October 24, 2011.

60. Cook interview.

61. Holley interview.

62. Root interview.

63. Jackie Stone, "States' Rights Resolution Fails in House, for Now," AP, May 20, 2009.

64. Perry interview, July 31, 2023.

65. Cook interview.

66. Rogers, *Turning Texas Blue*, 113.

67. Benkiser interview.

68. Root interview.

69. Kelley Shannon, "Democrats: Perry Should Disavow Secession Talk," AP, April 16, 2009.

70. Miller interview.

71. Jay Root, "Savvy Conservatism, Country Charm Led Perry to Win," AP, March 4, 2010.

72. Perry interview, July 31, 2023.

73. Monica Rhor, "Perry Rejects Stimulus Money for Unemployment," AP, March 13, 2009.

74. Kenneth P. Miller, *Texas vs. California: A History of Their Struggle for the Future of America* (New York: Oxford University Press, 2020), 218.

75. AP, "Letters, Emails Back Perry on Stimulus Rejection," April 18, 2009.

76. April Castro, "House Unanimously Approves $178 Billion TX Budget," AP, April 18, 2009.

77. AP, "Texas Democrats Tout Federal Stimulus Plan," July 30, 2009.

78. Root interview.

79. Burka and Hart, "Best and Worst Legislators [2009]."

80. "Kuempel Has Massive Heart Attack," *Gonzalez Enquirer*, May 13, 2009, https://gonzalesinquirer.com/stories/kuempel-has-massive-heart-attack-collapsed-in-elevator,13598.

81. Burka and Hart, "Best and Worst Legislators [2009]."

82. Burka and Hart, "Best and Worst Legislators [2009]."

83. Smith interview.

84. Kelley Shannon, "Governor's Office Defends $50 Million Grant," AP, March 25, 2009.

85. Jackie Stone, "Lawmakers Seek Accountability in Enterprise Fund," AP, March 27, 2009.

86. Jay Root, "State Officials Scrap Trans-Texas Corridor," AP, January 6, 2009.

87. Sullivan interview.

88. Perry interview, July 31, 2023.

89. Van de Putte interview.

90. Jim Vertuno, "Perry Signs Bill to Aid Storm Insurance," AP, June 19, 2009.

91. Van de Putte interview.

92. The law exempted businesses making $1 million or less in annual revenue from the new business tax. The previous low was $300,000.

93. Arelis Hernandez, "Perry Signs Tax Cut Bill for Businesses," AP, June 16, 2009.

94. Morgan Smith, "Debt Becomes Her?," *Texas Tribune*, May 14, 2010.

95. Wilbanks interview.

96. Suzanne Gamboa, "Aide Says Hutchison Planning to Run for Governor," AP, April 1, 2008.

97. Gamboa, "Aide Says Hutchison Planning to Run."

98. Weeks interview.

99. Jay Root, "Hutchison Kicks Off Campaign for Texas Governor," AP, August 16, 2009.

100. Lewis interview.

101. Carney interview.

102. Kelley Shannon, "Texas Gubernatorial Tussle Under Way," AP, January 31, 2009.

103. Johnson interview.

104. Draper, "Just a Texas-Governor Thing."

105. "How well does corrupt describe Rick Perry?," University of Texas/Texas Tribune Poll, October 2010, https://texaspolitics.utexas.edu/set/description-rick-perry-corrupt-october-2010.

106. AP, "Hutchison and White Sweep Newspaper Endorsements," February 18, 2010.

107. Carney interview.

108. McClellan interview.

109. Jay Root, "Hutchison Critics See Conflict in Husband's Work," AP, August 3, 2009.

110. Suzanne Gamboa, "Hutchison Takes Step towards Run for Governor," AP, December 5, 2008.

111. Shannon, "Texas Gubernatorial Tussle."

112. McClellan interview.

113. AP, "Perry Orders State Helicopters to the Border," March 18, 2010.

114. April Castro, "Perry: Arizona Immigration Law Not Right for Texas," AP, April 29, 2010.

115. AP, "Poll: Most Texas Voters Back Arizona-Style Ban," September 26, 2010.

116. Kelley Shannon, "Perry Voices Support for 'Choose Life' Plates," AP, December 19, 2008.

117. Kelley Shannon, "Hutchison Meets Campaign Supporters in Austin," AP, January 24, 2009.

118. Jay Root, "Perry Ponders Whether to 'Opt Out' of Health Plan," AP, November 2, 2009.

119. McClellan interview.

120. Jay Root, "Cheney Endorses Hutchison in Texas Governor Race," AP, November 18, 2009.

121. Root, "Cheney Endorses Hutchison."

122. AP, "Cornyn Criticizes Perry Campaign," March 4, 2009.

123. Root, "Cheney Endorses Hutchison."

124. April Castro, "Texas Emerging from Months-Long Economic Slump," AP, August 10, 2010.

125. Castro, "Texas Emerging from Slump."

126. Castro, "Texas Emerging from Slump."

127. His campaign reported that 41 of the 62 state executive committee members backed him. AP, "Perry Touts Endorsements from Party Activists," November 23, 2009.

128. Adam Doster, "A Former Texas Gubernatorial Contender, Anything but Retired," *Houstonia*, May 31, 2016.

129. Medina interview.

130. James C. McKinley and Clifford Krauss, "Yes for Texas Governor Is a No to Washington," *NYT*, March 2, 2010.

131. Medina interview.

132. Medina interview.

133. Medina interview.

134. Medina interview.

135. Michael Graczyk, "Medina Blames Gov's Race Opponents for 9/11 Flap," AP, February 12, 2010.

136. Kelley Shannon and Jay Root, "Governor Candidates Trudge across Texas," AP, February 27, 2010.

137. Medina interview.

138. April Castro, "GOP Challengers Fueled by Tea Party Activists," AP, February 1, 2010.

139. Castro, "GOP Challengers Fueled by Tea Party."

140. Shannon and Root, "Candidates Trudge across Texas."

141. Tom Benning, "Sen. Hutchison Wins Runner-up in 2009 'Porker of the Year' Contest," *DMN*, February 2, 2010.

142. Carney interview.

143. Shannon and Root, "Candidates Trudge across Texas."

144. Draper, "Just a Texas-Governor Thing."

145. AP, "Perry-Hutchison Dispute over Contacts with Clinton Escalates," March 30, 2010.

146. Kelley Shannon, "Poll: Perry Leads GOP Rivals Hutchison, Medina," AP, February 14, 2010.

147. Draper, "Just a Texas-Governor Thing."

148. Kronberg interview.

149. Jay Root, "Texas GOP Ousts Chair, Wants Arizona Immigration Law," AP, June 13, 2010.

150. Root, "Texas GOP Ousts Chair."

151. Kelley Shannon, "Texas Governor Perry Must Win in November before 2012 Talk," AP, March 6, 2010.

152. Charles Babington, "Tea Partiers Push GOP's 2012 Hopefuls to the Right," AP, April 8, 2010.

153. Shannon, "Perry Must Win in November."

154. Jay Root, "Democrats Try to Rally with Houston Mayor," AP, November 28, 2009.

155. Jay Root, "Texas Democrats at Crossroads in 2010 Elections," AP, March 21, 2009.

156. Perry's remarks to New Life Christian Center in San Antonio, August 3, 2009.

157. Root, "Savvy Conservatism, Country Charm."

158. Kelley Shannon, "Perry Courts Party's Right Early," AP, April 24, 2009.

159. Slater interview.

160. Slater interview.

161. Jim Vertuno, "Perry Still Courting Right at Glenn Beck Event," AP, April 25, 2010.

162. AP, "Perry at Evangelical Church in Frisco," January 11, 2010.

163. Jay Root, "Gov. Rick Perry Gets Endorsement from NRA," AP, September 17, 2010.

164. Jay Root, "Guns Could Be a Tough Topic for Texas Candidate," AP, June 5, 2010.

165. Evan Smith, "TribLog," *Texas Tribune*, April 27, 2010, https://www.texastribune.org/2010/04/27/rick-perry-shoots-coyote/; and Perry interview, August 4, 2023.

166. Carney interview.

167. Root, "Perry Gets Endorsement from NRA."

168. Jay Root, "White Kicks Off Texas Early Voting with Rallies," AP, October 17, 2010.

169. Kelley Shannon, "Come and Take It! Perry Fights Attacks Texas Style," AP, May 30, 2010.

170. Michael Graczyk, "White Wants 1,250 More Officers to Secure Border," AP, September 2, 2010.

171. Graczyk, "White Wants 1,250 More Officers."

172. After taking office, Mayor Annise Parker said that "for years we have spent more money than we have taken in," but added, "I inherited a city that was essentially well run." Jay Root, "Houston's Democratic Mayor Rips Texas Governor Perry," AP, September 29, 2010.

173. Kelley Shannon, "White Calls Perry's Officer Ad 'Shameless,'" AP, October 25, 2010.

174. Paul J. Weber, "Immigration in Back Seat in Texas Governor's Race," AP, September 22, 2010.

175. Jay Root, "New Conflict Questions for Bill White," AP, August 4, 2010.

176. Kelley Shannon, "White Raises Questions on Perry Donors, Appointees," AP, September 30, 2010.

177. Jay Root, "White Hunts for Votes in Former Democratic Bastion," AP, October 20, 2010.

178. April Castro, "Perry Says He'll Debate White if He Released Taxes," AP, September 2, 2010.

179. Paul J. Weber, "Perry Continues Refusal to Debate White," AP, August 30, 2010.

180. Castro, "Perry Says He'll Debate White."

181. Kelley Shannon, "Texas Lyceum Poll Shows Perry Leading White," AP, October 6, 2010.

182. Ross Ramsey, "The Mother's Milk," *Texas Tribune*, October 27, 2010, https://www.texastribune.org/2010/10/27/millions-fund-last-month-of-texas-campaigns. See also Texas Ethics Commission, Filer: Texans for Rick Perry (Filer ID 00015471), "8 Days before the General Election Report," November 24, 2010, http://bbs.ethics.state.tx.us/public/466187.pdf.

183. April Castro, "Independent Group Attacks Perry in Ads Statewide," AP, August 24, 2010.

184. AP, "No-Show Perry Attacked by Rivals at Debate," October 20, 2010.

185. AP, "Perry Says Poll Results Show Voters Hate Big Government," November 4, 2010.

186. David Koenig, "Perry Wins Reelection after Tapping Anti-DC Mood," AP, November 3, 2010.

187. "Perry Says Voters Hate Big Government."

188. Jay Root, "Timing, Mixed Messages Hurt White during Campaign," AP, November 3, 2010.

189. Philip Elliott and Paul J. Weber, "Obama to Campaign in Texas," AP, July 20, 2010.

190. Kelley Shannon and Jay Root, "Texas Candidates for Gov Trek across State," AP, October 19, 2010.

191. Jay Root, "Dem White Swimming Upstream in GOP Strongholds," AP, October 21, 2010.

192. Koenig, "Perry Wins Reelection."

193. Shannon, "Come and Take It!"

194. Shannon, "Lyceum Poll Shows Perry Leading White."

195. Koenig, "Perry Wins Reelection."

196. Dunnam interview.

197. Jay Root, "Perry, Gun-toting Conservative, Is Confident," AP, October 9, 2010.

198. Shannon, "Come and Take It!"

Chapter 9: The 2011 Session and the 2012 Presidential Election

1. Jay Root, "Perry Downplays Texas Budget Woes," AP, January 10, 2011.

2. Jay Root, "Anti-Tax GOP Confronts Budget Mess in Texas," AP, January 8, 2011.

3. April Castro, "Texas Lawmakers Faced with $15 Billion Shortfall," AP, January 10, 2011.

4. Jay Root, "House Speaker Wins Second Term in New Legislature," AP, January 11, 2011.

5. Legislative Reference Library of Texas online, Perry speeches, inaugural address,

1/18/11, https://lrl.texas.gov/legeLeaders/governors/searchproc.cfm?governorID=44&gov
DocTypeID=6.

6. The "Aggie" line was partially ad-libbed. The official House journal reported he said: "It took 154 years to get an Aggie into the governors office, and some of you are probably wondering if he'll ever leave," https://www.youtube.com/watch?v=xuutWXngVxM.

7. Quotes and paraphrases are from Perry, State of the State address, February 8, 2011, https://lrl.texas.gov/legeLeaders/governors/searchproc.cfm?governorID=44&govDocType ID=6.

8. Jay Root, "Texas Legislature Convenes Amid Budget Shortfall," AP, January 11, 2011.

9. Gary Scharrer, "Perry Puts Faith on Display but Offers Little for Collection Plate," *Houston Chronicle*, June 12, 2011.

10. April Castro, "Texas Raises Revenue Forecast by $1.2 Billion," AP, May 17, 2011.

11. April Castro, "Texas Budget Draft Cuts $13.7 Billion in Spending," AP, January 19, 2011.

12. AP, "Texas Governor, House Agree to Tap Reserve Fund," March 6, 2011.

13. Jim Vertuno, "Texas Senate Remains Divided over Budget Plan," AP, April 28, 2011.

14. Vertuno, "Senate Remains Divided."

15. Vertuno, "Senate Remains Divided."

16. AP, "Senate Rules Fight Fizzles," January 19, 2011.

17. "Senate Rules Fight Fizzles."

18. AP, "Senate Tentatively Passes State Budget," May 4, 2011.

19. April Castro and Jim Vertuno, "Texas Legislature Passes Budget that Cuts Billions," AP, May 29, 2011.

20. Governor Rick Perry, Executive Office, Papers of Mike Morrissey, HB1, 82nd Legislature, 2011, Republican Caucus Suggested Talking Points.

21. Chris Tomlinson, "Texas Legislature Passes Sonogram Requirement," AP, May 5, 2011. Three Democrats voted for the bill and four Republicans voted against it.

22. The rules, according to contemporary accounts: "A driver's license, personal ID card, military ID, passport or concealed handgun permit would be accepted. The last change approved by the Senate on Monday allows the state to issue free IDs to be used specifically for voting if someone does not have another acceptable form of identification. Voters without ID could cast provisional ballots but would have to show identification within six days to have their votes counted." Jim Vertuno, "Texas Senate Approves Voter ID Bill," AP, May 9, 2011.

23. AP, "Bills Pile Up as Perry Flirts with White House Run," June 16, 2011.

24. Jim Vertuno, "Perry Adds Pat-Down Ban to Special Session Agenda," AP, June 21, 2011.

25. Jim Vertuno, "Texas Lawmakers Pass Weakened Airport Groping Bill," AP, June 28, 2011.

26. Jim Vertuno, "Republicans Blame Each Other for Bill Failure," AP, June 29, 2011.

27. Staff, "Proof of Citizenship Required to Renew a Texas Driver's License," *CBS News*, June 30, 2011.

28. Jim Vertuno, "Budget Hearings Underway in Texas House, Senate," AP, June 2, 2011.

29. Will Wiessert, "Texas House Busy as End of Special Session Looms," AP, June 27, 2011.

30. Jay Root, "Texas Gov. Rick Perry Entertains Talk of 2012 Bid," AP, April 16, 2010.

31. Beth Fouhy, "Perry: Still Time to Decide on a White House Run," AP, June 15, 2011.

32. Fouhy, "Perry: Still Time to Decide."

33. Ivan Moreno, "Gov Perry: Marriage Is a States' Rights Issue," AP, July 23, 2011.

34. Limbaugh quoted in Chris Tomlinson, "Perry: Too Busy with Legislature for Presidency," AP, May 20, 2011.

35. Sullivan interview.

36. Perry interview, August 4, 2023.

37. Emily Ramshaw, "Perry's Surgery Included Experimental Stem Cell Therapy," AP, August 3, 2011.

38. Carney interview.

39. Beth Fouhy and Jim Davenport, "Texas Gov. Perry Jumps into 2012 Republican Race," AP, August 13, 2011.

40. Beth Fouhy and Steve Peoples, "Perry to Make Bid for GOP Nomination Official," AP, August 13, 2011.

41. Tilove interview.

42. Steve Peoples and April Castro, "No Tea Party for Perry as He Weighs Nomination Bid," AP, July 19, 2011.

43. Erik Schelzig, "Ramsey Defends Governor Perry for Backing Gore in '88," AP, August 10, 2011.

44. Maggie Haberman, "Clinton Calls Perry Good-Looking Rascal," *Politico*, August 15, 2011.

45. Smith interview.

46. Rick Perry, with Chip Roy, *Fed Up! Our Fight to Save America from Washington* (Little Brown and Co., 2010), 5.

47. Kelley Shannon and Jay Root, "White, Perry Rev Up Volunteers in Texas Gov Race," AP, November 2, 2010.

48. Frank James, "Rick Perry Stirs Firestorm by Accusing Fed Chair Bernanke of Near Treason," *NPR*, August 16, 2011, https://www.npr.org/sections/itsallpolitics/2011/08/16/139672998/rick-perry-stirs-firestorm-by-accusing-fed-chair-bernanke-of-near-treason.

49. James, "Perry Stirs Firestorm."

50. James, "Perry Stirs Firestorm."

51. Glenn Kessler, "Rick Perry's Made-Up 'Facts' about Climate Change," *Washington Post*, August 18, 2011.

52. Thomas Beaumont and April Castro, "Perry: Turn to God for Answers to Nation's Woes," AP, August 6, 2011.

53. "Strong," YouTube, https://www.youtube.com/watch?v=kxzONeK1OwQ.

54. Sullivan interview.

55. Thomas Beaumont, "Perry Calls Jobs Record a Big Plus," AP, August 15, 2011.

56. Beaumont, "Perry Calls Jobs Record Plus."

57. Republican Presidential Debate, Rochester, Michigan, November 9, 2011, https://www.youtube.com/watch?v=N7kl9TLzuAk.

58. Author's transcript, Florida Republican Presidential Debate, Tampa, November 23, 2012.

59. "Then and Now . . . Inflation," RedState.com, January 15, 2011, http://www.cbsnews.com/8301-503544_162-20110488-503544.html.

60. Selby interview.

61. Ratcliffe interview.

62. Sullivan interview.

63. Jeff Zeleny, "After Rocky Start, More Study, and Sleep, for Perry," *NYT*, October 9, 2011.

64. Amy Gardner and Phillip Rucker, "Rick Perry Stumbles Badly in Republican Presidential Debate," *Washington Post*, November 20, 2011, https://www.washingtonpost.com/politics/republican-presidential-candidates-focus-on-economy/2011/11/09/gIQA5Lsp6M_story.html.

65. Gardner and Rucker, "Perry Stumbles."

66. Gardner and Rucker, "Perry Stumbles."

67. Smith, interview.

68. Maria Recio, "Meet Dave Carney, Rick Perry's Karl Rove-like Political Guru," *Modesto Bee*, September 29, 2011, https://www.modbee.com/latest-news/article3137113.html.

69. Perry interview, August 4, 2023.

70. Smith interview.

71. Emily Ramshaw, "Even Perry's Critics Defend Him on Hunting Ranch Furor," *Texas Tribune*, October 3, 2011.

72. Ramshaw, "Even Perry's Critics Defend Him."

73. Tilove interview.

74. Perry interview, August 4, 2023.

75. Root interview.

76. Smith interview.

77. Zeleny, "After Rocky Start."

78. Chris Cillizza, "The 48 Seconds that Define Rick Perry's Political Career," *Washington Post*, September 12, 2015.

79. Michael R. Blood, "Texas' Rick Perry Faults Obama for Standoff," AP, October 5, 2013.

80. Kronberg interview.

81. Miller interview.

82. Freya Petersen, "Rick Perry Stumbles over Supreme Court Justices and the Name 'Sotomayor,'" *The World*, December 10, 2011, https://www.pri.org/stories/2011-12-10/rick-perry-stumbles-over-supreme-court-justices-and-name-sotomayor-video.

83. Felicia Sonmez, "Pelosi Mocks Perry's Debate Request," *Washington Post*, November 17, 2011.

Chapter 10: The 2013 Session, Indictment, and the 2016 Presidential Race

1. Manny Fernandez, "Texas Budget Surplus Proves as Contentious as a Previous Shortfall," *NYT*, January 8, 2013.

2. Paul J. Weber, "Expected Surplus Won't Lessen 2013 Budget Fight," AP, January 1, 2013.

3. Peggy Fikac, "Perry Has a Surprise in His State of the State Address," AP, January 29, 2013.

4. Fernandez, "Texas Budget Surplus Proves Contentious."

5. AP, "Timeline of Events in Texas Governor Rick Perry's Life," July 9, 2013.

6. Peggy Fikac, "Subdued Perry Saw Success in Regular Session," *SAEN*, June 2, 2013.

7. Nomaan Merchant, "Perry: Let Teachers Carry Guns in the Wake of Massacre," AP, December 18, 2012.

8. Alan Scher Zagier, "Perry Promotes 'Economic Freedom' Group in MO," AP, September 27, 2013.

9. Paul J. Weber, "Audit Finds Problems in Perry's Deal-Closing Fund," AP, September 25, 2014.

10. Aman Batheja, "Auditor: Perry's Business Fund Doled Out Millions without Proper Oversight," *Texas Tribune*, September 25, 2014.

11. Weber, "Audit Finds Poblems."

12. Paul J. Weber, "DA Investigating Texas' Troubled $3B Cancer Agency," AP, December 11, 2012.

13. Will Weissert, "Perry Taps Chief of Staff for Texas Supreme Court," AP, November 26, 2012.

14. John L. Mone and Betsey Blaney, "Texas Fertilizer Plant Blast Injures Dozens," AP, April 18, 2013.

15. Ramit Plushnick-Masti, "FEMA Denies Aid to Texas for Blast," AP, June 12, 2013.

16. Plushnick-Masti, "FEMA Denies Aid."

17. Will Weissert, "Perry Sending National Guard Troops to Border," AP, July 22, 2013.

18. Weissert, "Perry Sending Guard Troops to Border."

19. "Rick Perry Rejects Obama Handshake," *Daily Beast*, April 14, 2017.

20. Louise Stewart, "Perry Spurns Obama's Handshake, but Gets a Meeting on the Border Crisis," *Newsweek*, July 8, 2014.

21. Peggy Fikac, "Texas Pays Nearly $4 Million So Far to Sue Feds," AP, August 20, 2013.

22. Fikac, "Texas Pays Nearly $4 Million."

23. Paul J. Weber, "Texas Senate Passes $195.5B Two-Year Budget Plan," AP, March 20, 2013.

24. Robert T. Garrett, "Lawmakers Blasted over Budget Package," *DMN*, May 28, 2013.

25. Texas Digital Archive, Executive Office Records, Folder: Perry, Rick, Subject: Morrissey, Mike, Opperman to Morrissey (email), June 13, 2020.

26. Chris Tomlinson, "New Requirement Proposed for Texas Abortion Docs," AP, April 16, 2013.

27. Tomlinson, "New Requirement Proposed."

28. Chris Tomlinson, "Abortion Back on Texas Legislature's Agenda," AP, January 21, 2013.

29. Tomlinson, "Abortion Back on Agenda."

30. Will Weissert, "Perry Signs 'Merry Christmas' Bill into Law," AP, June 13, 2013.

31. Will Weissert, "Perry Vetoes 24 Bills, Makes Few Changes to Budget," AP, June 15, 2013.

32. Chris Tomlinson, "Texas DA: Veto Doesn't Take away Ethics Duties," AP, June 18, 2013.

33. Jim Vertuno and Paul J. Weber, "Perry Staying Mum as Special Session Talk Ramps Up," AP, May 25, 2013.

34. Chris Tomlinson, "Texas House Approves Redistricting Map," AP, June 20, 2013.

35. Will Weissert, "Perry Says No More Items for Special Session," AP, June 13, 2013.

36. AP, "What's the Deal with Rick Perry's $500 Hipster Glasses?," *Christian Science Monitor*, August 27, 2014.

37. Meghan Daum, "Will Smart Looking Glasses Do the Trick for Rick Perry?," *LA Times*, June 11, 2015.

38. Emily Heil and Helena Andrews, "Rick Perry's Glasses Make a Splash—But Don't Call Them 'Hipsters' Specs," *Washington Post*, February 25, 2014.

39. Tilove interview.

40. Mike Morrissey, Perry's deputy chief of staff; Ken Armbrister, legislative director; Rich Parsons, a Perry spokesman; and Mary Anne Wiley, the governor's general counsel, declined comment on their way in and out of the grand jury room. Jim Vertuno, "Perry's Aides Appear before Grand Jury in Veto Probe," *Lubbock Avalanche-Journal*, May 16, 2014, https://www.lubbockonline.com/story/news/state/2014/05/17/perrys-aides-appear -grand-jury-veto-probe/15041191007.

41. Paul J. Weber, "Texas' Perry Indicted for Coercion for Veto Threat," AP, August 16, 2014.

42. Will Weissert, "Prosecutor: Perry Wanted to 'Stymie' Public Corruption Unit," AP, February 14, 2015.

43. Perry interview, August 4, 2023.

44. At the time of writing, Buzbee is slated to serve as one of impeached Attorney General Ken Paxton's attorneys in his Senate trial, scheduled for September 2023.

45. Weber, "Perry Indicted."

46. Ken Thomas, "Texas Governor Perry Defends Veto that Led to Charges," AP, August 17, 2014.

47. Will Weissert, "Felony Indictment Energizes Texas GOP behind Perry," AP, August 24, 2014.

48. Weissert, "Indictment Energizes Texas GOP behind Perry."

49. Will Weissert and Paul J. Weber, "Texas Gov. Perry Booked on Abuse of Power Charges," AP, August 20, 2014.

50. Tilove interview.

51. Paul J. Weber, "Texas' Perry Says Disparaging Tweet Unauthorized," AP, September 1, 2014.

52. Paul J. Weber, "Texas Court Tosses Criminal Case against Former Gov. Perry," AP, February 24, 2014.

53. Weber, "Court Tosses Criminal Case."

54. AP, "Report: Perry Spent $2.6M on Attorneys to Beat Felony Case," July 15, 2016.

55. Will Weissert, "Abortion, Juvenile Crime Added to Texas Session," AP, June 11, 2013.

56. Steve Peoples, "Debate over Social Issues Emerges," AP, June 13, 2013.

57. Manny Fernandez, "You Call that a Filibuster? Texas Still Claims Record," *NYT*, July 4, 2013.

58. Dave Montgomery, "Senate Gives Up on Budget Deal: Special Session Looms," *Fort Worth Star Telegram*, May 20, 2011.

59. Sarah Tressler, "A Brief History of Leticia Van De Putte," *SAEN*, June 26, 2013.

60. Tressler, "Brief History of Leticia Van De Putte."

61. Katie McDonough, "Wendy Davis' Marathon Filibuster Kills Abortion Bill (For Now)," *Salon*, June 26, 2013, https://www.salon.com/2013/06/26/wendy_davis _marathon_filibuster_kills_texas_abortion_bill_for_now.

62. McDonough, "Wendy Davis' Marathon Filibuster."

63. McDonough, "Wendy Davis' Marathon Filibuster."

64. Chris Tomlinson, "Texas Senate Convenes to Debate Abortion Bill," AP, July 12, 2013.

65. Tomlinson, "Texas Senate Convenes."

66. Will Weissert, "Richards: Strict Texas Abortion Bill 'Lit a Fuse,'" AP, July 13, 2013.

67. Bill Barrow, "Abortion Returns to Forefront for 2014 Elections," AP, July 14, 2013.

68. Barrow, "Abortion Returns to Forefront."

69. Jim Vertuno, "Texas Lawmaker Pushing Back on Gov. Perry in 2013," AP, April 26, 2013.

70. Will Weissert, "Abbott Trumpeting His Conservative Credentials," AP, April 30, 2013.

71. Weissert, "Abbott Trumpeting Credentials."

72. Thomas Beaumont and Will Weissert, "Texas Dems See Chance to Become Relevant Again," AP, July 15, 2013.

73. The entire speech is found at Legislative Reference Library of Texas online, https://lrl.texas.gov/scanned/govdocs/Rick%20Perry/2015/speech011515.pdf.

74. Paul J. Weber, "GOP Rules Texas, but They're Talking Like They're on Ropes," AP, November 30, 2013.

75. Chris Tomlinson, "Chairman Says Texas Dems Have Much Building to Do," AP, August 15, 2013.

76. Tomlinson, "Texas Dems Have Much Building to Do."

77. Weber, "GOP Rules Texas."

78. Legislative Reference Library of Texas online, Perry address to the legislature, January 15, 2015, https://lrl.texas.gov/scanned/govdocs/Rick%20Perry/2015/speech011515.pdf.

79. Will Weissert, "Texas GOP Backs Away from Guest Worker Plan," AP June 8, 2014.

80. Paul J. Weber, "Nugent Backlash Reveals Rare Misstep for Texas GOP," AP, Friday 21, 2014.

81. Weber, "Nugent Backlash."

82. Chris Tomlinson, "Democrats Rally, but Have Far to Go in Texas," AP, July 28, 2013.

83. Tomlinson, "Democrats Rally."

84. Paul J. Weber, "Tea Party Poised for Big Wins in Texas GOP Runoffs," AP, May 26, 2014.

85. Weber, "Tea Party Poised for Big Wins."

86. Jon Blistein, "Rick Perry Launches Presidential Campaign with Rap Country Song," *Rolling Stone*, June 4, 2015.

87. The quotes from Perry's announcement come from Will Weissert, "Rick Perry Goes at It Again, Launches 2016 Bid," AP, June 4, 2015.

88. Will Weissert, "Perry Reshaped Texas, but Foundered Nationally," AP, July 8, 2013.

89. Steve Peoples and Thomas Beaumont, "Texas Gov. Rick Perry: 'I'm Ready' for White House Run," AP, January 17, 2015.

90. Gerry Mullany, "Rick Perry on the Issues," *NYT*, June 4, 2015.

91. Steve Peoples, "Perry-Paul Launch Foreign Policy War of Words," AP, July 14, 2014.

92. Erica Greider, "Rick Perry's Travails," *National Review*, September 7, 2015.

93. Erica Greider, "Rick Perry and Black Lives Matter," August 2, 2016.

94. Steve Peoples, "Hispanic Leaders Want GOP Field to Condemn Trump's 'Idiocy,'" AP, July 3, 2015.

95. Chris Cillizza, "The Awful Reality that Trump's Attacks on John McCain Proves," *CNN*, March 19, 2019, https://www.cnn.com/2019/03/19/politics/donald-trump-john-mccain-dead/index.html.

96. Ali Dukakis, "Rick Perry Calls Donald Trump a 'Cancer on Conservatism,'" *ABC News*, July 22, 2015.

97. Perry interview, August 4, 2023.

98. Dukakis, "Trump a 'Cancer on Conservatism.'"

99. See Trump Twitter Archive, https://www.thetrumparchive.com/, search term @GovernorPerry.

100. "Jeb Bush Calls Trump's Language 'Divisive' and 'Mean-Spirited,'" *Bay News 9*, July 22, 2015, https://www.baynews9.com/fl/tampa/news/2015/7/22/jeb_bush_calls_trump?cid=rss.

101. Abby Livingston, "Military Experts: Warship in Perry Video Was Russian," *Texas Tribune*, April 9, 2015.

102. Steve Peoples and Will Weissert, "Rick Perry to Exit 2016 Republican Presidential Race," AP, September 12, 2015.

103. Barbour would go on to run Jeb Bush's campaign in the South when Perry dropped out.

104. Will Weissert, "Can Super PAC Support Save Cash-Strapped Perry Bid?," AP, August 11, 2015.

105. Steve Peoples, "Trump Embraces Role as Bully, Bids Perry a Thorny Farewell," AP, September 13, 2015.

106. Wilbanks interview.

107. Wilbanks interview.

Chapter 11: An Underestimated Political Rebirth

1. Dawn M. Burkes, "Rick Perry Needs Help on Dancing with the Stars," *DMN*, September 20, 2016.

2. Abby Johnston, "Breaking Down Rick Perry's Performance on Dancing with the Stars," *Texas Monthly*, September 13, 2016.

3. Aurelie Corinthios and Mariah Haas, "Rick Perry Has a Whole New Appreciation for Dancers after Elimination," *People*, October 5, 2016, https://people.com/tv/dancing-with-the-stars-rick-perry-opens-up-about-elimination.

4. Brenna Williams, "The Play-by-Play of Rick Perry's DWTS Debut," *CNN*, https://www.cnn.com/2016/09/13/politics/rick-perry-dancing-with-the-stars-in-gifs/index.html.

5. Tom Benning, "Rick Perry Ascends Trump Tower to Meet President-Elect," *DMN*, November 21, 2016.

6. Alex Daugherty, "Rick Perry Sidesteps Question on Trump during 'Dancing with the Stars' Appearance," *McClatchy*, November 23, 2016.

7. Perry interview, August 4, 2023.

8. Tilove interview.

9. Perry interview, July 31, 2023.

10. Will Weissert, "Beyond 'Oops': Perry's Past May Raise Confirmation Questions," AP, December 13, 2016.

11. Jay Cassano, "How Texas Lawmakers Failed to Plan for Climate Change and Harvey Floods," *International Business Times*, August 29, 2017.

12. Matthew Daly and Will Weissert, "From 'Oops' to DOE Chief: Rick Perry Is Pick for Energy," AP, December 13, 2016.

13. Jim Malewitz and Kiah Collier, "Rick Perry's Complicated Energy Legacy in Texas," *Governing*, December 14, 2016, https://www.governing.com/archive/tt-rick-perry -energy-legacy.html.

14. Michael Collins, "Rick Perry: I've Changed my Mind about Eliminating Energy Department," *USA Today*, January 19, 2017.

15. Anthony Adrgana, "How Rick Perry Survives in Trump's Troubled Cabinet," *Politico*, April 3, 2018.

16. Michael Warren, "Rick Perry's Unlikely Third Act," *Washington Examiner*, August 13, 2018.

17. Ben Protess, "He Leaked a Photo of Rick Perry Hugging a Coal Executive. Then He Lost His Job," *NYT*, January 17, 2018.

18. Zahra Hirji, "The Energy Department Took Down Anti-Leaking Posters after an Investigation," *BuzzFeed News*, February 23, 2018, https://www.buzzfeednews.com /article/zahrahirji/energy-department-anti-leaking-posters.

19. Doyin Oyeniyi, "Energy Secretary Rick Perry Says Fossil Fuels Could Prevent Sexual Assaults in Africa," *Texas Monthly*, November 2, 2017.

20. Oyeniyi, "Energy Secretary Rick Perry."

21. Darius Dixon and Eric Wolff, "Energy Regulator Rejects Perry's Plan to Boost Coal," *Politico*, January 8, 2018.

22. Chris Tomlinson, "Trump and Perry Reject King Coal's Pleas," *Houston Chronicle*, August 24, 2017.

23. Jeremy Dillon and Geof Koss, "Mr. Congeniality: How Perry Uses Charm to Stay out of Trouble," *Politico*, April 2, 2019, https://subscriber.politicopro.com/article /eenews/1060139355.

24. Dillon and Koss, "Mr. Congeniality."

25. James Osborn, "How Rick Perry Bucked Congress's Energy Mandate," *Houston Chronicle*, April 10, 2020.

26. Matthew J. Belvedere, "Energy Secretary Rick Perry Contradicts Trump," *CNBC*, July 31, 2019, https://www.cnbc.com/2019/07/31/energy-secretary-rick-perry -humans-play-a-role-in-climate-change.html.

27. Simon Shuster and Ilya Marritz, "As Energy Secretary, Rick Perry Mixed Money and Politics in Ukraine: The Deals Could Be Worth Billions," *Texas Tribune*, September 10, 2020.

28. Shuster and Marritz, "Perry Mixed Money and Politics in Ukraine."

29. Justin Miller, "Rick Perry Exports His Pay to Play Politics to Ukraine," *Texas Observer*, November 13, 2019.

30. Shuster and Marritz, "Perry Mixed Money and Politics in Ukraine."

31. Miller, "Perry Exports His Pay to Play Politics."

32. Christopher Hooks, "The Rick Perry Show Is Back!," *Texas Monthly*, October 10, 2019.

33. Ben Lefebvre and Daniel Lippman, "Perry Pressed Ukraine on Corruption, Energy Company Changes," *Politico*, October 5, 2019.

34. Ben Lefebvre and Theodoric Meyer, "Energy Secretary Rick Perry Eyeing Exit in November," *Politico*, October 3, 2019.

35. Shuster and Marritz, "Perry Mixed Money and Politics in Ukraine."

36. "Full Letter from Secretary Perry to President Trump," Energy.gov, https://www .energy.gov/articles/secretary-perry-announces-resignation-effective-later-year.

Chapter 12: Legacy and Impact

1. John Egan, "Texas Explodes with 16 Percent Surge in Population, New Census Data Show," *Innovation Map*, https://houston.innovationmap.com/2020-census-population-surge-texas-2652813819.html.

2. Alejandro Serrano and Jordan Rubio, "Texas Continues to Lead US in Raw Population Growth, Census Bureau Estimates," *Houston Chronicle*, May 4, 2021.

3. "Texas Demographic Trends and Projections and the 2020 Census," Texas Demographic Center, https://demographics.texas.gov/Resources/Presentations/OSD/2021/2021_01_29_MexicanAmericanLegislativeLeadershipFellowship.pdf.

4. Dave Mann, "Whatever Rick Perry's Record Is, It's Not Conservative," *New Republic*, August 18, 2011, https://newrepublic.com/article/93902/rick-perry-record-liberal-conservative.

5. Will Weissert, "Texas GOP Taking Aim at Parts of Perry's Legacy," AP, June 4, 2014.

6. Paul J. Weber, "As Perry Mulls 2016, Abbott Cleans House in Texas," AP, February 6, 2015.

7. Weber, "Abbott Cleans House."

8. Michael Warren, "Rick Perry's Unlikely Third Act," *Washington Examiner*, August 13, 2018.

9. Erica Grider, "The Revolt against Crony Capitalism," *Texas Monthly*, February 17, 2014.

10. Carney interview.

11. Bill Hethcock, "Texas Outshines All Other States, by Far, in Luring California Headquarters Relocations," *WFAA*, June 26, 2021, https://www.wfaa.com/article/money/business/texas-california-corporate-relocations/287-7f02cfba-b6b8-478f-81ca-018c227252d1.

12. Herman interview.

13. Christopher Hooks, "Something Strange Is Going On with All Those Retiring Texans," *NYT*, September 7, 2019.

14. Tilove interview.

15. Matt Taibbi, "Rick Perry: The Best Little Whore in Texas," *Rolling Stone*, October 26, 2011, https://www.rollingstone.com/politics/politics-news/rick-perry-the-best-little-whore-in-texas-237514.

16. Slater interview.

17. Stenholm interview.

18. Carney interview.

19. Fikac, "Perry the Master of the Bold Move."

20. Wilbanks interview.

21. Miller interview.

22. Benkiser interview.

23. Wilbanks interview.

24. Thorburn, *Red State*, 191.

25. Fikac, "Master of the Bold Move.

26. Fikac, "Master of the Bold Move."

27. Gilbert Garcia, "Greg Abbott's Leadership Deficiencies Show in Property Tax Conflict," *SAEN*, June 3, 2023.

28. Rogers, *Turning Texas Blue*.

29. Arnold interview.

30. Stenholm interview.

31. Herman interview.

32. Hance, "Rick Perry: Part 1."

33. Dowd interview.

34. Stenholm interview.

35. Van de Putte interview.

36. Cook interview.

37. Steve Peoples and Paul Weber, "Kinzinger Goes to Texas in Search of Anti-Trump Republicans," AP, April 30, 2021.

38. Hooks, "Something Strange."

39. Julian E. Zelizer, *Burning Down the House: Newt Gingrich, the Fall of a Speaker, and the Rise of the New Republican Party* (New York: Penguin, 2020), 303.

40. Tim Alberta, "The Grand Old Meltdown," *Politico*, August 24, 2020, https://www.politico.com/search?q=Alberta%2C+Grand+Old+Meltdown.

41. Manny Fernandez and David Montgomery, "Governor Struggles to Lead as Texas Republicans Splinter into Factions," *NYT*, June 5, 2017.

42. Elaina Plott, "The GOP Won It All in Texas. Then It Turned on Itself," *NYT*, May 4, 2021.

43. William Cummings, "Rick Perry: Trump Is the 'Chosen One,'" *Austin American-Statesman*, November 25, 2019.

44. Stuart Stevens, "I Hope This Is Not Another Lie about the Republican Party," *NYT*, July 29, 2020.

45. Holley interview.

46. Andrew R. Graybill, "Are We Ready to Rehabilitate George W. Bush's Reputation?," *Texas Monthly*, October 2020.

47. Perry interview, August 4, 2023.

48. Hooks, "Something Strange."

49. Texas Hispanic Policy Foundation, "The 2020 Presidential and U.S. Senate Election Contests," https://static.texastribune.org/media/files/5efafcc57bd972cb32f8c47bc625d731/THPFFinalAug17.pdf, page 11.

50. Perry interview, July 31, 2023.

51. Patrick Svitek, "State Rep. Jake Ellzey Faces Mounting Opposition from His Right in Special Election to Replace Ron Wright in Congress," *Texas Tribune*, April 20, 2021.

52. Jonathan Swan, "Scoop: Trump Team Blames Conservative for Loser Endorsement," *Axios*, July 28, 2021.

53. Toomey interview.

54. Holley interview.

55. Herman interview.

56. Dunnam interview.

57. Dowd interview.

58. Jim Henson and Joshua Blank, "Analysis: A Reality Check for the Myth of the Texas Miracle," *Texas Tribune*, June 6, 2020.

59. Perry interview, July 31, 2023.

60. Toomey interview.

61. Jim Tankersley, "The 'Texas Miracle' Misses Most of Texas," *NYT*, July 7, 2019.

62. Erica Grieder, *Big, Hot, Cheap and Right: What America Can Learn from the Strange Genius of Texas* (New York: PublicAffairs, 2013), 13.

63. Max Ehrenfreund, "The Facts about Rick Perry and the 'Texas Miracle,'" *Wonkblog*, June 8, 2015, http://www.washingtonpost.com/blogs/wonkblog/wp/2015/06/08/the-facts-about-rick-perry-and-the-texas-miracle.

64. Texas Medical Association, "Quick Statistics on the Uninsured in Texas and the U.S.," June 23, 2010, https://www.texmed.org/Template.aspx?id=5519.

65. "2016 American Community Survey 1-Year Estimates," US Census Bureau, https://factfinder.census.gov/faces/tableservices/jsf/pages/pro-ductview.xhtml?pid=ACS_16_1YR_B19080&prodType=table.

66. "2016 American Community Survey 1-Year Estimates," US Census Bureau.

67. Gail Collins, "Fifty Shades of Trump," *NYT*, June 29, 2017.

68. Will Weissert, "Perry Reshaped Texas, but Foundered Nationally," AP, July 8, 2013.

69. Burka is quoted in Brian McCall, *The Power of the Texas Governor* (Austin: University of Texas Press, 2009), 3.

70. Robert T. Garrett, "Greg Abbott Confronts Coronavirus as Stronger Governor Than Texas Had 50 Years Ago," *DMN*, March 22, 2020.

71. Total offices equal 546, including state supreme courts, appeals courts, and district courts.

72. Justin Miller, "Rick Perry Exports His Pay to Play Politics to Ukraine," *Texas Observer*, November 13, 2019.

73. Reeve Hamilton, "Council's Report Cites Possible Grounds for Hall's Impeachment," *Texas Tribune*, April 8, 2014, https://www.texastribune.org/2014/04/08/report-possible-grounds-halls-impeachment.

74. Wayne interview.

75. Ratcliffe interview.

76. "When Perry Turned Republican."

77. Hoppe interview.

78. Hoppe interview.

79. Taibbi, "Best Little Whore in Texas."

80. Wayne interview; Rob Snyder, "Mark Griffin Re-Appointed to Texas Tech Board of Regents," https://kfyo.com/mark-griffin-re-appointed-to-texas-tech-university-system-board-of-regents. Governor Abbott reappointed Griffin to the board in 2019.

81. "Rick's Revolvers," Texans for Public Justice, http://info.tpj.org/reports/pdf/Rick Revolvers.sharkreport.pdf.

82. Meghan Ashford Grooms and Ciara O'Rourke, "Bill White Says Most of Gov. Rick Perry's Chiefs of Staff Have Been Lobbyists," *Politifact*, August 30, 2010.

83. Taibbi, "Best Little Whore in Texas."

84. Elbein, "Boy from Haskell."

85. Cook interview.

86. Aman Batheja, "Texas Governor Rick Perry Became a Millionaire While Serving in Office," *Miami Herald*, September 19, 2011.

87. Gary Scharrer, "Watchdog Group: Perry's Investments Show 'Pay to Play' Pattern," *Beaumont Enterprise*, September 21, 2011.

88. Conor Friedersdorf, "How Rick Perry Got Rich While Working Government Jobs," *The Atlantic*, August 30, 2011.

89. Friedersdorf, "How Rick Perry Got Rich."

90. Batheja, "Perry Became a Millionaire While in Office."

91. Holley interview.

92. Tilove interview.

93. Slater interview.

94. Paul J. Weber, "Texas Governor Stockpiles Cash, but Not for the Usual Reason," AP, February 24, 2019.

95. Silverstein, "The Great Campaigner."

96. Hart, "Perry's Party Now."

97. Cook interview.

98. Tom Benning, "Ex–Texas Governor Perry Enjoying New Home, Time out of Office," *DMN*, December 7, 2015.

99. Perry interview, July 31, 2023.

100. Jeremy Wallace, "Former Gov. Rick Perry Wades into Mask Debate in Texas Schools, with a Product Pitch," *Houston Chronicle*, August 23, 2021.

INDEX

Photo insert images are indicated by *p1, p2, p3*, etc.